北京外国语大学“双一流”建设重大（点）标志性项目“国家翻译能力理论框架与国家比较”（项目批准号：2022SYLA002）经费资助

北京外国语大学国家翻译能力研究中心专项经费资助

翻译世界中的合作

Collaboration in the World of Translation and Interpreting

任　文　主编

外语教学与研究出版社
FOREIGN LANGUAGE TEACHING AND RESEARCH PRESS
北京 BEIJING

图书在版编目（CIP）数据

翻译世界中的合作 ：汉文、英文 / 任文主编. -- 北京 ：外语教学与研究出版社，2023.9（2024.9 重印）
ISBN 978-7-5213-4744-9

Ⅰ. ①翻… Ⅱ. ①任… Ⅲ. ①翻译－国际学术会议－文集－汉、英 Ⅳ. ①H059-53

中国国家版本馆 CIP 数据核字（2023）第 150032 号

出 版 人　王　芳
责任编辑　李海萍
责任校对　闫　璟
封面设计　彩奇风
出版发行　外语教学与研究出版社
社　　址　北京市西三环北路 19 号（100089）
网　　址　https://www.fltrp.com
印　　刷　北京九州迅驰传媒文化有限公司
开　　本　650×980　1/16
印　　张　21
版　　次　2023 年 9 月第 1 版　2024 年 9 月第 2 次印刷
书　　号　ISBN 978-7-5213-4744-9
定　　价　76.90 元

如有图书采购需求，图书内容或印刷装订等问题，侵权、盗版书籍等线索，请拨打以下电话或关注官方服务号：
客服电话：400 898 7008
官方服务号：微信搜索并关注公众号“外研社官方服务号”
外研社购书网址：https://fltrp.tmall.com

物料号：347440001

记载人类文明
沟通世界文化
www.fltrp.com

序　言

翻译领域的合作，比如合作翻译（collaborative translation）或合译（co-translation），古已有之，不仅见诸历史上的佛经翻译、圣经翻译和文学翻译，也在近年来的笔译项目、团队口译和手语传译中屡见不鲜。如今，广义的合作已包括本地化、视听翻译、粉丝翻译和技术翻译等在内的众多翻译实践。任何涉及机器（辅助）翻译的项目都不可避免地涉及人类译员与翻译机器 / 人工智能之间的直接协作，翻译实践和教学人员与软件程序员之间的间接协作。除此之外，口译员之间也存在多种合作方式。社区口译中译员与医生护士、法官律师及其他利益相关方的合作，会议口译中同传译员之间的协作，可谓无处不在。特别是自 2020 年初新冠病毒感染疫情暴发以来，包括口笔译在内的应急多语服务更是凸显了语言与翻译服务过程中各相关方合作协同的重要性。

正是在这样的背景下，2022 年 6 月 25—26 日在北京举行的、由国际翻译家联盟、中国翻译协会联合主办，北京外国语大学承办的第十届亚太翻译论坛（APTIF10）将会议主题确定为“翻译世界中的合作：新时代、新变化、新模式”就显得恰逢其时，既回顾历史又启发当下，既关注学术研究又观照职业现实，对翻译界乃至整个社会都具有重要意义。

此次论坛为期 2 天，举办了 10 场主旨演讲、12 个常规主题论坛、4 个学术新芽（研究生）分论坛，来自美国、加拿大、英国、澳大利亚、韩国、新加坡、泰国、马来西亚、印度尼西亚、老挝、印度、俄罗斯、阿塞拜疆、乌兹别克斯坦、土库曼斯坦等 35 个国家和地区的近 300 名翻译界正式代表以线上或线下的方式参会，共同打造了一场高规格、高水平、高技术含量的区域性国际翻译盛会。中国网、腾讯会议、哔哩哔哩、译直播、微信视频号等众多平台同步直播，线上观看人数累计达 24.3 万人次，点赞量近 8 万，听众规模和参会代表区域多样性创国内外翻译学术会议和历届亚太翻译论坛历史记录。论坛得到新华社、人民网、光明网、中国日报、中国青年报、中国教育电视台等 30 多家主流媒体多渠道直播和广泛报道，赢得国内外翻译学界、业界广泛关注。

会议的成功举办，也让我们得以将会议中的部分发言结集成书，以论文集的形式呈现给读者，让我们有机会管窥作者们如何从不同视角、不同维度，呼吁、描述、阐释、拓展翻译中的合作问题。

杜占元、高岸明、杨丹分别作为翻译行业管理机构以及语言和翻译人才教育机构的领导者和决策者，从各自不同角度呼应着合作这一主题。杜占元指出，亚太地区是全球聚集人口和民族最多、经济文化发展最具活力、各国交流合作最为活跃、语言文化最为多元的地区；加强交流对话，共同致力于团结合作与和平发展，是亚太各国人民的共同呼声。他呼吁亚太翻译组织和翻译界同仁以论坛为抓手加强亚太翻译界的团结合作，共创团结进步的亚太翻译大家庭。高岸明同样倡导要加强亚太翻译界交流与合作。他汇报了中国语言服务业近年来在多元化人才培养、数字化和智能化创新、规范化监管以及国际交流等方面取得的成绩，并希望借此为亚太地区其他成员提供启示，引领推动实现更大范围的合作、发展与繁荣。杨丹则指出，合作是贯穿翻译事业永恒的主题。从两千多年前西方的圣经翻译，到中国汉唐时期的佛经翻译，均是通过多人相互协作才得以完成。今天，联合国、欧盟等超国家组织，以及国家机构之间和机构内部的翻译合作，新冠疫情、冬奥会和冬季残奥会等重大国际事件中的语言服务合作更是不可或缺，而技术驱动的人机合作也正在并将持续带来更多新的可能性。

在一定程度上，李宇明的论文可被视为就上述决策者对翻译合作的呼吁在语言领域的落地思考。李宇明指出，语言具有“沟壑”和“桥梁”的双重属性。要超越沟壑，构建无障碍社会，就必须培养公民具备包括翻译能力在内的“超语”能力。语言智能将为构建无障碍社会的“新桥梁”提供新的可能，但也需要警惕其可能成为某些人、某些群体交往的“新沟壑”。恰当的人机协同会是未来翻译发展的必由之路。

作为机器翻译和人机合作领域的专家型学者，Lynne Bowker 将机器翻译中人机合作模式的发展描述为“人在回路”（human-in-the-loop）、如过山车一般跌宕起伏的复杂历程。她进一步指出，在神经机器翻译时代，自适应机器翻译、交互式机器翻译和增强式翻译等不断发展，将再度引发 21 世纪的翻译如刺激的过山车般倾斜、下降、转弯和回环，我们须及时调整人机合作关系，充分利用人机合作，以迎接下一个跌宕起伏时代的到来。

在这个技术高速发展的时代，不仅需要建立起恰当的人机协作模式，翻译教育中的合作，包括合作式学习同样十分重要。Gary Massey 从 Don Kiraly 颇具影响力的著述《社会建构主义翻译教学》（*A Social Constructivist Approach to Translator Education*）中受到启发，认为合作学习是翻译教学的最佳实践，这种学习模式通常以合作项目中真实体验学习的形式进行，可给学习者带来更高的责任感、自主性、批判反思、自我调节、动机、主动性和自我效能，这些“软”技能在合作中至关重要，因而变得更加“硬化”，在译者能力模型和课程需求中占据核心位置。

任文、赵田园虽然聚焦一国翻译能力与其软硬实力之间关系的研究，但国家翻译能力的提升离不开各利益相关方之间的协作。她们的研究表明，国家翻译能力下的一级指标，即翻译管理、翻译服务和翻译发展能力基本都和经济硬实力与文化相关软实力指标呈显著正相关，但翻译服务与发展能力与硬软实力指标的正相关系数更高，凸显了翻译实践、翻译传播、翻译教育和翻译技术研发在提升硬软实力中更为重要的地位。建设国家翻译能力，需要协同社会网络中翻译活动的不同利益相关方，通过人才培养、科学研究、技术研发等提升多元主体的翻译实践及传播水平。

卞建华和张钰、李莹两组作者的论文都关注典籍翻译过程中的合作问题。卞建华和张钰针对《晏婴评传》的文本类型及合译模式，在“翻译标准多元互补论”视域下，采用比较和描写研究方法，对典籍合译时的翻译标准、翻译模式、译学路径进行了探讨。李莹以《聊斋志异》首部民族语朝文合译本为研究对象，结合阿皮亚提出的“深度翻译”策略，探析合译本《聊斋志异·卷一》中注释的“深度翻译”现象，期望为“聊斋学”和典籍外译研究提供参考。

朱玉犇、马志鹏和孙婷婷分别聚焦实战与模拟口译中新旧模式下译员的合作与技能融合问题。朱玉犇运用文献法、问卷法和案例研究法，对比分析了传统现场会议口译和远程同传模式下口译员合作情况的异同，发现两者在合作主题、角色分工及合作收益方面都出现了不同程度的变化。由于远程同传受到技术因素限制，整体合作的努力变少，合作收益降低；合作主题由原来的偏重信息抓取，转向偏重管理交接棒；合作手段更具侵入性，且无法做到准确、及时，需消耗更多精力；不同语种团队之间的沟通机会降低，无法有效建立默契关系，译员合作的可持续性受到威胁。马志鹏和孙婷婷通过实验方法，对比分析学生译员在同交传（Simultaneous Consecutive Interpreting，Sim-Consec）这一较新的口译模式与传统交传模式下口译表现的异同，发现学生在前者的表现优于后者。同交传这种新型的混合口译模式（hybrid mode）或可带来对交传和同传技能融合的需求。

郑金凤、许家绍以某公司开展的专利领域翻译实践为例，重点围绕“翻译实践”这一环节，从立足于高校的外围辅助层、定制开发层，到立足于企业的融合应用层、全面扩展层展开具体论证，探讨 MTI 学生从高校到企业、从理论到实践，最终成长为行业栋梁的完整历程，期冀为翻译人才培养的校企合作提供一种直通模式的借鉴。

余下的四篇论文虽未直接讨论合作问题，但当今几乎所有翻译活动，无论是笔译、口译还是机译，都不可能脱离某种方式的合作独立发生。Mayinuer Yusufu 等通过问卷调研，了解医学口译职业在中国的现状、困境和前景。陈靖怡基于中国知网数据库的相关文献，运用可视化软件 Citespace 绘制知识图谱，尝试厘清我国社区口译研究的源流与动态。王炎强、寿晨佳以《抗击新冠肺炎疫情的中国行动》白皮书的英译为例，借鉴社会学和翻译规范理论，讨论公共政策翻译规范问题。赵燕凤、柴橚通过分析源语文本、译者、译语文本与译语文化之间的多元动态关系，尝试细化勒菲弗尔的“折射”理论。除陈靖怡的论文外，其余三篇都是以合作方式开展的研究和写作，从另一个角度“演绎”了翻译研究中的合作实践。

本论文集虽然发端于第十届亚太翻译论坛及其主题——“翻译世界中的合作”，但正如杨丹校长文章的题目所言：“合作是贯穿翻译事业永恒的主题”，因而“合作”也必定成为翻译研究永恒的主题。

任 文

北京外国语大学西院

2023 年 7 月 26 日

目 录

一、决策者谈翻译合作

同筑行业合作之路　共架文明互鉴之桥

杜占元
中国翻译协会
中国外文出版发行事业局

摘　要：中国翻译界长期以来秉持全人类共同价值观，弘扬和平、发展、公平、正义、民主、自由等理念，与各国翻译组织加强交流合作，促进世界和亚太地区翻译行业共同发展。中国翻译协会作为中国翻译界唯一的全国性社会组织，一直以来积极推动中外语言翻译标准体系建设、组织文化产品译介、加强翻译人才队伍建设和翻译家国际交流等活动，受到国内外翻译界广泛认同。本文基于新时代宏阔背景，从中国外文出版发行事业局和中国翻译协会的角度出发，提出四点倡议：把握大势，服务亚太地区繁荣发展；健全体系，加快翻译行业标准化建设；深化交流，增进亚太地区文明交流互鉴；融合发展,推动翻译领域新技术应用。此外，本文介绍了中国翻译界对国际翻译组织的支持以及中国翻译协会开展的相关活动，并呼吁亚太翻译界团结合作，为亚太地区的和平发展和文明互鉴做出贡献。

关键词：交流合作；亚太地区；翻译界；中国翻译协会

A Path for Industry Collaboration, a Bridge for Cultural Exchange

Du Zhanyuan
Translators Association of China (TAC)
China International Communications Group (CICG)

Abstract: The translation industry in China is committed to upholding the common values of humanity, such as peace, development, fairness, justice, democracy, and freedom. It has strengthened its ties and collaborations with translation organizations from various countries, consolidating consensus, gathering strength, and promoting the growth of the industry both domestically and internationally, particularly in the Asia-Pacific region. As the national professional institution of translation, Translators Association of China (TAC) has been proactively promoting the construction of a translation standardization system, boosting cultural communication through translation, strengthening talent cultivation and international exchanges among translators, and encouraging dialogues between different civilizations. Its contributions have been globally recognized. From the perspective of the TAC and China International Communications Group (CICG), this paper proposes four initiatives: capitalizing on the current trend for the prosperity and development of the Asia-Pacific region, expediting the standardization of the translation industry, deepening cultural exchanges and mutual learning in the Asia-Pacific region, and integrating advanced technologies into translation. Additionally, this paper examines the contribution of the Chinese translation community to the world, as well as the related activities of the TAC. The paper concludes by calling for unity and further cooperation among the translation circles to promote peaceful development and cultural exchanges in the Asia-Pacific region.

Keywords: exchange and cooperation; Asia-Pacific region; translation community; TAC

盛夏时节，第十届亚太翻译论坛如约而至，很高兴同各位新老朋友相聚“云端”。在人类社会发展的历史进程中，翻译在推动文化交流、文明互鉴和社会进步方面发挥着不可替代的作用。尤其是在全球化、信息化深入发展的今天，翻译活动通过弥合语言沟通和文化交流的鸿沟，有效增进了各民族友好往来和国家互信合作，助力推动世界和平发展和人类共同进步。前不久召开的世界翻译大会，聚焦语言专业人士在构建文化、促进理解及建设永久和平方面的作用，正体现了新时代翻译工作的宗旨和追求。

20 世纪 90 年代，在国际翻译家联盟的支持下，中国翻译协会发起并创办了亚太翻译论坛，迄今已举办十届，日益发展成为亚太地区翻译界友好往来与交流合作的重要平台。自 2019 年第九届论坛举办以来，面对席卷全球的新冠病毒感染疫情和复杂变化的地区局势，亚太翻译工作者以高度的社会责任感和职业精神，为各国疫情防控和经济复苏提供了有力的语言支撑，为各国人民互联互通提供了便捷的语言服务，成为化解隔阂与误解、促进文明互鉴的重要力量。本届论坛以“翻译世界中的合作：新时代、新变化、新模式”为主题，就是希望以论坛为平台，深化对新时代背景下亚太地区翻译行业变革和未来发展的理解和认识，探索翻译合作新模式，促进亚太各国和平发展和文明互鉴。

长期以来，中国翻译界始终秉持和平、发展、公平、正义、民主、自由的全人类共同价值，与各国翻译组织加强交流合作，凝聚翻译共识、汇聚翻译力量，促进世界和区域翻译行业共同发展。作为中国翻译界唯一的全国性社会组织，中国翻译协会积极开展中外语言翻译标准体系建设，组织文化产品译介，加强翻译人才队伍建设和翻译家国际交流，推动中外文明对话，得到国内外翻译界广泛认同。我们将与亚太及世界各国翻译组织一道，探索新时代翻译合作发展之道，为推动中国和亚太地区乃至世界各国的文明互鉴做出新的贡献。为此，我提出四点倡议。

第一，把握大势，服务亚太地区繁荣发展。在国际交往中，翻译能够使信息准确、快速、广泛传播，发挥着增信释疑的重要功能。希望亚太翻译界持续关注亚太地区发展大势，发挥自身优势，多做促进沟通、解疑释惑的工作，拆除不同语言之间的藩篱，架起多元文化之间的桥梁，为地区繁荣发展做出翻译工作者应有的贡献。

第二，健全体系，加快翻译行业标准化建设。完善行业标准化体系，健全服务、管理与监督机制，是推动翻译行业与时俱进、创新发展的必由之路。希望本届论坛能够为亚太地区建立统一、科学、完善的翻译行业标准体系献计献策，推动各国在行业标准互认、人才评价等领域加强合作，增强翻译服务效能，提高社会对翻译行业和翻译工作者的认同，切实保护翻译工作者权益。

第三，深化交流，增进亚太地区文明交流互鉴。文明因交流而多彩、因互鉴而丰富。希望亚太翻译界在人员往来、信息交流、产品互换、技术研发等方面进一步团结合作，形成合力，提升亚太翻译界的整体实力、竞争力和影响力。加强与区域外国家和地区同行的交流，共享成果，以开放包容、合作共赢的姿态，推动行业发展和文明互鉴。

第四，融合发展，推动翻译领域新技术应用。近年来，人工智能、大数据、云计算等新技术的迭代发展，为翻译事业提供了新的助力。希望亚太翻译界密切跟踪翻译技术发展趋势，加强人工智能辅助翻译系统等翻译技术平台建设，创新应用场景和模式，深化技术合作，推动翻译事业向数字化、智能化更高水平迈进。

亚太地区是全球聚集人口和民族最多、经济文化发展最具活力、各国交流合作最为活跃、语言文化最为多元的地区。当前，世界经济重心正在加速向亚太地区转移，区域合作和一体化进程加快，亚太地区在全球发展格局中的战略地位不断上升。加强交流对话，共同致力于团结合作与和平发展，成为亚太各国人民的共同呼声。中国国家主席习近平在今年博鳌亚洲论坛开幕式上的讲话中指出："用对话合作取代零和博弈，用开放包容取代封闭排他，用交流互鉴取代唯我独尊，这是亚洲应有的襟怀和气度。"站在新的历史起点上，亚太翻译组织和翻译界同仁，要适应亚太发展的世纪大趋势，加强亚太翻译论坛联合委员会机制建设，扩大会员规模和代表性；探索举办形式多样、内容丰富的论坛配套活动，以论坛为抓手加强亚太翻译界的团结合作；积极参与国际翻译组织工作，在国际翻译界发出亚太声音、做出亚太贡献；适时成立亚太翻译联合组织，进一步扩大亚太翻译界的国际影响力和话语权，共创团结进步的亚太翻译大家庭。

本届论坛将集百家之长，把不同文明的优秀基因融合起来，把不同国家的利益融汇起来，将各国间的互信互助推向一个新的高度。衷心希望亚太翻译界的合作之路、友谊之路、创新之路越走越宽广，为亚太命运共同体建设传递更多的正能量，与全球译者共同筑就友谊合作之基、架设文明互鉴之桥，创造全球翻译事业更加美好的明天！

Strengthen Exchanges and Cooperation of the Asia-Pacific Translation Community Towards Better Development and Greater Prosperity

Gao Anming
APTIF Joint Committee
Translators Association of China (TAC)
China International Communications Group (CICG)
Federation of International Translators (FIT)

Abstract: With the aim of promoting exchanges among translation associations and individuals in the Asia-Pacific region, the APTIF has been a vital platform for communication and mutual learning over the past three decades. This paper provides an overview of the evolution and accomplishments of APTIF, with a focus on the role played by China. Additionally, it examines the distinctive features of China's language service industry in recent years, including exponential growth, diversified talent cultivation, digital and intelligent innovation, regulatory standardization, and orderly international exchanges, from the perspective of TAC. The goal is to offer insights to other members in the region. The paper concludes by discussing how the industry envisions the next generation of translation and how it can empower the Asia-Pacific translation community towards better development and greater prosperity. The paper suggests that a promising future for the translation industry in the Asia-Pacific region will be underpinned by diversity and vitality, supported by technological innovation, multi-disciplinary integration, and a rational support system.

Keywords: exchange; language service industry; cooperation and development

加强亚太翻译界交流与合作　推动实现更大发展与繁荣

高岸明
亚太翻译论坛联合委员会
中国翻译协会
中国外文出版发行事业局
国际翻译家联盟理事会

摘　要：本文首先回顾了亚太翻译论坛在过去三十年的发展和成就，探讨了中国在其中所扮演的重要角色。随后，以中国翻译协会的视角，进一步讨论了中国语言服务业近年来呈现出的特点，包括行业迅速发展、多元化人才培养、数字化和智能化创新、规范化监管以及井然有序的国际交流，借此为亚太地区的其他成员提供启示。最后，本文展望了语言服务行业未来的发展，探讨行业如何引领亚太翻译界进一步走向繁荣。本文认为，通过技术创新、多学科整合、科学规范化的支持系统，亚太地区翻译行业必将充满活力、异彩纷呈，走向光明的未来。

关键词：交流互鉴；语言服务行业；合作发展

Since its establishment in 1995, APTIF has taken it as its central mission to facilitate exchanges among translation associations and individuals within the Asia-Pacific region. The forum is committed to promoting connectivity and mutual learning among the Asia-Pacific and the international community. Under concerted efforts of all sides, the past three decades have seen successful conclusion of 9 APTIF sessions, which grew steadily with diversified themes, extensive communication, wider participation and rewarding outcomes, establishing itself as the most important platform for translation exchanges in the region.

The founding of the APTIF Joint Committee in 2016 marked a breakthrough in the history of the forum, charting a new course for international communication. In 2019, I was honored to be elected as the chair of the Joint Committee. During my term over the past three years, translation associations, educational institutions, and practitioners conducted extensive communication with each other on the platform. Every participant contributed to and at the same time, benefited from this grand get-together, bearing witness to the development of the forum. The COVID-19 pandemic in 2020 hit hard the T&I industry globally. The Joint Committee took quick responses, held a webinar with the theme of "Pooling the Strength of the Asia-Pacific Translation and Interpreting Community to Combat COVID-19" and issued an initiative to call on all parties in and beyond the region to unite as one through difficult times.

In December 2021, the Joint Committee held an on-line conference at which the first issue of *APTIF Bulletin* was released, serving as a new tool to facilitate mutual understanding and regional exchanges in the T&I profession. Now 6 issues of the *Bulletin* have been released, disseminating industry news from participating institutions and sharing experiences within the region. The publication is highly recognized by our members and attracts global attention as well, including FIT.

The APTIF dream started in Beijing 27 years ago. Today we gather here with our aspiration unchanged — common development for Asia-Pacific. As an important member in Asia-Pacific and the largest developing country in the world, China boasts a huge and booming market for translation activities. This paper discusses the characteristics of China's language service industry displayed in recent years, which may provide some food for thought for other members in the region, while drawing on their experiences and practices as well. This paper will conclude by elaborating on how the industry envisages the next-generation translation and how it can empower the Asia-Pacific translation community towards better development and greater prosperity.

The first part gives a brief introduction of TAC. Established in 1982, the Translators Association of China plays a pivotal role in the country's translation and language service industry, and is also one of the founding associations of APTIF. After 40 years of development, TAC now has some 7,000 members, and speaks for 980,000 professional translators and interpreters in the country.

As its membership keeps expanding, TAC has been promoting more exchanges among its branches and striving to improve services for its members and the industry. TAC, together with efforts of its members, has been working hard and contributing greatly to making its profession more specialized, well-organized, and systematic.

In the meantime, in a globalized world, TAC is fully aware that its development would be impossible without deeper integration with the international community. TAC joined FIT in 1987 and is now one of its largest members. It initiated APTIF in 1995 and co-hosted the 18th FIT World Congress in Shanghai in 2008. All these are part of its continued efforts to engage in international cooperation and exchanges.

As the national association for translation and interpreting in China, TAC keeps a close eye on dynamics of global translation industry. In the context of globalization and information age, countries are more interconnected than ever in terms of economy, culture, science and technology and many other fields. Translation is growing into an important part of national core competitiveness and cultural soft power and becoming a bridge for promoting cultural communication, economic and trade exchanges, knowledge sharing, and social progress. Translation and language services around the world are developing rapidly and vigorously in concert with peace and development of our times.

At the moment, China's translation and language service industry is showing many distinctive features. Remarkable progress has also been made in terms of growth, talent pool, technological innovation, management and international cooperation, which can be summarized as follows.

First, China's language service industry has grown exponentially.

The past four decades since China's introduction of the reform and opening-up policy, especially the last decade during which the country's development has entered a new era, have been a critical period for China to interact more deeply with and open wider to the world. It has also been a time for China's translation and language service industry to adapt to national development and advance both in depth and scope as the country integrates more profoundly with the rest of the world.

Through a continuous nationwide survey first launched in 2012, TAC has been conducting systematic research and analysis of the current situation, characteristics, problems and trends of the industry. The survey results have shown a continuous expansion and steady growth of output in the translation and language service industry over the past decade. Figures are shown in Table 1 below. And this output made up about 17 percent of the global figure.

Table 1 The situation, characteristics, problems and trends of the language service industry in 2021

The number of enterprises engaged in language service-related business in China in 2021	420,000
And the number of enterprises with language service as their main business in 2021	Nearly 10,000
The total output value of language service enterprises in 2021	RMB55.5 billion (USD8.67 billion)
And the annual average growth rate of total output value in 2021	11.10%
Total output value in 2021 as a proportion of global language service forecast	16.80%
People engaged in providing translation and language service in 2021	5.38 million
Growth rate of language professionals in the past decade	40%

Among the disciplines, language education and training, information and communication technology, and intellectual property rights-related services rank as the top three in terms of business turnover. Translations from and into Chinese are still the mainstay and has become more balanced, which is 37 percent for each, while translation between international languages other than Chinese has grown to about a quarter of the total volume.

Second, China's language service industry is cultivating a diverse talent force to promote cross-sector and integrated development.

During the last four decades, China's translation and language service industry has leveraged the world's largest higher educational system to enjoy rapid development rarely seen in the world. According to the latest survey data, most translators in China are under the age of 45 and hold at least a bachelor's degree, while master's degrees are becoming increasingly common and higher degrees are not at all rare. The team of translators is clearly tiered. Close exchanges and integrated development of disciplines has enhanced market demand to the point where employers constantly expect more from practitioners, raising the bar for everyone. Multi-disciplinary talent with not only foreign language proficiency but also expertise in other fields, such as international relations, journalism & communication, economics or management science, become considerably more competitive with their employers. This table shows the number of professionals and part-time practitioners in 2021. There were 980,000 professional translators last year, up 53 percent from 10 years ago.

The next three charts (charts 1, 2, 3) show enrollments of postgraduate programs in translation and interpreting, the number of higher-education institutions offering postgraduate programs in T&I, and the number of languages with postgraduate programs in T&I, all going up steadily.

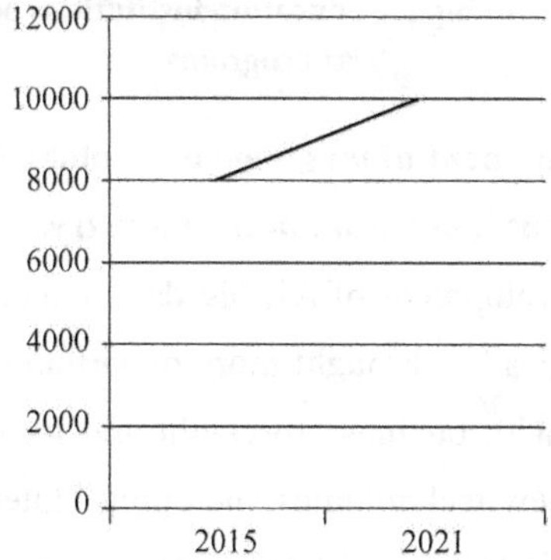

Chart 1 The enrollments of postgraduate T&I programs

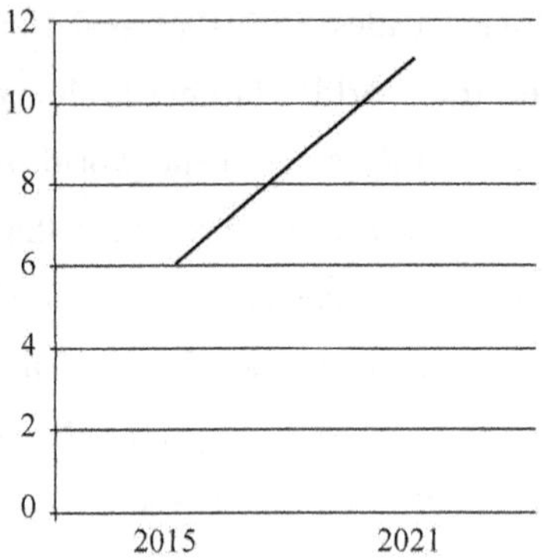

Chart 2　The number of languages with postgraduate T&I programs

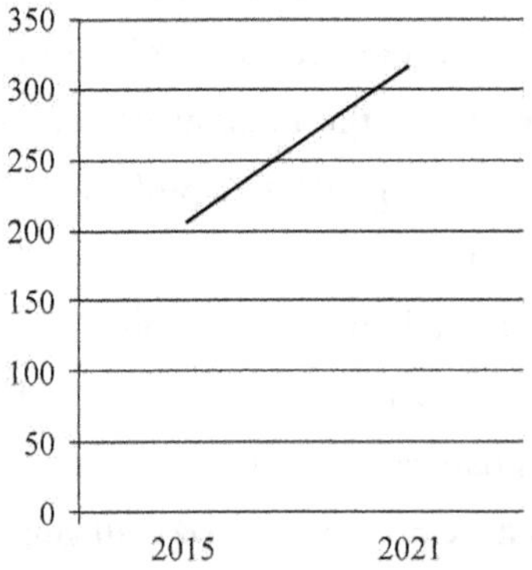

Chart 3　The number of higher-education institutions offering postgraduate T&I programs

Third, the development of language technology drives the application of digital and intelligent innovation in the industry.

The vigorous development of AI, big data, cloud computing and other information technologies has brought more opportunities than challenges for the industry. People with business foresight and tech savvy entrepreneurs are eager to harness new technologies and apply "Internet Plus" thinking to the language service industry and hence opened a vast ocean for language technologies to help build both a more globalized and localized future.

Stellar examples are set by Alibaba Group, one of the largest e-commerce companies in China, and iFLYTEK Co., one of the big techs in China specializing in AI. Both have made key contributions in machine translation and natural voice recognition.

From these cases, it can be observed that the high-tech firms strive not only for breakthroughs in world-leading research and innovation, but also to meet actual market demand. Their language technologies have not only made translation more efficient, cost-effective and dynamic, but also benefited users in China and around the world.

Fourth, China is promoting standardization to better regulate the industry.

A survey found that more than 70% of language service users believe that standardization and sound regulation are good for sustained operations of language service providers and will guarantee quality.

In recent years, supported by its members and industry players, TAC has introduced initiatives to promote standardization and self-regulation in the industry. It has conducted joint research on standardization with domestic and foreign specialized agencies, and organized compilation of five national standards and 23 institutional standards and industry norms. TAC also have organized certification of language service enterprises across the industry, and promoted international mutual recognition of language service standards. In this way, a quantifiable standardization system has gradually taken shape.

TAC considers translation infrastructure building tremendously important to the profession. It has collaborated with both domestic and overseas foreign language colleges and universities and language technology enterprises to develop and establish data platforms such as multilingual foreign translation corpus and terminology databases to provide guide to standardized translation of terminology in various industries. TAC has improved resources available and basic conditions for translation work by leveraging our powers as an industry organization to improve the profession by regulating, guiding and supporting practitioners.

Fifth, China is promoting platform-based, institutionalized openness and cooperation in international exchanges.

With the deepening of globalization, China has seen its exchanges and trade with other parts of the world multiply by leaps and bounds. During the process, the country's translation sector has become increasingly open to and integrated into the global community, enabling language services to prosper. It is fair to say that without competent translation and language services, China would not have achieved its development miracles. And mutual learning among different cultures would not be as effective as it is today.

TAC has taken much efforts and practical measures in recent years to advance exchanges between China's translation community and its global partners. It is fair to say that all efforts are well paid off. On the recently concluded FIT Statutory Congress, nominated by TAC, Mr. Frans De Laet, who is entitled as the overseas expert, honorary advisor of FIT and its former secretary general, and who was professor here at BFSU in 2010—2013, stood out from many candidates and was awarded one of FIT's most prestigious honors—the Pierre-François Caillé Memorial Medal. In the meantime, TAC's leaders have been serving on the council of FIT for many years now and involved in decision-making of global translation affairs, offering solutions and wisdom from China and the wider Asia-Pacific region to international community.

China's translation industry grows stronger alongside the Asia-Pacific family where people communicate, interact and bond as one. APTIF brought T&I professionals to Beijing, Seoul, Hong Kong, Bogor, Macao, Penang and Xi'an. Friends and experts at APTIF, though being in different time zones and thousands of miles away from each other, managed to meet online or offline for this grand showcase of knowledge-sharing, close cooperation, and mutual assistance.

As an old Chinese saying goes, a wise learner knows how to overcome his own shortcomings by drawing on advantages of others. Asia-Pacific is the most dynamic region in the world and holds huge potential for future development. It is true that countries in the region differ a lot in their national conditions, ethnic groups, cultures, and languages, but they coexist and interact with each other along the way, producing rich fruits accordingly. China is ready to share with all countries in the region our experiences in advancing T&I industry for common development.

Among all exceptional cases in the region, the T&I educational system in the Republic of Korea, which offers much food for thought, stands out. In 2019, it impressively delivered the 9th APTIF meeting, paving the way for further development. A close partner of the Joint Committee, the Graduate School of Interpreting and Translation (GSIT) of Hankuk University of Foreign Studies is a world-class educational institution for translators and interpreters. The school is also the first in Asia to join CIUTI as a regular member. Without doubt, it has a lot to offer in terms of their experience in educational philosophy, talent training, curriculum arrangement, faculty, and international exchanges. In the future, the potential of APTIF could be fully unleashed to meet the needs in communicating with others, sharing academic results and ideas, and accessing practices and experiences.

Domestically, Beijing Foreign Studies University (BFSU), the organizer of this forum, has experiences to offer as well. Last month, BFSU released the 2021 Global Translation Index, analyzing translation capabilities of 193 countries and regions. It is noted that among the top 50 on the list, there are 12 from the Asia-Pacific region, accounting for 24% of the total number, which illustrates the importance of the region in global translation landscape and the exceptional achievements China have made in terms of translation management, language service and development potential. But there is another fact that requires extra attention. Only 4 out of 20 top seats on the list were from Asia-Pacific (beside China, the other three are Japan, the Republic of Korea and Australia), whereas 16 were taken by Europe and North America. There is much more to be done to expand our influences and empower our translation community.

Yet, the industry is presented with various opportunities brought by new business forms and more emerging technologies in various sectors. In the new era, we embrace the next-generation translation which, I believe, will empower Asia-Pacific region, and push the development of translation industry to new heights.

This paper believes that the next-generation translation will make the language service industry more equal, diversified and inclusive.

Exchange in spoken and written languages is an important component of cultural exchanges, and the translation of classics by Chinese and foreign translators has effectively promoted exchange and mutual learning among different cultures.

The world-famous translation theorist George Steiner observed: "Every language is a world. Without translation, we would inhabit parishes bordering on silence."

Today, about 40% of the world's more than 6,700 remaining languages are on the verge of extinction, with one disappearing from the planet every two weeks. It is the common responsibility of the international translation community to protect rare and endangered languages and cultural heritage, protect the right to preserve the spoken and written languages of the vulnerable groups, including those with visual and hearing impairments, and promote common development in the world.

This paper sees that the next-generation translation community, empowered by modern technology, will develop broader vision and stronger capacity to ensure the values of equality, diversity, and inclusiveness in the translation community, and robustly promote exchanges, mutual learning, and integrated development of diverse cultures.

Next-generation translation will be empowered by and in due course propel more intelligent, efficient, greener technological innovation that will benefit all in the language service industry.

From index cards to computer keyboards and speech recognition, advancements in technology have empowered translation and interpreting activities, injecting much vitality into the industry, by bringing people separated by mountains and seas to meet face-to-face in person or virtually on the cloud.

Indeed, when machine translation becomes more mature and is widely adopted, ordinary translation jobs that do not require explicit accuracy will likely be replaced by AI assisted computer translation. In fact, this is already happening on an increasing scale. Nevertheless, modern technology may also serve to drive down the cost of switching among languages, therefore creating more demand that would not happen without easier access.

The next-generation translation technologies are expected to fully emancipate and therefore boost productivity, and allow language professionals to focus more on creative translation activities that better promote human wellbeing. The industry should actively seek to promote the power of intelligent, efficient, green translation and interpreting services and enhance shared benefits from interaction in technology development, standards formulation and industrial development.

Next-generation translation will attract more people to the sector for the noble cause of promoting equality, cultural inclusiveness and shared values.

Inclusiveness is a basic indicator of the progress of human civilization, and with it the value of translation activities increases. The world needs more language professionals who are globally minded, thoughtful, competent, responsible and enterprising, to create a vibrant scene in the industry.

With demand driving supply, this paper anticipates that next-generation translation and interpreting services will attract more people to the sector, who will sharpen their capabilities through interdisciplinary and multidisciplinary communication, strengthen cross-cultural communication skills alongside deepening international cooperation, break down cultural barriers, and engage in international cooperation more readily and more confidently. They will be able to promote exchanges and mutual learning among cultures with a broader mind, contribute wisdom and promote mutual respect, openness and inclusiveness.

Last but not least, next-generation translation will help build a more scientific, rational, specialized and standardized support system.

In the future, translation and interpreting services will take on more forms, language technology will continue to evolve, the language service market will expand, and language services will cover virtually all economic and social spheres. TAC will continue to uphold the principles of joint consultation and cooperation for shared benefits, rely on APTIF and other platforms, strengthen communication and coordination among translation organizations in various countries to align standards, coordinate mechanisms and share outcomes to create more growth points for international cooperation in language services, and build a diverse, interactive international translation community that works towards common development.

Next-generation translation organizations are expected to act more proactively to unite diverse stakeholders, protect the rights and interests of translators and interpreters, improve the language service support system, and drive high-quality development of the global language service industry.

As an international academic forum, APTIF has come a long way and we are now at its 10th session. Over the past 27 years, the forum has enabled mutual learning and exchanges between our region and the world, contributing considerably to the sustainable development of translation industry of participating countries and regions. APTIF also played a big role in spreading the voice of Asia-Pacific to the international community, building the image of Asia-Pacific and strengthening the global influence of our region. A strong and unified Asia-Pacific will in turn enable regional members to prosper.

合作是贯穿翻译事业永恒的主题

杨　丹　北京外国语大学

摘　要: 第十届亚太翻译论坛由国际翻译家联盟和中国翻译协会联合主办，北京外国语大学承办，主题为“翻译世界中的合作：新时代、新变化、新模式”。翻译作为跨语言、跨文化、跨国跨地区的社会活动，在历史上一直扮演着重要角色，并随着世界融合与技术发展而发生日新月异的变化，对传统意义上的翻译实践、翻译教学、翻译研究均提出了新要求，也凸显了合作的重要性。本文认为翻译合作作为其中永恒不变和重要的主题，必将持续引领翻译事业的发展。本文期冀论坛能够聚集中外专家智慧，共同探讨翻译领域的新发展、新挑战及解决途径。

关键词: 亚太翻译论坛；合作交流；翻译事业；发展

Collaboration, an Evergreen Theme in the World of Translation and Interpreting

Yang Dan
Beijing Foreign Studies University

Abstract: The 10th Asia-Pacific Translation and Interpreting Forum (APTIF 10) organized under the auspices of the International Federation of Translators (FIT) and the Translators Association of China (TAC) was held at Beijing Foreign Studies University (BFSU). The theme of the forum is “Cooperation in the Translation World: New Era, New Changes, New Models”. Translation is a crucial social activity that serves to help cross the barriers between languages, cultures, countries, and regions. It has played a significant role in history and is undergoing new changes due to the integration of the world and technological advancements. This has resulted in new requirements for traditional translation practices, translation teaching, and translation research. This paper argues

that collaboration, as an evergreen theme in the world of translation and interpreting, will continue to lead the development of translation. The forum is expected to bring together experts from around the world to discuss new developments, challenges, and solutions in the field of translation.
Keywords: APTIF; cooperation and exchange; translation practice; development

自 1995 年创立以来，三年一届的亚太翻译论坛已经成功走过 27 个年头，如今已成为亚太地区乃至国际翻译学界业界交流与合作的重要平台之一。今天，第十届亚太翻译论坛再次回到她的诞生地北京，作为会议承办方，北京外国语大学对此深感荣幸。北外被称为新中国外交官的摇篮，也是翻译国家队的摇篮，从建立之初就以培养高端外语和翻译人才为己任。在 81 年的办学历程中，北外为国家领导人、国家部委、联合国等国际组织培养了人数最多的高层次多语翻译人才。目前，北外共开设了 101 个语种，也是中国开设语种最多的高校。感谢国际译联和中国译协对我们的信任，把承办第十届亚太翻译论坛的机会交给北外。此次论坛以"翻译世界中的合作：新时代、新变化、新模式"为主题，恰合时宜，意义重大。

首先，新时代赋予翻译新的历史使命。作为一项跨语言、跨文化、跨国跨地区的社会活动，翻译在人类文明发展的不同时期都扮演着极其重要的角色。以中国为例，我们在历史上就曾经历了两汉至唐宋的佛经翻译、明末清初的科技翻译、鸦片战争至五四运动的西学翻译、新中国成立初期到 20 世纪 70 年代中后期的东西方文学翻译，以及改革开放至今百花齐放的翻译等五次高峰。在西方，翻译活动也曾助力罗马帝国的强盛，西方基督教文明的发展，文艺复兴的发端，以及二战前后的联合国、欧盟等现代国际组织的诞生。不同时期的翻译活动无不紧扣时代主题。进入 21 世纪，世界各国在经济、社会、文化等各方面进一步高度融合，密切交流，当今世界没有哪一个国家或民族可以脱离翻译活动而取得长久蓬勃的发展。近年来，世界格局风云变幻，逆全球化浪潮此起彼伏，全球合作受阻，单边主义和保护主义抬头。与此同时，新冠病毒感染疫情引发的不确定性也给各国发展及前途命运蒙上了一层阴影。历史告诉我们，越是在这样的时期，我们就愈发需要沟通心灵，谋求合作，加强文明互鉴，这也正是当今时代赋予翻译新的崇高使命。亚太地区作为世界上最具发展活力与潜力的地区，在维护世界和平稳定，推动全球合作发展方面发挥着独特作用。翻译界同仁应当互学互鉴，为推动构建人类命运共同体做出更大贡献。

其次，新变化对翻译事业发展提出新要求。伴随大数据、云计算、人工智能、虚拟现实等技术的快速发展，翻译行业不断涌现出新的业态，机器翻译、网络众包以及国际化浪潮下催生的语言服务产业，对传统意义上的翻译实践、翻译教学、翻译研究带来新的挑战。特别是新冠病毒感染疫情暴发以来，不少国家和地区的翻译实践与教学活动被迫转到线上，由此产生的影响值得我们展开深入研究。近年来，北京外国语大学着眼时代的新发展、新模式、新需求，勇于创新、开拓进取，在语种开设、翻译专业设置、复合型、复语型人才培养等方面取得了一系列重要进展。北京外国语大学目前正在积极实施全球战略，战略重点可以概括为“三个全球”，即全球语言、全球文化、全球治理。“全球语言”就是要构建全球领先的语言教育、研究、服务、保护平台，打造全球多语言航空母舰；“全球文化”重点就是用外语、外嘴、外脑“讲好中国故事”；“全球治理”重点就是构建全球知识体系，推动中国的全球治理体系和治理能力现代化，提升中国全球领导力，而这三个“全球”战略的推进都离不开语言和翻译的基础性作用。2021 年 5 月 22 日，北外正式成立全国首个国家翻译能力研究中心，汇聚各方专家力量，全球独家研发了 193 个国家的国别翻译能力指数以及 454 所中国大学翻译能力指数。作为能够反映当今各国国家翻译能力现状，以及中国大学翻译教学、实践、研究和社会服务发展状况的晴雨表，这两个指数对引领国家翻译能力建设及翻译学科发展无疑具有重要意义。长期以来，各国翻译学界都在以各自的方式开展着丰富多彩的翻译实践、翻译教学与翻译研究，以回应当今时代的文化诉求与社会需要。在本次论坛上，我们将会聆听中外专家在这些重要议题上分享真知灼见，凝聚集体智慧，共同应对这些新变化、新挑战。

再次，新模式是新时代新变化给翻译带来的必然结果。翻译教学方面，机辅翻译实验室、交传同传实验室只能是翻译专业的标配。远程教学、虚拟仿真教学以及各种智能设备正在进入越来越多的课堂。各种令人眼花缭乱的质化、量化工具日益丰富翻译研究的手段，而 eye-tracker（眼动仪）、EEG（脑电图）、ERPs（事件相关电位）、fMRI（功能性磁共振成像）、fNIR（近红外光学脑成像系统）、MEG（脑磁图）、PET（正电子发射计算机断层扫描）等最新技术让我们得以探究“翻译中的大脑”（the translating brain），并不断接近那个神秘的“黑匣子”。机助人译、人助机译、远程口译等翻译实践新模式更是深刻地改变了译者的生活和工作方式。

最后，合作是贯穿翻译事业永恒的主题。如果说这世上有哪一条原则能够指导所有类型的翻译活动，那一定是合作。我认为，合作应当是翻译的天然属性之一，小到一次翻译任务，大到一个国家的翻译战略，再到联合国等国际社会有组织的翻译职能，无不需要人与人之间的合作才能顺利开展。两千多年前，西方圣经翻译就有了依靠多人协作才完成的《七十士译本》。无独有偶，在一千多年以前的东方，中国的佛经翻译也是依靠译主、证义、度语、笔受等多个角色的相互配合才得以实现。时间快进到两千年后的今天，联合国、欧盟等超国家组织，以及国家机构之间和机构内部的翻译合作，新冠疫情、冬奥会和冬残奥会等重大国际事件中的语言服务合作更是不可或缺。北外 20 多个语种的老师参与由中国外文出版发行事业局组织的《习近平谈治国理政》三卷本的翻译审校，北外五个语种的中外专家合作译审《习近平总书记教育重要论述讲义》等，也都是合作翻译的典型案例。而当下，技术驱动的人机合作也正在并将持续为我们带来更多新的可能性。

本次盛会将带领我们回顾历史、启发当下。在会议期间，与会专家会在现场和云端分享各自的研究成果，他们的真知灼见必将对亚太翻译界乃至整个社会产生重要意义。我们相信，无论世事如何改变，合作的主题亘古不变，历久弥新。翻译界如此，其他领域也莫不如是。

二、超语实践中的沟通与合作

语言是文化的鸿沟与桥梁[1]

李宇明　北京语言大学

摘　要：语言与文化群体具有互促互育关系，语言是文化群体内沟通关联的纽带和认同标记，且对外具有封闭性和排他性。对内认同、对外封闭排他的特点，使语言成为文化间的“沟壑”。“语言沟壑”有利于维护人类文化的多元性。但语言又具有沟通不同文化的“桥梁”作用，不同文化群体通过语言相互交流，文化也随之外溢而益外，成为人世间的共同财富；不同文化群体也可在交流中相互理解，变“他者”为“友者”，甚至为“我者”。在超语时代、数字时代，全面认识语言的“沟桥二重性”很有意义。全世界有六七千种语言，许多语言还有地方方言、社会方言和用于特殊人群的手语、盲文等。语言、方言等使人世间布满了文化沟壑，而要超越沟壑，构建无障碍社会，必须培养公民的“超语”能力，其中包括翻译能力。语言智能为发挥语言的桥梁作用提供了新可能，人机协同是自动翻译发展的必由之路。语言机器人是构建无障碍社会的“新桥梁”，但也需要警惕，它也可能成为某些人、某些人群交往的“新沟壑”。

关键词：语言；超语时代；文化沟通；翻译；无障碍社会

1　本文根据“第十届亚太翻译论坛”（2022年6月25日，北京外国语大学）上的报告修改而成，当时的报告题目为“促进社会无障碍沟通——超语时代翻译的社会担当”。相关内容，曾以“构建信息无障碍社会”为题，在“中国民族语言学会民族语文应用专业委员会第三次学术研讨会暨中国民族语文应用第二届高端论坛”上做过学术报告（2022年4月9日）；曾以“语言信息化与语言权利”为题，在武汉大学举行的“中国语言学话语体系建设与国际传播学术研讨会”上做过学术报告（2022年5月27日）；以“语言是文化的鸿沟与桥梁”为题，在宁波诺丁汉大学人文专家大讲堂做过学术报告（2022年6月28日）。本文得到国家社科基金重大项目“‘两个一百年’背景下的语言国情调查与语言规划研究”（项目批准号：21&ZD289）的支持。吴艳为本文的写作提供了不少帮助。

Language as Both a Gap and a Bridge of Cultures

Li Yuming
Beijing Language and Culture University

Abstract: Language and culture are intertwined. Language serves as a unifying force for people within a particular culture, providing a means of group identification. However, language can also act as a barrier, excluding those from other cultural backgrounds. This inward identity and outward exclusiveness of language can create a "gap" between cultures. While this gap can help preserve the diversity of human cultures, language can also serve as a "bridge" for cross-cultural communication, enabling cultures to spread and benefit one another. This ultimately leads to mutual understanding, transforming the "other" into "friends" and eventually into the "we". In the age of translanguaging and digitalization, it is crucial to recognize the dual nature of language as a gap and a bridge. With over six or seven thousand languages in the world, along with regional dialects, sign language, and braille, cultural barriers are pervasive. Therefore, promoting "translanguaging" skills, including translation, is essential to building an inclusive community. Language intelligence can help bridge cultural gaps, and human-machine collaboration is crucial for automatic translation. Language robots can also serve as a bridge for an accessible community, but they may also create a "new gap" for some individuals and groups.

Keywords: Language; the age of translanguaging; cultural communication; translation; accessible community

1. 引言

文化多元化仍是国际社会的重要话题，各种文化相互尊重、相互借鉴、共同进步仍是国际社会的基本主张。语言与文化的关系十分密切，语言具有文化阻隔和文化沟通的双重功能，本文称之为“沟桥二重性”。世界一体化由于新冠病毒感染疫情、国际政治等原因出现了一些逆流，但是人类之间的互动交往不可能因此而“熔断”，托马斯·弗里德曼（Thomas L. Friedman，2006）关于“世界是平的”的判断仍在应验，无障碍社会的构想及其实践正在使世界变得更加平坦。特别是由于互联网的广覆盖和数字化的大发展，人类在理念和技术上都更有条件进行超语实践（translanguaging practice），亦即超越语言、方言及其他语符进行交往，利用快速进步的语言智能进行交往。在文化多元化、世界一体化仍为世界重要话题的时局下，对于身处超语时代和数字时代的我们，认真审视语言的“沟桥二重性”具有学术和现实的双重意义。

本文首先从语言属性，特别是语言与文化的关系入手，讨论语言的“沟桥二重性”，然后从超语和无障碍社会的视角，进一步认识跨越语言沟壑、充分发挥语言桥梁作用的意义。本文强调公民“超语”能力的培养，促进自动翻译事业的发展，重视语言智能在数字时代构建无障碍社会的新桥梁作用。

2. 语言的“沟桥二重性”

语言具有对内认同、对外封闭排他的特点，如同“文化沟壑”，同时也具有文化间相互沟通的功能，如同“文化桥梁”。这便是语言的“沟桥二重性”。要全面、深入地认识语言的“沟桥二重性”，需要先了解语言是什么。

2.1 语言

语言是语言学的研究对象。任何学科对其研究对象几乎都难以确切地定义，这是因为不同时代、不同学派、不同学者都可能从不同的角度、在不同层面上来认识自己学科的研究对象，由此而形成不同的学术观点乃至不同的学派。这种现象在外学科或不从事科学研究的人看来有些奇怪，其实这是十分正常的学术现象，甚至也可以理解为学科不断发展进步、兴旺发达的一种表现。

语言学是一门古老而年轻的学科，而且是横跨人文科学、社会科学、理工科的“大学科”，对语言有不同的学科认识更为正常，据说关于语言的定义不下 300 种。潘文国（2001）曾经搜集 19 世纪初叶以来有代表性的关于语言的观点68则，并对这些观点逐条列举，审慎评述，可谓集其大成。潘先生在此基础上将语言定义为“语言是人类认知世界及进行表述的方式和过程”，是有独到见地的。当然，这又为语言的定义增加了一种。

本文对语言的各种定义不做刻意评价，只打算做些综合汇聚工作。综合前人时贤的观点，可以这样来描述语言：

1）语言是人类用于交际和思维的最为重要的符号体系；

2）语言是文化最为重要的组成部分，是文化最为重要的构建者、阐释者、记录者、负载者和传播者，且常常具有民族“图腾”（totem）的作用；

3）语言能力是“元人力资本”，语言数据是数字经济的关键生产要素。

关于上述三个方面，第一个是关于语言的交际、思维两大职能的界定，这两大职能是语言的基础功用，是语言的其他功能的基础；符号是语言的本质属性，如果不具备符号的性质，语言就难以发挥好交际和思维的职能。第二个是关于语言与文化的关系的表述，特别强调了语言作为文化的“构建者、阐释者、记录者、负载者和传播者”角色。第三个是关于语言经济属性的认识。过去人们较少从经济学的角度去看待语言，其实语言一直在人类的经济生活中发挥着不可或缺的重要作用，特别是社会进入数字时代，再忽视语言的经济属性，就可能出现严重的缺陷了。

人们还可以从其他的视角来看待语言和研究语言，但能够从上述三个视角来观照语言，已经较为全面了。认识语言以上三个方面的属性，特别是第二个方面的属性，有助于全面而深入地了解语言与文化群体的各种复杂关系。

2.2 语言与文化群体

人是社会化动物，交际是人类的本性，新生儿甚至胎儿就对母亲的声音特别敏感。在研究人类群体的发展时，学者们常常将人类共同生活的群落大小和人类原始文明的突发性进步作为语言产生的一个标志。原因就是语言产生之后，人类的信息沟通能力和生产力大大提升，由此才能维持较大的群落聚集，才能带来经验的大集聚、智力的大提升和文明的大飞跃（胡明扬，1983；尤瓦尔·赫拉利，2014）。

语言产生之后，就与人类的文化群体构成互促互育的关系。在社会交际和人类的认知思维中，在阐释、记录、传播人类文化的过程中，语言不断发展完善，词汇量不断增加，语法系统越来越缜密，语用手段不断丰富，并且还产生了文字系统，发展出书面媒体，之后又发展出有声媒体、网络媒体和融合媒体。而人类也在语言交际中形成不同的文化群体，并不断发展壮大，形成古今各种文明，由原始社会进入农业社会、工业社会和数字社会。语言是文化群体的建构者和阐释者，也是群体文化的记录者和负载者。人类因使用不同的语言而构成不同的文化群体，如英语与英语文化群体、法语与法语文化群体、德语与德语文化群体、日语与日语文化群体、汉语与汉语文化群体等。当然，文化群体之间的差异并不仅仅是语言，还有宗教信仰、文化传统、风俗习惯、生活方式等，但是语言往往成为文化群体的显性标识或显性标识之一，甚至发挥着类似图腾的作用。世界上很多国家都把国语与国旗、国徽、国歌同等看待，这就是语言与文化关系的一种重要证明。

2.3 语言沟壑

语言是文化之间的鸿沟。就文化群体而言，语言对内具有认同性，对外具有封闭性、排他性。也就是说，语言会把人分为“我者”和“他者”。说同样语言的人，是“我者”，是自己人，属于同一文化群体，这就是语言的认同性。而说其他语言的人，是“他者”，是外人，非我族类其心必异，这就是语言的封闭性、排他性。对“我者”而言，语言是同群体相互关联的纽带；对“他者”而言，语言形成了隔离群体的鸿沟。

在现实生活中，语码转用常常意味着文化认同的更换。“他者”文化群体的人，改说“我者”的语言，常被视作对“我者”文化和文化群体的认同；反过来，“我者”文化群体的人放弃“我者”的语言，改说“他者”的语言，也被视为背离原有文化群体、皈依“他者”文化群体的行为。历史上，有许多统治者通过“语言同化”来实现文化同化，其中有成功的事例，但也有被统治者拼死抗争而最终同化失败的案例。直到今天，许多地方、许多人群仍在讲述着自愿同化和被迫同化的语言故事，仍在引发各种语言矛盾甚至导致语言战争。

联合国教科文组织最新公布的数据认为人类语言有 7,000 多种，其中包括手语 150 多种。这一语言数据虽然未必准确，未必得到普遍认可，但足以说明人类语言之多。如果把语言看作文化群体之间的沟壑的话，那么可以说人世间布满语言的沟壑。认真说起来，语言沟壑远不止如此之数，因为不仅语言具有认同性和排他性，语言的各种变体也具有类似的功能。当前，被语言学家较多研究的语言变体起码有四大类型：地域变体、社会变体、特殊变体和机器变体。

2.3.1 地域变体

地域变体指的是一种语言的地域方言，地域方言形成方言区。有些语言的地域方言很少，方言间的语言距离不大，如中国的东乡语、水语、布依语，几乎可以看作没有方言的语言，虽然其各自内部也可以分出一些土语差别来。而有些语言的地域方言多，方言间的语言距离很大，如中国的汉语方言、藏语方言等。汉语的南北方言相互之间不大能听得懂；藏语的卫藏方言（拉萨话）、康巴方言（德格话、昌都话）、安多方言（青海藏区）这三大方言之间的差别，也达到了相互不能通话的地步。

而有些地域方言，其书面语由于各种原因甚至采用了不同的字母表。例如，语言学传统上把内蒙古的蒙古语和蒙古国的蒙古语看作同一种蒙古语，把印度的印地语和巴基斯坦的乌尔都语看作印地–乌尔都语，把前南斯拉夫地区的塞尔维亚语和克罗地亚语看作塞尔维亚–克罗地亚语。然而，内蒙古的蒙古语使用传统蒙古语字母，蒙古国的蒙古语使用基立尔字母；印地语使用天城体字母，乌尔都语使用阿拉伯字母；塞尔维亚语使用基立尔字母，克罗地亚语使用拉丁字母。当一种语言的地域变体采用不同的字母表时，常有分化为不同语言的可能性，比如印地语与乌尔都语、塞尔维亚语与克罗地亚语，都有将其看作独立语言的主张，在现实语言生活中也被当作不同的语言在使用，其语言鸿沟比一般的地域变体自然也就更为深阔。

2.3.2 社会变体

社会变体又称社会方言，是比照“地域方言”创造出来的术语。社会人群因性别、年龄、职业、社会阶层等不同而分化为不同的社会群落，不同社会群落在语言使用上有各自的特点，特别是在词汇和表达方式上有各种语言特点，有时在语音、语法上也有特征性差别。特别是不同的职业和不同的学术专业，词汇差异很大，有些职业还使用电报代码、旗语、灯语等特殊的符号系统。社会语言学发展起来之后，人们也重视对社会方言的研究，不同社会群落的社会方言也有内部认同和外部排他的特性。

2.3.3 特殊变体

听障人士常使用手语，视障人士使用盲文，特殊交际还有旗语、灯语等。手语、盲文、旗语、灯语等与自然语言都有一定的关系，因而可以视为语言的特殊变体。手语使用手的指式、动作、位置和朝向，配合以面部表情，按照手语语法规则来进行交际（杨军辉，2022），手指的不同指式等表示不同的字母，由此与一定的自然语言发生关联，手语中也常加入一些自然手势。手语不仅有汉语手语、英语手语等差别，其内部也有地区差异，比如中国手语就有南北差别、有大陆与台湾地区的差别（刘艳虹等，2013）。中国的手语也有规范化和推行国家通用手语的任务。

盲文用凸点的不同排列表示字母，是可以触摸的拼音文字。现代盲文以方为单位，每方六个点位，由法国盲人路易•布莱尔（Louis Braille）1824 年创造，为纪念他的贡献，国际上通称盲文为“布莱尔”。盲文与特定的语言联系在一起，且其内部也常有“方言性”的差异。中国的盲文有大陆（内地）、台湾地区、香港地区的差异，也有新老盲文的差异，规范化和推行国家通用盲文也是一项重要的语言任务。

2.3.4 机器变体

随着语言信息化的发展，计算机逐渐参与人类的语言活动，如自动翻译、信息自动检索、自动摘要、智能写作、社交机器人等。人类的语言活动也更加依赖机器，“人–机–机–人”的交际成为交际常态。“人–机–机–人”的交际包括“人–机”交际、“机–机”交际、“机–人”交际。“人–机”交际需要人具有一定的语言技术能力，能够与机器进行对话；“机–机”交际需要形成机器设备之间信息沟通的网络；“机–人”交际需要机器具有一定的与人对话的能力。特别是随着数字化、智能化的发展，计算机逐渐发展出语言智能，其角色将从与人简单对话发展为人类的助手，亦即“AI 助手”。未来人工智能发展的重要任务，就是为人类的特定行业、特定人群配备 AI 助手，协助特定行业、特定人群的交际、工作和生活。这样的 AI 机器，不仅要有一定的智慧，有行业或人群的有关知识，还需要有一定的语言能力。不管是"人–机"交际、"机–人"交际，还是人与 AI 助手的语言交际，机器变体都构成新时代重要的语言变体。机器变体的认同性可能不如上述三大语言变体，但是排他性也确实是客观存在，造成排他性的根本原因是掌握现代信息技术的能力和条件。

2.4 语言桥梁

语言及其变体形成文化的沟壑，这只是语言一个侧面的特点，它还有与之相反的功能，即语言及其变体也是架设在沟壑之上的文化间相互沟通的桥梁。语言是文化的阐释者和传播者，它不仅向本社团阐释文化以使文化能纵向传承，它还向其他社团阐释文化以使文化得以横向传播。

语言的桥梁功能首先是由"跨语人"发挥出来的。跨语人包括过去所谓的双语人、双言人、多语人、多言人等，他们可以在不同文化群体间穿行，通过各种翻译活动使不同文化沟通起来、交流起来，并使单语人也能受益。方言区之间也有"双言人"帮助沟通，健全人与聋人间、健全人与盲人间也通过既懂手语、盲文也懂自然语言的跨语人相互沟通。当前，社会方言之间的沟通还没有形成外语翻译、民语翻译、方言翻译、手语翻译之类的职业群体，了解机器变体也主要靠每个人的信息化实践，尚缺乏社会的、理性的推动规划，特别是教育规划。

语言沟通可以使不同文化群体相互理解、共享文化。通过相互理解可以减少矛盾冲突，变"他者"为"友者"，甚至变"友者"为"我者"。通过语言沟通使文化外溢到其他文化社团中，使本属于某社团的文化通过外溢而发挥益外的作用，甚至发展为人类共享的公共产品。共享文化不仅可以将某群体的地方性文化国际化，也可以将国际文化地方化，人类在文化共享中共同发展、共同进步，成为命运共同体。

曼德拉（Nelson R. Mandela）有段名言："如果你用一个人听得懂的语言与他交流，他只会记在脑子里；如果你用他的母语与他交流，他将会记在心中。"（If you talk to a man in a language he understands, that goes to his head. If you talk to him in his language, that goes to his heart.）李宇明（2015）提出，语言有"表情达意、通事通心"之别，共同语主要起"达

意、通事”的作用，而母语、方言还可以“表情、通心”。这一观点与曼德拉的看法很契合。在语言生活中，在各个层面的语言交际中，要重视“通事”之语，但也绝对不能轻视“通心”之语。人类用民族共同语及方言等进行“通事–通心”沟通，加强本民族的交往与团结，构建起民族共同体；用国家通用语言和本国的其他语言、方言等进行国内的“通事–通心”沟通，建立起国家共同体；用外语、母语等进行国际间的“通事–通心”沟通，促进人类命运共同体的构建。

3. 人类的超语时代

3.1 超语概念萌生

超语（translanguaging）概念源自威尔士语的复兴研究。1994 年，威廉姆斯（C. Williams）在其关于威尔士语振兴教育的博士论文中提出了“超语”概念，大力提倡双语教学策略：在课堂教学过程中，教师有计划、有意识地在同一节课上使用两种语言，交替进行输入、输出活动，系统地建构双语教学模式（Williams, 1994）。

2001 年，威廉姆斯的博士导师贝克（Colin Baker），在 *Foundations of Bilingual Education and Bilingualism* 一书中，将威廉姆斯的研究成果引介到英语世界，自此吸引了来自语言学、教育学、认知科学、新闻传播学和文化研究等领域研究者的兴趣。李嵬、沈骑（2021）曾经指出，在谷歌学术中以 translanguaging 作为关键词进行搜索，截至 2020 年 12 月，有超过 152,000 个词条的标题或摘要中包含 translanguaging。“超语”概念由威廉姆斯提出、贝克向学界引介，经过 20 余年的使用，已经超出了双语教学的范畴，也超出了语言复兴的范畴，发展成为“利用各种语符进行沟通”的宏观理念。

3.2 对超语的认识

今天，世界范围内有数千种语言及相关符号在不同范围、不同场合为不同人群所使用，并通过现代语言技术聚拢在互联网上。人们在同一交际活动中，也常常不停地切换语码，或是混用不同语符。人类已经进入一个不同语符、不同媒体同现共用的“超语时代”（the translanguaging age）。置身超语时代，我们对“超语”应有以下四点认识。第一，超语不只是关注不同语符的共用与切换，更强调以积极的态度看待语符的共用与切换。语符的共用与切换其实是意义建构的动态过程，是变换新表达、产出新意义、塑造新知识、获得新经验的过程。第二，“超语”之“超”（trans-），其含义不仅是字面意义的“超越”，也应是“融合”，强调的是语言使用者超越某种语符边界的能力，强调的是“融合”使用多种语符的能力，亦即跨文化的沟通能力和兼容、借鉴、融化吸收多种文化的能力 。第三，“超语”之“语”（languages）早期主要指称不同的语言，特别是双语，之后发展到语言的地域变体，再发展到语言的特殊变体、社会变体，而今发展到具有信息传递功能的各种事物（可称为“语符”），包括图表、视频、体态语、表情包、语言文字之外的各种符号甚至交际场景等。具有使用多种语符能力的人，就是“超语人”。第四，人机对话也属于超语范畴。机器变体的问题在超语研究中还较少提及，但在“人-机-机-人”的交际成为交际常态的当下，在语言智能快速发展、许多行业和特殊人群将要配备 AI 助手、语言机器人将要广泛参与人类社会生活的明天，机器变体必然成为超语之“语”，成为超语研究的重要内容之一。

超语时代是对未来语言生活的一种描述，也将是面对遍地语言沟壑的社会新应对，是语言桥梁作用充分发挥的一个新时代。超语时代蕴含着、催生着许多新的语言观念，比如：

1）原来被很多人信奉的“语言纯洁观”，可能不再适应现在的语言生活；

2）语言和文字虽然还是人类用于交际的主要符号系统，但在语言生活中人们会较多地、有意识地使用语言文字之外的各种符号；

3）单语人将被超语人取代，合格的社会成员都应具有一定的超语能力，语言教育应是培养学生超语能力的新教育；

4）语言翻译也将由“语言”翻译扩大到“超语”翻译，并且得到 AI 翻译助手的更多帮助。

这些的新的语言观念，将会带来语言学、翻译学等一系列新变革，甚至产生一些新学科或分支学科，发展出新的语言技术，使语言学、翻译学等学科具有社会新担当。

4. 无障碍社会的构建

4.1 无障碍社会

无障碍社会是近 30 年来国际社会倡导的新理念。特别是 2000 年以来，随着信息化时代的发展，国际社会不仅关注残障人士的衣食住行问题，也关注其信息无障碍问题，并由特殊人群的无障碍发展到社会全域的无障碍。

据刘晓宇（2022）研究，无障社会的理念，最早可以追溯到 1959 年欧洲议会通过的《方便残疾人使用的公共建筑的设计与建筑的决议》。该决议旨在通过对公共建筑物进行特殊改造，为残疾人无障碍（barrier-free）出行提供便利。1974 年，联合国残疾人生活环境专家会议提出“无障碍环境”（barrier-free environment）的理念，旨在构建无障碍的物理空间。1990 年，美国颁布《美国残疾人法案》，规定就业、交通、公共设施、政府服务和电信等各方面对残疾人应是“可及的”（accessibility），无障碍理念从改变环境向合理便利的房县发展。1993 年，联合国大会第 48 届会议通过了《残疾人机会均等标准规则》，要求各国政府应“对待任何类别的残疾人……在提供信息和交流方面实现无障碍”。2000 年 7 月，在日本冲绳举行的 G8 首脑会议上，美国、日本、德国、英国、法国、意大利、加拿大和俄罗斯等八国领导人发表了《实现全球信息化社会的冲绳宪章》，这就是所谓的《IT 宪章》或《东京宣言》。《IT 宪章》旨在促进信息通信技术发展，缩小国家间、地区间信息技术发展差距，其中也特别提到了残疾人和老年人在信息技术方面的特殊需求与困难。2002 年，联合国经济及社会理事会的亚洲及太平洋经济社会委员会在日本滋贺县大津市举办第二届“亚太残疾人十年”活动，通过了《琵琶湖千年行动纲要》。《琵琶湖千年行动纲要》明确提出，为亚洲及太平洋地区的残疾人“努力缔造一个包容、无障碍和以权利为本的社会”。2004 年起，中国工业和信息化部、中国残疾人联合会、中国互联网协会、中国残疾人福利基金会每年联合主办一届“中国信息无障碍论坛”，信息无障碍理念不断在中国社会传播，信息无障碍措施不断付诸实施。2006 年，联合国特别会议通过了《残疾人权利公约》，提出“促使残疾人有机会使用包括因特网在内的新的信息通信技术和系统”，“在设计、开发、生产、推行等早期阶段促进无障碍信息和通信技术和系统”。2016 年 3 月，中国残疾人联合会、国家互联网信息办公室联合印发《关于加强网站无障碍服务能力建设的指导意见》。2020 年 9 月，中国工业和信息化部、中国残疾人联合会联合发布《关于推进信息无障碍的指导意见》。2020 年 11 月，国务院印发《关于切实解决老年人运用智能技术困难的实施方案》。2021 年 7 月，国务院印发《“十四五”残疾人保障和发展规划》。2021 年，工业和信息化部陆续发布《互联网应用适老化及无障碍改造专项行动方案》《工业和信息化部关于切实解决老年人运用智能技术困难 便利老年人使用智能化产品和服务的通知》《工业和信息化部办公厅关于进一步抓好互联网应用适老化及无障碍改造专项行动实施工作的通知》等政策文件。2021 年 12 月，中央网络安全和信息化委员会印发《“十四五”国家信息化规划》。2022 年 5 月，中国信息通信研究院发布《信息无障碍白皮书（2022 年）》。

近些年来，中国无障碍社会建设的步伐，特别是信息无障碍的步伐，明显加快。无障碍社会是一个不断丰富的理念，是一个不断发展的过程。这种发展，可以概括为四大发展趋势：第一，从残障人群到老年人群，从特殊人群到一般人群，无障碍是社会全域的无障碍；第二，从出行、生活到学习、工作，无障碍是人生全域的无障碍；第三，从生活无障碍到信息无障碍，信息无障碍从信息服务渠道无障碍到信息沟通内容无障碍，从物质生活领域发展到精神生活领域，无障碍是生活全域的无障碍；第四，从建筑业到媒体、信息产业，再到语言服务业及社会其他行业，无障碍需要社会各行业的支持。

4.2 语言与无障碍社会

“社会全域、人生全域、生活全域、各行业支持”的无障碍社会理念包含许许多多内容，但从当前的无障碍社会建设的实践来看，主要集中在生活无障碍和信息无障碍两大部分以及四个方面的内容上。第一，生活无障碍，包括道路出行、社区居住、室内生活、工作场合、学习场景、语言景观、各种指引标识及信息提示等无障碍；生活无障碍还可以再概括为生活设施无障碍和标识指引无障碍。第二，信息无障碍，包括信息设施、信息提供、终端接收、媒体形态、语言文字、语体表现等无障碍；信息无障碍还可以再概括为信息服务渠道无障碍和信息沟通内容无障碍。

语言的桥梁作用是构建无障碍社会的保障性力量。其一，在生活无障碍中，第二部分内容中的标识指引无障碍主要是语符使用的问题，其中包括提供多语多文信息及标识符号。其二，在信息无障碍中，第二部分中的信息沟通内容无障碍主要是语言文字问题，具体而言，主要包括以下四个方面：

1）国家通用语言、民族语言、方言、外语等语种的应用及受众的接受能力，以及这些语种的教育、翻译等；

2）手语、盲文及其他符号系统的创制改进、教育、应用等，涉及听障人群与健全人群、视障人群与健全人群等，也包括手语机器人、盲文机器人的研发；

3）平面媒体、有声媒体、网络媒体、融媒体等媒体形态的语符等，以及各类人群对这些媒体形态的适应，比如，老年人比较适应传统媒体，喜欢大字体，年轻人比较适应新媒体，听障人士可通过“听障字幕”观看影视，视障人士可通过“口述影像”，在看不见画面的情况下享受电影之乐，实现“媒体普惠”（鲁伟、李德凤，2022）；

4）语言内容在表达上的深奥还是浅显、文雅还是通俗等。

上列四方面所涉及的语种及其各种变体、语言媒体、语言风格等都直接影响信息内容的良好传递与顺畅理解，而信息内容的良好传递与顺畅理解是信息无障碍的根本目标，也是评价信息无障碍的重要指标。

其三，在信息无障碍中，第二部分中的信息服务渠道无障碍从表面看是设备与技术的问题，其实也与各人群的语言使用习惯、能够接受的语言技术等有一定关系。语言使用习惯、语言技术等也是重要的语言文字问题。

无障碍社会建设，体现的是人人生而平等的社会理念。生活无障碍是生存、生活层面的问题，是保障特殊人群能够融入大众生活、参与大众的各种活动。信息无障碍是要消除特殊人群乃至全社会的数字鸿沟，实现信息平等，保证信息获取的机会无障碍；进一步说，就是保证特殊人群乃至社会人人都能平等地、方便地、安全地获取信息、使用信息和进行信息沟通。信息无障碍是对生活无障碍的重要补益，是生活无障碍理念在信息领域的体现，是社会发展到数字时代的必然要求。

无障碍社会建设，由生活无障碍发展到信息无障碍乃至生活全域，由残障人群发展到老年人群乃至社会全域、人生全域，都体现了时代的进步和人类生活的进步。但总体来看，当前的无障碍社会建设还多在硬件与技术方面，如道路、场馆、房舍、信息通道、信息器件等，对信息沟通内容无障碍等与语言文字相关方面的关注还不够，这需要引起政府、社会、学界和技术等部门的重视。

5. 结语

近些年来，翻译的概念在不断扩展。翻译的理念在不断变化（蓝红军，2015；许均，2015），翻译范畴已经包括语内翻译（intralingual translation）、语际翻译（interlingual translation）和符际翻译（inter-semiotic translation）等（黄忠廉，2012），这与“超语”之“超”、“超语”之“语”的理念已经非常接近。翻译的使命就是发挥语言的桥梁作用，促进社会沟通无障碍，把一种文化群体的知识变为另一种文化群体的知识，把某群体的知识变为全人类的知识，而且在社会沟通、文化扩展中，带来人类的相互理解和情感接近，减少各种误解和矛盾冲突。在超语时代，翻译担当的社会无障碍沟通责任更为重大。

鼓励社会实施多语制度，加强全面的多语教育，包括鼓励健全人学点手语、学点盲文。一般社会成员应具备多语能力，包括翻译能力。超语视野下的翻译能力其实就是社会成员在不同文化群体、亚群体之间穿行的能力，是当代人的语言能力素养。

信息时代最为重要的是避免被信息边缘化，掌握一定的现代语言技术非常重要。就社会而言，要重视发展机器自动翻译水平。实践已经表明（任文，2019；王华树、王鑫，2021），自动翻译对社会一般成员的跨语言交流是颇有帮助的，而且也会促进翻译行业的发展。自动翻译的发展与应用，都不可能离开翻译专业人员的介入，翻译人员与机器的互动互助是自动翻译水平提升的方式，也是翻译实践的模式。

此外，利用语言智能来为特殊人群服务，提升特殊人群的信息沟通无障碍水平，是重要的发展方向。未来是人与机器互动互育的时代，研发具有语言智能的机器人，为特殊行业、特殊人群配备智能机器人（AI

助手），是社会发展大势。语言机器人将帮助人类更好地进行社会沟通，成为人类社会沟通的新桥梁。不过，语言机器人也可能成为社会新的鸿沟。语言的沟桥二重性，随着语言智能化时代的到来，将有新的表现形式。

参考文献

[1] 胡明扬. 语言和语言学 [M]. 湖北：湖北教育出版社，1983.
[2] 黄忠廉. 方言翻译转换机制 [J]. 北京理工大学学报（社会科学版），2012（2）：144-147.
[3] 蓝红军. 翻译本质的追寻与发现——“何为翻译？——翻译的重新定位与定义”高层论坛综述 [J]. 东方翻译，2015（2）：92-95.
[4] 李嵬，沈骑. 超语实践理论的起源、发展与展望 [J]. 外国语（上海外国语大学学报），2021（4）：2-14.
[5] 李宇明. “一带一路”需要语言铺路 [J]. 中国科技术语，2015（6）.
[6] 李宇明. 构建信息无障碍社会 [J]. 语言战略研究，2022（2）.
[7] 刘晓宇. “十四五”时期关于语言障碍者的信息无障碍问题与对策 [J]. 待刊，2022.
[8] 刘艳虹，顾定倩，程黎，魏丹. 我国手语使用状况的调查研究 [J]. 语言文字应用，2013（2）：35-41.
[9] 鲁伟，李德凤. 无障碍传播：发展历史与研究现状 [J]. 解放军外国语学院学报，2022（4）：88-96.
[10] 潘文国. 语言的定义 [J]. 华东师范大学学报（哲学社会科学版），2001（1）：97-128.
[11] 任文. 机器翻译伦理的挑战与导向 [J]. 上海翻译，2019（5）：46-52.
[12] 托马斯·弗里德曼. 世界是平的——21 世纪简史 [M]. 何帆、肖莹莹译. 长沙：湖南科学技术出版社.
[13] 王华树，王鑫. 人工智能时代的翻译技术研究：应用场景、现存问题与趋势展望 [J]. 外国语文，2021（1）：9-17.
[14] 许钧. 关于新时期翻译与翻译问题的思考 [J]. 中国翻译，2015（3）：8-9.

[15] 杨军辉. 中国手语和汉语双语教育初探 [J]. 中国特殊教育，2002（1）：33.

[16] 尤瓦尔·赫拉利. 人类简史：从动物到上帝 [M]. 林俊宏译. 北京：中信出版社，2014.

[17] Williams, C. An evaluation of teaching and learning methods in the context of bilingual secondary education [D]. Bangor: University of Wales, 1994.

三、翻译中的人机协作

Loop the Loop: Riding the Roller Coaster of Human-Computer Collaboration in Machine Translation

Lynne Bowker
University of Ottawa

Abstract: Machine translation (MT) is an area of translation where collaboration between humans and computers has been through a series of ups and downs. From the early days when it was thought that computers could "go it alone" and produce fully automatic high-quality translations with no help from humans to the present-day "human-in-the-loop" (HITL) situation, it has been a veritable roller coaster ride with both parties contributing to collaborative translation efforts to a greater or lesser degree at different points in the history of MT. In this paper, we first look back at some of the major twists and turns in the collaborative relationship between humans and computers in the context of MT to understand how we got to this point. Then we will look ahead to consider what changes are taking place in the relationship now as we strive to get the most out of human-computer collaboration in the age of neural machine translation (NMT), where new developments such as adaptive MT, interactive MT and augmented translation are presenting additional inclines, descents, curves and loops to be navigated as part of the thrill ride of translation in the 21st century. Hang on to your hat!
Keywords: human-in-the-loop; artificial intelligence; augmented translation; adaptive machine translation; data-driven machine translation; fully-automatic high-quality translation (FAHQT); interactive machine translation; neural machine translation

机器翻译中跌宕起伏的人机合作模式

Lynne Bowker　渥太华大学

摘　要: 在机器翻译（MT）领域中，人机合作经历多次起伏。从早期认为计算机可以“单打独斗”，无须人类帮助即可全自动产出高质量翻译，到目前的“人在回路”（HITL）情境，此过程确如过山车般跌宕起伏。在机器翻译各个历史阶段，人机双方对合作翻译均有或多或少的贡献。本文首先回顾人机合作关系在机器翻译背景下主要的曲折反复，以理解现状背后的发展过程，之后展望未来，思考在神经机器翻译（NMT）时代应如何调整人机合作关系，充分利用人机合作。在此时代，自适应机器翻译、交互式机器翻译和增强式翻译等不断发展，再度引领21世纪的翻译如刺激的过山车般倾斜、下降、转弯和回环。我们需做好准备，进入一个跌宕起伏的时代。

关键词: 人在回路；人工智能；增强式翻译；自适应机器翻译；数据驱动机器翻译；全自动高质量机器翻译（FAHQT）；交互式机器翻译；神经机器翻译

1. Introduction

Google's English dictionary (provided by Oxford Languages, 2022) tells us that a roller coaster is “an amusement park attraction that consists of a light railroad track with many tight turns and steep slopes on which people ride in small fast open cars”. The entry goes on to note that the concept can also be used figuratively, and even as a verb, where it means “move, change, or occur in the dramatically changeable manner of a roller coaster”. Ironically, roller coasters themselves have experienced something of a figurative roller coaster ride. According to Wikipedia (n.d.), the first modern roller coaster was constructed in Paris in 1817, and although it spawned a number of imitators, their popularity soon declined. Roller coasters returned to fashion during France's *Belle Époque* period, which lasted from around 1887 until the First World War in 1914. Following the war, roller coasters spread to amusement parks around the world and began an era in the roller coaster industry often referred to as the Golden Age, which lasted until the end of the 1920s. Unfortunately, the Great Depression in the 1930s significantly impacted the amusement park industry and brought an end to the rapid growth experienced during the Golden Age. Over next few decades, roller coasters were still constructed with varying degrees of success from one location to the next. However, it was not until 1959 that there was a major design breakthrough when Disneyland introduced the tubular track, which allowed the track to bend in sharper angles in any direction, thus permitting the incorporation of loops, corkscrews and inversion elements. This sparked a new era of roller coaster enthusiasm, which led to a resurgence across the amusement park industry.

So what does this have to do with machine translation (MT)? Well, like roller coasters, MT tools have experienced rises and falls in popularity as they met with initial enthusiasm (e.g., Weaver's memorandum), followed by difficult circumstances (e.g., the ALPAC Report), which led to determined perseverance (e.g., the METEO system), eventual breakthroughs (e.g., data-driven approaches), and finally a new era of popular interest. While these developments may not have taken place at the literal speed of a roller coaster ride, we must remember that MT has been around for less than 75 years, meaning that this technology, its context of use, and the attitudes towards it have witnessed a lot of changes in a relatively short period. Of particular interest in this paper is the way in which the collaboration between translators and computers has changed throughout the history of MT. We begin by looking back at some of the major twists and turns in the collaborative relationship between translators and computers in the context of MT to understand how we got to this point. Then we will look ahead to consider what changes may lie ahead in the translator-computer collaborative relationship in the age of neural machine translation (NMT), where developments such as adaptive MT, interactive MT and augmented translation are presenting additional inclines, descents, curves and loops to be navigated as part of the thrill ride of translation in the 21st century. Hang on to your hat!

2. Early days of machine translation: Not much collaboration and that's a FAQHT!

MT systems using computer technology were first developed in the period following the Second World War. In 1949, an American mathematician named Warren Weaver published a relatively short paper entitled simply "Translation", in which he laid out some ideas for how MT systems could work, drawing inspiration in part from cryptography techniques used during the War (Locke & Booth, 2003). This paper, now commonly referred to as "Weaver's Memorandum", was highly influential and it served to launch MT research both in the United States and around the world (Weaver, 1949). At the time, Weaver was employed by the Rockefeller Foundation, which is a science-driven philanthropic organization, and his proximity to founders also proved instrumental in fostering early MT research (Poibeau, 2017). In 1951, the first full-time researcher in MT was appointed: Yeoshua Bar-Hillel at the Massachusetts Institute of Technology. The following year, Bar-Hillel organized the first international conference on MT, and by 1954, the results of collaborative research between Georgetown University and IBM were shared in a public demonstration (Hutchins & Somers, 1992). Money was flowing, enthusiasm was high, researchers were working hard — MT research was off to a flying start!

From the beginning, the prevailing assumption was that the goal of MT research should be the creation of fully automatic high-quality translation (FAHQT), and indeed the idea was that MT systems would largely be able to replace human translators in many contexts (Hutchins & Somers, 1992). The early attempts at MT approached translation as a linguistic issue, and developers created detailed sets of grammar rules and very large bilingual dictionaries in an approach now referred to as rule-based machine translation (RBMT) (Hutchins & Somers, 1992). However, human translators use knowledge that goes far beyond syntax and vocabulary in order to translate successfully, and it soon became clear that translation was a more complex task than MT system developers had first imagined.

By the end of the 1950s, Bar-Hillel began to express strong doubts about continuing to pursue FAHQT as the main goal (Poibeau, 2017). This was an early inkling that perhaps computers did not have what it takes to tackle the task of translation alone. Not long after Bar-Hillel raised these concerns, the funders of MT research in the US became concerned about the relative lack of progress, so they commissioned an independent committee to produce an evaluation of the state of MT. The Automatic Language Processing Advisory Committee (ALPAC) was formed in 1964, and two years later, it delivered the now infamous APLAC Report (1966). This report essentially found that MT was too slow, too costly, and too poor in quality to be of use for most purposes, and it also determined that there was no pressing need for MT since the demand for translation at that time could comfortably be met by the existing workforce of professional translators.

Certainly, the MT systems that existed in the mid-1960s were not capable of replacing professional translators, and so the ALPAC Report recommended that researchers reorient their attention to doing more fundamental research in linguistics and that they more or less drop research into MT proper and instead look into developing computer aids intended to assist, rather than replace, translators (Hutchins, 2003). Although ALPAC's recommendations led to a missed opportunity for more direct collaboration in MT specifically, they did pave the way for translator-computer collaboration in translation technologies more generally, and it became common to view translation as a spectrum. As presented in Hutchins & Somers (1992), at one end of the spectrum lies FAHQT, while at the other end lies human translation involving no mechanical aids whatsoever. Meanwhile, two new concepts emerged in the space between these two extremes, referring to different types of collaboration: human-aided machine translation (HAMT) and machine-aided human translation (MAHT). Essentially, HAMT describes the use of MT systems to produce translations with the assistance of humans before, during or after the computerized translation process, whereas MAHT refers to the use of computer-based tools as aids for professional translators. Essentially, the difference lies in which partner — human or computer — is playing the central role of translator and which is playing the supporting role of assistant.

According to Hutchins & Somers (1992), the notions HAMT and MAHT both fall under the umbrella of computer-aided translation (CAT), and this latter term and acronym are both still widely used today. CAT covers a broad range of tools and resources (e.g., terminology management systems, translation memory systems, various types of corpora and corpus analysis tools, localization tools). As this paper specifically addresses MT, we will try to focus the discussion on tools where the computer takes responsibility for generating at least some original translated text (rather than only retrieving existing translations from elsewhere). We acknowledge, however, that the boundary between MT and other CAT tools is becoming increasingly blurred. Readers interested in an exploration of human-computer collaboration in CAT more broadly can find more details in O'Brien (2012).

3. The proper place of humans and computers in MT? Collaborating... a bit

In 1980, Martin Kay wrote a visionary article entitled "The Proper Place of Men and Machines in Language Translation", which was later reprinted in full in the journal *Machine Translation* (Kay, [1980]1997a). At the time Kay wrote this canonical piece, those who were still working on MT research were doggedly continuing to pursue the goal of FAHQT using rule-based approaches (Hutchins & Somers, 1992). Although there were some limited successes, such as the domain-specific METEO system used to translate weather forecasts (Lehrberger & Bourbeau, 1988), Kay lamented the general state of MT research, noting "The proper thing to do is therefore to adopt the kinds of solution that have proved successful in other domains, namely to develop cooperative man–machine systems" (Kay, [1980]1997a: 3). Along with the word "cooperative", Kay also uses terms such as "collaborator" and "collaborating" (*Ibid:* 22) to describe the nature of the relationship to be encouraged between the human and the computer in order to achieve the best outcomes. In Kay's opinion, a team effort where people and computers work together offered a better chance for success than a fully automated approach.

The heart of Kay's proposal is the development of a tool that he described as a "translator's amanuensis" (Kay, [1980]1997a: 13), and this proposal sowed the seeds for what we now largely recognize as a translation memory (TM) system — a type of computer-aided translation tool. This is not to say that Kay was against the idea of MT; he saw the translator's amanuensis as the beginning of an incremental approach to MT. In other words, Kay definitely believed in the possibility of MT, but he felt it should be a cooperative venture where both computers and translators had a role and where each played to their own strengths:

> I want to advocate a view of the problem in which machines are gradually, almost imperceptibly, allowed to take over certain functions in the overall translation process. First they will take over functions not essentially related to translation. Then, little by little, they will approach translation itself. The keynote will be modesty. At each stage, we will do only what we know we can do reliably. Little steps for little feet! (Kay, [1980]1997a: 13)

Nearly two decades later, in 1997, Kay penned a short follow-up commentary entitled "It's Still the Proper Place", in which he emphasized that "little has happened to change the overall assessment we should make of the proper place of humans and machines in language translation" (Kay, 1997b: 35). In other words, Kay believed that a collaborative approach was still the correct way forward; however, a major paradigm shift in the underlying approach to MT was beginning to gain momentum, and it relegated translators to a less visible role than the one that Kay had championed.

4. Data-driven approaches: Putting human collaborators in the back seat

During the 1990s, computers had become faster and more powerful, and an increasing number of translators were writing and sharing documents in electronic form, creating a wealth of machine-readable translation data. Therefore, developers began to conceive of a new way of getting computers to process language which was data-driven. While computers had not been very good at processing linguistic rules, they were strong in areas such as pattern matching and rapid calculations, and so the notion of statistical machine translation (SMT) was born (Koehn, 2010). Rather than making use of linguistic rules and dictionaries, SMT adopts a data-driven approach that relies on huge corpora—both monolingual corpora and bilingual parallel corpora, the latter of which consist of previously translated texts aligned with their original source texts. In very simple terms, developers feed these texts into the SMT system, which consults them to look for patterns of how a given phrase has been translated in the past and to calculate probabilities that it should be translated that way again in a new text. By the 2000s, SMT had superseded RBMT to become the dominant paradigm, but research into other data-driven approaches continued, and in 2016, the first MT tools using artificial neural networks and machine learning techniques appeared (Koehn, 2020). These neural machine translation (NMT) systems also require vast bilingual parallel corpora to use as training data. By looking at the training corpus of previously translated texts, NMT systems can learn to translation new texts.

On the surface, both SMT and NMT give the appearance of being fully automatic approaches with no collaboration required from translators. However, as pointed out by Kenny (2011) and Moorkens (2022), the truth is that neither SMT nor NMT could function without the fundamental contribution of human translators, who generate the large volume of high-quality data needed to train these MT systems in the first place. Without this training data, there would be no MT output. Translators therefore play an essential, though not highly visible, role in this collaborative process. Unfortunately, the valuable contribution that human translators make to data-driven approaches is often overshadowed because an impression has been created that data is a sort of natural resource that simply exists and that can be harvested, mined or collected by anyone. In truth, translation data has been painstakingly created by skilled human translators, who unfortunately lose both credit for and control over this data once it leaves their hands and is made available in public spaces, such as the web, from where it can be scraped and repurposed as training data for data-driven MT systems (Moorkens & Lewis, 2020). The false impression that data-driven systems do not require human collaboration is also reinforced by simplistic media reporting. For example, Vieira (2020: 109) relays that between 1986 and 2019, many of the English-language press articles that present MT to the general public lack nuance and "often put forward conceptualisations of MT as a technology with at times human-like, at times 'magical' powers." Meanwhile, the fact that data-driven approaches would be completely unable to function without human-supplied high-quality data is not discussed.

Moreover, it is not only the popular media that create this impression. Some researchers have also claimed that human parity for MT systems is within sight (e.g., Wu *et al.*, 2016) or even that it has been achieved (e.g., Hassan *et al.*, 2018), suggesting that the goal of FAHQT that had eluded RBMT systems might now be within reach. Although other researchers (e.g. Toral *et al.*, 2018) have countered that the definitions of human parity as well as the means used to judge it in these articles are not problem-free, the myth of human parity still persists in many circles. Even though human parity has not been achieved, it is widely acknowledged that SMT produced a considerable improvement in quality over the older rule-based systems, and that NMT has introduced yet another leap in quality (Castilho *et al.*, 2017). However, it is equally widely accepted that raw, unedited MT output is not suitable for all contexts of use, and so the need for humans to post-edit MT output has begun to gain more prominence.

5. Human collaborators as "the clean-up crew"

Post-editing is not a new idea, but in the period of RBMT, the quality of MT output was often so poor that post-editing was either tedious (e.g., requiring a translator to fix basic linguistic errors that a person would rarely make) or more time-consuming than translating a text from scratch (e.g., trying to make sense of unintelligible nonsense) (Krings, 2001). Because it was not practical in most instances, post-editing did not become a regular practice in the translation industry during the era of RBMT. This situation has changed in recent years, however, since the output of NMT systems may be of a sufficiently good quality to act as a viable first draft. Now, in many circumstances, NMT output can be post-edited efficiently thus contributing to an overall productivity boost. Not surprisingly, clients are enthusiastic about potential cost savings owing to this improved efficiency, and this can in turn lead to a greater volume of material being translated (O'Brien, 2020).

Nonetheless, translators are not always enthusiastic about working as post-editors. For example, Kelly (2014: n.p.) has likened post-editing to "linguistic janitorial work" and described human post-editors as "the clean-up crew" who are responsible for fixing the mistakes made by the computer (and typically receiving a lower rate of pay to do so). Meanwhile, investigations into the application of NMT to creative texts reveal that translators find it constraining to post-edit rather than translate literary work, leading to translations that readers deem to be of lower quality than purely human translations (e.g., Kenny & Winters, 2020; Guerberof Arenas & Toral, 2022).

6. Human-in-the-loop: Adaptive MT

In an effort to make the task of post-editing both more appealing and more efficient, researchers have since introduced *adaptive MT*. As noted above, NMT uses machine learning, which is a branch of artificial intelligence that focuses on the use of data and algorithms to imitate the way that humans learn, gradually improving its accuracy. Most machine learning models rely on data that has been prepared by humans, and as we explained previously, in the case of NMT, the system needs a massive parallel corpus of previously translated texts aligned with their source texts to use as training material. However, with adaptive MT, translators can contribute to machine learning at other points in the process too. More powerful machine learning systems are designed to allow both parties — humans and computers — to interact regularly through a mechanism usually referred to as human-in-the-loop (HITL) (Monarch, 2021). The term HITL is not particularly well chosen since it gives the impression that the computer is the one in charge; however, humans actually play a very important role. Essentially, HITL aims to achieve what neither a person nor a computer can accomplish independently. When a computer cannot solve a problem, a person intervenes. This process results in the creation of a continuous feedback loop. With regular feedback, the algorithm learns and goes on to produce better results in the future (Monarch, 2021).

In adaptive MT, if a translator is post-editing a text, the system can learn on the fly and store the corrections as soon as they are made (Etchegoyhen *et al.*, 2021). The adaptive MT system can then apply the newly learned choice to a future translation. In the words of DePalma (2017, n.p.):

> It [adaptive MT] adapts to the content they [translators] work on, automatically learning terminology and style. It remembers what linguists have previously translated at the sub-segment level, and goes beyond translation memory to help translate text it has never seen before in a way that is consistent with how the individual professional works. Rather than post-editing MT output of dubious quality, linguists see the results as

suggestions they can choose to use or not. The more they use the system, the better these suggestions will become.

7. Better integration for improved collaboration: interactive MT

While the greater involvement of humans offered by the HITL design has been welcomed, translators still often find themselves constrained to participating at the beginning and end of the loop. For example, humans are involved *before* the translation process (e.g., by providing the translations used as training data for the NMT system) and *after* the translation process (e.g., by post-editing the raw NMT output). Even adaptive MT still assumes that an MT system will attempt to produce a complete translation and that the translator will then post-edit this complete draft. However, a more genuinely collaborative approach is implemented in interactive NMT, which presents a translator with predictive on-the-fly hints and suggestions (e.g., word-level or sentence-level autocompletion) as they work (Santy *et al.*, 2019; Xiao *et al.*, 2022).

Interactive MT is not a completely new idea; there were attempts in the 1980s and early 1990s to integrate this feature into RBMT systems (e.g., ALPNET). However, as noted by Hutchins & Somers (1992), this approach was not popular at the time because there were often so many interactions for a single sentence that it would have been quicker for the user to translate from scratch. Now that MT technology has advanced and uses neural approaches, interactive MT is making a comeback.

Using the Lilt tool, Martikainen (2022) conducted an experiment with Master's-level translation students to explore how these users felt about working with interactive MT. On the whole, the reaction of the students was positive, and they found that having choices was both empowering and practical, leaving translators feeling less constrained than if they had had a translation solution imposed on them, as is the case in the more traditional post-editing approach. On the downside, students found that the real-time adaptation function was not always up to the task, although this may be resolved as technologies become more powerful and developers come up with new solutions. For example, Xiao *et al.* (2022) have recently proposed a bilingual text-infilling approach that aims to improve efficiency over existing lexically constrained decoding techniques. In spite of challenges faced by students with regard to obtaining real-time solutions, Martikainen's (2022) overall conclusion is that interactive MT does indeed have the potential to offer a better experience for translators than post-editing static MT output, although working interactively does come with a learning curve.

8. What's next? Broadening collaboration networks with augmented translation and responsive MT

A few years ago, DePalma (2017, n.p.) suggested that the translation industry is "on the cusp of a disruptive transformation that will redefine how professional linguists work". Referred to as *augmented translation*, this approach seeks to place translators in a technology-rich environment where artificial intelligence will be used to enrich their access to relevant information. According to DePalma (2017), the historic focus of tools developers on speeding up the translation process and lowering the costs has left translators feeling alienated from the aspects of their work that originally attracted them to the translation profession (e.g., solving challenging problems, creative aspects of language). Augmented translation will put translators in the centre of a platform that will incorporate not only adaptive MT but also other technologies and techniques (e.g., terminology management, translation memory, automated content enrichment, lights-out project management) in order to make the translation process more efficient while also granting translators more control (Lommel, 2017). It will be the combination of technologies that eliminates inefficiencies and permits translators to focus on what they do best. Augmented translation also seeks to support project management by freeing up managers to focus on delivering quality customer service and addressing problems, rather than transferring files back and forth.

Moreover, according to Lommel (2021), MT systems will soon be looking to collaborate not only with translators but potentially with clients or end-users as well. So-called *responsive MT* will take on board feedback from various sources. In principle, this increased wealth of information will mean better input for augmented translation workflows, which will in turn make work simpler for translators and will free them up to focus on the more interesting and challenging parts of their job. Although no existing platforms currently meet the requirements for responsive MT, Lommel (2021) believes that it will not be long until this even broader collaborative approach becomes a reality.

9. Discussion

The focus of this paper has been on human-computer collaboration in the context of MT. Table 1 summarizes the main nature of the collaboration between translators and computers during key periods of MT history, revealing how the roles have shifted with the introduction of new technologies and techniques.

Table 1 The main nature of the collaboration between translators and computers during key periods of MT history

Period	Key characteristic	Nature of collaboration between translators and computers in MT
1949 to late 1960s	Goal is FAHQT	No collaboration; MT intended to replace human translators
1970s and 1980s	MT is recast as a type of CAT (HAMT vs MAHT, initial identification of strengths and limitations of both humans and computers)	Reduced focus on RBMT and more attention on developing CAT, which put humans into the picture and shifted the computer to a supporting role

(To be continued)

(Continued)

Period	Key characteristic	Nature of collaboration between translators and computers in MT
1990s to 2010s	Data-driven approaches (e.g., SMT, NMT)	Computers take centre stage again, overshadowing the critical contribution of humans (i.e. providing essential training data)
Mid-2010 to present	Post-editing and adaptive MT	HITL gives humans a greater role, but the contributions of computers and translators are more consecutive than collaborative, with humans still mainly to contributing before and after the translation process
Late 2010s to present	Interactive MT	More genuinely collaborative with humans and computers playing to their strengths
2020s	Augmented translation and responsive MT	Not yet fully realized, but potentially expanding the collaborative network (e.g., to include project managers, clients, end users)

As illustrated in Table 1, the roller coaster ride representing the collaborative relationship between translators and computers has taken a number of twists and turns, from an early stage where there was no role foreseen for translators, to an increased level of responsibility for translators as the conceptualization of MT gave way to CAT, followed by an overshadowing of translators when data-driven approaches were introduced, to a situation where computers and translators carried out their duties consecutively rather than in true collaboration as translators were simply left to post-edit the complete draft produced by the MT system.

Looking back at the historical timeline of MT development, we can observe that the least successful periods — as illustrated by the ALPAC Report that followed the early drive for FAHQT, by Kelly's (2014: n.p.) contention that many translators "hate technology" in large part because they were isolated from the translation process and left to work as "the clean up crew", or by the ethical concerns raised by Kenny (2011) — were the were period where collaboration was low and where translators felt that they were being ignored or exploited, rather than operating as full partners in the translation process. In contrast, the most productive periods were those when collaboration was more genuine, such as following Kay's ([1980]1997a) push to reconceptualize MT as being under the CAT umbrella, or the more recent move to integrate post-editing more fully into the translation loop (e.g., through adaptive and interactive MT), rather than isolating the translator's contribution to the end of the process.

The most recent developments, such as interactive MT and elements of augmented translation, show a greater recognition that computers and people have very different strengths. Computers are good at pattern matching and rapid calculations, meaning that they can lead to improvements such as increased consistency and productivity, which can in turn mean that a greater volume of texts can be translated. Meanwhile, people excel at creativity and accuracy, which contribute to the production of a quality product appreciated by end users. The combination of computer "brawn" and human "brains", which allows each party to play to its own strengths, has created a situation that is more favourable to desired outcomes (i.e., greater throughput of quality products) than could be achieved by either party working alone.

It has been convenient for the purpose of this paper to focus on the nature of the collaboration between the two main parties — computers and translators. However, it is important to recognize that other factors can also influence the nature of the collaboration between these two. For instance, some of the reasons that translators have been reluctant to work with technology stem not from concerns about the tools themselves but rather from the business practices surrounding their use (e.g., LeBlanc, 2017). For example, the downward pressure on rates, or a client's decision to impose the use of a particular tool or workflow, can certainly impact a translator's willingness to work in a collaborative fashion with MT. We note that the most recent developments in the world of MT, such as aspects of augmented translation or responsive MT, seek to expand the collaborative relationship beyond the core pair of translator and computer to include others such as project managers, clients and end users. It will be interesting to observe how this expanded network affects and is affected by the collaborative process in the years to come.

10. Concluding remarks

The 75-year history of collaboration between translators and computers in the context of MT has been full of ups and downs, and twists and turns. O'Brien (2020: 337) suggests that over this period, the translation profession has gradually changed to the point where translators have become almost "symbiotic with the 'machine'", requiring a close and constant collaboration between the two. The relationship is not always easy, but it persists nonetheless. Indeed, it seems that this view of translator-computer collaboration as a necessary precursor for success is starting to be recognized more widely. Although we noted earlier that Vieira's (2020) study of the English-language media identified a sometimes problematic portrayal of MT, where this technology was often presented as being on a par with or even superior to humans, this attitude is not necessarily universal nor representative of the current state of affairs. The data in Vieira's study covered the period from the mid-1980s to mid-2019, thus capturing some of those periods where translators found themselves in the back seat. However, Wang & Ping (2020) conducted a similar investigation in the Chinese media, focusing on 50 articles published between 2017 and 2019, thus more specifically revealing current attitudes. Wang & Ping's (2020) findings show that the most prominent theme in the news stories is "progress", occurring in 68% of the articles. However, the second-most prominent theme appearing in these news stories is "human-machine cooperation and coexistence", which appeared in 64% of the articles (Wang & Ping, 2020: 7). According to these researchers, human-machine cooperation is put forward as a solution to the question of whether translators will be replaced by computers, with news articles portraying the belief that humans and machines should complement each other. Wang & Ping (2020) even found that this particular concept of collaboration resulted in the creation of some new Chinese-language terms and expressions in the media articles, all of which share a similar meaning of the cooperation between humans and machines.

This is an encouraging note on which to end the paper, although it remains to be seen how the next round of collaboration will play out when new techniques for language processing are discovered and as new business models are introduced to the translation industry. One thing that seems certain, however, is that the roller-coaster ride is not over yet!

References

[1] Automatic Language Processing Advisory Committee. Language and machines — Computers in translation and linguistics [Z/OL]. Washington, D.C.: National Academy of Sciences, National Research Council, 1966. https://web.archive.org/web/20110409070141/http://www.mt-archive.info/ALPAC-1966.pdf

[2] Castilho, S., Moorkens, J., Gaspari, F., *et al.* A comparative quality evaluation of PBSMT and NMT using professional translators [R/OL]. In Proceedings of the 16th Machine Translation Summit (MT Summit XVI) (pp.116-131)[C]. 2017. http://aamt.info/app-def/S-102/mtsummit/2017/conference-proceedings/

[3] DePalma, D. A. Augmented translation powers up language services [Z/OL]. CSA Research Blog, February 15, 2017. https://csa-research.com/Blogs-Events/Blog/ArticleID/140

[4] Eriguchi, A., Rarrick, S. & Matsushita H. Combining translation memory with neural machine translation [R/OL]. In Proceedings of the 6th Workshop on Asian Translation (pp.123-130) [C]. Hong Kong, China.

Association for Computational Linguistics, 2019. https://aclanthology.org/D19-5214/

[5] Etchegoyhen, T., Ponce, D., Gete, H., & Ruiz, V. Online learning over time in Adaptive Neural Machine Translation [R/OL]. In Proceedings of the International Conference on Recent Advances in Natural Language Processing (RAPNLP 2021) (pp. 411-420) [C]. 2021. https://aclanthology.org/2021.ranlp-1.47/

[6] Guerberof Arenas, A. & Toral, A. Creativity in translation: MT as a constraint for literary texts [J/OL]. Translation Spaces, 2022. https://benjamins.com/catalog/ts.21025.gue

[7] Hassan, H., Aue, A. & Chen, C. *et al*. Achieving human parity on automatic Chinese to English news translation [R/OL], 2018. https://arxiv.org/abs/1803.05567

[8] Hutchins, W. J. & Somers, H. L. Machine Translation: An Introduction [M]. London: Academic Press, 1992.

[9] Hutchins, J. ALPAC: The (in)famous report [A]. In Nirenburg, S., Somers, H. L. & Wilks, Y. A. (eds.). Readings in Machine Translation (pp.131-135) [C]. Cambridge: The MIT Press, 2003.

[10] Kay, M. The proper place of men and machines in language translation [J]. Machine Translation, 1997,12 (1/2): 3-23.

[11] Kay, M. It's still the proper place [J]. Machine Translation, 1997, 12 (1/2): 35-38.

[12] Kelly, N. Why so many translators hate translation technology [Z/OL]. Huffington Post Blog, July 19, 2014. https://www.huffpost.com/entry/why-so-many-translators-h_b_5506533

[13] Kenny, D. The ethics of machine translation [A/OL]. In Ferner, S. (ed.). Reflections on Language and Technology — The Driving Forces in the Modern World of Translation and Interpreting. Proceedings of the 20th New Zealand Society of Translators and Interpreters National Conference [C]. Auckland: New Zealand Society of Translators and Interpreters, 2011. Retrieved from http://doras.dcu.ie/17606/

[14] Kenny, D. & Winters, M. Translation, ethics & the literary translator's voice [J]. Translation Spaces, 2020, 9(1): 123-149.

[15] Koehn, P. Statistical Machine Translation [M]. Cambridge: Cambridge University Press, 2010.

[16] Koehn, P. Neural Machine Translation [M]. Cambridge: Cambridge University Press, 2020.

[17] Krings, H. P. Repairing Texts: Empirical Investigations of Machine Translation Post-Editing Processes [M]. Kent, OH: Kent State University Press, 2001.

[18] LeBlanc, M. "I can't get no satisfaction!" Should we blame translation technologies or shifting business practices? [A]. In Kenny, D. (ed.). Human Factors in Translation Technology (pp.45-62) [C]. London: Routledge, 2017.

[19] Lehrberger, J. & Bourbeau, L. Machine Translation: Linguistic Characteristics of MT Systems and General Methodology of Evaluation [M]. Amsterdam: John Benjamins, 1988.

[20] Locke, W. N., Booth, A. D. & Weaver, W. Translation [A]. In Nirenburg, S., Somers, H. L. & Wilks, Y. A. (eds.). Readings in Machine Translation (pp.15-23) [C]. Cambridge: The MIT Press, 2003.

[21] Lommel, A. How augmented translation affects the language services industry [Z/OL]. CSA Research Blog, July 5, 2017. https://csa-research.com/Blogs-Events/Blog/How-Augmented-Translation-Affects-the-Language-Services-Industry

[22] Lommel, A. Augmented translation: Are we there yet? [Z/OL]. CSA Research Blog, November 4, 2020. https://csa-research.com/Blogs-Events/Blog/augmented-translation-2020

[23] Lommel, A. Responsive machine translation: The next frontier for MT [Z/OL]. CSA Research Blog, August 17, 2021. https://csa-research.com/Blogs-Events/Blog/responsive-MT-Test

[24] Martikainen, H. Ghosts in the machine: Can adaptive MT help reclaim a place for the human in the loop? [Z/OL], 2022. https://hal.archives-ouvertes.fr/hal-03548696

[25] Monarch, R. Human-in-the-loop Machine Learning: Active Learning and Annotation for Human-Centred AI [M]. Shelter Island, NY: Manning, 2021.

[26] Moorkens, J. Ethics and machine translation [A]. Machine Translation for Everyone: Empowering Users in the Age of Artificial Intelligence [C]. Berlin: Language Science Press, 2022.

[27] Moorkens, J. & Lewis, D. 2020. Copyright and the reuse of translation as data [A]. In O'Hagan, M. (ed.). The Routledge Handbook of Translation and Technology [C]. London: Routledge.

[28] O'Brien, S. Translation as human-computer interaction [J]. Translation Spaces, 2012, 1 (1): 101-122.

[29] O'Brien, S. Translation, human-computer interaction, and cognition [A]. In Alves, F. & Jakobsen, A. L. (eds). Routledge Handbook of Translation and Cognition (pp. 376-388) [C]. London: Routledge, 2020.

[30] Oxford Languages. Roller coaster [A/OL]. Google English Dictionary [Z], 2022. https://www.google.com/search?q=define+roller+coaster

[31] Poibeau, T. Machine Translation [M]. Cambridge: The MIT Press, 2017.

[32] Santy, S., Dandapat, S., Choudhury, M. & Bali, K. INMT: Interactive neural machine translation prediction [A/OL]. In Proceedings of the 2019 Conference on Empirical Methods in Natural Language Processing and the 9th International Joint Conference on Natural Language Processing (EMNLP-IJCNLP): System Demonstrations (pp.103-108) [C]. Hong Kong, China. Association for Computational Linguistics, 2019. https://aclanthology.org/D19-3018/

[33] Toral, A., Castilho, S., Hu, K. & Way, A. Attaining the unattainable? Reassessing claims of human parity in neural machine translation [A]. In Proceedings of the Third Conference on Machine Translation: Research Papers (pp.113-123) [C]. Brussels, Belgium. Association for Computational Linguistics, 2018.

[34] Vieira, L. N. Machine translation in the news: A framing analysis of the written press [J]. Translation Spaces, 2020, 9(1): 98-122.

[35] Wang, B. & Yuan, P. Perceptions of machine translation and computer-aided translation by professionals and the general public: A survey study based on articles in professional journals and the media [J]. International Journal of Translation, Interpretation, and Applied Linguistics, 2020, 2(2): 1-14.

[36] Weaver, W. Translation [Z/OL], 1949. https://mt-archive.net/50/Weaver-1949-original.pdf

[37] Wikipedia. Roller coaster [Z/OL], 2022. https://en.wikipedia.org/wiki/Roller_coaster

[38] Wu, Y., Schuster, M., Chen, Z., *et al.* Google's Neural Machine Translation System: Bridging the gap between human and machine translation [Z/OL], 2016. https://arxiv.org/abs/1609.08144

[39] Xiao, Y., Liu, L., Huang, G., *et al.* BiTIIMT: A bilingual text-infilling method for interactive machine translation [A/OL]. In Proceedings of the 60th Annual Meeting of the Association for Computational Linguistics (Volume 1: Long Papers) (1958–1969) [C]. Dublin, Ireland: Association for Computational Linguistics, 2022. https://aclanthology.org/2022.acl-long.138/

四、翻译教学中的合作

Soft Skills Are Getting Harder: Collaboration and Competence in Translator Education

Gary Massey
Zurich University of Applied Sciences

Abstract: Since Kiraly's influential *A Social Constructivist Approach to Translator Education*, collaborative learning has become best practice in translator education. Combining individual reflection with collaborative knowledge-building, it marks an evolution from a transmissionist to a transformationist perspective on learning as "a personal, holistic, intrinsically motivating and socially effectuated construction process" (Kiraly, 2000: 23). Characteristically implemented as authentic experiential learning in collaborative projects involving real-world praxis partners (or simulated equivalents), it aims for students to become "proactive seekers of knowledge" and teachers "partners in learning" (Kiraly, 2013: 214-215). A range of qualitative studies have shown student outcomes to include greater responsibility, autonomy, critical reflection, self-regulation, motivation, initiative and self-efficacy. Collaboration places a premium on such soft, transferable skills which, under the umbrella of service provision, interpersonal and personal competences, have been "hardened up" to occupy an increasingly central position in translator competence modelling and curricular demands. But it can be notoriously hard to operationalize, monitor and assess their development. This paper traces the development of collaboration in translation pedagogy, discussing the shift towards soft, transferable skills in competence models and job profiles. It explores collaborative competence development among the various actors engaged in translator education on the basis of social

constructivist and emergentist concepts associated with student learning.
Keywords: social constructivism; emergentism; collaboration; language industry profiles; hard skills; soft skills; transferable skills; portfolio assessment

软技能的硬化趋势：翻译教育中的合作与能力

Gary Massey　苏黎世应用科学大学

摘　要：自吉拉里（Don Kiraly）颇具影响力的著述《社会建构主义翻译教学》问世以来，合作学习就成为翻译教学的最佳实践。合作学习将个人反思与合作性知识建构相结合，标志着看待学习的视角从知识传递演变为知识革新，将学习视为“个人的、全面的、受内在激励和社会影响的建构过程”（Kiraly，2000：23）。合作学习通常以合作项目中真实体验学习的形式进行，项目有现实世界的实践伙伴（或模拟者）参与，旨在使学生成为“主动的知识寻求者”，使教师成为“学习伙伴”（Kiraly，2013：214-215）。诸多定性研究表明，合作学习的能带来更强的责任感、自主性、批判反思、自我调节、动机、主动性和自我效能。此类可迁移的“软”技能在合作中相当重要，但在服务供应、人际和个人能力的范畴内，这些技能已逐渐“硬化”，在译者能力建模和课程需求中占据更核心的位置，但无论是将此类技能的发展可操作化，还是对其进监测和评估，都颇具难度。本文追溯了翻译教学法中合作的发展，讨论了在能力模型和工作评估中针对可迁移的“软”技能的转向。此外，本文依托社会建构主义和涌现论两大概念中与学生学习相关的部分，探究了从事翻译教育的各个行动者的合作能力发展路径。。
关键词：社会建构主义；涌现论；合作；语言行业概况；硬技能；软技能；可迁移技能；组合评估

1. Introduction

Don Kiraly’s influential work, *A Social Constructivist Approach to Translator Education* (2000), quintessentially “holds that meaning, knowledge, and the mind itself are inextricably embedded in our personal interactions with other people" (Kiraly, 2000: 7). It was published at a time when, with something of a time-lag compared with pedagogies in other, related disciplines such as language teaching, translation pedagogy was entering a new phase of epistemological awareness and began questioning many of the assumptions that has hitherto shaped the self-concepts of the educators. It set out to challenge the predominantly transmissionist perspective on learning that Kiraly saw in translations training up to that point, where learners were passive consumers of knowledge distributed by all-knowing teachers in "digestible chunks" (Kiraly 2000: 22).

Transmissionist approaches had dominated translator training in the 1970s and early 1980s. They had been identifiably teacher-centric, based on the trainers' "performance magistrale" (Kiraly, 1995: 7) and echoed in Newmark's (1991: 130) famous view that success in teaching translation rested "65% on the personality of the teacher, 20% on the course design and 15% on the course materials". Although a more systematic objectives-based pedagogy of professional translation began emerging in the 1980s (e.g., Delisle, 1980), followed in the next decade by functionalist approaches (e.g., Nord, 1997; Colina, 2003) derived from skopos and translational action theory (Holz-Mänttäri, 1984; Reiss & Vermeer, 1984), together with sporadic situated learning initiatives through authentic project work (e.g., Vienne, 1994), it is Kiraly's book that marks the most radical move away from transmissionism towards a transformationist pedagogy that presented learning as "a personal, holistic, intrinsically motivating and socially effectuated construction process" (Kiraly, 2000: 23). The approach combines Schön's (1987) personal reflective practice and action with collaborative knowledge-building, operationalized by student teamwork on simulated and, increasingly, authentic translation assignments with real-world clients, briefs, deadlines and even publication of target documents. The teachers become "partners in learning rather than distributors of knowledge", while their students are "proactive seekers of knowledge" (Kiraly, 2013: 214-215). Crucially, a range of qualitative studies have shown student outcomes to include greater responsibility, autonomy, critical reflection, self-regulation, motivation, initiative and self-efficacy (e.g., González-Davies & Enríquez Raído, 2017; Kiraly & Massey, 2019; van Egdom *et al.*, 2020).

In parallel, and partial reciprocity, with teaching approaches and practices, cognitive research into the nature and development of competent translation performance and expertise has increasingly informed translator education as it has sought to establish models of translation and broader language mediation competence. Arguably the best-known model derived from such translation process research (TPR) is the PACTE group's (2003), which presents translation competence as a set of interacting sub-competences — bilingual, extralinguistic, knowledge about translation, instrumental and strategic — supported by the activation of psycho-physiological components.

The PACTE group claim to have empirically validated their model in two decades of TPR experiments and questionnaire surveys, and they have used it as the basis for the NACT[1] translation competence framework (e.g., PACTE, 2018). This is a set of performance level descriptors for translator training and assessment that covers the components language competence, cultural, world knowledge and thematic competence, instrumental competence, translation service provision competence, and finally, translation problem-solving competence — the central strategic competence governing the deployment of all the others to solve various problem types.

The PACTE competence model forms the starting point for other componential models of translation competence, a major example being the empirically researched TransComp model (Göpferich, 2008). Elements are also visible in the European Master's in Translation (EMT) competence profile for professional translators (EMT Expert Group, 2009). The EMT model places service provision competence at the hub of the wheel used to visualize its various sub-competences, which otherwise comprise.

1 "Establishing Competence Levels in the Acquisition of Translation Competence in Written Translation", see grupsderecerca.uab.cat/pacte/en/nactproject (accessed June 30, 2022).

The EMT profile indicates a move away from *translation* competence to *translator* competence as a fully integrated member of the professional translator community, initially proposed by Kiraly (2000: 13). Its second iteration, the 2017 EMT Competence Framework (EMT Board, 2017), goes further in this direction by putting even more emphasis on socio-technical knowledge and the socio-cognitive personal and interpersonal competences needed in work contexts, including a number of what its authors refer to as "soft skills" (EMT Board, 2017: 10). In casting such an overtly wider net, the framework appears to be in lockstep with a progressive shift over the last two decades of TPR focussed on competence and expertise development towards a cognitive translatology paradigm (e.g., Muñoz Martín, 2016) that presents cognition as embodied, embedded, extended, enacted and affective (4EA cognition).

This brief rundown of translation pedagogy depicts the background against which the present paper will discuss in greater detail its main topic, namely the way that collaboration in learning, and more pertinently in the professional settings for which translation students are educated, places a premium on soft or transferable skills. As we shall see, these skills have, under the umbrella of service provision, interpersonal and personal competences, progressively been "hardened up" to occupy an increasingly central position in translator competence modelling, curricular implementations and the job profiles of language industry professionals.

Nevertheless, they remain hard to pin down. They are, by and large, ill-defined and poorly delineated, suggesting that a more systematic approach to identifying, describing and measuring these increasingly crucial soft skills is badly needed. The present article suggests ways in which this might be done. In doing so, it also explores the issues of collaborative competence development among the various actors engaged in translator education on the basis of social constructivist and emergentist concepts associated with student learning.

2. Definitions and delineations

The *Oxford English Dictionary* (Oxford University Press, n.d.) defines "soft skills" as "abilities which enable effective communication and social interaction with other people; interpersonal skills [...]", though it provides no entry for hard ones. The latter are, however, described in the *Oxford Dictionary of Human Resource Management* (Heery & Noon, 2017a) as "competencies that employees possess such as numeracy, literacy, fluency in a foreign language, and specific job-related technical abilities". Wholly appropriately in the present context, the same entry also points out the growing shift towards soft skills as a necessary complement to the hard ones. For Heery & Noon (2017b), "soft skills" are "associated with activities such as customer handling, communication, problem-solving, and teamworking", including "loyalty, enthusiasm, punctuality, and a strong work ethic".

On the surface, the distinction between hard and soft would appear to be clear-cut, but as soon as attempts are made to anchor it in particular professions or types of (vocational) training, the contours seem to blur. Even Heery & Noon (2017b) concede in their entry that critics argue that what they list are not really skills but rather "qualities or attributes" — and by extension beyond the reach of skills training and development in the traditional sense.

In the field of library and information science, Matteson *et al.* (2016) evocatively refer to "soft skills" as "a phrase in search of meaning". Although there are overlaps among the various lists of soft skills that have been investigated by researchers — Matteson *et al.* (2016: 75) cite, for example, "sociability, self-management, communication skills, ethics, diversity sensitivity, teamwork skills, problem-solving or critical thinking abilities, customer service competencies, emotional intelligence, and leadership skills" — they stress the need to first delineate terms such as "skills", "dispositions", "attitudes", "beliefs" and "values" before trying to identify the particular skills that can be designated "soft" (Matteson *et al.*, 2016: 74). They (Matteson *et al.*, 2016: 75-80) compellingly show how confusing and contradictory the definitions of, and the management research on, soft skills have been, concluding that this makes it impossible to connect research findings across studies and that the lack of clear "taxonomies of discrete soft skills makes it challenging for the idea of soft skills to truly gain traction in research or in practice" (Matteson *et al.*, 2016: 80-81).

As elsewhere, translation studies and pedagogy demonstrate no obvious consensus on what exactly soft skills are, nor on which skills to focus. The EMT competence framework (EMT Board, 2017: 10) assigns "soft skills", which "enhance graduate adaptability and employability", to personal and interpersonal competence. The skill descriptors themselves cover time, stress and workload management; compliance with instructions; teamwork in virtual, multicultural and multilingual environments; responsible use of social media; adaptation to ergonomic demands; self-evaluation; and autonomous and collaborative competence development. Yet, these, too, only partially coincide with the "soft skills" listed across other disciplines and are not even consistent with other approaches and taxonomies within translation studies itself. Hubscher-Davidson & Lehr (2021: 79-80), for instance, address soft skills through the prism of emotional intelligence (EI), with which, they claim, proper training could usefully address the issues of occupational stress, motivational problems, isolation and technological impacts on health and well-being that translators are known to experience. Galán-Mañas *et al.* (2020) align soft skills with entrepreneurship. O'Brien & Rossetti (2020: 116) focus their concept of soft skills on communication, flexibility and critical thinking. Chan (2015), who prefers the synonymous term "transferable skills", locates them above all in general knowledge, entrepreneurship and ethics.

Despite the divergent heuristics in play, however, there is no doubting the fact that soft, transferable skills in general are very much in demand in the language industry and professions, even to the extent that they are becoming less easy to distinguish from their "harder" equivalents. The next section briefly looks at how this has come about and what the likely reasons are.

3. Soft skills in professional contexts

Although taxonomies and definitions of soft, transferable skills remain blurry and sometimes contradictory, there is convincing evidence that they have been regarded as increasingly core, "hard" elements of competent performance in the various strands of the language industry. Recent translation studies research shows soft, transferable skills to feature constantly and large in graduate and employer self-report, job advertisement data, and industry hiring processes.

Ringgenberg's (2022) small-scale snapshot sample of job ads for language mediators on the GALA website[1] reveals that nearly two-thirds partly or wholly mentioned skills that other studies, including those cited above, refer to as soft or transferable: time, stress and workload management; commitment to quality, tasks or employers; attention to detail; self-organization; communication and interpersonal skills; self-development; collaboration; independence; proactivity; service-mindedness; professionalism; innovativeness and creativity; ethics; adaptability; problem-solving; motivation. Bernadini *et al.* (2022) report on the results of a large-scale international corpus-based study of job posts targeting emerging jobs at the crossroads of languages and technology from the Erasmus+ UPSKILLS[2] project. Their analysis of the skills, competences and tasks that technologically competent translation students could aspire to demonstrates that, alongside "harder" data analysis, research, technical and disciplinary skills, there is a major role for transferable soft ones: written and oral communication, attention to detail, analytical skills, problem-solving and the "ability to thrive in a fast-paced environment" are those expressly listed. Angelone (2022) concentrates in his study presentation on the transferable soft skills related to flexibility and adaptability, exploring the evolving need for adaptive expertise in response

1 GALA Globalization and Localization Association: https://www.gala-global.org/. 33 advertisements were sampled on February 5, 2022.

2 https://upskillsproject.eu/(accessed on August 31, 2022)

to the dynamic diversification and transformation of tasks that translators undertake in the language industry. Adaptive expertise involves optimal performance across tasks when these require flexibility in problem-solving or are ill-defined. Using alumni interview data collected in early 2022, he describes the ill-defined tasks experienced by professionals working in various parts of the language industry and the adaptable expertise needed to address them: coping with varying specifications, clients, project managers, deadlines, industry strands, stakeholder constellations, technologies, virtual and physical spaces, and compensation. Finally, Risku *et al.* (2022) present a qualitative interview study on the criteria used by employers to hire in-house translators for translation departments and agencies. It reveals a pronounced emphasis on soft skills, personality and adaptability as elements of a pragmatic-cooperative notion of lived expertise in context, involving interaction, cooperation, communicative skills, self-presentation and appearance, team skills, respect for employer values and processes, conscientiousness, stress resistance, feedback processing and critical self-awareness (of one's strengths and limitations).

How can we account for such developments? All of the above-mentioned studies were conducted against the background of a diversifying and rapidly evolving language industry. In 2020, Slator listed 700 job titles for core language industry tasks (Slator, 2020: 11-17), compared to a wholly compatible survey that it had commissioned two years previously and that had uncovered 100 fewer titles (Bond, 2018). This evidence is enhanced by an analysis of buyer intentions in Slator's 2022 *Language Industry Market Report* (Slator, 2022: 15), which demonstrates just how layered buyer demands have become when commissioning language services. Primary intentions that drive spending across all verticals ranges from market access, at a rounded 35% of the percentage market share, through regulatory compliance (18%), customer acquisition (11%), public accessibility (10%), process management (7%), people management (5%), customer retention (5%), event and reaction monitoring (4.5%), and discovery (3.3%).

In an attempt to capitalize on increasingly diverse and complex demand patterns, language service providers have progressively positioned themselves as strategic business partners (Hickey & Agulló García, 2021: 40). As a result, the language industry has seen an expansion of services upstream and downstream of core translation and localization services towards multilingual content creation, on the one hand, and services like compliance, accessibility, publishing, distribution, consultancy, and the management of content, data and quality, on the other. Service providers obviously need the staff with the fundamental skills and attributes to service demand in these, and as yet unanticipated, areas of work in a hugely dynamic language industry.

On a market hallmarked by rapidly diversifying jobs, roles and tasks, the capacity to adapt to ever-changing socio-technical environments is predicated on possessing skills that help graduates transition smoothly to new professional contexts and demands which cannot be handled by the routines of established knowledge, procedures and approaches in stable, pre-defined professional settings. Giving graduates the competences to act as human experts in the multiple loops of the current and future language industry (Massey & Ehrensberger-Dow, 2021) is the crucial current and future task of translator education. It will rely to a considerable degree on how a combination of "hard" skills, such as those making up multilingual and intercultural competence and language technology competence, and much-needed transferable "soft" ones are learned and assessed.

The increasingly prevalent cognitive paradigm of translator education of the past few years, 4EA cognition, recognizes how the essential situatedness of translation in particular, and of other core and ancillary language services in general, presupposes an interdependence between language mediators and their human and technological work environments. Inevitably, therefore, the paradigm lends considerable credence to the application of social constructivist and emergentist educational approaches based on scaffolded simulated, and more particularly authentic, experiential learning (e.g., Kiraly & Massey, 2019). Their most visible and obvious expression is in the mentorships and work placements, translation projects, student companies, agency simulators and so on (e.g., Astley & Torres Hostench, 2017; Buysschaert *et al.*, 2017) that have featured repeatedly and increasingly in translation pedagogy literature and practice, prompting educators to work ever closer together with the language industry in order to increase graduate employability (Rodríguez de Céspedes, 2017). The naturally corollary has therefore been a premium placed not just on "hard" technology skills, subject-specific knowledge and core linguistic, cultural and mediation knowledge, but the growing amount of attention afforded to "soft" or transferable skills, to closely associated entrepreneurship ones and to what have been — rather nebulously — termed personal attributes (e.g., Schnell & Rodríguez, 2017; Galán-Mañas *et al.*, 2020).

One way of accounting for the growing awareness of soft, transferable skills, and indeed for what appears to be their growing convergence with hard ones, appears to lie in the increasing recognition of the embeddedness of language mediation within a socio-technical environment. Another major factor in the eroding distinctions between hard and soft, core and transferable skills lies quite patently in the nature of language mediation itself. Indeed, the overwhelming majority of soft skills inventories outside the study and practice of language mediation give prominence to communication and problem-solving, both of which are considered core, hard skills in translation competence models and profiles. Language mediation is self-evidently communication enacted to serve the communicative goals of embodied human actors or the organizations they populate within their various extended socio-cultural settings. Thus, the ability to mediate *per se* across and within languages must intrinsically require an amalgam of hard and soft skill sets that are often indistinguishable from one another. This matter is implicitly but nevertheless lucidly raised by Calvo (2011: 14), who in her deliberations on curriculum design quite appositely asks whether translation is to be seen and presented as a purely vocational, highly specialized type of knowledge, or as an adaptable, multi-purpose, transferable one. It would appear that a combination of competence modelling and market forces are now feeding into the latter understanding — though in tandem with the former and not to its exclusion.

Two examples should suffice to demonstrate the point. The influential European Master's in Translation (EMT) network's *European Master's in Translation Competence Framework 2017* (EMT Board, 2017) presents a transversal description of the many situated cultural, intercultural, transcultural and multicultural aspects of what translators do: "sociolinguistic, cultural and transcultural knowledge and skills" are "the driving force behind all the other competences" (EMT Board, 2017: 6). Translators should obviously be able to translate and mediate in specific intercultural contexts and work in multicultural, multilingual teams and environments (EMT Board, 2017: 8-10), which are seen as indicators of translation competence (mediating in intercultural contexts) and of personal and interpersonal competence (teamwork in multicultural and multilingual environments), respectively. The ability to do so is therefore directly related in the framework with a set of "generic skills, often referred to as 'soft skills', that enhance graduate adaptability and employability" (EMT Board, 2017: 10). Here we note that what used to be a clear distinction between core hard and transferable soft skills — witnessed, for example, in the previous iteration of the EMT competence profile (EMT Expert Group, 2009) — seems to have become rather fuzzier as an increasingly 4EA conceptualization of cognition as embodied, embedded, extended, enacted and affective has come to exert a decisive influence on how competent professional translation should be regarded.

This incipient fusion extends beyond core translation activity to what were once considered supplementary value-adding activities (ISO 17100, 2015: 18), but which have now evolved into their own discrete professional profiles in a diversifying language industry. Post-editing, for example, has its own standard (ISO 18587, 2017) and competence models (Nitzke & Hansen-Schirra, 2021: 69-77). From the perspective of the present paper, what is most interesting about the models are the semiotics of their visual representations. Nitzke and Hansen-Schirra (2021: 73) depict a "house of PE [post-editing] competence [with] three pillars [that] are framed by a roof, which represents soft skills for post-editors". Though it is not always completely transparent what these soft skills are, the following are explicitly listed (Nitzke & Hansen-Schirra, 2021: 72-74): consulting, risk assessment and service competences, concentration, attentiveness, stress resistance, logical reasoning, analytical thinking and quick-wittedness. An affinity with the latest technology, an adequate professional self-perception and appropriately ethical behaviour are also highlighted.

While this enumeration of soft skills makes practical sense in the context of profiling the professional post-editor, it is again quite divergent from the others we have encountered. As yet, there appears to be no uniform framework for defining and delineating the soft, transferable skills that the language industry patently demands. Furthermore, translator education still appears to have to work on embracing them adequately. The next section attempts to address these issues.

4. Defining, teaching and assessing soft skills

From what we have noted so far, soft skills are indeed still in search of a meaning, at least with respect to the language industry. It is therefore self-evident that a more coherent, systematic approach in researching, teaching and assessing such skills would be warranted.

UNICEF's flagship *Global Framework on Transferable Skills* (2019) provides an eminently practicable starting point. Barely know in the field of translation studies and pedagogy, the framework applies a consummate working definition of transferable skills that encompasses three interrelated skill categories: the cognitive (the ability to focus, solve problems, make informed choices, set plans and goals, etc.), the social (the ability to communicate, collaborate, resolve conflicts, negotiate, etc.) and the emotional (understanding and regulating one's own emotions, coping with stress, understanding others' emotions, empathy, etc.). These are activated in four learning dimensions, oriented on four principal outcomes to guide the holistic development of learners: the cognitive dimension of learning (education, lifelong learning), the instrumental dimension of employability (employment, entrepreneurship), the individual dimension of personal empowerment and the social dimension of active citizenship (values) (UNICEF, 2019: 9-20).

The framework is expressly designed to be adaptable to local needs, seeking engage users "in a process of identifying and analysing a breadth of transferable skills" rather than "name specific skills in a context of competing definitions" (UNICEF, 2019: 15). It has already been operationalized by Middle East and North African (MENA) countries and has provided a springboard for others to elaborate their own conceptual and programmatic framework (CPF) of transferable skills development.

By way of illustration, the MENA CPF identifies twelve core skills, three for each of the outcomes named above: creativity, critical thinking, problem-solving (for the learning outcome), cooperation, negotiation, decision-making (for the employability outcome), self-management, resilience, communication (for the personal empowerment outcome), respect for diversity, empathy, participation (for the active citizenship outcome) (UNICEF, 2019: 17). These are further broken down into sub-skills, such as divergent and analytical thinking (learning outcome), teamwork, risk-taking and autonomy (employability outcome), self-efficacy, reflective thinking and self-development (personal empowerment outcome), and agency, social awareness and ethical decision-making (active citizenship outcome).

I propose that the framework could readily be adapted not only to geographical needs, but also to sectorial ones — such as those of the language industry. In this case, the learning, employability and empowerment outcomes can transition more or less seamlessly to a language industry framework, while the MENA CPF's socio-politically oriented outcome of active citizenship can be re-calibrated to accommodate an industry-oriented organizational dimension that focuses on ethically grounded agency within a socially responsible corporate value-system as its prime outcome. Agency has hitherto been defined in the MENA CFP as a sub-skill, but in the broader industry and organisational contexts of language mediation, it has been regarded by those who have been researching language mediators' status and self-concept (e.g., Katan, 2016; Kuznik, 2016; Massey & Wieder, 2019; Schäffner, 2020) as a key outcome for the profession if, in an age progressively dominated by artificially intelligent language technologies, it is truly to provide the added value of embodied human intelligence and intervention. It would then be necessary to review and re-weight the core skills and the sub-skills. Exploring the results of such a review goes well beyond the scope of the present paper, but even at this early stage of deliberation what is abundantly clear is that the personal empowerment core skill labelled "communication" could benefit from being replaced by a more nuanced alternative — a selection that would depend very much on the particularities of the locale in which the CPF should apply.

Once sufficiently "localized" to meet the sectorial demands of the language industry and, wherever necessary, regional and geographical particularities, the framework needs to be operationalized in concrete teaching scenarios. There still appears to be a blind spot when it comes to achieving an adequate balance between hard and soft skill development in curricular design. In the UK context, Havergal (2015) speaks of the need to redress the imbalance in broader university education between hard and soft skills. O'Brien & Rossetti (2020: 115) recognize full well that "success in the workplace seems to rely on an array of transferable, soft skills" but are still forced to ask how training institutions can adequately prepare students for career paths in localization. Galán-Mañas *et al.* (2020: 7) appeal for "a new pedagogical approach that entails changes in the combination of specific and soft skills, in the teaching and learning methodologies and in the roles of students and teachers".

The questions regarding translator/language mediator education are somewhat puzzling, as the pre-requisites and conditions are, to a very great extent, already in place. The fundamental socio-technical embeddedness of soft, transferable skill sets squares exceedingly well with the aspirations of the now widespread social constructivist and emergentist approaches to the education of translators and related language professionals. We recall that social constructivism sees meaning, knowledge and cognition embedded in personal interactions. We are also reminded that repeated studies of collaborative, authentic, experiential learning in projects that engage students and teachers with industry partners, professional partners and/or end-users encompass outcomes that encompass the development of soft skills — responsibility, autonomy, critical reflection, self-regulation, motivation, initiative, self-efficacy, and so on. The sole but still necessary refinement, from the emergentist point of view, would be to continue breaking down the artificial boundaries between teaching and learning and finally accept both as "mutually specifying, co-emergent, pervasive and evolving practices" (Davis & Sumara, 1997: 110). In other words, translator education still has to fully realize the student-teacher-industry learning partnerships that have been achieved in other disciplines (e.g., Bovill *et al.*, 2011; Healey *et al.*, 2015; Tong *et al.*, 2018). Only then will all stakeholders, from students to teachers to professionals, be able to benefit equally from such holistic learning events.

One thorny issue remains. As Cimatti (2016: 112) suggests, assessing soft, transferable skills is a potentially delicate and difficult undertaking in educational and professional contexts that are directed almost exclusively towards evaluating hard subject-specific, technical skills and knowledge. This is made all the more difficult as assessment of learner and professional performance in language mediation is still almost exclusively based on the quality of the final product, obviously coupled with the temporal-quantitative dimension of productivity, but not necessarily linked to the multifarious processes by which the products have come about. Moreover, time and resource constraints on educators and their institutions present an ever-heightening barrier to teaching and assessing hard skills, let alone the transferable ones that have, as we have seen, have become such an important part of job profiles in the current language industry.

That having been said, authentic experiential learning in collaborative settings creates an ideal framework for the situated assessment of both hard and soft, transferable skills. Although the modalities of assessing transferable soft skills have not often been considered in translation pedagogy, there are notable exceptions. Rotheneder (2007: 8-17) is one. She makes the case for e-portfolios in hard and soft skills assessment. E-portfolios are both an effective online tool for distance learning and a "method for planning, reflecting, documenting, and evaluating learning processes and products" (Rotheneder, 2007: 9). Students plan their development goals, reflect on their learning, and collect and present evidence of their achievements to illustrate their progress. E-portfolios promote reflection on skills and their development, and they make those skills visible not only to teachers but also to potential employers. They can also be deployed after graduation as a reflective record of lifelong learning and employability.

Rotheneder's contribution is virtually unique in translation studies literature, but the utility of e-portfolios has been more consistently recognied in other disciplines. Particularly in the assessment of soft skills, Cimatti (2016: 111-112), for example, argues cogently in favour of e-portfolios and stresses the particular importance of triangulation of multiple sources of feedback and assessment in doing so. This would suggest that the most effective way of evaluating transferable soft skill development could and should be centred on a longitudinal, 360-degree situated assessment that deploys an e-portfolio tool. Such a solution would allow students during their studies, and the professionals they become afterwards, to document permanently the work they do, their reflections on their performance in terms of both processes and products, and the feedback they receive on it. To remain wholly congruent with the social constructivist and emergent principles of learning partnerships among teachers, students and other partners involved in learning events, it should involve constructive situated assessment rather than norm-referencing (Kiraly, 2000: 152-163). In addition to learner self-report and self-assessment alongside coach or teacher assessment, there should be space for continuous feedback from peers, industry partners, practitioners, employers, real-world clients and end-user groups. This would provide all stakeholders in the processes and products of language mediation education and practice to identify the extent to which students and graduates working as language professionals have developed the necessary skills. In short, consistent deployment of e-portfolios supplies the means to conduct a holistic assessment of the full range of integrated, complementary hard and soft skills that the language industry demands.

5. Conclusion

The growing perception in the language industry and in translator education is that transferable soft skills are key to the employability and success of translation graduates. Competence modelling and job profiles have seen a convergence of hard and soft skill sets and an increasing fuzziness in distinguishing them. This is the result of a growing realization that language mediation is embedded in complex, interactive socio-technical environments, and of the quite obvious fact that it is, intrinsically, the enaction of embodied communication among human actors in extended socio-cultural and organisational settings.

Authentic experiential learning in collaborative projects offers a ready means of teaching both hard and soft, transferable skills. However, there are still issues surrounding how to identify and categorize transferable skill sets, and how to assess their development. UNICEF's *Global Framework on Transferable Skills* (2019) offers an excellent starting point for developing applicable taxonomies, while portfolio methods and the digital tools that support them provide a workable means of implementing longitudinal, situated assessments of students and, later, graduate professionals based on self-reflection that can be triangulated with feedback from peers, teachers, employers, clients and end-users.

References

[1] Angelone, E. Documenting adaptive expertise, diversification and ill-defined tasks in the language industry [R]. Paper presented on the 10th EST Congress: Advancing Translation Studies, Oslo, Norway, 2022.

[2] Astley, H. & Torres Hostench, O. The European graduate placement scheme: An integrated approach to preparing master's in translation graduates for employment [J/OL]. The Interpreter and Translator Trainer, 2017, 11(2-3): 204-222. https://doi.org/10.1080/1750399X.2017.1344813

[3] Bernadini, S., Ferraresi, A. & Petrovic, M. M. A curious mindset and love of experimentation: A corpus perspective on emerging language industry jobs [R]. Paper presented on the 10th EST Congress: Advancing Translation Studies, Oslo, Norway, 2022.

[4] Bond, E. The stunning variety of job titles in the language industry [N/OL]. Slator News, June 1, 2018. [30-06-2022]. https://slator.com/features/the-stunning-variety-of-job-titles-in-the-language-industry/

[5] Bovill, C., Cook-Sather, A. & Felten, P. Students as co-creators of teaching approaches, course design, and curricula: Implications for academic developers [J/OL]. International Journal for Academic Development, 2011, 16(2): 135-145. https://doi.org/10.1080/1360144X.2011.568690

[6] Buysschaert, J., Fernandez Parra, M. & van Egdom, G.-W. Professionalising the curriculum and increasing employability through authentic experiential learning: The cases of INSTB [J/OL]. Current Trends in Translation Teaching and Learning E, 2017, 4: 78-111. [30-06-2022]. http://www.cttl.org/uploads/5/2/4/3/5243866/cttl_e_2017_3.pdf

[7] Calvo, C. Translation and/or translator skills as organising principles for curriculum development practice [J/OL]. The Journal of Specialised Translation, 2011, 16: 5-25. [30-06-2022]. https://jostrans.org/issue16/art_calvo.pdf

[8] Chan, A. General education in the new undergraduate translation curricula: The case of Hong Kong universities [J/OL]. Current Trends in Translation Teaching and Learning E, 2015, 2: 97-138. [30-06-2022]. http://www.cttl.org/uploads/5/2/4/3/5243866/chapter_4_chan_general_education_clean.pdf

[9] Cimatti, B. Definition, development, assessment of soft skills and their role for the quality of organizations and enterprises [J/OL]. International Journal for Quality Research, 2016, 10(1): 97-130. https://doi.org/10.18421/IJQR10.01-05

[10] Colina, S. Translation Teaching from Research to the Classroom: A Handbook for Teachers [M]. New York: McGraw-Hill, 2003.

[11] Davis, B. & Sumara, D. Cognition, complexity, and teacher education [J/OL]. Harvard Educational Review, 1997, 67(1): 105-126. https://doi.org/10.17763/haer.67.1.160w00j113t78042

[12] Delisle, J. L'analyse du discours comme méthode de traduction: Initiation à la traduction française de textes pragmatiques anglais, théorie et pratique [M]. Ottawa: Université d'Ottawa, 1980.

[13] van Egdom, G.-W., Konttinen, K., Vandepitte, S., Fernández-Parra, M., Loock, R. & Bindels, J. Empowering translators through entrepreneurship in simulated translation bureaus [J/OL]. HERMES — Journal of Language and Communication in Business, 2020, 60: 81-95. https://doi.org/10.7146/hjlcb.v60i0.121312

[14] EMT Board. European Master's in Translation. Competence Framework 2017 [R/OL]. European Commission, 2017. [30-06-2022]. https://ec.europa.eu/info/sites/info/files/emt_competence_fwk_2017_en_web.pdf

[15] EMT Expert Group. Competences for professional translators, experts in multilingual and multimedia communication [R/OL]. European Commission, 2009. [30-06-2022]. https://ec.europa.eu/info/sites/info/files/emt_competences_translators_en.pdf

[16] Galán-Mañas, A., Kuznik, A. & Olalla-Soler, C. Entrepreneurship in translator and interpreter training [J/OL]. HERMES–Journal of Language and Communication in Business, 2020, 60: 7-11. https://doi.org/10.7146/hjlcb.v60i0.121307

[17] González-Davies, M. & Enríquez Raído, V. (eds.). Situated Learning in Translator and Interpreter Training: Bridging Research and Good Practice [C/OL]. London: Routledge, 2017. https://doi.org/10.1080/1750399X.2016.1154339

[18] Göpferich, S. Translationsprozessforschung: Stand – Methoden – Perspektiven [M]. Tübingen: Gunther Narr, 2008.

[19] Havergal, C. UK engagement survey: Universities have limited impact on students' "soft" skill development [R/OL]. Times Higher Education, 2015. [30-06-2022]. https://www.timeshighereducation.com/news/uk-engagement-survey-universities-have-limited-impact-students-soft-skill-development

[20] Healey M., Bovill, C. & Jenkins, A. Students as partners in learning [A]. In Lea, J. (ed.). Enhancing Learning and Teaching in Higher Education: Engaging with the Dimensions of Practice (pp. 141-163) [C]. London: Open University Press, 2015.

[21] Heery, E. & Noon, M. Hard skills [A/OL]. A Dictionary of Human Resource Management (3rd Ed.) [R]. Oxford: Oxford University Press, 2017a. [30-06-2022]. https://www.oxfordreference.com/view/10.1093/acref/9780191827822.001.0001/acref-9780191827822-e-1638

[22] Heery, E. & Noon, M. Soft skills [A/OL]. A Dictionary of Human Resource Management (3rd Ed.) [R]. Oxford: Oxford University Press, 2017b. [30-06-2022]. https://www.oxfordreference.com/view/10.1093/acref/9780191827822.001.0001/acref-9780191827822-e-1828

[23] Hickey, S. & Agulló García, B. The 2021 Nimdzi 100 [M/OL]. 2021. [30-06-2022]. https://www.nimdzi.com/nimdzi-100-2021/

[24] Holz-Mänttäri, J. Translatorisches Handeln: Theorie und Methode [J]. Annales Academiae Scientarum Fennicae, 1984.

[25] Hubscher-Davidson, S. & Lehr, C. Improving the Emotional Intelligence of Translators: A Roadmap for an Experimental Training Intervention [M/OL]. New York: Palgrave Macmillan, 2021. https://doi.org/10.1007/978-3-030-88860-2

[26] ISO 17100. Translation Services — Requirements for Translation Services [S]. International Organization for Standardization, 2015.

[27] ISO 18587. Translation Services — Post-editing of Machine Translation Output — Requirements [S]. International Organization for Standardization, 2017.

[28] Katan, D. Translation at the cross-roads: Time for the transcreational turn? [J/ OL]. Perspectives, 2016, 24(3): 365-381. https://doi.org/10.1080/0907676X.2015.1016049

[29] Kiraly, D. Pathways to Translation [M]. Kent: Kent State University Press, 1995.

[30] Kiraly, D. A Social Constructivist Approach to Translator Education [M/OL]. Manchester: St. Jerome, 2000. https://doi.org/10.4324/9781315760186

[31] Kiraly, D. Towards a view of translator competence as an emergent phenomenon: Thinking outside the box(es) in translator education [A]. In Kiraly, D., Hansen-Schirra S. & Maksymski K. (eds.). New Prospects and Perspectives for Educating Language Mediator (pp. 197-224) [C]. Narr Francke Attempto, 2013.

[32] Kiraly, D. & Massey, G. (eds.). Towards Authentic Experiential Learning in Translator Education (2nd Ed.) [C]. London: Cambridge Scholars, 2019.

[33] Kuznik, A. Work content of in-house translators in small and medium-sized industrial enterprises. Observing real work situations [J/OL]. The Journal of Specialised Translation, 2016, 25: 213-231. [30-06-2022]. . https://www.jostrans.org/issue25/art_kuznik.pdf

[34] Massey, G. & Ehrensberger-Dow, M. Language mediation professions: Humans in multiple loops [A/OL]. In ZHAW Angewandte Linguistik

(eds.). Angewandte Linguistik in Sprachberufen (pp.157-160) [C]. Berlin: De Gruyter, 2021. https://doi.org/10.21256/zhaw-23109

[35] Massey, G. & Wieder, R. Quality assurance in translation and corporate communications: Exploring an interdisciplinary interface [A/OL]. In Huertas Barros, E., Vandepitte, S. & Iglesias Fernánde, E. (eds.). Quality Assurance and Assessment Practices in Translation and Interpreting (pp. 57-87) [C]. London: IGI Global, 2019. https://doi.org/10.4018/978-1-5225-5225-3.ch003

[36] Matteson, M. L., Anderson, L. & Boyden, C. "Soft skills": A phrase in search of meaning [J/OL]. Portal: Libraries and the Academy, 2016, 16(1): 71-88. https://doi.org/10.1353/pla.2016.0009.

[37] Muñoz Martín, R. (ed.). Reembedding Translation Process Research [M]. Philadelphia: John Benjamins, 2016.

[38] Newmark, P. About Translation [M]. Clevedon: Multilingual Matters, 1991.

[39] Nitzke, J. & Hansen-Schirra, S. A Short Guide to Post-editing (Translation and Multilingual Natural Language Processing 16) [M/OL]. Berlin: Language Science Press, 2021. https://doi.org/10.5281/zenodo.5646896

[40] Nord, C. Translating as a Purposeful Activity [M]. Manchester: St. Jerome, 1997.

[41] O'Brien, S. & Rossetti, A. Neural machine translation and the evolution of the localisation sector: Implications for training [J/[OL]]. The Journal of Internationalization and Localization, 2020, 7(1-2): 95-121. https://doi.org/10.1075/jial.20005.obr

[42] Oxford University Press (n.d.). Soft, adj. [EB/OL] In OED Online. [30-06-2022]. https://www.oed.com/view/Entry/183898?redirectedFrom=%22soft+skills%22#eid1199266090.

[43] PACTE. Building a translation competence model [A/OL]. In Alves, F. (ed.). Triangulating Translation: Perspectives in Process Oriented Research (pp. 43-66) [C]. Philadelphia: John Benjamins, 2003. https://doi.org/10.1075/btl.45

[44] PACTE. Competence levels in translation: Working towards a European framework [J/OL]. The Interpreter and Translator Trainer, 2018,12(2): 111-131. https://doi.org/10.1080/1750399X.2018.1466093

[45] Reiss, K. & Vermeer, H. J. Grundlegung einer allgemeinen Translations Theorie [M]. Tübinegen: Niemeyer, 1984.

[46] Rodríguez de Céspedes, B. Addressing employability and enterprise responsibilities in the translation curriculum [J/OL]. The Interpreter and Translator Trainer, 2017, 11(2-3): 107-122. https://doi.org/10.1080/1750399X.2017.1344816

[47] Rotheneder, N. E-learning and employability in translator training: Introducing e-portfolio and personal development planning at the University of Vienna [J/OL]. Translating and the Computer, 2007, 29: 1-20. https://aclanthology.org/2007.tc-1.11.pdf

[48] Ringgenberg, I. Human added value in language mediation: An analysis of the perceived importance of translation and employability competence models [D]. Winterthur: Zurich University of Applied Sciences, 2022.

[49] Risku, H., Schlager, D., Milosevic, J. & Rogl, R. The social construction of translation expertise in the language industry [R]. Paper presented on the 10th EST Congress: Advancing Translation Studies, Oslo, Norway, 2022.

[50] Schäffner, C. Translators' roles and responsibilities [A/OL]. In Angelone, E., Ehrensberger-Dow, M. & Massey, G. (eds.). The Bloomsbury Companion to Language Industry Studies (pp.63-89) [C]. New York: Bloomsbury Academic, 2020. https://doi.org/0.5040/9781350024960.0008

[51] Schnell, B. & Rodríguez, N. Ivory tower vs. workplace reality. Employability and the T&I curriculum — balancing academic education and vocational requirements: A study from the employers' perspective [J/OL]. The Interpreter and Translator Trainer, 2017, 11(2-3): 160-186. https://doi.org/10.1080/1750399X.2017.1344920

[52] Schön, D. A. Educating the Reflective Practitioner: Toward a New Design for Teaching and Learning in the Professions [M]. New York: Jossey-Bass, 1987.

[53] Slator. Slator 2020 Language Industry Market Report [R/OL]. 2020. [30-06-2022]. https://slator.com/slator-2020-language-industry-market-report/

[54] Slator. Slator 2022 Language Industry Market Report [R/OL]. 2022. [30-06-2022]. https://slator.com/slator-2022-language-industry-market-report/

[55] Tong, V. Shaping higher education pedagogy with students in a consortium setting [A/OL]. In Tong, V., Standen, A. & Sotiriou, M. (eds.). Shaping Higher Education with Students: Ways to Connect Research and Teaching (pp. 3-13) [C]. London: UCL Press, 2018. https://www.uclpress.co.uk/products/95121

[56] UNICEF. Global Framework on Transferable Skills [S/OL]. UNICEF Education Section, 2019. [30-06-2022]. https://www.unicef.org/media/64751/file/Global-framework-on-transferable-skills-2019.pdf

[57] Vienne, J. Towards a pedagogy of translation in situation [J/OL]. Perspectives: Studies in Translation Theory and Practice, 1994, 2(1): 51-59. https://doi.org/10.1080/0907676X.1994.9961222

五、翻译利益相关方之间的合作

国家翻译能力及其与经济硬实力和文化软实力之间的关系研究

——兼谈翻译利益相关方之间的合作如何助推翻译能力发展[1]

任　文　赵田园　北京外国语大学

摘　要：通过对国家语言能力、国家翻译实践、翻译机构和机构翻译等相关文献的梳理及理论反思，我们提出了一个包含四个子能力的国家翻译能力框架。在此基础上，采用德尔菲法和层次分析法（AHP），构建了一个具有三级可测量指标的国家翻译能力指标体系。通过权威官网查询、正规渠道采购以及合作单位提供等方式获取数据，计算出 2021 年全球 193 个国家的国家翻译能力排名，并尝试考察一国翻译能力和次级能力与其经济硬实力和文化软实力之间的关系。研究结果表明：1）全球国家翻译能力大致可分为三个梯队，大部分国家在翻译管理能力、翻译服务能力和翻译发展能力方面发展不平衡；2）一国翻译能力总体上与其经济硬实力和文化相关软实力指标呈正相关，但与文化软实力的关系更为密切；3）一国翻译能力与其语言多样性之间不存在直接相关，通过 GDP 和贸易总额变量的中介调节后相关性增强；4）一国的贸易出口总额、国际声誉和媒体及传播水平三个指标拟合后能够显著预测一国的翻译能力；5）一国的翻译服务和翻译发展能力与其经济硬实力和文化相关软实力关系更为密切。国家翻译能力研究具有重要意义：在学术方面，可以增加

1　本文系北京外国语大学“双一流”重大（点）标志性项目“国家翻译能力理论框架与国际比较”（项目批准号：2022SYLA002）的研究成果。本文根据任文教授在第十届亚太翻译论坛的主旨发言整理而成，部分内容已经发表在《跨学科视角下国家翻译能力概念再思与指数构建研究》（任文、赵田园，2023）、《中国翻译》（2023 年第 1 期，第 44-52 页）以及《指数全球》（杨丹等，2021）。

翻译研究的跨学科维度；在实践方面，有助于我们更好了解一国翻译能力如何为国家经济和文化发展做出贡献。

关键词：国家翻译能力；指标体系；经济硬实力；文化软实力；利益相关方的合作

A Study on the Correlation Between a Country's Translation Capacity and Its Economic Hard Power and Cultural Soft Power with an Analysis on the Role of Stakeholder Cooperation in Promoting Translation Capacity at the Country Level

Ren Wen Zhao Tianyuan
Beijing Foreign Studies University

Abstract: Based on the notions of and discussions about National Language Capacity (NLC), State Translation Program (STP), translating institutions and translation in institutions, a comprehensive National Translation Capacity (NTC) framework with four sub-capacities is constructed. Building on this framework — and adopting the methods of Delphi and the analytic hierarchy process (AHP) — an NTC index with three-level measurable indicators is formulated. On top of this, drawing on data provided by official websites and cooperative institutions and sourced from authoritative organizations, a league table of the NTC of 193 countries in 2021 is developed to examine the potential correlation that a country's translation capacity and sub-capacities may have with its cultural soft power and economic hard power. The research results show that: 1) the translation capacities of all the countries can be roughly divided into three tiers, with most countries developing unevenly in capacities of translation management, translation service, and translation development; 2) a country's translation capacity is generally positively correlated with its economic hard power and cultural soft power indicators, but the relationship with cultural soft power is closer; 3) there is no direct correlation between a country's translation capacity and its language diversity, but the correlation is strengthened through the mediating effect of GDP and total trade variables;

4) fitting the three indicators of a country's total exports, international reputation, and media and communication development can significantly predict its translation capacity; 5) a country's translation service and development capacities are more closely related to its economic hard power and cultural soft power. Research on NTC is of great significance: Theoretically, it increases the interdisciplinary dimensions of translation studies; practically, it helps us better understand how a country's translation capacity contribute to national and regional economic and cultural development.

Keywords: National language capacity; NTC index; economic hard power; cultural soft power; cooperation of stakeholders

1. 引言

新时代，翻译作为一国国际传播的重要基础和桥梁，已然成为一国文化软实力的重要组成部分；翻译产品和翻译行业也因其能够产生红利，成为能够为一国经济发展做出贡献的产业之一。既有研究也表明，翻译实践催生的翻译产品以及对这些产品的规划和国际传播产生的影响力对提升和彰显国家的软硬实力都起着越来越大的作用（许建忠，2013：90；许建忠，2014：VIII；任文、李娟娟，2021：5；杨丹等，2021：199；杨枫，2021：18；赵田园、徐秀玲，2021：124；高乾、裘禾敏，2022：129；高玉霞、任东升，2022：7；黄友义，2022：13）。然而，以上研究结论主要基于专家的主观经验判断和理论思辨得出。迄今为止，学界尚未有研究通过量化方式，具体考察一国翻译能力，也未见实证探索一国翻译能力及其子能力与该国文化软实力、经济硬实力以及文化软实力和经济硬实力中主要构成要素的相关关系的研究，致使以上结论缺乏数据支撑和纵深分析。基于此，我们通过对国家语言能力、国家翻译实践、翻译机构和机构翻译等相关文献的梳理及理论反思，提出了一个包含四个子能力的国家翻译能力框架。在此框架基础上，采用德尔菲法和层次分析法（AHP），构建了一个具有三级可测量指标的国家翻译能力指标体系。通过权威官网查询、正规渠道采购以及合作单位提供等方式获取数据，我们计算出了

2021 年全球 193 个国家的国家翻译能力排名，并尝试基于此数据，通过相关分析、多元线性回归、中介效应建模等统计学方式，考察了一国翻译能力及一级子能力与其总体经济硬实力和文化相关软实力指标的关系，以期更为充分地论证一国翻译能力与一国国家经济和文化发展的关系，同时为国家翻译能力发展及翻译利益相关方合作提供建议。

2. 国家翻译能力概念和要素梳理

目前为止，关于国家翻译能力的深入讨论并不多见，关涉国家翻译能力的相关论述主要有两条路径：一是从语言学视角出发，或将国家翻译能力隐含于国家外语能力要素中（赵世举，2015；文秋芳，2016 等），或将其等同于国家话语外译能力（文秋芳，2017）；二是从翻译学路径出发，或将其行为主体限定为一国政府及代表政府的机构与个人（任东升，2019），或将其视为国家实力的一部分（蓝红军，2020），或主要关注中国的国家翻译实践，特别是中译外问题（杜占元，2022）。

任文、李娟娟（2021）基于以上研究中的要素和视角以及自身对国家翻译实践主体和范围的思考，首次提出了较为全面的国家翻译能力概念和构成要素，为国家翻译能力评价研究提供了理论基础和方向，被视为新时代我国译学发展的一种开拓性工作（杨枫，2021：19）。该概念系首次提出，意在引发学界思考和关注，概念界定略为繁杂，且未涉及对国家翻译能力评价的具体要素以及对国家翻译能力的具体评价。为此，任文、赵田园（2023）结合管理学中的 OGSM 模型和相关跨学科理论，在任文、李娟娟（2021）基础上，进一步提炼简化了国家翻译能力概念定义，即“一国依靠多元主体，通过翻译实践与传播，以及翻译管理与发展等活动，推动国内外不同语言间开展符合国家利益的对话交流与知识互鉴，服务一国软硬实力和国际话语权提升的能力”，并在此概念框架宏观指引下，提出了更为明确具体的国家翻译能力概念要素框架（表 1），同时指出可借鉴经济学中具有通过简化、量化模型对各类现象进行描述、刻画和展示优势（杨丹等，2021：2）的指数研究方法具体开展国家翻译能力评价研究，为本文研究奠定了理论框架和方法论基础。

表 1 国家翻译能力概念要素框架

一级指标	二级指标	三级指标
国家翻译管理能力	翻译立法和规划能力	翻译立法
		翻译政策与规划
		翻译标准
	职业 / 行业管理能力	翻译协会
		翻译证书考试
		翻译证书市场效用
	应急翻译管理能力	应急翻译管理规定
		应急翻译资源储备调配
国家翻译实践能力	行业翻译能力	语言服务企业翻译产值
		全国人均语言服务产值
		语言服务行业从业人数
		翻译服务岗位语种数量
	机构翻译能力	机构翻译服务提供量
		机构翻译人数
		机构翻译语种数量
	应急翻译能力	应急翻译服务提供量
		应急翻译人才储备
		应急翻译语种数量
国家翻译传播能力	翻译产品媒介能力	媒介种类
		媒介融合程度
	译入译出产品影响力	市场销量
		图书馆藏量
		借阅量
		媒体评论量
		媒体评论态度
		翻译产品衍生产品量

（待续）

（续表）

一级指标	二级指标	三级指标
国家翻译传播能力	国内语言互译产品影响力	市场销量
		图书馆藏量
		借阅量
		媒体评论量
		媒体评论态度
		翻译产品衍生产品量
国家翻译发展能力	翻译教育能力	开设翻译专业的学校数量
		翻译专业涵盖的语种数量
		开设翻译专业教学层次
		翻译专业毕业生数量
		从事翻译工作的毕业生数量
	翻译研究能力	翻译论文发表数量
		翻译专著、教材数量
		翻译资源库创建数量
	翻译技术能力	自然语言处理（翻译相关）专利数量
		语音识别（翻译相关）专利数量

3. 国家翻译能力指数研究

指数研究包括指标体系构建和指标体系测算两部分，前者是首要和基础环节（杨丹等，2021），需要科学理论、原则支撑，后者则需要研究者选用科学的赋权、数据收集来源和数据预处理方式。完成以上两部分工作，方能合理可信地计算出各国国家翻译能力得分，计算其与文化软实力、经济硬实力及其中各要素的相关程度。我们将在本小节重点论述国家翻译能力指数研究过程及其结果。

3.1 国家翻译能力指数指标体系构建

我们基于表 1，参照指标体系构建的相关原则，如“科学性与客观性相结合”“系统性与全面性相结合”“数据可测性与可获得性相结合”“精简性与平衡性相结合”“国别包容性与可比性相结合”等原则，删除了部分数据暂时不可获得或无法通过统一渠道获得的指标，如“机构翻译能力”“应急翻译能力”“翻译产品媒介能力”“市场销量”“借阅量”“媒体评论量”“媒体评论态度”“翻译产品衍生产品量”“国内语言互译产品影响力”等。同时也将指标数量较少、在国家翻译能力中功能相近的指标同类合并，保持各维度指标数量平衡，如将“国家翻译实践能力”和同样在国家翻译能力提升中作用外显的“国家翻译传播能力”合并，统称为“国家翻译服务能力”。

参照以上思路，我们最终构建了一个三级可测量的国家翻译能力指数体系。该体系包含“国家翻译管理能力”“国家翻译服务能力”“国家翻译发展能力”三个一级指标，每个一级指标下设若干相互关联的二级和三级指标（见表 2）。具体来说，“国家翻译管理能力”一级指标主要指一国在翻译领域进行宏观管理的能力，细分为“翻译立法及规划能力”“职业 / 行业管理能力”“应急翻译管理能力”三个二级指标。“翻译立法及规划能力”通过“翻译立法”“翻译政策和规划”“翻译标准化建设”三个指标量化，主要指一国是否具有规范翻译活动所需的法律法规、政策规划及各类标准。“职业 / 行业管理能力”通过“翻译协会”和“翻译认证考试”两个指标量化，主要指一国是否有专门的翻译协会和翻译认证考试；“应急翻译管理能力”通过“应急翻译管理规定”量化，主要指一国是否有在突发重大事件中有序提供应急翻译服务的相关规定。为了增加指数数据的颗粒精细度，我们还细化了部分三级指标，如将“翻译立法”指标细分为有专门的翻译立法、翻译相关立法和两者都有；“翻译认证考试”指标细分为通用领域考试、垂直领域考试和两者皆有等。

表 2　国家翻译能力指数指标体系

一级指标	二级指标	三级指标
国家翻译管理能力（19.59%）	翻译立法及规划能力（73.06%）	翻译立法（43.49%）
		翻译政策和规划（33.80%）
		翻译标准化建设（22.71%）
	职业 / 行业管理能力（18.84%）	翻译协会（50%）
		翻译认证考试（50%）
	应急翻译管理能力（8.10%）	应急翻译管理规定（100%）
国家翻译服务能力（50.85%）	翻译行业服务能力（75%）	全国翻译服务行业产值（38.67%）
		全国人均翻译产值（12.81%）
		翻译服务从业人数（24.82%）
		翻译服务岗位语种数量（23.70%）
	翻译传播能力（25%）	翻译传播数量（100%）
国家翻译发展能力（29.57%）	翻译教育能力（48.06%）	开设翻译专业的学校数量（50%）
		翻译专业涵盖的外语数量（50%）
	翻译研究能力（40.54%）	翻译相关论文发表（50%）
		翻译相关专著、教材出版（50%）
	翻译技术研发能力（11.40%）	自然语言处理（翻译技术相关）专利数量（50%）
		语音识别（翻译技术相关）专利数量（50%）

"国家翻译服务能力"一级指标主要指一国翻译实践能力以及翻译实践产品产生的影响力，细分为"翻译行业服务能力"和"翻译传播能力"两个二级指标。前者通过"全国翻译服务行业产值""全国人均翻译产值""翻译服务从业人数""翻译服务岗位语种数量"四个指标量化。后

者因数据可获得性和可比性原则，目前仅通过“翻译传播数量”指标量化，指一国国家图书馆在统计年度内收藏的译入译出作品数量总和。

“国家翻译发展能力”一级指标指一国在翻译领域的可持续发展能力。三个二级指标中，“翻译教育能力”通过“开设翻译专业的学校数量”和“翻译专业涵盖的外语数量”两个三级指标量化；“翻译研究能力”通过“翻译相关论文发表”和“翻译相关专著、教材出版”两个三级指标量化，主要指一国在 SCI、SSCI、A&HCI 来源期刊发表的翻译类论文数量，以及公开出版的翻译类专著和教材数量；“翻译技术研发能力”通过“自然语言处理（翻译技术相关）专利数量”和“语音识别（翻译技术相关）专利数量”两个三级指标量化，主要考察一国在全球专利数据库中拥有的翻译技术相关专利总数。

3.2 国家翻译能力计算方法

本部分主要阐述表 2 中指标体系的赋权、数据搜集、数据预处理和总分计算方法。

3.2.1 指标体系赋权方法

综合考虑本研究的目的和数据特点，我们选取近年来广泛应用于指标体系权重测算的层次分析法（AHP），结合定性和定量数据计算指标体系权重。主要思路是邀请评价领域专家，对指标体系中同一层级内指标的重要性两两循环对比打分，构建同层级指标重要性打分矩阵，归一化求解矩阵并进行矩阵一致性检验（随机一致性比率 CR 小于 0.10 即合格），得出体系中每一层级的权重（刘健、王小菲，2022）。专家打分问卷使用“9 标度法”，即 9、7、5、3、1 分别对应同一层级内一个指标相对于另一指标是绝对重要、十分重要、比较重要、稍微重要，还是同样重要，8、6、4、2 表示重要程度介于相邻的两个等级之间。

我们充分考虑到打分专家的权威性、代表性和独立性，邀请了 10 位来自国内不同区域的翻译教学、研究和实践领域专家，单独对表 2 中指数体系的指标相对重要性开展“9 标度”打分。

10 位专家问卷返回率为 100%，我们对专家打分数据进行汇总，发现专家打分除一级指标外，整体分歧不大，这说明打分的权威程度、积极程度和协调程度都较高。我们取10位专家打分的几何平均数，构建了层次分析矩阵，并运用了MATLAB对打分矩阵进行归一化计算求解矩阵，确定权重，检验权重分配一致性，得到国家翻译能力指数指标体系各层级指标的权重结果，详见表2。

3.2.2 数据搜集方法和渠道

本着权威性、可获取性和口径可比性原则，我们主要通过官网查询、报告检索、数据库检索、权威渠道购买、关键词网络检索等方式搜集数据。

官网查询主要包括查询中国商务部的全球法规网、各国翻译行业主管部门网站、ISO网站、世界银行网站、各国本地招聘网站、Lingohaus全球招聘网、各国国家图书馆官网、各国翻译协会官网、国际大学翻译学院联合会官网等。以“翻译标准化建设”指标为例，我们在ISO网站以及各国标准库进行检索。若该国有自建翻译标准或该国属于ISO成员，有可遵循的翻译标准即为有效数据。

报告检索主要包括参考CSA Research发布的《全球语言服务市场报告》和部分国家的国家图书馆年度信息公报。以“全国翻译服务行业产值”为例，参考《全球语言服务市场报告》中全球八大地区语言服务产值，按照世界银行统计发布的各地区各国GDP占比，计算各国翻译行业服务产值。

数据库检索主要包括检索Web of Science以及WorldCat数据库。以“翻译相关论文发表数量”为例，在Web of Science数据库检索界面中检索标题或主题含有translat* 或 interpret* 的论文，文献类型限定为article。

权威渠道主要指购买由英国Minesoft专利资讯公司联合RWS专业翻译集团共同打造的Patbase数据库，检索各国与翻译相关的自然语言处理和语音识别技术。

关键词网络检索主要指使用“国名 + 关键词”检索方式在百度和google中搜索相关信息。以“翻译协会”这一指标为例，本研究主要以“国家名 +translator association”或“国家名 +interpreter association”方式在google中检索。

通过以上方式获得数据后，进一步进行人工判断、整理和交叉核实，剔除无效及错误数据。此后，再和前一年数据对比，二次查证年度间明显的异常数据，尽力提升数据准确性。各指标体系数据来源如图 1 所示。

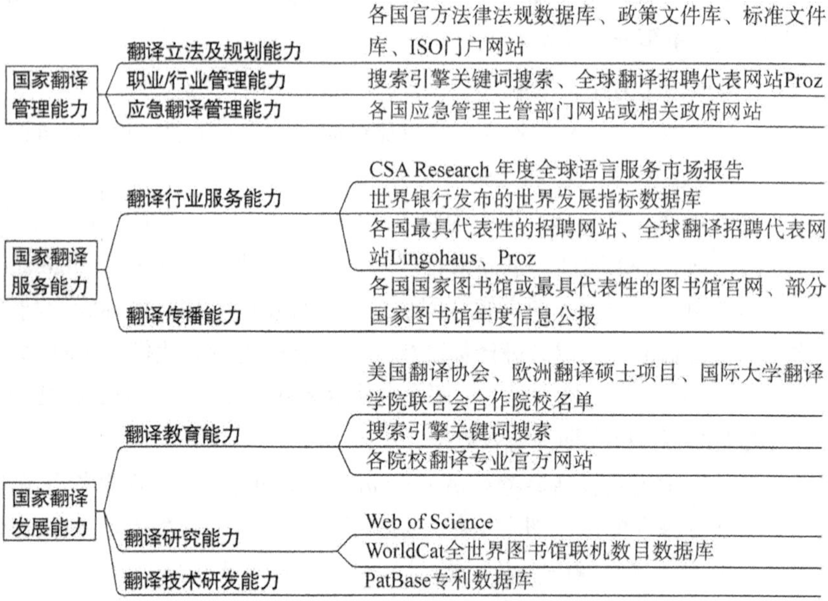

图 1　国家翻译能力指数指标体系数据来源说明

3.2.3　数据预处理方法

数据预处理是对指数数据进行分析与挖掘的前提。我们主要面临缺失值插补、不同量纲数据标准化处理两大技术问题。

在缺失值处理方面，考虑到缺失值主要存在于“国家翻译服务行业产值”和“全国人均翻译产值”两个指标中，且都是少数经济落后国家，很难参考其他国家数据，通过取均值、众数等方式插入缺失值。因此，我们将其统一视为 0，降低该数据缺失对最终得分和排名的影响。

在数据标准化处理方面，首先将搜集到的分类指标数据赋分，并转化为定量数据。例如，“翻译政策规划”“翻译协会”“应急翻译管理规定”为二分类指标，原始数据为“有”或“无”两类。通过专家咨询并参照通用的二分类指标定量转化方式，将“有”赋值为虚拟变量 1，“无”赋值为虚拟变量 0。其他指标如“翻译标准化建设”“翻译认证考试”等，参考专家建议，将其不同的分类变量分别赋值为 0.5、0.8 和 1 不等。

随后，根据各指标定量数据分布特征，我们用数据平滑后极差归一化和直接极差归一化两种处理范式，剔除数据量纲差异的影响。例如，“全国翻译行业服务产值”“全国人均翻译产值”“翻译传播数量”“开设翻译专业的学校数量”“翻译相关论文发表”“翻译相关专著、教材出版”“自然语言处理（翻译技术相关）专利数量”“语音识别（翻译技术相关）专利数量”等指标的数据服从幂律分布，首先通过取对数方式对数据进行平滑处理。其他指标数据相对符合正态分布,则保留原始数据。随后，我们运用极差法将所有数据进行极差归一化处理。该方法的好处是，以数据指标的极值为参照系，对原始数据进行线性变换，映射至［0–1］的范围内，使数值之间差异缩小，分布紧凑（韩晶，2021）。

3.3 各国国家翻译能力得分与排名

基于以上指标体系权重及数据测算方法，我们采用层级递归加权方式，即将三级指标得分加权，合成二级指标分数，再将二级指标和一级指标得分加权，最终计算出各国翻译能力得分。

数据表明，就总分而言，2021 年，全球国家翻译能力差距较为明显，主要可以分为三个梯队。第一个梯队共有 7 个国家，分别是美国、中国、英国、德国、西班牙、澳大利亚、奥地利，标准化后总分均超过 0.6 分；第二个梯队得分在 0.3–0.6（不等于 0.6）之间，共 52 个国家，以意大利、法国、加拿大、比利时、芬兰、瑞士等为代表。我们可以将以上国家视为世界翻译大国；第三梯队得分小于 0.3，共 134 个国家，以克罗地亚、哈萨克斯坦、缅甸、秘鲁、伊朗、亚美尼亚、斯里兰卡等为代表，我们认为这些国家的翻译能力相对较弱。由于篇幅限制，我们仅在此处通过图 2 和图 3 展示国家翻译能力排名前 20 和排名后 20 的国家及其总分。

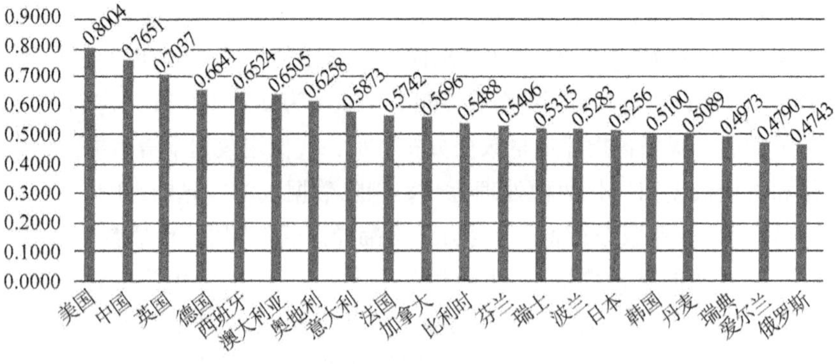

图 2　2021 年国家翻译能力排名前 20 的国家得分情况

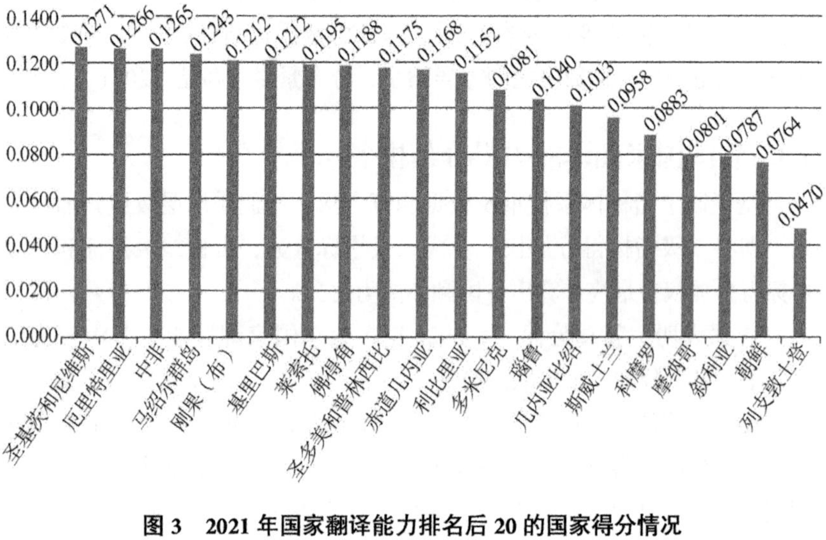

图 3　2021 年国家翻译能力排名后 20 的国家得分情况

以上数据表明，2021 年排名前 20 的国家中，欧洲占据 14 个之多，展示了欧洲作为多语社会在翻译能力方面的传统优势；北美两国悉数进入排名前 20，且美国延续了其在榜单上排名第一的位置；东亚三国（中国、日本、韩国）表现均不俗，中国更是因近年来实施“中国文化走出去”、加强国家文化软实力和国际传播能力建设等，翻译能力不断攀升，超越英国跃居第二。

在以上分析基础上，我们继续分析了各国在国家翻译能力下各一级子能力的得分及排名情况。就国家翻译管理能力而言，经过数据标准化处理后，有 20 个国家得分达到了 0.8，是国家翻译管理能力强国，分别是美国、奥地利、爱沙尼亚、阿尔巴尼亚、荷兰、芬兰、加拿大、德国、英国、中国、意大利、印度尼西亚、阿根廷、新西兰、新加坡、韩国、日本、瑞士、澳大利亚、西班牙，其他得分高于 0.6、小于 0.8 的国家有 60 个。就国家翻译服务能力而言，经过数据标准化处理后，仅有美国、中国、德国、英国、澳大利亚、奥地利等 6 个国家得分超过 0.6，其余 187 个国家得分均低于 0.6，列支敦士登得分最低，为 0 分。就国家翻译发展能力而言，同样只有 6 个国家得分标准化处理后超过 0.6，分别是中国、美国、英国、西班牙、意大利、澳大利亚，另有 63 个国家在该项能力上得分为 0。我们可以看出，2021 年，全球各国的翻译管理能力普遍优于翻译实践能力和翻译发展能力，部分国家的翻译发展能力严重不足。

为了进一步了解各翻译大国和翻译发展水平较弱的国家在国家翻译能力各一级指标能力上的发展平衡情况，我们同样统计了 2021 年全球翻译能力排名前 20 国家和后 20 国家在翻译管理能力、翻译发展能力和翻译教育能力的得分情况，详见图 4 和图 5。

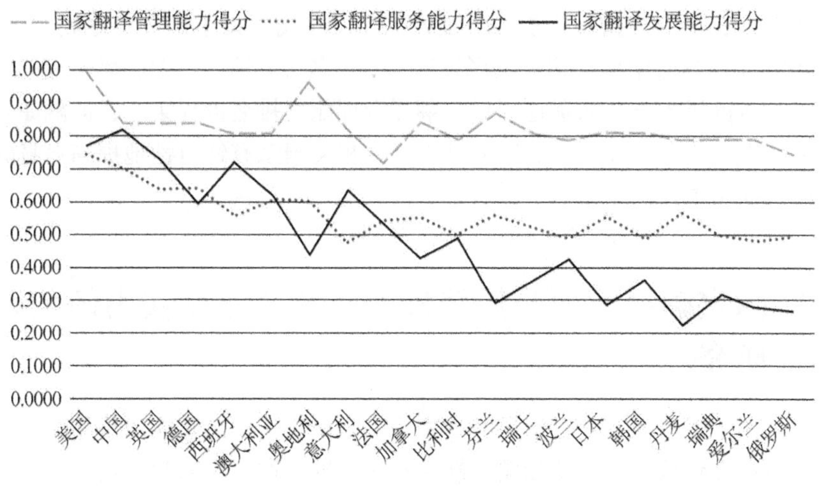

图 4　2021 年国家翻译能力排名前 20 国家的一级指标得分对比

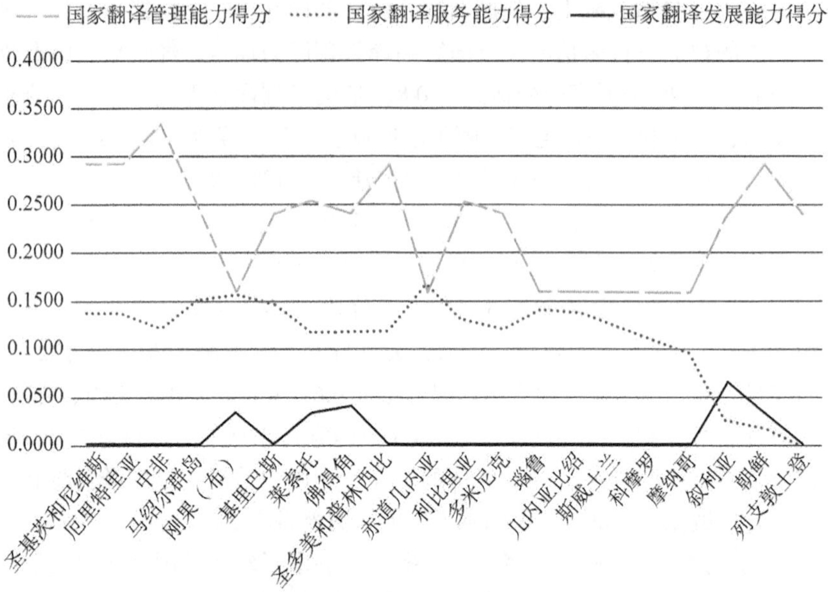

图 5　2021 年国家翻译能力排名后 20 国家的一级指标得分对比

以上数据表明，2021 年，无论是全球翻译能力排名前 20 的国家，抑或是排名后 20 的国家，都有接近一半国家在翻译管理、翻译服务、翻译发展三个一级指标子能力方面发展不太平衡。以中国和奥地利为例，2021 年，尽管中国的国家翻译发展能力排名世界第一，但翻译管理能力仅排名世界第五，而奥地利尽管翻译管理能力排名世界第二，但翻译发展能力仅排名世界第十。以上结果可供相关国家有针对性地提高自身的国家翻译能力。

4. 国家翻译能力与经济硬实力和文化软实力的关系研究

鉴于既有研究均基于研究者主观判断指出一国翻译能力与其经济硬实力和文化软实力密切相关，缺乏量化数据支撑。我们尝试基于前文计算出的 2021 全球各国翻译能力得分与其经济硬实力和文化软实力发展相关指标得分开展分析，具体通过相关性分析、多元线性回归和中介调节建模方式开展，力图为既有研究成果提供数据支撑，同时凸显一国翻译能力与其经济硬实力和文化软实力的关系。

为了实现以上研究目标，我们选取了若干可以通过官方权威渠道获得并且常用于评价各国的经济硬实力和文化软实力的指标，作为和国家翻译能力进行关系分析的参照变量。通常来说，在经济硬实力测量方面，各国经济衡量指标主要包括总体经济指标（如国内生产总值、失业率、价格指数、收入指标等）和各领域经济指标（如财政政策指标、货币政策指标、国际收支指标、金融市场指标等）（高琼华、王庆春等，2015）。考虑到世界银行数据库的经济与增长指标中，总体经济增长指标如 GDP 增长率和 GDP（现价美元）以及贸易领域的支出（现价美元）和收入（现价美元）四项指标数据基本覆盖了所有国家，且数据始终保持动态更新（目前已更新至 2021 年）。其他指标或更新不及时，或覆盖国家数量较少，故我们选取了以上四个指标和各国国家翻译能力进行关系分析。

在国家文化软实力测量方面，近年来，总部位于伦敦的全球著名咨询公司 Brand Finance 基于既有研究中对于软实力的概念和公司内部积累的大型数据库，连续若干年发布了覆盖全球大部分国家的全球软实力指数[1]（Global Soft Power)。在该排名中，软实力主要从 11 个方面测量，分别是国际知名度（Familiarity)、国际声誉 (Reputation)、国际影响力 (Influence)、商务和贸易（Business & Trade)、政府治理（Governance)、国际关系（International Relations)、文化和遗产（Culture & Heritage)、媒体与传播（Media & Communication)、教育与科技（Education & Science)、公民特质与价值观（People & Values)、新冠病毒感染疫情应对（COVID-19 Response）等。考虑到政府治理、国际关系、新冠病毒感染疫情应对这几个指标和文化软实力不太相关，我们将以上三个指标删除。此外，考虑到翻译是不同世族语言之间的相互沟通理解的方式，具有多语言符号转换性（许钧，2005），我们有理由假设如果一国之内语言符号越多样，那么就需要更多翻译服务来保障及维护区域人民和文化顺利交流。换言

1 详见 Global Soft Power Index | Brandirectory。

之，一国的翻译能力可能与该国语言文化多样性存在正相关关系。因此，我们基于世界语言网站[1]数据库，抓取了世界各国语言数量这一指标。综上，我们选取了国际知名度、国际声誉、国际影响力、商务与贸易、文化与遗产、媒体与传播、教育与科技、公民特质与价值观、语言多样性等 9 个指标和各国国家翻译能力进行关系分析。

在做数据分析的过程中，有两点需要说明。其一是指标缺失值处理方式。由于国家翻译能力指数研究测算了全球 193 个国家的翻译能力，而我们选取的经济硬实力和文化软实力相关指标由于统计源或多或少都存在国别缺失，因此我们在做相关系数测算、线性回归以及中介建模时，若对应的两组指标数量不一致，则以小样本指标的国家数为准，避免人工插补缺失值造成的数据分析偏差。其二是指标数据预处理方式。由于我们选取的部分指标原始数据波动较大，如全球国家的 GDP，数据不符合正态分布，不适宜做相关、线性回归等分析，因此我们首先采用数据最大最小归一化处理方法，对不符合正态分布的数据进行平滑处理，再开展相关系数测算和多元线性回归，力求从技术层面提升数据分析的有效性。

数据测算显示，在宏观层面，国家翻译能力总分与经济指标中的 GDP、贸易出口、贸易进口指标呈显著正相关，相关系数分别达到了 0.544、0.661 和 0.678，与软实力中和文化因素相关的 7 个指标均呈显著正相关，其中和一国国际声誉、国际影响力、媒体和传播、教育和科技发展指标的相关系数均超过 0.7，具体相关系数如表 3 所示。

表 3　2021 年国家翻译能力总分与经济硬实力和文化相关软实力指标的相关性分析

变量	皮尔逊相关性（国家翻译能力总分）
GDP 增长率	0.076
GDP（现价美元）	0.544**[2]
贸易出口（现价美元）	0.661**

（待续）

1　详见 https://www.ethnologue.com/。

2　本文所有 ** 表示在 0.01 级别（双尾），相关性显著。

（续表）

变量	皮尔逊相关性（国家翻译能力总分）
贸易进口（现价美元）	0.678**
国际知名度	0.692**
国际声誉	0.815**
国际影响力	0.763**
文化和遗产	0.677**
媒体和传播	0.820**
教育和科技	0.810**
公民特质与价值观	0.649**
语言多样性	0.160

在以上分析基础上，我们将 12 个指标作为自变量，将国家翻译能力总得分作为因变量进行逐步回归分析（逐步 stepwise 法），最终余下贸易出口、国际声誉、媒体和传播三项指标为对国家翻译能力得分具有显著影响的因素。三项指标与国家翻译能力得分线性回归拟合的模型为“总得分 =0.178 + 0.355* 贸易出口 + 0.171* 国际声誉 + 0.299* 媒体传播”。该模型 R 方值为 0.817，意味着贸易出口、国际声誉、媒体和传播水平可以解释国家翻译能力总得分的 81.7%，且该模型通过 F 检验 (F=141.202, p=0.000<0.05)，说明模型有效，模型拟合详情参见表 4。

表 4　2021 年国家翻译能力总分与经济硬实力和文化相关软实力指标的回归分析

逐步回归分析结果 (n=99)						
变量	非标准化系数		标准化系数	*t*	*p*	VIF
	B	标准误	***Beta***			
常数	0.178	0.012	–	15.222	0.000**	–
贸易出口	0.355	0.061	0.305	5.780	0.000**	1.449
国际声誉	0.171	0.060	0.304	2.868	0.005**	5.833
媒体和传播	0.299	0.081	0.420	3.711	0.000**	6.644

（待续）

（续表）

逐步回归分析结果 (n=99)						
变量	非标准化系数		标准化系数	*t*	*p*	VIF
	B	标准误	***Beta***			
R^2	0.817					
调整 R^2	0.811					
F	*F* (3,95)=141.202, *p*=0.000					
D-W 值	1.329					

在中观方面，我们继续分析了国家翻译能力的一级指标子能力与 12 个经济和文化相关的软实力指标的关系，以期能够为翻译领域如何贡献国家经济硬实力和文化相关的软实力提供更为翔实的数据支撑。数据表明，国家翻译管理能力、国家翻译服务能力和国家翻译发展能力除了与经济指标中的GDP增长率以及软实力指标中的语言多样性不显著相关外，和其余指标值都达到了统计学意义上的显著正相关，但和各指标的相关程度大小存在差异，详见表 5。

表 5　2021 年国家翻译能力一级指标得分与经济硬实力和文化相关软实力指标的相关分析

变量	皮尔逊相关性（国家翻译管理能力）	皮尔逊相关性（国家翻译服务能力）	皮尔逊相关性（国家翻译发展能力）
GDP 增长率	0.049	0.090	0.051
GDP（现价美元）	0.375**	0.604**	0.571**
贸易出口（现价美元）	0.411**	0.625**	0.719**
贸易进口（现价美元）	0.427**	0.638**	0.738**
国际知名度	0.556**	0.692**	0.799**
国际声誉	0.566**	0.815**	0.735**
国际影响力	0.479**	0.763**	0.835**

（待续）

（续表）

变量	皮尔逊相关性（国家翻译管理能力）	皮尔逊相关性（国家翻译服务能力）	皮尔逊相关性（国家翻译发展能力）
文化和遗产	0.484**	0.677**	0.770**
媒体和传播	0.566**	0.820**	0.814**
教育和科技	0.549**	0.810**	0.763**
公民特质与价值观	0.494**	0.649**	0.620**
语言多样性	0.163	0.123	0.161

通过总结和对比表 3、表 4 和表 5 中的数据，我们可以得出如下几个方面结论与启示。

其一，我们证实了既往研究中提出的一国翻译总体能力与经济硬实力和文化方面软实力关系确实密切，存在较为显著的正相关关系，但相对于经济硬实力而言，一国翻译能力与文化方面的软实力关系更为密切。因此，各国在加强文化软实力建设过程中，要充分重视翻译能力建设的助推作用，同时为翻译能力建设提供良好的文化环境。

其二，我们的数据不直接支持既有研究中指出的一国翻译能力与语言多样性呈显著的正相关。但是我们的数据分析表明，当 GDP 和贸易进出口总额成为调节变量时，一国的翻译能力和语言多样性的正相关关系更加显著，即只有当一国的语言多样性能够对其商务和贸易进出口产生正向促进作用，才能够促进一国翻译能力提升。囿于篇幅限制，此处仅展示 GDP 对于语言多样性与国家翻译能力的中介调节作用（见表 6、表 7）。通过表 6 和表 7，我们可以得到中介模型，即“国家翻译能力总得分 0.324−0.100* 语言数量 +0.704*GDP”，GDP 为语言数量促进总得分增长的完全中介变量。该结论可通过部分例证得以论证，如欧洲国家语言多样，经济相对发达，其国家翻译能力得分也相对更高，而非洲地区国家虽然语言多样，但受制于经济发展水平落后，不同语言民族间交流相对闭塞，由此产生的贸易进出口和翻译需求极少，因此国家翻译能力也随之落后。该现象部分说明了商务和贸易发展对于不同语言民族间交往及由此产生的翻译需求的促进作用，也从另一方面凸显了翻译能力建设对

表 6　GDP 对于一国语言多样性和国家翻译能力的中介调节作用

变量	总得分					GDP					总得分				
	B	标准误	*t*	*p*	*β*	*B*	标准误	*t*	*p*	*β*	*B*	标准误	*t*	*p*	*β*
常数	0.341**	0.017	20.058	0	–	0.024	0.014	1.66	0.100	–	0.324**	0.014	23.160	0	–
语言数量	0.027	0.091	0.295	0.768	0.03	0.180*	0.076	2.358	0.020	0.233	–0.100	0.076	–1.309	0.194	–0.111
GDP											0.704**	0.099	7.138	0	0.605
R^2	0.001					0.054					0.347				
调整 R^2	–0.009					0.044					0.334				
F 值	$F(1,97)=0.087, p=0.768$					$F(1,97)=5.562, p=0.020$					$F(2,96)=25.543, p=0.000$				

* $p<0.05$ ** $p<0.01$

表 7　GDP 对于一国语言多样性和国家翻译能力的中介调节作用结果检验

项	c	a	b	a*b	a*b	a*b	a*b	a*b	c'	检验结论
	总效应			中介效应值	(Boot SE)	(*z* 值)	(*p* 值)	(95% BootCI)	直接效应	
语言数量=>GDP=> 总得分	0.027	0.180*	0.704**	0.127	0.072	1.774	0.076	0.039–0.319	–0.100	完全中介

* $p<0.05$ ** $p<0.01$

于语言保有量较多国家的重要性，即这些语言数量较多的国家更需要加强翻译能力建设，打破国内多语沟通壁垒，以此推动本国民众以及与外部世界的交流，提升本国经济发展。

其三是一国的贸易出口、国际声誉、媒体和传播发展水平三个指标能够显著预测一国的国家翻译能力，我们认为其原因主要在三方面。首先，贸易出口需要翻译服务尤其是机器翻译服务的支持为商品走出去提供高质量的多语言服务，如翻译多语种产品说明书，提高海关文件处理效率，降低商品通关时间，获得国际社会商品流通规则等信息。其次，一个国家良好的国际声誉有赖于一国的国际传播能力建设，以达到自塑形象或者影响他国形成对本国正确认知的目的，而翻译作为跨语言符号转换的桥梁，是国际传播的重要和基础环节。再次，一国的媒体和对外传播需要跨越语言文字壁垒，良好的翻译能力能够减少媒体对外传播过程中的信息损耗和信息误传，提升媒体和对外传播水平。综上所述，我们认为通过线性回归模型拟合出的一国贸易出口总额、国际声誉以及媒体和传播水平组合能够在较大程度上反映一国的翻译能力确有其学理和现实基础。为此，要注重加强翻译跨语言大数据平台、多语种语料库、本地化技术、机器翻译系统等建设，为提升贸易出口、国际声誉以及媒体和传播水平做出贡献。

其四是从中观层面来看，国家翻译能力各一级子能力与经济硬实力和文化相关软实力的紧密程度存在差异。数据表明，虽然国家翻译管理能力、国家翻译服务能力和国家翻译发展能力基本都与经济硬实力和文化相关软实力指标的相关性达到了统计学意义上的显著，但国家翻译服务能力和国家翻译发展能力与经济硬实力和文化相关软实力指标的正相关系数更高，凸显了翻译实践、翻译传播、翻译教育和翻译技术研发在提升国家经济硬实力和文化相关软实力中更为重要的地位，也说明相对于国家翻译管理能力而言，国家翻译服务和国家翻译发展能力的作用更为外显。为此，在建设国家翻译能力过程中，一国需要在保持对国家翻译实践和教育有序规划前提下，协同社会网络中翻译活动的不同利益相关方，通过人才培养、科学研究、技术研发等大力提升国家多元主体的翻译实践及传播水平。

5. 结语

本文首先基于对语言学和翻译学的研究成果以及跨学科理论思辨，提出了国家翻译能力概念要素框架，并结合“科学性与客观性相结合”“系统性与全面性相结合”“数据可测性与可获得性相结合”“精简性与平衡性相结合”“国别包容性与可比性相结合”等原则和德尔菲、层次分析等方式，对要素框架进行了降维和赋权处理，构建了一个包含国家翻译管理能力、国家翻译服务能力和国家翻译发展能力三个一级指标在内的三级可测量的国家翻译能力指标体系。

在此基础上，我们通过权威数据查询和计算，展示了 2021 年全球 193 个国家的翻译能力得分和排名情况，指出 2021 年全球国家翻译能力大致呈金字塔状态分布，可以分为三个梯队，大部分国家的翻译管理能力、翻译服务能力和翻译发展能力得分不平衡。我们还在本文最后一部分运用相关分析、多元线性回归分析和中介效应建模方式，尝试考察了一国翻译能力和次级能力与其经济硬实力和文化相关软实力之间的关系，通过数据证实了一国翻译能力总体上与其经济硬实力和文化相关软实力指标呈正相关关系，但与文化软实力的关系更为密切；一国翻译能力与其语言多样性之间不存在直接相关，通过 GDP 和贸易总额的中介调节作用后相关性增强；一国的贸易出口、国际声誉以及媒体和传播水平三个指标拟合后能够显著预测一国的翻译能力；相较于翻译管理能力，一国的翻译服务和翻译发展能力与其经济硬实力和文化相关软实力的关系更为密切。我们希望本文研究能够从学术层面为既有研究中国家翻译能力与经济硬实力和文化软实力相关的假设和结论提供数据支持，为未来研究提供检验假设，增加翻译研究的跨学科维度。在实践层面，能够帮助学界和业界更深入了解一国翻译能力如何为国家经济和文化软实力提升做出贡献，同时也呼吁新时代背景下，社会网络中不同翻译相关行动者之间的加强协调合作，为国家翻译能力发展营造良好积极的大环境。

参考文献

[1] 杜占元. 推动国家翻译能力建设 服务党和国家工作大局 [EB/OL]. [2022-04-26]. https://epaper.gmw.cn/gmrb/html/202204/26/nw.D110000gmrb_20220426_1-06.htm
[2] 高乾，裘禾敏. 中国文化外译与国家翻译实践 [J]. 中国翻译，2022（4）：129-132.
[3] 高琼华，王庆春. 经济指标解读 [M]. 重庆：重庆大学出版社，2015.
[4] 高玉霞，任东升. 做好国家翻译实践规划，助力国家翻译实践能力提升——任东升教授专访 [J/OL]. 北京第二外国语学院学报：1-12. [2022-12-11]. https://journal.bisu.edu.cn/CN/abstract/abstract717.shtml
[5] 韩晶. 2021 中国低碳发展指数报告—区域比较 [M]. 北京：经济日报出版社，2022.
[6] 黄友义. 强化国家对外翻译机制，助力国际传播能力提升 [J]. 英语研究，2022（1）：12-19.
[7] 蓝红军. 国家翻译实践——从现实需求到理论建构 [J]. 外国语文，2020（5）：112-118.
[8] 刘健，王小菲. 基于层次分析法的高校图书馆网站用户满意度评价指标体系构建研究 [J/OL]. 情报科学：1-16. [2022-07-19].
[9] 任东升. 国家翻译实践概念体系构建 [J]. 外语研究，2019（4）：68-73+112.
[10] 任文，赵田园. 跨学科视角下国家翻译能力概念再思与指数构建研究 [J]. 中国翻译，2023（1）：44-52.
[11] 任文，李娟娟. 国家翻译能力研究：概念、要素、意义 [J]. 中国翻译，2021（4）：5-14+191.
[12] 文秋芳. 国家话语能力的内涵——对国家语言能力的新认识 [J]. 新疆师范大学学报（哲学社会科学版），2017（3）：66-72.
[13] 文秋芳. 国家语言能力的内涵及其评价指标 [J]. 云南师范大学学报（哲学社会科学版），2016（2）：23-31.
[14] 许建忠. 翻译经济学 [M]. 北京：国防工业出版社，2014.

[15] 许建忠. 全球化时代的翻译经济 [J/OL]. 外语教育研究，2013（1）：88-91. DOI:10.16739/j.cnki.cn21-9203/g4.2013.01.035.

[16] 许钧. 文化多样性与翻译的使命 [J]. 中国翻译，2005（1）：41-44.

[17] 杨丹，等. 指数全球 2021 [M]. 北京：外语教学与研究出版社，2021.

[18] 杨枫. 国家翻译能力建构的国家意识与国家传播 [J]. 中国翻译，2021（4）：15-19.

[19] 赵世举. 全球竞争中的国家语言能力 [J]. 中国社会科学，2015（3）：105-118.

[20] 赵田园，徐秀玲. 新时代翻译能力研究的国家视角与跨界融合——兼评首届“国家翻译能力：理论建构与实践探索”学术研讨会 [J]. 当代外语研究，2021（5）：121-128.

六、典籍翻译中的合作

翻译标准多元互补论视域下典籍合译研究

——以《晏婴评传》笔译实践为例

卞建华　张　钰　青岛大学

摘　要:《晏婴评传》是目前研究晏婴最为完备的著作，该书深入考证、辨析了大量的史载材料，引用典籍四十余部，是典籍翻译实践及其研究的范本。针对《晏婴评传》的文本类型及合译模式，笔者在“翻译标准多元互补论”的视域下，采用比较和描写研究法，对典籍合译时的翻译标准、翻译模式、译学路径进行了探讨。实践和研究表明，为选取以“中国味”为旨归的翻译策略和方法，典籍合译在规约性翻译、语言翻译以及二度翻译问题中，客观存在着绝对标准下的具体标准多元化及其标准互补的实际价值。

关键字: 典籍英译；多元互补；翻译标准；合作翻译

Research on Collaborative Translation of Chinese Classics from the Perspective of “Pluralistic and Complementary Translation Standards” — A Case Study of the Translation of *A Critical Biography of Yan Ying*

Bian Jianhua, Zhang Yu
Qingdao University

Abstract: The book titled *A Critical Biography of Yan Ying* (*Yan Ying Ping Zhuan*《晏婴评传》) provides a comprehensive study of Yan Ying, drawing from over 40 volumes of ancient records. It is a valuable resource for scholars interested in Chinese classics translation and the relevant research. The authors employ comparative and descriptive research methods to analyze collaborative translation standards, co-translation modes and translation studies approaches for Chinese classics. It is concluded that practice and research have shown that in selecting translation strategies and methods that aim to capture the "Chinese characteristics", there objectively exist pluralistic and complementary specific standards under the absolute standard in the co-translation of Chinese classical works, language-related problems in translation, and retranslation.

Keywords: English translation of Chinese classics; pluralism and complementarity; translation standards; co-translation

1. 引言

所谓“观乎人文，已化成天下”，弘扬传播中国文化一直是治国安民的重要途径，而典籍就是其重要的载体。在倡导中国文化“走出去”、文化“双创”和建立国家翻译实践体系的背景下，中国典籍外译迅猛发展。典籍英译“不仅是一个语言转换的过程，更是一种跨文化传播的活动”（张德福，2021：50），“也是中国文化走向世界、实现中西文化对等交流、达到世界文化融合的一条重要途径”（王宏印，2009：1）。

然而，即便是作为国家重大出版工程立项的《大中华文库》，“除个别几个选题被国外相关出版机构看中购买走版权外，其余绝大多数已经出版的选题都局限在国内的发行圈内，尚未真正‘传出去’”（谢天振，2014：2）。中国经典英译尚且如此，更不必说因缺乏“四部”体系内现存的注释疏解，抑或系统权威的今人述评而被边缘化的典籍，而此类典籍的翻译模式及其研究正是对中国文化体系更加多元、全面的补充。

由此可见，典籍英译任重道远，边缘典籍的英译模式更亟待实践。由此，笔者特选择《晏婴评传》展开合译研究，一探典籍合译之玄妙。

2. 典籍英译深入探究

本节主要在前人研究的基础上，深入挖掘典籍英译的现存问题。将典籍翻译研究从译本为导向转为以问题为导向，层层剥离，论中有述。

笔者将分类讨论以下四点：1）“典籍”的概念界定与“典籍英译”的主要特征；2）“边缘典籍”的含义及其特点；3）典籍译者的自身观照；4）典籍翻译中常见的翻译策略及方法。

2.1 “典籍”的界定与特征

目前，学界对“典籍”的概念界定没有统一标准的答案。以文本时间和形式为界定依据，典籍一般是指“1911年以前历朝的刻本、写本、稿本、拓本等”（李正栓、杨丽华，2012：42）。以文本内容和性质为界定依据，“典籍是记载自然、人文、哲学理念和重要典章制度的文献”（汪榕培，2006：66）。以文本的价值意义为界定依据，典籍是“历史文化的重要载体”（汪榕培、黄中习，2008：164）。“原则上，在中国文化史上出现过的一切重要的基本文献，都可以归入文化典籍的范畴。”（王宏印，2009：2）

通过对《孟子·告子下》《说文解字》《梦溪笔谈》《辞海》《汉英大词典》中“典籍”之意的比对，“典籍”一词的定义经历了一个不断拓宽的过程——“今天的‘典籍’可以理解为中国古代流传至今的重要文献，是一个国家的文化基因和最深层次的智慧结晶”（罗选民、李婕，2020：84）。

综合比较“典籍翻译”的现有概念，得出其本质属性中有两个最重要的元素——“古代”和“国家重要文献”。这两个限定条件衍生出了典籍翻译的两个内涵特征：“首先，典籍是由中国古代语言写成的。这一点决定了典籍翻译存在一个二度翻译过程。其次，典籍作为国家重要文献，其翻译行为常常是由国家政府机构力量主导的。”（罗选民、李婕，2020：84）

究其第一个内涵特征——二度翻译，其过程包括：语内翻译和语际翻译。以二度翻译为讨论核心，王宇弘、潘文国（2018：93-95）谈到典籍英译过程中原文理解的三道关卡：“第一关是语言文字关。第二关是古代文化关。第三关是中国文化最核心的一些词语，比如文学艺术上的‘韵、味、神、骨、比、兴’。”

而跨越原文理解的三道关卡，正是译文准确与灵活表达的前提和先决条件。比如，典籍多基本术语及文化概念，其正确译介的前提是要透彻理解中国文化的核心词语；典籍多复杂晦涩的遣词造句，其灵活翻译的前提是要熟悉文言文的语法和字词含义；典籍多灵活多变的行文风格，时而气势恢宏，时而工整严谨，时而隽永清秀，其广度和深度的制衡更是对译者双语能力严峻的考验。

通过以上描述，针对《晏婴评传》英译实践中有关“原文理解”和“译文表达”的难点，笔者在下文归纳总结了实际的普遍性问题，并尝试提出解决方法。

2.2 “边缘典籍”及其特点

在描述典籍英译的概念界定、主要特征后，典籍英译的基础或必备条件便得以凸显——即典籍注解与今注述评。“中国文化典籍的整理与注译，包含了文化典籍文本本身的分类与版本的鉴定，即古籍整理和文献的注释与疏解，或所谓的古文今注今译。这两个方面的工作是古文外译的基础，也构成典籍英译的基础。”（王宏印，2009：197）

而典籍的整理分类是语料建构和搜索的前提条件。笔者总结古代官方的编目叙录发现，中国文献及图书的分类始见于西汉刘向刘歆父子的《七略》，东汉班固的《汉书·艺文志》采用的就是刘氏父子的体系；唐代之后，四部之分（经、史、子、集）成为中国典籍目录学的主流；至清代，《四库全书总目》对古代文献的“经、史、子、集”四分法最为完备。

在前人对典籍概念界定与分类的基础上，笔者辅之以知网计量可视化分析，在本文创造性地提出“边缘典籍”的概念：因缺乏“四部”体系内现存的注释疏解，甚至系统、权威的今人述评，导致译者难以客观、全面地理解和参透典籍文本，从而使该古代文献在典籍外译过程中成为被边缘化的对象；该过程称为典籍外译的边缘化，该对象称为边缘典籍。

以上对“边缘典籍”的概念界定和古代文献的分类描述，旨在拓宽典籍英译的研究范围，寻求“典籍英译”的外延概念，以及呼吁各方重视边缘典籍的今注今译，促进学界创造性发展、创造性转化优秀中国传统文化。

2.3 典籍译者的自身观照

从译者主体间性、译者因素研究考虑，“翻译不是译者单方面的译介行为，应该由读者决定接受或拒绝翻译。不同种类的读者需要不同类型的译本”（Lefevere，2002：10-14）。因此，“中国典籍需要不同的译本，以满足不同类型的读者需求，从而共同推动中国典籍‘走出去’”（魏泓，2020：59）。

所以在译介过程中，译者可以针对读者的不同需要采用不同的翻译策略。比如，偏向文学效果的归化策略或偏向历史典章、精确再现的异化策略。此外，译者应结合实际情况，为提升文化译介和传播效果，选取合适的翻译模式，如合作翻译或独立翻译。

由此可见，“典籍译者兼具典籍语言转换者和跨文化传播者的双重身份，发挥着举足轻重的纽带和桥梁作用”（张德福，2021：52）。典籍译者不仅需要精通双语及其背后的社会文化规约，还需要考虑文化站位问题，具备文化传播和话语研究意识；语言现象有时是一种商品运作，其消费对象需要不断推敲和斟酌。

综上所述，典籍译者要明晰文化站位的概念，从文化译介和传播效果出发，选择合理的翻译模式，继而靠近具体的翻译标准，做好“一仆二主”的中间体。

2.4 常见翻译策略及方法

近几年，为了能完整传递源语文化，文化文本语境内的“深度翻译法”成为讨论热点。在典籍翻译中，译者通常采用厚译或深度翻译（thick translation）的方法（陆振慧，2013：55-61；葛厚伟，2017：139；钟达锋，2017：124）。

所谓厚译或深度翻译，指“通过附注（annotation）或文内注释（accompanying glosses），将（目标语）文本置于丰富的（源语）文化或文本语境（cultural and linguistic context）的翻译方法”，其目的是为了帮助读者深度理解源语文本的相关文化信息（Appiah，1993：812；817）。总的来说，厚译最终须通过增译副文本信息的翻译手段来实现。

然而，翻译思维局限在某一方向势必不是完美的，一个问题的解决后会产生新的问题，思维的各个方向需要彼此间多元互补。虽然厚译为译者所青睐，但若添加的位置不合理或过多增添译注和副文本信息，势必会降低译文叙事的流畅和连续性。

为提升深度翻译后译文的流畅和连续性，译者可采用与其互补的翻译方法——添加译者“声音”。通过对多部典籍的描写翻译研究，“收集‘可观察’的文本证据，‘重构’翻译规范、提炼普适性翻译法则”（Toury, 2004：15，2012：93-115），研究发现叙事典籍英译中“声音”策略，即增添译者评价声音，可有效地保证文本的衔接和连贯。此现象从侧面验证了翻译策略多元化的客观存在及其互补的实际价值。下文将在多元互补论视域下，在具体实例中具体分析翻译实践中的译学路径。

3. 翻译标准多元互补论

理论的存在，在西方逻辑学中，是指导各事物相互作用、发展趋势的客观规律；在中国哲学中，就是道器论里形而上和形而下的辩证和统一。相比于中国特色的理论体系，西方的科学理论缺乏工匠化理念和本土化传承。中国文化是历久弥新、一脉相承、厚重且成熟的系统体系，而西方之文化以发散为特点，包罗万象，不同学科发展之间存在明显的不连续性或间断性（discontinuity）。如若用西式学术方式研究中国之文化，不免存在割裂中国文化之嫌。但是，因西方科学理论与本土观念之间的异同，不同语系之间语言转换所遵循的指导理论的差异，我们一直缺乏中国特色的理论指导。

所以，建立中国特色的翻译理论迫在眉睫，这一说法与现阶段国家翻译实践理论的建设相得益彰。通过对典籍英译研究中常出现的翻译策略、方法和手段的类比分析，笔者认为对于典籍英译中的翻译问题，无法找到共同的翻译标准。在查阅历年有关典籍英译的文献资料，比对熟悉相关翻译描述、翻译策略后，笔者特选取辜正坤的“翻译标准多元互补理论”指导中国特色的翻译实践，以寻求理论的实际意义，补充中国特色翻译理论体系。

3.1 具体标准的标准

关于翻译标准的认知，多元互补论认为——具体翻译标准不可能只有一个，绝对的“信”不是“不容易做到”，而是根本就做不到。“翻译标准问题是翻译理论的核心问题，也是一个哥德巴赫猜想式的问题。”（辜正坤，1989：16）

翻译标准是一个标准体系，其构成方式是绝对标准（原作）、最高标准（抽象标准、最佳近似度）、具体标准（分类）。绝对标准是最高标准的标准，最高标准是具体标准的标准（辜正坤，1989：18）。

在具体的翻译实践中，“译者应依据时代特点与翻译标准来确定翻译原则、制定翻译策略。……中国典籍的译介可采用多种方式。译者可酌情采用节译、全译、释译、编译、转译、译述、漫画等方式来满足不同读者的需求”（魏泓，2020：59）。由此可见，翻译标准不同，对译者产生直接影响，进而影响翻译质量；对读者产生间接影响，进而影响文化译介与传播。

总的来说，翻译标准多元互补论具有辩证法精神，推翻了“唯一的具体翻译标准”的设想，从具体标准的群落研究到抽象标准研究，即个性与共性研究。其次，多元互补论是系统科学与哲学的中介理论，明晰了绝对标准一元化和具体标准多元化对立统一的关系及其背后原因。此外，它合乎翻译的实际，在具有包容性的同时，还映射了中国文化思想。

3.2 多元的客观存在

没有绝对标准不等于说没有任何标准。恰恰相反，“能够用以指导翻译实践并判断译作价值的具体标准不但有，而且不止一个，即是有若干个，这种情形称作翻译标准多元化”（辜正坤，1989：17）。

究其原因，在于翻译功能和目的多元化。“人类的审美情趣具有多样性，读者、译者具有多层次，翻译手法、译作风格、译作价值因而势必多样化，最终导致具体翻译标准的多元化。”（辜正坤，1989：17）比如上文所述，读者决定接受或拒绝翻译，不同种类的读者需要不同类型的译本。

同样，译者的多层次也导致翻译标准的多元与互补。举例而言，汪榕培坚持的翻译标准是“传神达意”，达意是翻译的出发点，译文要试图准确地体现译者的理解和阐释。以上观点与当代的“读者接受论”“译者主体性”乃至“解构主义”等观点有相通之处，译者在译文中就是要表现翻译的解读思路。

然而，单纯的“达意”还不够，必须是“传神地达意”，既包括传递外在的形式，也包括传递内在的意蕴（汪榕培，2007：33-36）。换言之，翻译既要注重形似，又要追求神似。

由此可见，翻译标准的多元化是客观存在的，其理论的深入研究势必会打破译者的思维局限，鼓励译者从多角度、多方位思考翻译问题。

3.3 互补的实际意义

关于多元互补理论的研究思维模式——立体思维，可谓前无古人，后难有来者。“立体思维强调思维的空间性，暗示思维主体者的作用，宛如是一种全息式观照。”（辜正坤，1989：17）

简而言之，“一个翻译标准所具有的优点，正是别的翻译标准所具有缺点。所以翻译标准的多元化本身就意味着翻译标准的互补性。各式各样的翻译标准代表了译作价值的各个方面，每个标准在独自发挥自己的功能的同时，其实就是在和所有的标准相辅相成，起着弥补其他标准缺陷的作用”（辜正坤，1989：19）。比如，“厚译策略解决叙事典籍翻译中的翻译问题，的确有助于目标语读者深度理解源语文化，然而一贯地增添译注和副文本信息，势必会降低译文叙事的流畅和连续性”（桑仲刚，2021：95）。但是，若因此大量采用声音策略，“由于叙述评论是叙述者的情感、态度、立场、心智等的流露，为此也被称为叙述者的‘声音’或叙述‘干预’”（Zhao，1995：48；72-74）。

所以，在特定的情况下选择翻译手段时，不能局限于一种、一概而论，要“兼而有之”“博采众长”。这同时也验证了具体翻译标准之间的互补能使翻译质量更加接近绝对标准，靠近最佳近似度。

3.4 理论的研究价值

翻译标准多元互补论是一个自成体系的翻译理论。“作为当代中国翻译理论的重要代表，其理论构建深受儒、释、道等中国传统文化的影响，

背后贯穿着一多相应、虚实相生、动静相宜等中国传统思维方式，并由此形成其鲜明的中国理论特色。”（王剑，2013：155）

结合文化转向后的翻译标准，游贤育（2016：43）指出，“多元互补论中影响具体标准的因素与文化转向后翻译研究的内容一脉相承，多元互补论既包含了译者因素，也包含了各种文本外因素对翻译的影响”。

在理论指导实践中，译者要力求在“多角度、全方位、多层次”的立体思维中理解原文，灵活表达。“在不同文本语境和文化中，以推动文化交流为原则，权衡取舍翻译策略、翻译方法以及翻译手段，在多元中寻求互补，以此靠近最佳近似度。”（辜正坤，1989：73）

综上所述，以翻译标准多元互补论为指导进行典籍英译研究，具有实际价值意义。在实践中采用中国特色的翻译理论，译介具有中国特色的文化负载词、准确表达作者观点、详细描述历史事件、综合把握语言风格，也是《晏婴评传》英译的亮点和难点。

4. 翻译模式及研究对象

在合作翻译中，如何平衡借鉴、相互启发，最终要落到实践上。笔者选择多元互补理论指导《晏婴评传》翻译实践的原因，一是著作分为行文论述和典籍引用两部分，文本类型不同；二是引用的典籍各自的体裁、史书类型、语言表现等也不同；三是合作翻译涉及译者的任务分工与协调，实践中存在多元的分工方式、多元的翻译问题，更存在互补的翻译视角、互补的翻译策略。

本节将具体分析《晏婴评传》的翻译模式、翻译价值和相关语料的翻译问题。

4.1 合作翻译的分工及协调

翻译模式基本有两种：一是个人独立完成，即从原本选择到阅读理解，再到翻译成文，仅凭一己之力，也就是我们常说的严格意义上的翻译；二是两人或多人分头负责，协力完成，我们将其称为合作翻译，简称“合译”。传统合作翻译模式主要分为口述加笔受的合作翻译模式、主译加辅译的合作翻译模式以及集体分工协作的翻译模式（刘杰辉、冯书彬，2009：23）。本次翻译实践则选取了分工协作的翻译模式。但不同于以往按书内章节分工的集体合译模式，本次实践将根据问题的多元与译者的互补，从方法论出发，将实践中不同翻译问题的解决途径分门别类，再依次分工。例如，译者 A 的任务是从古文献学视域下整理归纳、比较分析书中各处典籍引文，疏通理解难点；译者 B 的任务是从历史学角度，在不同历史语境中，逐一为各类术语翻译正名，或以训诂学、译介学、知识论等视角解决翻译过程中涉及不同学科的翻译问题……以此类推，分工协作、合并成文，并展开研究。

此合译方式具有两个突出优势。第一，统一性。由于以往合译方式常根据章节分工，不可避免地存在同一译作前后具有不同翻译水平和语言风格的问题，甚至出现译作前后译名不统一的现象。但若根据多元的翻译问题和译者互补的翻译层次分工协作，将有效地避免“断裂式”表达，保持译者风格和内容理解的协调统一。第二，专业性。从翻译辩证思维方面来看，“多元”概念的提出，正突显了翻译过程中专业问题的“唯一”性，比如文献整理或者历史分析，抑或文化传播、译者行为等各类专业问题。多元的客观存在，更需要不同的实践者分担“专业”的问题，将多元问题用“唯一”的方式解决。

4.2 《晏婴评传》的翻译价值

《晏婴评传》的创新之处与主要特点，一是该书为目前研究晏婴的最为完备的著作；二是材料翔实，考证扎实，辨析深入；三是细致入微，匡谬正误，新见迭出。

作为目前研究晏婴最为完备的著作，《晏婴评传》尚未出现译本。作者战化军为不作空泛之论，在书中深入考证、辨析了大量的史载材料，如《史记》《晏子春秋》《左传》《礼记》《论语》《孟子》《管子》《论语》等典籍 50 余部，其中先秦典籍近 20 部。书内相关的典籍英译是本翻译实践中的亮点、重点和难点。

由此可见，《晏婴评传》的翻译价值不仅局限于个人传记、一本书的译介，更是一系列典籍整理、史料比对、语料搜集与译介的系统工程。从翻译内容看，该书的译介是对相关典籍译本更加多元、全面的补充；

从翻译模式看，此次合译模式及分工方式是促进译者转变翻译思维、跨学科研究的契机；从指导理论看，该研究丰富并验证了中国特色的翻译理论。换言之，《晏婴评传》的英译实践是以一带多、促进边缘典籍英译、带有中国特色的翻译实践。

4.3 相关语料的翻译问题

在先秦典籍中，《晏子春秋》现存英译本出现时间较晚，且两个译本的译者都为国外著名的汉学家。西方首部《晏子春秋》英语全译本于2016年由欧洲著名出版社博睿出版社（Brill）出版发行，译者为英国汉学家、翻译家米欧敏（Olivia Anna Rovsing Milburn）。

而国内首部《晏子春秋》的英译本作为2018年中以合作、国家出版基金项目《晏子春秋（汉英对照版）》姗姗来迟，英译者为以色列著名汉学家欧永福（Yoav Ariel），同时译本入选中国国家文化名片《大中华文库》。

在对比分析两个译本的翻译过程、翻译难点中，笔者认为导致《晏子春秋》英译本出现时间晚、版本少的最主要的原因在于"缺乏前人的系统考注与述评"。正如米欧敏在回顾《晏子春秋》翻译难点时说："如果原作文本中的某些部分意义不清楚，那么译者理解起来就很困难。另外，《晏子春秋》也没有任何早期的评论可资参考，所以我们也不知道人们过去是如何看待这本书，或者他们是如何解释书中的这些难解段落的。"（孙继成、杨纪荣，2019：3）

笔者发现，在两个译本的翻译过程中，都存在参考书目较少、前人注释评述不够全面的问题。米欧敏说在翻译过程中，主要参考了吴则虞的《晏子春秋集释》（1977）和王更生的《晏子春秋研究》（1976）两本书目，这无疑减弱了典籍理解的准确性。同样，由欧永福撰写、吴洋翻译的《晏子春秋（汉英对照版）》前言《历史中的晏子形象与〈晏子〉文本》也从侧面证实了这一点（王琼，2019：37）。

由此可见，译者不应闭门造车，要广泛研究比较相关古今通释。米欧敏和欧永福的《晏子春秋》译本是《晏婴评传》翻译的主要语料，二者的比对不仅加深了笔者对原著的理解，也拓宽了资料的搜寻范围。

5. 翻译策略及方法分析

在翻译研究中，翻译问题常分为“因双语文化习惯、规约（conventions）、规范（norms）等的不同而产生的规约性翻译问题（convention-related translation problems），由词汇、语法等语言差异而造成的语言翻译问题，因源语文本的标记性特征导致的语篇翻译问题，以及由于双语文本在各自交际情景中功能的不同而造成的语用翻译问题四类”（Nord，2006：174-176）。

结合以上分类，并基于对原文语境和指导理论的深入理解，笔者通过分析讨论译者的思维过程及其对多元翻译策略的权衡和取舍，总结归纳了以下四点：规约性翻译的策略互补、语言翻译问题的多元处理、语篇内的衔接与连贯、二度翻译的近似标准，旨在提供能靠近最佳近似度的翻译方法。

5.1 规约性翻译的策略互补

在本节笔者以“声音”策略和“厚译”策略为例，论述翻译策略之间的互补价值。“声音”策略，是指在译文中增加译者的叙述评论。此处“叙述”是指叙述行为、叙述方式及内容等。所谓叙述评论，“指叙述者对叙述内容（人物、场景、事件）、叙述话语及其叙述行为所做的概括与解释、判断与评价，是叙述者‘声音’的显性表达”（Chatman，1978：228）。“厚译”策略是指译者对译文中副文本的添加和选择。通常，译者会采用增加脚注、尾注、文内注等副文本信息的手段，补充与源语相关的文化、语言、语篇及文本语境信息。

例 1：

原文：《晏子春秋》中有数处提及晏婴与齐灵公的关系。

初译： In *The Spring and Autumn Annals of Master Yan* (*Yanzi Chunqiu*), there are several references about relationship between Yan Ying and Duke Ling of Qi.

采用“声音”策略后的译文： In *The Spring and Autumn Annalsof Master Yan* (*Yanzi Chunqiu*), there are several references about the master-servant relationship founded on mutual respect between Yan Ying and Duke Ling of Qi.

对于不了解春秋时期历史及相关人物关系的读者，此句在文中第一次出现时，可能会造成理解障碍，不得不翻看书后章节或者查阅相关史料厘清晏婴和齐灵公的主仆关系，方能理顺文内逻辑和作者观点。

为避免以上问题，译者根据语境及客观事实，通过查找《晏婴评传》文内的评注、线索和《晏子春秋》等相关史料补充验证，增加译文“评判声音”。从读者角度出发，寻求多元、互补的翻译方法，使读者更好地理解晏婴在“一人侍三主”的区别和特点。

例 2：

原文：齐庄公元年，与晋国等诸侯盟于澶渊，承认晋国的盟主地位，但实际上，齐庄公一直积蓄武力，伺机报平阴之役之仇。

初译：In the first year of Duke Zhuang of Qi period, Duke Zhuang and some feudal princes of Jin State formed an alliance in Chan Yuan, and acknowledged Jin was the leader state. However, Duke Zhuang had been accumulating force under the table and seeking for the revenge for the Battle of Pingyin.

增加副文本后的译文：In the first year of Duke Zhuang of Qi period (794 BC), Duke Zhuang and some feudal princes of Jin State formed an alliance in Chan Yuan (澶渊), and acknowledged Jin was the leader state. However, Duke Zhuang had been accumulating force under the table and seeking for the revenge for Duke Ling's lost in Battle of Pingyin (平阴) in 555 BC.

增加“794 BC”意在给予读者更清晰的时间概念，在学术译著中能更方便地搜索与研究。另外，增加“盟于澶渊”的注释一是为了让读者了解历史，二是为了防止读者将其与“澶渊之盟”（Chanyuan Treaty in 1005）混淆。

“平阴之役”是春秋时期齐晋争霸中的著名战役，发生于公元前 555 年 10 月至 555 年 12 月，位于山东平阴。而原文对于此历史叙述过于单薄，缺少对参战方、参展结果及主要指挥官的解释。国内读者或许容易理解，但很难让国外读者理清思路、了解人物背后的真实意图以及盟于澶渊的背景。为了不影响读者阅读的流畅性，笔者在实践过程中，尽量将副文本以从句或句内成分形式呈现，与原句完美融合。

5.2 语言翻译问题多元处理

针对由词汇、语法等语言差异而造成的语言翻译问题，笔者将其归纳为两类：成语、谚语、俗语方言的异化翻译原则；概念、术语、中国特色词的语用翻译法。

“中国古典文化典籍英译的难点之一在于基本概念因人而异，而其中最困难的问题又在于古代文章中许多概念缺乏明确的界定，由此造成概念的模糊不清与术语的游走不定。”王宏印指出，“应进一步结合术语的语用情况以及其他术语的相互关系，划分术语的使用范围，建立包括下位术语在内的整个术语系统”（王宏印，2003：41）。

在这里中国特色词包含了我们常说的文化负载词等。笔者尝试用中国特色的翻译理论指导特色词语的翻译，目的就是让外国读者更好地了解中国文化，如同潘文国教授在《中籍英译通论》里对于格义和正名的辩证：“格义意为从自己的语言文化看别人的语言文化。正名，意为注意语言和文化的体系性，牵一发而动全身；译者要慎用音译，敢创新词。”（潘文国，2017：141-147）

在特色的理论指导下，笔者在本次实践中特别注意如官职、纪年、历史事件等翻译，在历史语境中究其概念的内涵和外延，多采取“音译（英文释译 + 中文）”翻译方法。

例 3：

原文：齐庄公“为车五乘之宾”。

译 文：The Duke Zhuang of Qi equipped “Yong Jue”, the courageous peerage, with five-horses-drawn carriage and treated them as guests.

原文意为“齐庄公享受五乘爵禄的侍卫队伍”。“五乘之宾”为享受五乘爵禄的人，五乘是先秦的一种爵禄，似以车辆为计算单位。在原文的语境中，包含更加详细的说明，“齐庄公设立‘勇爵’，给予五乘战车的人员装备，并待之如宾客，当时的勇武之士都以得到此待遇为荣”。

在文化外译策略及多元理论指导下，笔者在此选择异化的翻译策略，使读者更加具象地了解中国古代的阶级意向与标志。值得注意的是，笔者在译文中添加宾语 Yong Jue 及其归化的解释，对应上下文的语境，这也是多元互补论指导实践的生动体现——在一个句子中，为不同的翻译目的和效果，在不同情况下采取不同方法。

官职的译法常出现四类：直译、对应译法、加注（注释考证或说明）和语境内灵活处理。在此实践中，译者主要用到了《英汉古代官职词典》，采用对应译法（音译 + 注释 / 中文）的方法，旨在将中国官职文化对外译介出去。

例 4：

原文：大夫

译文：Grand Master (ta-fu, the 2nd official highest category of officials)

需要注意的是，在不同时代，即使名称相同的官职，所代表的职责并不相同，需仔细查找史料和相关词典，明确职责范围、厘清历代区别。为靠近“达意通理”的翻译标准，可适当添加注释，为读者带来方便。

5.3 二度翻译的近似标准

多元标准互补论中对标准的讨论，纠正了译者对于“忠实”的误解。如上文所述，我们应该在具体问题中讨论具体的方法和标准，以达到与原文的近似。本节就多元互补论如何指导二度翻译的英译实践进行详细讨论。

首先，减少语内翻译的理解成本是二度翻译的难点。语内翻译的理解成本主要是指译者在敲定译稿前所用时效和工具使用，典籍英译中主要以二度翻译的语内翻译为讨论核心。原作的注、疏、今译等在对原文的理解中起着至关重要的作用，是典籍英译研究必须关注的课题（王宏、刘性峰，2015：73）。因此，在理解文本过程中，除了译者本身的知识储备外，还需要对相关知识强大的搜索能力以及对语料、注与考、平行文本的梳理技巧。

其次，在典籍翻译中，译者要培养自己的训诂能力，读懂文言文，了解相关书籍，学会查找和归类相关用法。比如，在古文今译中文言词语的特点多以单音节词为主、通假字、对偶排比的对文见义；在词语翻译中常有一字多义、同义合成；在文言句法和结构中多见古今对应、不对应、语气词和语内增减。

唯有此，才能在多元理解中，互相补重，降低局限性和主观性。

例 5：

原文：纪子伯莒子盟于密。

译文（理）： Tsze-pih of Ke and the count of Keu made a covenant at Meih.

王韬《春秋左氏传集释》说："密，莒邑，在今莱州府昌邑县东南十五里有密乡故城。"杜预说："密是莒国一城（在今莱州府昌邑县），这座城相距莒非常远，尽管距离纪很近。此说可以接受，但令人疑惑的是，相距如此之远的一个地方怎么会是莒国之地。"所以，笔者在拿来理雅各的译文时，首先查证了"春秋时代形势图"，具体分析原文所指，经考证得知"莒"并非指"莒国"（与齐国和鲁国接壤），而是指齐国的"莒县"；"密"位于齐国昌邑县，距离"纪"较近，而距"莒"较远。于是采用了理雅各的译文。

5.4 互文与理解系统构建

法国著名语言家朱莉娅·克里斯蒂娃（Julia Kristeva）（1969：133）认为，单独的文本是不存在的，所有的文本都存在相互关系。后来，菲利普·索莱尔斯（Philippe Sollers）重新定义"互文性"，认为"每一篇文本都联系着若干文本，并且对这些文本起着复读、强调、浓缩、转移，和深化的作用"（转引自萨莫瓦约，2003：4）。

相比于西方的互文理论，中国的互文只是一个修辞格。"互文性指构成文本的每个语言符号都与本文之外的其他符号相关联，在形成差异时显出自己的价值。"（张隆溪，1983：99）

在此次合译实践中，笔者巧妙地将互文的思想运用到典籍翻译里，尤其是在《晏婴评传》的古文献整理和比对中。笔者认为，互文与理解系统的构建是促进文本理解、提高二度翻译准确性的有效途径之一。在本节中，笔者创造性地分为两部分：基于作者自身的考证研究和基于逻辑线索的史料比对。

以《晏子春秋》与《老子》互文建构为例，作者在第六章将《老子》（第二十二、四十四、四十六、五十八、六十七、七十六、七十七、七十八章）的中心思想与《晏子春秋》中“贵柔、尚水、谦下、商俭、知足、廉而不伤、反对厚藏”的相似精神类比分析，通过自身考证，准确表达了中国特色的文化术语及其概念。此举不仅方便笔者找到相关术语及概念的英汉权威语料，重复使用，还能利用互文特点，减少不必要的工作量，以达到翻译仿拟的目的。

再比如书中对含有“草莱”相关字眼的引用：

> 《盐铁论·轻重》：“辟**草莱**而居。”
>
> 《国语·齐语》：“通齐国之鱼盐于**东莱**……”
>
> 《汉书·地理志下》：“太公以齐地负海潟卤，少五谷而人民寡，乃劝以女工之业，通鱼盐之利，而人物辐辏。”
>
> 《史记·货殖列传》：“（齐）地潟卤，人民寡，于是太公劝其女功，极技巧，通鱼盐，则人物归之，繦至而辐辏。”

笔者在搜索查证相关史籍后，做出系列总结，一举攻克对原文中“草莱”的理解。通过搜集仿拟相似语料的权威译文，提高翻译效率。更重要的是，此举加强了语内翻译的准确性。

此外，我们不仅可以寻求作者在文中的解释考证，还可以自己查找相关史料，按照逻辑线索，如对时间、人物、地点等进行比对，加深理解。举例如下：

> 《史记·田敬仲完世家》：“陈完至齐，齐桓公欲使陈完为卿，陈完力辞……田桓子无宇有力，事齐庄公……”
>
> 《史记集解》：“始食菜地于田，由是改姓田氏。”
>
> 《史记索隐》：“敬仲奔齐，以陈田二字声相近，遂以为田氏。”

《史记正义》："敬仲既奔齐，不欲称本国故号，故改陈字为田氏。"

《史记·十二诸侯年表》："齐自是称田氏。"

在笔者不理解"陈完"为何在下文译为"田氏"后，通过查找相关史料才知"陈完后来改姓田氏"，并在译文中补充相关副文本，不仅表明了自身的翻译思路，也使读者更能详细地了解历史背景及人物经历，体会中心思想。

6. 小结

将"典籍合译"作为研究主题，除了源于当下传统文化输出的紧迫性和翻译研究的创新性，还源于笔者对传统文化的敬仰和对典籍文字感知的渴望。笔者以《晏婴评传》为翻译实践与研究对象，用中国特色翻译理论——多元标准互补论为指导，试图为边缘典籍的合译实践提出可复制的翻译方法，创新固有思维，拓宽典籍英译的研究范围。

在研究中，笔者描述了"典籍英译"的内涵和外延，并尝试给出边缘典籍及典籍翻译边缘化的概念；在实践中，笔者创新合译方式，归纳翻译策略，如互文观照中"基于作者自身的考证研究"与"基于逻辑线索的史料比对"等翻译方法。此外，笔者针对不同语境下复杂多变的翻译问题，构建多元、互补的翻译策略，创新分工协作模式，归纳翻译方法。

翻译的过程离不了治学与研究，暂不论用词的考究，对资料的搜索比对就是磨性子的差事。对译者来说，典籍翻译最基本的要求是"走出去"能"回得来"。译文回溯对文化理解至关重要，尤其是学术文本译介。其中，跨学科视角下术语翻译的正本清源就是间接的文化站位。另外，文本内部的互见与校对必不可少，这区别于译者自身搜索的注与考。

以上种种，都需要译者提前构想、研究，通过比对、分析相关语料和译本风格，结合自身翻译模式，对翻译策略和手段进行取舍和谋划。

参考文献

[1] 葛厚伟. 民族文化典籍的深度翻译策略 [J]. 贵州民族研究，2017(3): 139-142.

[2] 辜正坤. 翻译标准多元互补论 [J]. 中国翻译，1989（1）: 100-105.

[3] 辜正坤. 中西诗比较鉴赏与翻译理论 [M]. 北京：清华大学出版社，2003.

[4] 辜正坤. 翻译学体系框架略论——《译学津原》序 [J]. 外语与外语教学，2007（1）: 66-67.

[5] 李正栓，杨丽华. 21 世纪初中国典籍英译小议 [J]. 浙江外国语学院学报，2012（6）: 42-47.

[6] 陆振慧. 论注释在典籍英译中的作用——兼评理雅各《尚书》译本 [J]. 扬州大学学报（人文社会科学版），2013（6）: 55-61.

[7] 理雅各. 中国经典（卷 3）[M]. 上海：华东师范大学出版社，2011.

[8] 刘杰辉，冯书彬. 中国传统合作翻译模式刍议 [J]. 唐山师范学院学报，2009（31）: 23-25.

[9] 罗选民，李婕. 典籍翻译的内涵研究 [J]. 外语教学，2020（6）: 83-88.

[10] 潘文国. 从“格义”到“正名”——翻译传播中华文化的必要一环 [J]. 华东师范大学学报（哲学社会科学版），2017（5）: 141-147.

[11] 潘文国，王宇弘. 典籍翻译的道与器——潘文国教授访谈录 [J]. 纵横论译，2018（5）: 93-101.

[12] 萨莫瓦约，绍炜译. 互文性研究 [M]. 天津：天津人民出版社，2003.

[13] 桑仲刚. 叙事典籍翻译的“声音”策略：以敦煌遗书《孔子项讬相问书》的英译为例 [J]. 外国语，2021（4）: 94-102.

[14] 孙继成，杨纪荣. 访英国汉学家米欧敏：从晏子到麦家“解密”中国文化 [J]. 中国社会科学报，2019（2）: 1-5.

[15] 王宏，刘性峰. 当代语境下的中国典籍英译研究 [J]. 中国文化研究，2015（2）: 69-79.

[16] 王宏印. 中国文化典籍英译 [M]. 北京：外语教学与研究出版社，2009.

[17] 王宏印，荣立宇. 典籍翻译，任重道远——王宏印教授访谈录 [J]. 燕山大学学报（哲学社会科学版），2013，14（3）：1-6.
[18] 王宏印. 中国文化典籍翻译——概念、理论与技巧 [J]. 大连大学学报，2010（1）：127-129.
[19] 王剑. “翻译标准多元互补论”的中国传统文化阐释 [J]. 华侨大学学报（哲学社会科学版），2013（3）：155-160.
[20] 王琼. 国家出版基金项目《晏子春秋（汉英对照版）》简评 [J]. 传播与版权，2019（2）：36-40.
[21] 汪榕培. 为中国典籍英译呐喊——在第三届全国典籍英译研讨会上的发言 [J]. 中国外语，2006（1）：66.
[22] 汪榕培.《诗经》的英译——写在“大中华文库”版《诗经》即将出版之际 [J]. 中国翻译，2007（6）：33-35.
[23] 汪榕培，黄中习. 加强民族典籍的英译，弘扬民族优秀文化 [J]. 广西民族研究，2008（4）：164-165.
[24] 魏泓. 中国典籍如何“走出去”“走进去”“走‘深’进去”？——以《史记》英译为例. 语言与翻译，2020（1）：58-63.
[25] 谢天振. 中国文学走出去：问题与实质 [J]. 中国比较文学，2014（1）：1-10.
[26] 游贤育. 文化转向后翻译标准之再思考 [J]. 上海翻译，2016（5）：40-44.
[27] 张德福. 试论中国典籍跨文化传播模式的构建 [J]. 上海翻译，2021（1）：50-53.
[28] 张隆溪. 结构的消失——后结构主义的消解式批评 [J]. 读书，1983（12）：95-105.
[29] 钟达锋. 康达维译《文选 · 赋》：学术研究型深度翻译 [J]. 外语教学与研究，2017（1）：124-134.
[30] Appiah, K. Thick translation [J]. Callaloo, 1993(4): 808-819.
[31] Chatman, S. Towards a theory of narrative [J]. New Literary History, 1975 (2): 295-318.
[32] Kristeva, J. Semiotics: Researches for a Semiotic Analysis [M]. Paris: Seuil, 1969.

[33] Lefevere, A. Translation/History/Culture: A Sourcebook [M]. London: Routledge, 2002.

[34] Nord, C. Text Analysis in Translation: Theory, Methodology, and Didactic Application of a Model for Translation-Oriented Text Analysis [M]. Beijing: Foreign Language Teaching and Research Press, 2006.

[35] Zhao, Y. H. The Uneasy Narrator: Chinese Fiction from the Traditional to the Modern [M]. Oxford: Oxford University Press, 1995.

《聊斋志异》民族语朝鲜语版合译本的翻译策略

李　莹　北京外国语大学

摘　要：2021 年由黑龙江朝鲜民族出版社出版发行的民族语朝鲜语版《聊斋志异》是首部《聊斋志异》民族语朝鲜语合译本，由我国两位朝鲜族译者朴正阳和李光在合译完成。本文结合美国学者阿皮亚提出的“深度翻译”策略，以该合译本《聊斋志异·卷一》中的注释为主要研究对象，对照其源语翻译底本注释，探析合译本中的“深度翻译”现象，期冀为“聊斋学”和典籍外译研究提供一定的参考价值。

关键词：《聊斋志异》；深度翻译；注释；翻译策略

On the Translation Strategies in the Co-translated Korean Version of *Liaozhai Zhiyi*

Li Ying
Beijing Foreign Studies University

Abstract: The Chinese Korean version of *Liaozhai Zhiyi* (or *Strange Tales of a Lonely Studio* in English), published by Heilongjiang Korean Nationalities Publishing House in 2021, is the first Korean version of *Liaozhai Zhiyi* co-translated by two Chinese Koreans Piao Zhengyang and Li Guangzai. This paper aims to explore the phenomenon of "thick translation" proposed by American scholar Kwame Athony Appiah in the translated version of *Liaozhai Zhiyi* Volume I, with the annotations in the translation as the main research object. It is hoped that this paper will provide valuable reference for the "Liaozhai Studies" and the translation of China's ancient books into foreign languages.

Keywords: *Liaozhai Zhiyi*; thick translation; annotation; translation strategies

1. 引言

清代小说家蒲松龄的《聊斋志异》在中国文学史上占有举足轻重的地位，马瑞芳（2007）称其为与莫泊桑、契诃夫、欧·亨利齐名的“世界短篇小说之王”。《聊斋志异》全书共12卷，收录491篇中短篇小说，内容丰富，题材广泛，不仅吸收了中国历代传奇志怪小说的精华，而且糅合了史传文学的独特形式，不仅是情节离奇曲折的志怪小说，也是一部中国文学和中国传统思想的百科全书（孙雪瑛，2016：7）。《聊斋志异》不仅于国内，在世界也颇具影响力，是学界公认的海外译介最多、传播影响最广的中国古典文学作品之一。1766年，历史上最早的《聊斋志异》刊印本青柯亭刻本问世，18年后的1784年，该刻本便由轮船海运到日本，开启了《聊斋志异》的海外传播之旅。到目前为止，已有日语、英语、法语、德语、俄语、韩语（朝鲜语）、意大利语、西班牙语和越南语等20余个外语语种的《聊斋志异》译文，是拥有外文翻译语种最多的一部小说，同时也是中国古典文学作品中外文版本最多的一部，达近百种（孙雪瑛，2016：15）。《聊斋志异》于18世纪中期传入朝鲜半岛，但由于当时朝鲜王朝的文人多通晓汉语，长久以来《聊斋志异》都是以汉语原文的形式在朝鲜半岛被传阅（宋华伟，2008：10）。直到20世纪初朝鲜半岛才出现正式的《聊斋志异》朝鲜语译文，即朝鲜近现代小说家、翻译家梁白华1915年发表于朝鲜半岛佛教学刊《佛教振兴会月报》的《续黄粱》篇译文。后直到20世纪60年代，韩国才出现第一部韩语（朝鲜语）译本，即1966年汉城乙酉文化社出版的崔仁旭《聊斋志异》译本，之后韩国又陆续出版多部节译本和编译本，2002年民音社出版的由韩国汉学家金惠经翻译的《聊斋志异（1—6卷）》共翻译《聊斋志异》491篇小说，是韩国第一部真正意义上的《聊斋志异》韩文（朝鲜语）全译本。自此近10年后的2021年，我国黑龙江朝鲜民族出版社出版发行了民族语朝鲜语版《聊斋志异》，这是首部《聊斋志异》朝鲜语合译本，由我国两位朝鲜族译者朴正阳和李光在合译完成。该译本采取怎样的翻译策略来向朝鲜语读者传递《聊斋志异》艰深晦涩的语言、深邃的文化内涵、生动传奇的志怪故事？以此为研究问题，本文将结合美国学者阿皮亚（K. A. Appiah）

提出的“深度翻译”策略，以该合译本《聊斋志异·卷一》中的注释为研究对象，对照其源语文本注释，探析合译本中的“深度翻译”现象。

2.《聊斋志异》民族语朝鲜语版合译本概况

2021年由黑龙江民族出版社出版的《聊斋志异》民族语言朝鲜语译本共翻译《聊斋志异》491篇短篇，与韩国金惠京所译《聊斋志异》篇目数相同，也是一部全译本。同时，该译本也是一部由两位译者合作完成的第一部朝鲜语合译本。译者朴正阳和李光在同是任教于我国高校朝鲜语（韩语）系的朝鲜族教授，朴正阳教授于朝鲜金日成综合大学获文学博士学位，著有《朝鲜乐府诗研究》(朝鲜语)、《中国文学史》(朝鲜语)等多部专著和《金瓶梅（朝鲜语版）》等译著。李光在教授于韩国忠北大学获文学博士学位，著有《中韩无产阶级文学运动比较研究》《比较文学概论》《中国现代文学史》《中国现当代文学》等著作。可见，两位译者不仅从事翻译实践,在中朝鲜语（韩语）文学等学术研究领域也卓有成就，是典型的具有学者身份的“学者型译者”。学者型译者是翻译活动的重要群体，学者角色与译者角色相互配合，或在文化的引进和输出上有助于合理选择，或在语言文字的转换中减少信息失真，或在传播异质文化信息中创造出新的文化成果或新的文化现象，如新词、新句法等，或可建构新的翻译理论，在翻译领域起到重要作用（章方，2007：56-64）。

该合译本的封底页明确交代了翻译原文底本，指出“本书根据中华书局出版社2015年4月第1版翻译出版”，即中华书局“中华经典名著全本全注全译丛书”的三全本《聊斋志异》。该底本采用2010年中华书局出版的孙通海、王秀梅等八位先生翻译的文白对照本《聊斋志异》的译文部分，在此基础上加以校改润色，并约请《聊斋志异》研究专家于天池先生做注释、题解，对原文中难理解的字词句、专有名词和典章制度等传统文化知识出注诠释，使得该底本文章整体晓畅易懂（于天池等，2015：13），是学界公认的权威《聊斋志异》版本之一。该底本共四册十二卷491篇短篇小说，每篇由四部分构成，除了蒲松龄所著文言文原文以外，还有题解、注释、白话文译文三部分。《聊斋志异》民族语朝鲜语译本在构成上与翻译底本相同的地方在于共四卷翻译《聊斋志异》491篇短篇，不同点在于朝鲜语译本省去了文言文原文和题解部分，由民族语朝鲜语译文和注释两部分构成。

3. “深度翻译”与注释

“深度翻译”（Thick Translation），也译作“厚翻译”“厚译”等，最早由美国哲学家阿皮亚在“深度描写”（thick description）（也作“深描”等）概念的基础上提出。其本质是尊重异质文化，深入异质文化内部以异质文化持有者视角观察和理解该文化，具体方法是“通过注释、序跋、评论等为译文构筑文化、社会和文本等丰富的语境”（吴冰、朱健平，2018：75）。王雪明和杨子（2012）、张璐（2020）等研究都曾指出“深度翻译”对典籍翻译具有重要指导意义，王晔（2018）、于海鹏（2020）、张璐（2020）、胡作友和刘倩倩（2021）等认为注释作为翻译补偿的有效手段，是“深度翻译”策略的重要表现。

基于对译者和译本特征的考察，本文结合美国学者阿皮亚提出的“深度翻译”策略，以该合译本《聊斋志异·卷一》中的注释为主要研究对象，对照其源语文本注释，探析该译本中的“深度翻译”现象。本文对翻译底本和合译本注释译文文本细读一一比对后，运用定量和定性相结合的研究方法展开分析，定量方法按类型和功能分别统计注释数量，定性方法则结合实际翻译案例，对注释翻译进行定性描写。

4. 从注释看《聊斋志异》合译本“深度”翻译

注释通常包括文内夹注、脚注、尾注、文内隐注等类型（张璐，2020：78），结合翻译底本和译本特征，本文在此考察译本脚注，经笔者统计，朴李合译本中脚注共有 149 处。

以译本 149 处脚注为二级样本，将其区分为“翻译型注释”和“译者主体型注释”进行考察，翻译型注释即由源语文本注释直接翻译而来的译语注释，译者主体型注释则是译者发挥译者主体性，融入个人意图和观点等，在译文中自行添加的注释，原文注释或有或无。经考察，二级样本中“翻译型”注释脚注 131 个，“译者主体型”注释脚注 18 个。

张璐（2020）将译注的功能总结为四类：语义疏通、文化阐释、比照指涉、沟通读者。语义疏通功能指对原文中的地名、朝代、度量衡、人名、植物等名物典故进行解释，对文本中艰涩难懂的词汇语句进行释义疏通，为读者扫清阅读障碍。文化阐释功能即对原文中涉及的文化或社会现象进行解释与补充。比照指涉功能，指译者利用不同文化间的共通性，把不同空间的诗学距离和不同的文化概念在注释中并置起来，借用目标语国家的概念来比照源语中的概念，希望通过一定形式的互文比照唤起读者熟悉的记忆，达到审美共鸣和文化传递的目的。沟通读者功能，指译者出于需要直接现身，对自己译文中的不足或翻译时的感悟向读者沟通说明（张璐，2020：79）。本文按照译注这四种功能划分，对 131 个翻译型注释脚注和 18 个译者主体型注释脚注进行了统计，统计结果如表 1。

表 1　译本注释统计表

注释类型＼功能		语义疏通	文化阐释	比照指涉	沟通读者	总计
译本	翻译型注释	95	36	0	0	131
	译者主体型注释	9	5	2	2	18
总计		104	41	2	2	149

由表 1 可知，朴李合译本第一卷中的注释主要为语义疏通和文化阐释类，其中语义疏通类所占数量最多。

4.1　语义疏通类注释

语义疏通类注释多见于对地名、人名、官职名等名物专有名词翻译时所添加的脚注，其中翻译型注释 95 个，译者主体型注释 9 个，翻译型注释占比明显高于译者主体型注释。

具体来说，对于地名翻译型注释，如《崂山道士》篇中的“崂山”一词，译者采用“朝鲜语汉字词直译 + 汉字标注 + 原文注释直译”的翻译策略，将“崂山”译作“로산（嶗山）”，并按照原文内容添加脚注“로산 혹은 뢰산(牢山)이라고도 한다. 지금 청도시(青島市)동북쪽에

있는데 남쪽으로는 황해(黄海), 동쪽으로는 로산만(崂山灣)에 련결돼있고 상청궁(上清宮)과 백운동(白雲洞) 등 절간이 많아 명성을 날렸다.(原文注释：也称‘崂山’或‘牢山’，在今山东青岛东北，南滨黄海，东临崂山湾，有上清宫、白云洞等名胜古迹。)”，原文注释中交代了“崂山”所处位置及其道教名山的特点，译者在翻译时并未将其忽略，而是对原文注释进行直译以与原文注释传达的信息保持一致。人名翻译型注释如《聊斋自志》中“才非干宝，雅爱搜神”中“干宝”一词的翻译，原文对其作以脚注“干宝，字令升，东晋文学家，‘撰集古今神祇灵异人物变化，名为《搜神记》’(《晋书》本传)”，在脚注中对“干宝”的身份及其主要贡献进行介绍。朝鲜民族语合译本采取“朝鲜语汉字词直译＋汉字标注＋原文注释直译”的翻译策略，文中将其译作“간보(干宝)”，并在脚注中将原文注释直译为“자는 령승(令升)，동진(东晋)의 문하가, 고금의 신기한 이야기들을 모아〈수신기(搜神记)〉를 편찬했다”，翻译内容与原文一致。再如与科举制度相关的人员名称的翻译，例如，“予姊丈之祖，宋公讳焘，邑廪生。”出自《考城隍》篇，其中“廪生”一词在原文注释中解释为“廪生：廪膳生员。明洪武二年(1369)始，凡考取入学的生员(习称‘秀才’)，每人月廪食米六斗，以补助其生活。后生员名额增多，成化年间改为定额内者食廪，称廪膳生员，省称廪生增额者为增广生员和附学生员，省称增生和附生。清沿明制，廪生月供廪银四两，增生岁、科两试一等前列者，可依次升廪生，称补廪”，译文将“廪生”译作“름생(廪生)”，并对该词原文注释的全部内容进行直译。诸如此类的注释翻译案例颇多，在此不一一举例，通过对这些例子的分析来看，语义疏通类翻译型注释的注释对象多为地名、人名、植物名、官职名称、制度名称等名物专有名词，多采用“朝鲜语汉字词直译＋汉字标注＋原文注释直译”的翻译策略。

在语义疏通类注释中，译者主体型注释占比虽远小于翻译型注释，但其重要性却是不容忽视的，因为或增或减的注释内容里，藏有译者的个人意图和观点等，值得探究。其中，人名的译者主体型注释如《聊斋自志》篇中“披萝带荔，三闾氏感而为骚”，原文在脚注中对“三闾氏”进行解释，“三闾氏，指屈原。屈原(约前340—前227)，名平，战国时楚国伟大诗人，出身贵族，曾做过三闾大夫，掌楚王族昭、屈、景三姓之事”，

朝鲜民族语朴李合译本在翻译时，正文中并没有采取“朝鲜语汉字词直译+汉字标注”的翻译方法，而是将其“三闾氏”按照其所指代的意义译作“굴원（屈原）”，并作脚注“전국 시대 초（楚）나라의 시인으로이름은 평（平）이고 삼려대부（三闾大夫）를 지냈다. 초사체（楚辞体）의 대표작으로 일컬어지는《리소（离骚）》와《구가（九歌）》등을 창작하였다”。与原文注释相比，译文注释删除了“掌楚王族昭、屈、景三姓之事”，增添了“초사체（楚辞体）의 대표작으로 일컬어지는《리소（离骚）》와《구가（九歌）》등을 창작하였다.（笔者译：创作了楚辞体的代表作《离骚》合《九歌》）”。在译文注释中，“昭、屈、景”即为“三闾”，王逸对“三闾”解释为：“三闾之职，掌王三族三姓，曰昭、屈、景”，这是目前对其最早也是最具影响的诠解，表面看来译文注释将此删减似有不妥。然而，这恰是译者发挥主体性，体现其治学严谨和对读者负责的地方，因为史学研究领域对“三闾大夫”的解释尚存争议，“关于屈原的‘三闾大夫’，也是屈原研究中争议颇多并没有确切定论的一个难点”（郑志强，2011：77），如此删减可以减少歧义，为读者带来更好的阅读体验。再如“刘孝廉”，译者同样采用“朝鲜语汉字词对应+汉字标注”译法，译作“류효렴（劉孝廉）”，后在注释中向读者交代“孝廉”并非人物名字，而是代指“举人”。官职等制度名“译者主体型”注释，如“王公大人”该成语意为国君重臣，后泛指高官贵人，汉文语境读者对此十分熟悉，但对于朝鲜语语境读者来说则较难理解，因此译者在对其进行“朝鲜语汉字词对应+汉字标注”译作“왕공대인（王公大人）”后，在注释中解释该成语是指代“身份地位高的贵族”，疏通语义，减少歧义，便于读者理解。

4.2 文化阐释类注释

文化阐释类注释是对原文中涉及的文化或社会现象进行的解释与补充，其中翻译型注释 36 个，译者主体型注释 5 个。文化阐释类译者主体型注释，例如：

原文：后人犬俱寸磔以死。(《犬奸》)

白话文：后来人和狗都用剐刑处死了。

原文注释：寸磔：千刀万剐。磔，古代酷刑，即凌迟，俗称剐刑。

译文：후에 사람과 개는 모두 한치씩 도려내여 죽이는 벌을 받고 죽었다.

译文注释：원문은 촌책（寸磔）이다. 촌（寸）은 한치라는 뜻이고 책（磔）은 고대의 형벌의 일종으로 사지를 찢어내거나 혹은 사람을 여러 토막을 내여 죽이는 벌을 말한다.

译者在此并没有采取"朝鲜语汉字词对应＋汉字标注"译法，而是在理解原文注释内容后，将其意译到译文中，在译文中已将"寸磔"的意思译出，但为了进一步拓展译文读者的文化视野，译者对"寸磔"一词在译文中又给予了文化阐释，分别指出"寸"和"磔"的意思后，对"寸磔"之刑的实施方法向译文读者说明。再如《犬奸》篇中对"夜叉"的注释：

原文：夜叉伏床，竟是家中牝兽。(《犬奸》)

白话文：夜叉伏在床上，竟是家里的雌畜。

原文注释：无。

译文：야차（夜叉）가 번듯이 침대에 누워 있으니 필경 짐승의 암컷이고....

译文注释：야차（夜叉）：불교에서 사천왕에게 딸린 여덟 귀신 즉 건달파（乾闥婆），비사사（毗舍阇），구반다（鳩槃茶），아귀，제용중，부단나（富單奴），야차（夜叉），라찰（羅刹）을 팔부라고 하는데 그중의 하나인 야차는 사람을 괴롭히거나 해친다는 사나운 귀신이다.

"夜叉"一词来自梵语，是梵语 Yakṣa 的译音，意为"捷疾鬼""轻捷""勇健"，又被译成"药叉"等。汉典对其解释为"能啖鬼或捷疾鬼，佛教徒所说的一种吃人恶鬼或腾飞空中、速疾隐秘之恶鬼。印度神话中一种掌握太阳运行轨迹的半神小神灵”[1]，有地行夜叉、虚空夜叉、天夜叉三种，是印度传统文化的重要内容，也是佛教研究中不能忽视的文化现象。译者在译文中没有对其做过多解释，以“朝鲜语汉字词对应＋汉字标注”的译法直译该词，后于注释中对这一文化现象进行补充解释，并将其文化内涵扩大至“八部鬼众”。“八部鬼众”是佛学术语，一般指四大天王所率领的八类鬼神，即乾闼婆、毗舍阇、鸠槃荼、薜荔多、诸龙、富单那、夜叉、罗刹。[2]在使读者理解文义的基础上向朝鲜语读者阐释其文化内涵。

4.3 比照指涉类注释

比照指涉类注释指借用目标语国家的概念来比照源语中的概念，样本中比照指涉类译者主体型注释两个：

> **原文**：河南有故绅子，……（《长清僧》）
>
> **白话文**：河南有个旧官绅的公子，……
>
> **原文注释**：故绅子：老豪绅的儿子
>
> **译文**：그때 하남의 한 작고한 신사（紳士）의 아들이 ......
>
> **译本注释**：신사（紳士）：신（紳）은 허리에 매는 큰 띠를 가리킴.〈례기·옥조（礼记·玉藻）〉에“선비의 허리띠는 석자이고 허리띠는 두자반이다”라는 기재가 있다. 옛날에 권세와 지위가 있는 사람들이 띠를 둘렀기때문에 이런 명칭이 생겨났는데 후세에는 관직에 있거나 혹은 과거에 급제했지만 벼슬에서 물러나 향으로 돌아간 사람들을 일컬어 신사 혹은 향신（豪绅）이라고 하였다.

“故绅子”，翻译底本中作注“老豪绅的儿子”，然而译本中没有按照汉字词对译法将其翻译为“호신（豪绅）”，而是采用韩国本土概念，将

1 参见 https://baike.baidu.com/item/%E5%A4%9C%E5%8F%89/761?fr=aladdin（访问日期：2023-3-20）

2 参见 https://foxue.bmcx.com/babuguizhong__foxued/ 佛学大词典–八部鬼众（访问日期：2023-3-20）

其比照翻译为“신사”，但韩语（朝鲜语）“신사”对应中文“绅士”“神社”“神思”等至少20种，因此译者在括号内标注汉字繁体“紳士”。然而“绅士”一词在现代社会，无论是中文还是朝鲜语（韩语）语境，为人所熟之的语义皆为“举止优雅、待人谦和、谈吐得当的男士”，主要来源于英国绅士，因此译者进一步在注释中对此予以阐释，指出“신”字的来历和文化内涵，深度拓展目标语读者的文化视野。再如：

原文：……，彩楼鼓吹赴藩司，……（《长清僧》）

白话文：……，都要扎起五彩楼牌，敲锣打鼓地到藩司衙门去祝贺……

原文注释：藩司，即布政使。明代为一省的行政长官，清代则为总督、巡抚的属官，专管一省的财赋和人事。这里指藩司衙门。

译文：...... 곱게 장식한 루각모형을 만들어 세워들고 북을 치고 춤을 추면서 성청（省廳）으로 행진하는 축하놀이마당을 별렸는데 ......

译本注释：성청（省廳）：원문은 번사（藩司）인데 한성（省）의 인사와 재무를 주관하던 관리 포정사（布政使），안찰사（按察使）등의 성급（省级）관리를 지칭하는것으로 보아야 한다.

“藩司”，官名，明清时“布政使”的别称，又称“藩台”“方伯”，清制为从二品，主管一省之行政和财赋之出纳，可通过特旨除授、廷臣推荐、吏部开列具题等方式选任。[1] 译者在此没有将其对译为“번사”，这是因为朝鲜语（韩语）中，“번사”一词对应汉字“燔師”，意为“陶瓷烧制时烧火的人”，容易给译文读者带来歧义，因此译者在翻译时，借用朝鲜语语境中意义相似的概念来比照源语中的概念，将其翻译为“성청（省廳）”，并在注释中予以解释。

1 参见 https://www.zdic.net/hans/%E8%97%A9%E5%8F%B8 汉典 - 藩司（访问日期：2023-3-20）

4.4 沟通读者类注释

沟通读者类注释是指译者基于意图，对自己译文中的不足或翻译时的感悟向读者沟通说明，样本中沟通读者类“译者主体型”注释2个，主要是对词、曲、诗等的注释，举例如下：

> **原文**：仙仙乎，而还乎，而幽我于广寒乎！（《崂山道士》）
>
> **白话文**：轻盈起舞呀！你快回来呀！你为什么幽闭我在广寒宫里呀！
>
> **原文注释**：仙仙：轻盈起舞的样子。《诗·小雅·宾之初筵》：“屡舞仙仙。”幽：幽禁。广寒：月宫名。旧题汉郭宪《洞冥记》：“冬至后月养魄于广寒宫。”
>
> **译文**：춤을 추네 춤을 추네
> 인간세의 춤을 추냐
> 아니면 갇혀있는 광한궁의 춤을 추냐！
>
> **译文注释**：이 노래는 달속에서 날아오는 상아가 벽에 붙은 달을 보고 인간이 만든것인지，아니면 하늘에 실제로 있는것인지 분간할수 없다는 뜻에서 부른 것이다.

该曲出自《聊斋志异·崂山道士篇》，是被王生师父用法术召唤来的嫦娥在跳完《霓裳羽衣舞》之后唱起的歌，译者基于自我意图，在注释中对译文加以补充说明，指出“这首歌是月宫嫦娥看着墙上的月亮，无法分辨是人类制作的，还是天空中实际存在的”，起到沟通读者的功能。

5. 结语

基于对黑龙江朝鲜民族出版社出版发行、朝鲜族“学者型”译者朴正阳和李光在教授翻译的民族语朝鲜语版《聊斋志异·第一卷》注释的定量统计、底本比较、定性分析，发现《聊斋志异》民族语合译本的注释可区分为翻译型注释和译者主体型注释两类，按照注释功能对其进一步考察后发现不同功能的注释中，知识型内容的语义疏通和文化内容阐释型注释占绝大多数，由此可见译者在翻译时将译文的文义畅通置于首位，并“深度”拓展读者的文化视野，为译文读者构建“深度”语境，帮助读者更好的理解作品。采取以注释补偿为主的深度翻译策略对典籍朝鲜语（韩语）翻译具有一定的借鉴意义，值得深入探究。

参考文献

[1] 胡作友，刘倩倩. 注释与源语文化的异域重构——以理雅各《论语》英译本为例 [J]. 重庆工商大学学报（社会科学版），2021（2）：124-135.

[2] 马瑞芳. 马瑞芳说聊斋 [M]. 北京：作家出版社，2007.

[3] 蒲松龄. 聊斋志异 [M]. 孙通海，于天池，译，于天池，注. 北京：中华书局，2015.

[4] 蒲松龄. 聊斋志异 [M]. 朴正阳，李光在，译. 黑龙江：黑龙江朝鲜民族出版社，2021.

[5] 宋华伟. 接受视野中的《聊斋志异》[D]. 济南：山东师范大学，2008.

[6] 孙雪瑛著. 聊斋志译：诠释学视阈下的聊斋志异翻译研究 [M]. 上海：上海三联书店，2016.

[7] 王晔.《聊斋志异》俄、英译本注释中的文化解读 [J]. 外语教学与研究，2018（5）：779-788.

[8] 王雪明，杨子. 典籍英译中深度翻译的类型与功能——以《中国翻译话语英译选集》（上）为例 [J]. 中国翻译，2012（3）：103-108.

[9] 吴冰，朱健平. 认同与异变：深度翻译在我国的接受研究 [J]. 语言与翻译，2018（3）：73-79.

[10] 于海鹏. 从文本注释到文化传播——由莫言短篇小说的日译本谈起 [J]. 浙江工商大学学报，2020（2）：11-20.

[11] 章方. 学者型译者在翻译中的跨角色互动 [J]. 北京邮电大学学报（社会科学版），2007（4）：59-64.

[12] 张璐. 注释作为典籍英译翻译补偿手段有效性的实证研究 [J]. 外语学刊，2020（4）：78-83.

[13] 郑志强. 屈原“左徒”、“三闾大夫”新诠 [J]. 中国文化研究，2011（3）：75-79.

[14] Appiah, K. A. Thick translation [A]. In Venuti, L. (ed.). The Translation Studies Reader [C]. London: Routledge, 2000.

七、口译中的合作

疫情下的同传译员合作

——基于远程会议平台的案例分析[1]

朱玉犇　北京外国语大学

摘　要：2020年初暴发的新冠病毒感染疫情推动了远程同传的大规模应用。在远程模式下，口译搭档常常分处不同的物理空间，这给团队成员的合作提出新的挑战。学界虽不乏针对远程口译的讨论，但聚焦口译员合作的著述尚不多见。本研究基于Sylvia Kalina提出的口译过程分析框架，运用文献法、问卷法和案例研究法，系统梳理传统会议口译下各个任务阶段的口译员合作主题、角色分工及合作收益，并与远程模式下的口译员合作进行对比分析。研究发现，远程同传下的口译员合作在角色分工、合作主题和合作收益等方面都发生了较大改变。具体而言，受技术因素影响，口译员传统角色分工被打破，导致整体合作努力变少，合作收益降低；合作主题由过去的偏重信息抓取，转向偏重交接棒管理；合作手段更具干扰性，且无法做到准确及时，导致更多精力消耗；不同语种间的沟通机会降低，团队无法有效建立默契关系，未来合作的可持续性受到威胁。在此基础上，本研究对远程口译兴起后的会议口译实践、教学及研究提出相关建议。

关键词：远程同传；团队合作；相同空间；新冠病毒感染疫情；中国

1　原文发表于：Zhu Y., Exploring booth-mates' teamwork in the time of a pandemic: A case study, *Across Languages and Cultures*, 2022, 23(2): 206-225。本文在原文基础上略有改动。笔者对参与问卷调查的140名会议口译员表示感谢。承蒙北京外国语大学高级翻译学院任文教授审读并提出意见，特此感谢！

Exploring booth-mates' teamwork in the time of a pandemic: A case study

Zhu Yuben
Beijing Foreign Studies University

Abstract: Co-location is a crucial precondition for simultaneous interpreters' teamwork. However, it is becoming increasingly difficult to secure amid the COVID-19 pandemic, as conference interpreters across the world are forced to embrace distance interpreting due to anti-covid public health measures. This article aims to examine how the pandemic's disruption to co-location has changed interpreters' teamwork and to what effects. Drawing on the analysis framework of Pre-process, Peri-process, In-process, and Post-process proposed by Sylvia Kalina, the study explores the changing reality in China by combining micro-macro analysis of one case study and a survey involving 136 conference interpreters in the country. Results show that the pandemic has unleashed unprecedented disruption to interpreters' teamwork in spite of their proactive efforts to maintain it. More specifically, a new teamwork pattern featuring major shifts in collaboration themes, division of roles, and fewer benefits is emerging. Findings from the research may shed light on the changing realities not only in China, but possibly in the wider world. Practical suggestions and future research needs are also identified.

Keywords: simultaneous interpreting; teamwork; co-location; COVID-19; China

1. 引言

同声传译要求口译员同步处理多个任务，因此被视为一项具有认知挑战性的工作（Gile，2007）。为缓解疲劳，同传团队通常由至少两人组成，成员间彼此帮助（AIIC，2016a）。例如，被动译员（指正处于休息间歇的口译员）需要随时关注主动译员（指正处于工作状态的口译员）是否遭遇困难，并在必要时伸出援手，帮对方记录数字、查找术语或寻找文件等。主动译员也可以通过眼神、声音或其他肢体语言主动向被动译员寻求帮助。

值得注意的是，此类合作的顺利开展需要口译员同处一个空间。然而疫情之下，这一前提条件时常无法满足。为反映新的职业现实，AIIC（2020a）对后疫情时代的会议口译实践做了新的分类。根据发言人和口译员的相对位置不同，这四种情景分别是：1）口译员与部分参会者在一起，剩余参会者远程参会；2）不同语种的口译员全部在一起，参会者全部远程参会；3）同一语种口译员在一起，但其他语种口译员远程参会；4）口译员各自远程参会，但能够与搭档远程交流。新模式对口译团队合作产生的影响不一，其中第 4 种情景被视为只应在极端情况下采用（AIIC，2020b）。然而，在部分地区，第 4 种情景似乎正在成为疫情下的职业常态，而以往文献对远程口译中的合作探讨并不充分。鉴于此，本文将运用文献法、问卷法和案例研究法，系统梳理传统会议口译各阶段的合作主题、角色分工及合作收益，并与远程会议中的口译员合作情况进行对比分析。在此基础上，本研究对远程口译兴起后的会议口译实践、教学及研究提出相关建议。

2. 文献综述和分析框架

全球首例远程口译实验发生在 20 世纪 70 年代，而涉及同传模式的远程口译实验则开展于 20 世纪 90 年代（Amato *et al.*，2018：40）。早期远程口译研究侧重于其技术可行性（Symphonie Experiment Study Group，1978；Mouzourakis，1996），直到近年来人们才逐渐将目光转向口译员本身，从人体工程学、心理学、口译产品和表现等不同视角对远程同传下的口译员进行了多维度描写（Kurz，2002；Mouzourakis，2003；Moser-Mercer，2005；Braun，2006；Roziner & Shlesinger，2010；Braun，2016；Wang，2018；Seeber *et al.*，2019）。总体而言，过往文献对团队合作的关注比较有限，究其原因或许是以往远程同传模式下，口译员仍能够拥有同处空间，远程会议模式对口译员内部合作影响较小。而新冠疫情的暴发打破了这一局面，给团队合作带来新的不确定性。根据 AIIC 的一份报告，第 4 种情景甚至会导致“零团队合作”（AIIC，2020c）；鉴于团队合作对会议口译至关重要，有学者指出居家办公恐将重新定义会议口译。口译用户有必要了解不同类型的口译活动存在的现实问题（Ghinos，2020)。然而，任何用户教育都需要证据支持，否则只能事倍功半。目前，学界尚未对此话题开展充分的针对性研究。已有的少量研究仅关注了口译任务进行阶段的口译员团队合作，而现实中口译员在会议开始之前以及结束后都会开展合作。在此背景下，本研究试图厘清新冠病毒感染疫情下口译员团队合作模式的新变化，为学界提供有益参考。为方便对照疫情前后变化，本文参考 Kalina（2002）的口译过程分析框架，将整个口译过程分为四个阶段：任务前期（Pre-process）、任务临近（Peri-process）、任务中（In-process）和任务后（Post-process），采用文献法对疫情前的会议口译实践进行系统性回顾。

口译员的团队合作在任务前期就已经开始（杨柳燕等，2014）。例如，为避免重复劳动，口译组长会代表全体口译员向主办方索要会议资料（AIIC，2003）。Han（2015）通过对中国会议口译员的问卷调查发现，许多会议材料，特别是对口译工作较为有用的材料通常会在任务临近甚至任务中才提供给口译员。这意味着许多准备工作需要在“任务临近”阶段开展。迫于时间压力，口译员可能会将材料做内部分工，分头准备不同的发言内容（鲍刚，2005：326）。任务开始前，组员之间还要商定工作次序，工作时长以及交接棒程序等问题（Chmiel，2008）。如果涉及多语同传，不同语种间也会相互配合。例如，主办方可能临时向其中一组译员提供发言手稿，其他语种的口译员会通过对手稿拍照等方式获得副本，以便熟悉内容。

相较于“任务前期”和“任务临近”阶段，学界对“任务中”合作的关注明显更多。对同传译员而言，坐在身旁的搭档可以帮助记录数字等易丢失的信息，其重要性不言而喻（Jones，2002：119；Gile，2009：202）。以书面形式提供帮助似乎是最受欢迎的方法，因为其干扰性较小（Jensen，2006；Albl-Mikasa，2012；刘德周，2019）。此外，被动译员还可以帮助查找文件、查阅词汇，并监控主动译员的麦克风和输出频道（鲍刚，2005：317；仲伟合、詹成，2009：88）。如遇突发状况，成员之间还会相互救急（刘德周，2019），该做法已被纳入 ISO/FDIS 23155 标准（Ghinos，2020）。

“任务中”合作的另一项内容是术语一致性（Jensen，2006）。如果口译员对同一主题使用不同术语，听众可能会误以为主题本身发生了变化（Jones，2002：86）。事实上，围绕一致性的合作并不局限于术语，还涉及一般性的应对策略。例如，在笔者参与的一次任务中，口译组长在开始时选错了输出频道。到交接棒时，组长迅速向笔者说明情况，两人决定将错就错，沿用这一频道设置，这是因为此时听众已经熟悉了现有的频道安排，再去调整可能引发不必要的混乱。

与“任务中”合作相比，关于“任务后”合作的论述并不多见。Albl-Mikasa（2012）通过对 10 名德国专业口译员的访谈发现，口译员会在任务后做相互反馈和集体反思。据笔者观察，这一操作并不仅限于德国市场，许多口译员都会在任务后进行反思性交谈，有些甚至会对照彼此的口译笔记，更新词汇表并相互分享。口译能力的提升离不开大量的刻意练习,而“信息反馈”是刻意练习的重要前提（Shreve,2006）。因此，“任务后”的反思性交谈无疑有助于提高团队成员的口译表现，同时增进感情，为未来合作奠定基础。

由此可见，传统会议口译的团队合作贯穿任务全程，角色分工明确，合作主题多元，口译员可以从合作中获得诸多收益（见表 1，圆括号中的内容代表不同任务阶段隐含在主要角色关系下的次要角色关系）。

表 1　传统会议口译模式下的译员合作

任务阶段	合作主题	角色分工	合作收益
任务前期	获取材料； 确保工作条件	组长与组员	效率
任务临近	获取材料； 准备工作	平等伙伴 （组长与组员）	效率
任务中	信息保存； 处理突发事件； 监控设备； 管理交接棒； 保持一致性	主动与被动 （组长与组员）	干扰低； 响应迅速； 节约精力
任务后	反思	平等伙伴 （组长与组员）	附带学习； 增进感情

综上所述，过往文献主要论及传统口译环境中的团队合作，缺乏针对远程模式的深入探讨。本研究对中国市场 136 名会议口译员开展了问卷调查，在此基础上结合一项真实远程口译任务的案例分析，从宏观和微观双重维度深入剖析新冠病毒感染疫情下的口译员合作。具体而言，本研究尝试回答以下两个问题：

1）疫情之下，口译员的团队合作模式发生了哪些变化？

2）这种变化带来了哪些影响？

借助对此类问题的探究，笔者希望能够为用户教育、推广最佳行业实践以及后疫情时代的口译教学提供有益参考。

3. 研究方法

3.1 问卷调查

本节分别介绍笔者于 2021 年初开展的一项问卷调查，以及于 2021 年 6 月参与完成的一次远程口译任务。

本研究中的问卷调查采用方便抽样和滚雪球抽样法（Hale & Napier, 2013）。笔者首先通过微信将电子问卷发送至一部分具备丰富经验的会议口译员，再由他们转发给自己结识的有经验的口译员。为确保调查对象了解疫情前后的不同口译实践情况，问卷要求口译员具备至少两年的工作经验。数据收集于 2021 年 1 月至 3 月期间完成。最终共有 140 名口译员完成了问卷填写，其中有 4 人因数据不符合问卷要求被剔除，最终有效人数 136 人，包含男性 50 人，占比 36.8%；女性 86 人，占比 63.2%。会议口译从业时间为 2—5 年的 28 人，占比 20.6%；5—10 年的 47 人，占比 34.6%；10 年以上的 61 人，占比 44.8%。

问卷内容主要包含李克特 5 级量表、单选题、多选题和部分开放式问题，以便受访者就特定主题交流想法。本研究仅节选了问卷中与团队合作直接相关的题目数据（见附录第Ⅱ部分）。

3.2 案例研究

3.2.1 背景信息

在回答“自新冠疫情以来，您在哪些会议平台上做过口译（交传或同声传译）”的问题时，超过 90% 的受访者选择了 Zoom，可见 Zoom 是目前中国使用最广泛的远程国际会议平台（见图 1）。本案例中的口译任务正是在 Zoom 上完成的，因此具有较强的代表性。本次口译任务涉及三组口译员（包括 2 名中文—英文口译员、1 名韩语—英文口译员和 2 名日语—英文口译员），三组译员共同为一家跨国软件公司（以下简称“公司”）组织的网络会议提供同传服务。会议总长 90 分钟。会议开始时公司代表首先结合 PowerPoint 做了发言，之后与亚太地区的合作伙伴进行问答。会议的工作语言为英语，同传服务的对象是来自中国、日本和韩国的参会者。

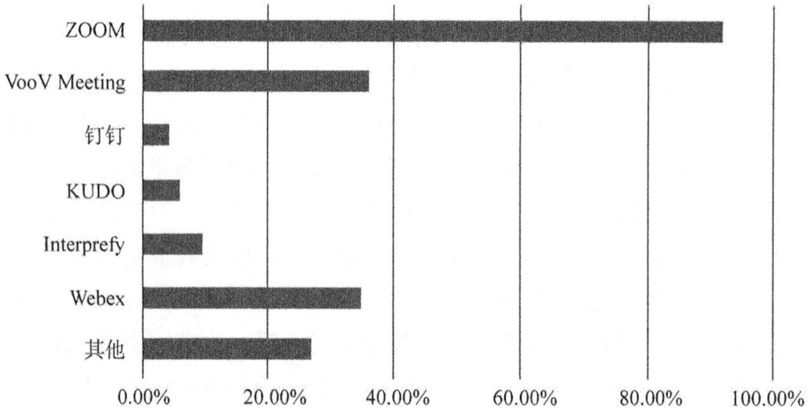

图 1　中国广泛使用的远程国际会议平台的问卷调查情况

笔者和搭档各自居家办公，通过 Zoom 聊天功能和微信保持沟通，符合上文描述的第 4 种情景；日语口译员在一起线下工作，符合第 3 种情景；韩语口译员独自一人工作，因此她的工作条件与 AIIC 提出的四类情景均不相符（见第 1 节）。

3.2.2 数据收集与编码

会议原始数据由录屏软件抓取。为监听彼此的口译输出，笔者与搭档全程保持微信语音通话，并用录音笔记录双方全部口译输出。此外，译员之间的微信信息和 Zoom 会议屏幕截图也被转录以供分析。数据通过定性数据分析软件 NVivo 11 进行编码和分类。本研究采用了演绎法（预设编码方案），即依照表 1 中已经列明的合作主题，对数据中出现的合作行为进行归类。为简洁起见，笔者采用英文缩写指代不同合作主题（缩写表见附录第 I 部分）。例如，2021 年 6 月 15 日的微信交流文字的编码过程示例如下（数据已做匿名化处理）：

CN°-1：6.27，跟上次 XYZ 一样，12：30-13：30，可能只需要干到 13：00。有空吗？
CN°-2：是个周日，没问题，感谢队长。

在上述的简短交流中，口译组长在任务开始的 9 天前向搭档介绍了任务时长、工作方式、薪酬和工作条件等信息。CN°-2 称 CN°-1 为队长，以明确双方在这一阶段的关系性质是组长与组员。由此，双方成功确立分工，CN°-1 将代表两人向客户索取材料。在 NVivo 11 中，这段文本数据被归入子节点 Cond-Pre（协商工作条件–任务前期）和 Matl-Pre（索要材料–任务前期），放在主题节点 Pre-process（任务前期）之下。编码完成后，每个主题节点下的合作尝试次数可通过其节点计数统计显示。

4. 分析结果与讨论

根据编码结果，共确定了 21 次成功或失败的合作尝试（见表 2）。

表 2　案例中识别的团队合作尝试

合作主题	尝试次数	百分比 (%)
Pre-process	—	—
Cond-Pre	1	—
Matl-Pre	1	—
小计	2	9.5

（待续）

（续表）

合作主题	尝试次数	百分比 (%)
Peri-process	—	—
Cond-Peri	1	—
Matl-Peri	1	—
Prep-Peri	3	—
小计	5	23.8
In-process	—	—
Equip-In	7	—
Cont-In	0	—
H/O-In	5	—
Cns-In	0	—
Info-In	1	—
小计	13	61.9
Post-process	—	—
Rapp-Post	0	—
Rflt-Post	1	—
小计	1	4.8
总计	21	100

初步统计显示，有 61.9% 的团队合作发生在“任务中”阶段，这一结果也解释了过往文献对此阶段合作的更多关注。令人惊讶的是，设备监控和交接棒管理成为最突出的两大合作主题，合计占总尝试次数的一半以上，这与以往文献的研究结论似乎有些矛盾。以往文献认为与信息相关的协助（如记录数字、查找术语和文件等）最为突出（Chmiel, 2008）。下文将具体讨论这一变化的成因。

4.1 任务前期团队合作

分析表明，远程口译破坏了传统的角色分工。如前所述，任务前期中的团队合作主要围绕获取材料和协商工作条件展开。本案例中，主办方直到任务前夕才提供相关材料，这与前人研究结果相吻合（Han, 2015）。在向 CN°-2 转发材料时，CN°-1 解释道，与该公司举办的以往活动不同，此次任务将涉及四种语言，包括中文、英文、日文和韩文。但主办方已向他明确说明，在问答环节，非英语国家的参会者都将在 Zoom 聊天框中用英文提问，因此各语种口译员全程只需要负责将英译译回自己的母语，任务不涉及接力同传（见图 2）。

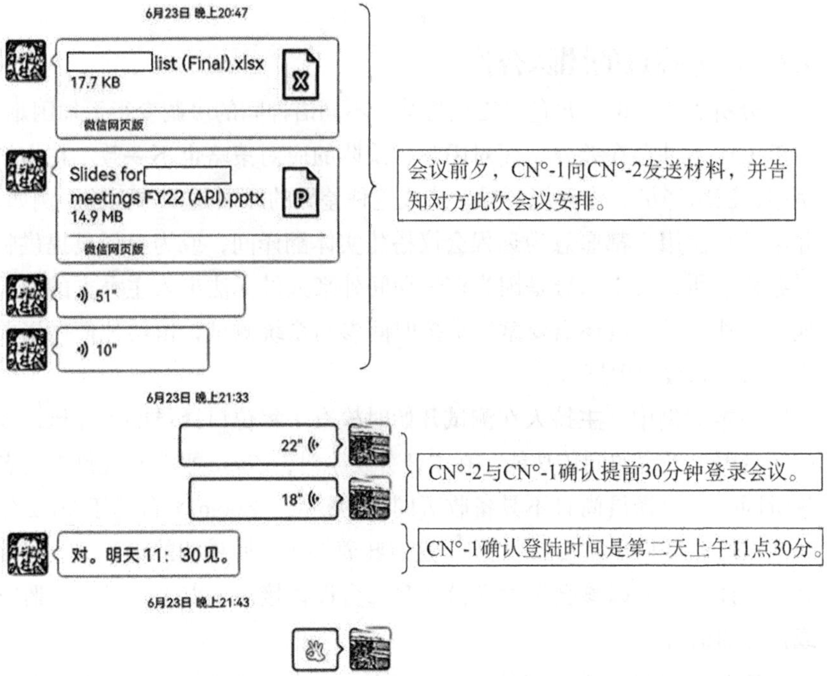

图 2　任务前夕中文口译员之间的微信交流

通常情况下，如果一场会议涉及多名口译员，客户会倾向于委托一名口译组长负责组建整个口译团队并负责总体协调。在本案例中，日语组和韩语组由主办方单独招募，这种新的聘用模式在后疫情时代绝非孤例。受疫情影响，不同地区的参会者可能会出于各种考虑从当地招聘口译员。例如，出于保密需要，参会者可能会在会议期间将手稿借给口译员参考，待会议结束后再收回。远程会议则不具备这样的便利，这导致参会者不得不在保密性和口译效果之间做取舍。部分参会者会选择从本地招聘口译员，共同远程参会，以兼顾以上两种需求，这一趋势也在问卷调查结果中得到印证。调查结果显示，自疫情以来，近 60% 的受访者有过与异地译员远程合作的经历，传统角色分工受到影响，给团队合作带来了许多挑战。具体而言，本任务中不是只有一名口译组长，而是三名，这直接导致三组译员之间缺乏沟通，中文组并不清楚日文组和韩文组是否也了解此次会议无须接力。下文将详细介绍这给合作带来的挑战。

4.2 任务临近的团队合作

分析表明，由于角色分工被打乱，不同语种间的协调变得更加困难。由于工作条件存在差异，面对困难各团队的应对策略也不一致。在本案例中，三组译员工作环境各异，造成这种差异的原因是多方面的。例如，并不是每位用户都愿意为远程会议搭建实体翻译间，或为口译员提供临时办公场所，其中部分是因为疫情期间外来人员无法出入主办方的办公地。此外，口译员还需要拿出更多时间参与系统测试，留给他们做译前准备的时间被大大挤占。

在本案例中，主持人在测试开始时检查了每位口译员的麦克风，随后便启用了平台的同传功能。在本任务发生时，Zoom 平台只允许参会者收听同传，口译员尚且不具备收听同传的权限（Zoom 平台已于 2022 年初推出口译员相互监听的功能），这意味着要想监听搭档的输出或进行接力，口译员需要以参会者的身份从第二台设备接入，点击自己想要监听或接力的语言。

KN° 提出自己听不到其他团队的声音，无法开展接力。这意味着韩语组事先并不清楚本场会议不需要接力的安排。主持人回应道如果有参会者使用非英语发言，她会收听对应语种的英语翻译，然后再以主持人的身份将英语译文复述，给所有译员听。CN°-1 则表示他此前获悉的任务说明是本场会议无须接力。此时，JP°-1 简单咨询了自己的同事，然后宣布日语组可以用第二台设备登录并收听其他语种输出，因此不需要主持人重复。这一提议获得了KN°的支持，但却遭到CN°-1和CN°-2的反对，因为二人居家办公，需要用第二台设备保持内部沟通和监听对方译文（见图3）。由此可见，即便为应对远程口译挑战做了积极准备，第4种情景中的口译员仍面临较大障碍。

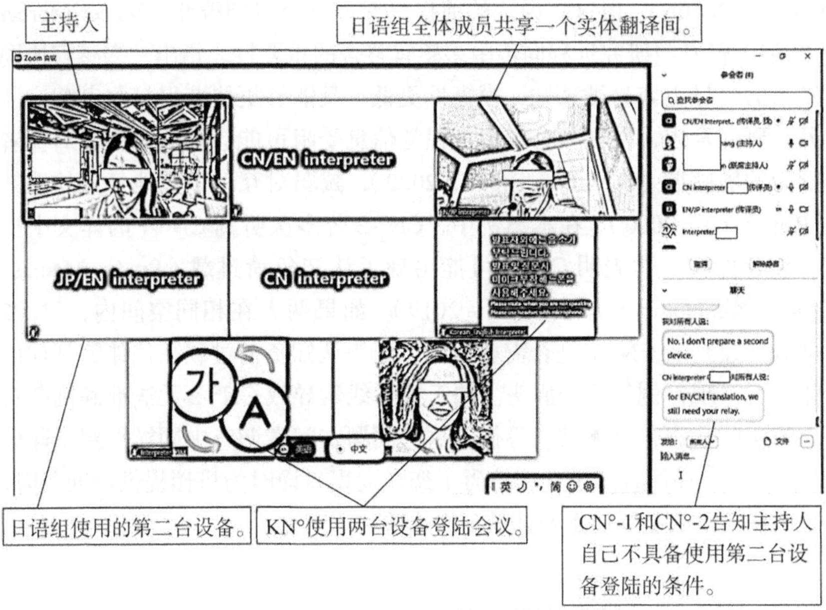

图3　口译员与主持人讨论接力安排

各方经过反复讨论，最终确定了以下解决方案：每当参会者用韩语或日语发言时，主持人将收听英语同传，暂停会议并向中文组译员复述英文，中文组再将主持人复述的英文翻译成中文；如果原始发言为中文，那么日语组和韩语组直接收听中文组的英文输出，做接力同传。整个系统测试完成后，留给口译员做最后准备的时间已经所剩无几。

会议开始前，CN°-1在微信上提醒CN°-2，目前的接力方案太过复杂，可能会对主持人和口译员造成困难，而后续发展的确如此。

4.3 任务中的团队合作

4.3.1 信息抓取

表 1 的统计结果显示，围绕信息抓取的团队合作大幅减少。第 4 种情景下的口译员很难准确识别搭档是否需要帮助。AIIC 在介绍会议口译员职场礼仪时指出，“口译员是否需要搭档帮助，通常是很容易看出来的”（AIIC，2016b），但这一说法的前提是双方可以看到彼此。Moser-Mercer（2005）曾专门研究远程同传中多感官整合的重要性，指出“多感官协同发出的信号更容易被感知，模糊性更低，且能够更快获得接收者响应”。另有研究发现，在视频会议中，视觉信息受阻可能会降低参会者对他者行为的敏感度（Davitti & Braun，2020），减弱对互动中其他各方的感知（Robertson，2000）。在本案例中，CN°-2 曾多次听到 CN°-1 的译文中出现较长停顿，这表明 CN°-1 可能出现了认知负荷过载（Pradas Macías，2006；Koutsombogera & Vogel，2019）。如果两人在相同空间内，CN°-2 可以迅速判断 CN°-1 是否需要帮助，因为认知负荷过载往往伴随其他肢体语言出现，例如紧皱眉头。缺乏视觉线索导致 CN°-2 无法准确判断对方的实际状态，只能被动等待。这一问题在问卷调查中同样得到了印证（见图 4），在回答“是什么妨碍了您在远程口译时为搭档提供帮助”时，缺乏视觉输入是受访者勾选最多的选项。

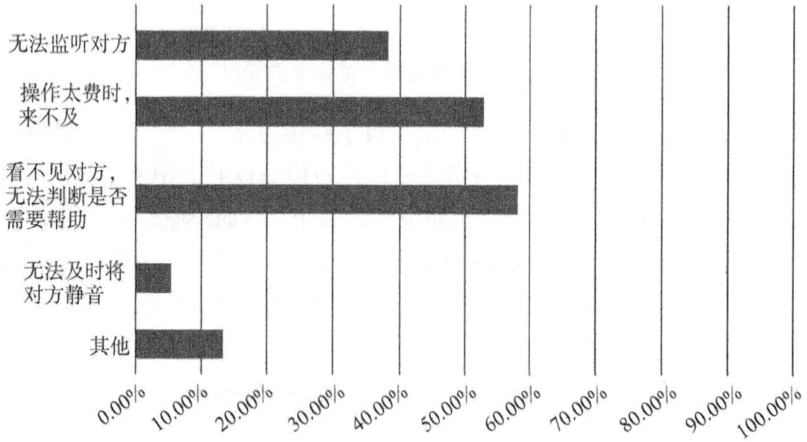

图 4 关于妨碍远程口译中为搭档提供帮助的问卷调查情况

值得注意的是，即使发现搭档遇到了困难，提供帮助的手段也更具侵扰性。在会议接近尾声时，CN°-2 突然收到 CN°-1 在 Zoom 聊天区发来的一条私聊信息（见图 5）。由于看不见对方，CN°-2 误以为这是 CN°-1 误操作，于是提醒对方他的信息发在了私聊窗口。但 CN°-1 并没有回应，而是继续发来了第二条信息，内容同样令 CN°-2 感到费解。直到会议结束 CN°-2 才明白，原来这些是韩国代表先前的提问，主持人已经把英语译文发给了 CN°-1，而 CN°-1 又试图将这些内容转发给正在口译的 CN°-2。这一系列操作不仅没有起到帮助作用，反而促使正在口译的 CN°-2 花费额外精力回复 CN°-1 的消息。

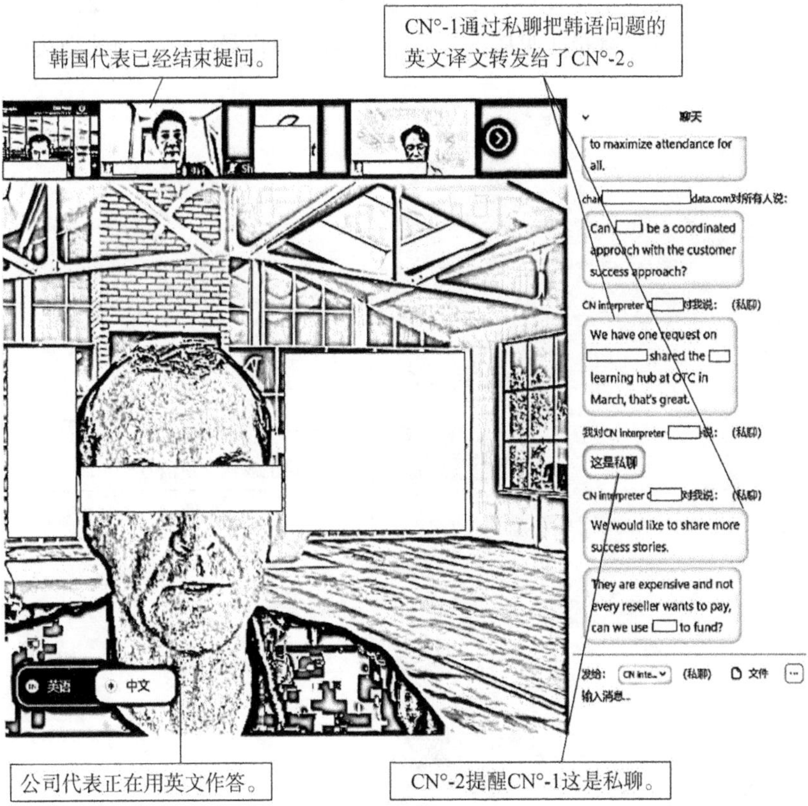

图 5 韩语问题信息输入不同步造成 CN°-2 理解混乱

远程口译中的团队合作效率也明显下降。在传统环境中，求助需求可以更迅速地被发送和被感知，远程会议则无法实现及时同步。如图5所示，CN°-2在收到CN°-1转来的问题时，公司发言人已经在对问题作答。两个信息输入不同步是造成CN°-2理解混乱的主要原因。即使CN°-2能准确判断出这是问题的英文译文，也早已错过了翻译问题的机会。

4.3.2 交接棒

远程会议中的交接棒管理需要消耗更多精力，也更容易出现失误。为了管理交接棒，中文组译员采用了一种临时办法，即被动译员在微信上发送1，提示主动译员自己已经做好准备；主动译员回复2，即表示同意交接给被动译员（见图6）。这种被国内口译员广泛采用的交接棒程

图6 交接棒前CN°-1和CN°-2在微信上互发信号确认

序有几大缺点。首先，口译员必须在临近交接棒时一边翻译，一边回复微信消息，消耗更多精力；其次，该做法打乱了正常的交接棒顺序。在传统的交接棒程序下，主动译员应当先关闭麦克风，然后接棒的被动译员再打开自己麦克风（AIIC，2016b）。主动译员通过关闭麦克风这一个动作，即表示了自己同意交接，也顺势完成了交接，可谓一举两得，非常高效。而在本案例中，交接棒的授权信号和麦克风关闭操作是分开的，增加了交接棒的失误概率。例如，在其中一次交棒给 CN°-1 后，CN°-2 忘记在 Zoom 上将自己静音，直到下一次接棒时才发现自己的失误。

4.3.3 监测设备

在远程会议中，监控搭档设备变得更加困难。目前，Zoom 上的口译员麦克风图标不显示信号强度变化，只显示是否静音。由于许多口译员使用的耳麦都带有线控功能，Zoom 上的麦克风图标被激活并不代表线控也是开启状态。在本案例中，被动译员可以通过微信通话监控搭档的输出，也可以在 Zoom 上查看对方的麦克风图标是否已解除静音，但却无法确定对方的线控是否已经打开。根据表 2，设备监控占据了"任务中合作"尝试的较大比例。这是因为每当有语种切换时，被动译员就必须刻意检查搭档的输出频道是否正确。在传统模式下，口译输出频道的切换可以被多感官即时感知，如口译员伸手触摸控制台旋钮、按钮被按下的声音、控制台上的频道占用指示灯切换等。而在 Zoom 平台上，被动译员必须退出全屏，转到参会者列表，特意查看搭档的图标状态才能确认对方的频道设置。

4.3.4 应急处置

自新冠疫情以来，围绕处理突发状况的团队合作大幅增加。问卷调查显示，近 70% 的受访者在远程口译中曾遇到因网络连接不畅导致的突发状况（见图 7）。在本案例中，CN°-2 在任务临近阶段的系统测试时短暂掉线，CN°-2 随即与 CN°-1 商定，在接下来的会议中一旦发生掉线情况，应立即在微信上告知对方。

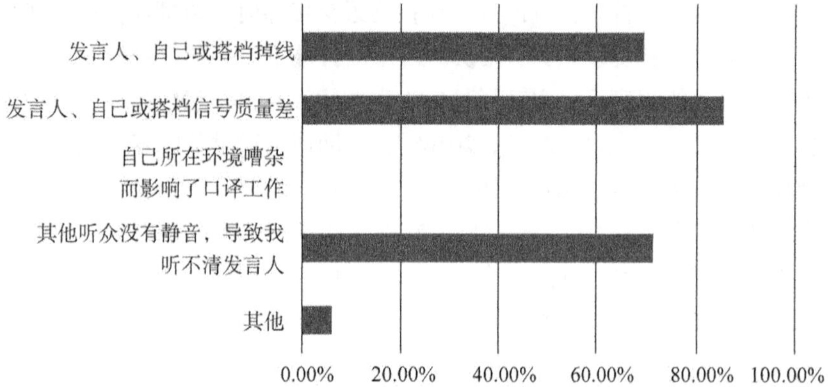

图 7　远程模式下网络连接引发的问题情况

4.3.5　保持一致性

虽然术语一致性没有受到太大影响，但由于缺乏沟通，口译员在应对策略协调方面遇到了挑战。如前文所述，主持人在会议开始前承诺每当有韩语或日语发言时，会暂停讨论并向中文组复述英语译文。但这一承诺在后来的会议中并未兑现。会议开始时，所有参会者被邀请做简短的自我介绍。轮到韩国和日本嘉宾发言时，主持人并没有向中文组转述英语翻译，正在翻译的 CN°-1 迅速决定借助事先获取的演讲者简历做总结性介绍，以保障会议的顺利进行，对此中文听众并未察觉任何异常。然而，在问答环节，这一策略便不再可行。当其中一位韩国参会者发言时，CN°-2 直接向听众解释道主持人稍后会用英语转述韩国代表的问题，请大家稍候。但主持人似乎已经忘记了先前的约定。出于自我保护（Monacelli，2009），CN°-2 需要向听众表示自己并未收到主持人转述的问题，所以只能直接翻译公司代表对该问题的回答。这一情况在会议期间数次上演，影响了中文听众的整体体验。

4.4　任务后的团队合作

围绕联络感情的合作同样受到严重影响。会后，CN°-1 和 CN°-2 对会议过程中的挑战进行了反思。他们终于有机会解开私聊信息的谜团。CN°-1 解释说自己原本可以在转发信息时说明信息的用途，但那样耗时太长，可能会导致 CN°-2 失去翻译的机会。两人对三个口译小组之间缺乏协调表示遗憾。由于平台会议室很快便被主持人关闭，口译成员没有任何机会建立联系，未来合作的可能性大大降低。

4.5 团队合作新模式

案例分析指向一种新的团队合作模式（见表 3）。就合作主题而言，口译员在协商工作条件、处理突发状况和管理交接棒方面花费了更多精力（用“+”表示）。在信息抓取、设备监测和保持一致性方面所做的努力较少（用“–”表示）。对其他主题的努力基本保持不变（用“≈”表示）。

围绕角色分工的合作发生两大变化。在任务前期和任务后，角色分工的清晰度下降（用“–”表示），这主要归因于多个小组负责人的出现。此外，受技术因素影响，主动译员和被动译员的角色划分变得更加泾渭分明（用“+”表示），即主动译员不得不更加主动，而被动口员则变得更加被动。

总体而言，团队合作产生的收益明显减少。口译员缺乏迅速有效的互助手段，提供和接受帮助的过程更加耗时耗力，不同团队之间建立融洽关系更加困难。

表 3　远程会议口译的团队合作新模式

任务阶段	任务主题	角色分工	合作收益
任务前期	获取材料 ≈ 确保工作条件 +	组长与组员 –	效率 –
任务临近	获取材料 ≈ 准备工作 ≈	平等伙伴 （组长与组员 –）	效率 ≈
任务中	信息抓取 – 处理突发状况 + 监测设备 + 管理交接棒 + 保持一致性 –	主动与被动 + （组长与组员）	干扰低 – 相应迅速 – 节约精力 –
任务后	反思 ≈	平等伙伴 （组长与组员）	附带学习 ≈ 增进感情 –

新的工作模式意味着后疫情时代的口译培训和口译实践需要做出相应调整。团队合作一直被视为口译培训的重要内容（Gile，2009：44；Setton & Dawrant，2016：309）。虽然休息时的口译员不一定总会留在翻译间内随时待命（Jalón，2004：158），但业界的共识是被动译员应随时准备在对方需要时提供帮助。未来的毕业生应具备与远程会议相关的情景意识，以应对新兴模式带来的诸多挑战。此外，不同利益攸关方之间需要建立共识，以确保口译员获得包括实体翻译间在内的适当工作条件。目前，我国仍然缺乏有关工作条件的标准。由于此前远程口译采纳程度较低，最新的行业准则（中国翻译协会，2019）也并未包含远程口译。国内外现行的诸多行业准则虽然要求口译员拒绝接受工作条件不利的任务（任文、殷明月，2020），但考虑疫情的冲击，口译员的工作机会已经大幅减少。在新的共识产生之前，拒绝所有不符合传统会议工作条件的口译任务近乎是一种奢望。鉴于此，行业协会或可在维护口译员正当权益方面发挥更大作用。此外，口译用户应当尽可能从同一地区招聘口译员，以提高口译员空间共享的可能性；同时应当尽量避免通过平台招聘口译员，因为后者更倾向于雇用来自不同地区的口译员。

值得注意的是，任何形式的远程口译都会给口译员带来额外负担，因此总体上绝非最佳选择（Moser-Mercer，2003）。新冠疫情在加速技术应用的同时也放大了与技术相关的挑战。本案例揭示出的诸多问题并不限于 Zoom 平台，其他具备增强功能（如允许口译员监控搭档的输出或有技术人员全程在线提供支持）的平台仍无法摆脱缺乏视觉信息和高干扰等弊病。即使口译员可以借助摄像头看到搭档，平台的人体工学设计以及虚拟和物理空间之间的频繁切换也会使口译员丧失临场感（Moser-Mercer，2005；Davitti & Braun，2020），妨碍团队合作。因此，第 1、2、3 种情景远非理想之选。我们希望随着技术进步，这些挑战能够在未来逐步得到解决。

5. 结论

新冠疫情的暴发给会议口译造成巨大冲击。本文聚焦其对口译团队合作产生的影响。案例研究和问卷调查相结合使本研究得以综合微观、宏观两种视角，使分析更加细致深入，且兼具代表性。研究结果表明，尽管口译员在积极克服外在限制，其合作仍然受到负面影响。一种新的团队合作模式正在涌现，合作主题和合作效果较传统模式都发生较大变化。口译行业和口译培养单位都需要适应不断变化的新环境。

需要指出的是，影响口译团队合作的因素是多元的，并非所有错失的合作机会都可以直接归咎于技术或远程会议模式。考虑到技术带来的好处，本研究认为我们不应完全否定技术，但有必要通过实证研究揭示技术对口译活动的复杂影响。笔者希望本研究能激发更多学者对该问题的关注，以充分评估疫情对口译职业产生的深远影响。

参考文献

[1] 鲍刚. 口译理论概述 [M]. 北京：中国对外翻译出版有限公司，2005.

[2] 刘德周. 同传译员口译任务的分工与合作 [J]. 中国科技翻译，2019（3）：16-18.

[3] 杨柳燕，苏伟，戴炜栋. 口译教程：学生用书 [M]. 上海：上海外语教育出版社，2014.

[4] 中国翻译协会. 中国职业译员道德规范 [S/OL]. 2019. [2022-4-1]. http://www.tac-online.org.cn/uploadfile/2019/0929/20190929041750755.pdf

[5] 仲伟合，詹成. 同声传译 [M]. 北京：外语教学与研究出版社，2009.

[6] AIIC (International Association of Conference Interpreters). Practical guide for professional conference interpreters [S/OL]. 2003. [2021-8-4]. https://aiic.org/document/547/AIICWebzine_Apr2004_2_Practical_guide_for_professional_conference_interpreters_EN.pdf.

[7] AIIC. AIIC professional standards [S/OL]. 2016a. [2021-9-4]. https://aiic.org/document/6304/Professional_standards_ENG.pdf.

[8] AIIC. Booth manners [S/OL]. 2016b. [2021-9-4]. https://aiic.org/document/561/AIICWebzine_JunJul2004_7_SANT’IAGO_RIBEIRO_Booth_manners_EN.pdf.

[9] AIIC. AIIC Covid-19 distance interpreting recommendations for institutions and DI hubs [S/OL]. 2020a. [2021-7-28]. https://aiic.org/document/4839/AIIC%20Recommendations%20for%20Institutions_27.03.2020.pdf.

[10] AIIC. Position paper [S/OL]. 2020b. [2021-7-21]. https://aiic.ch/wp-content/uploads/2020/04/aiic-un-sector-position-paper-15042020.pdf.

[11] AIIC. Reference guide to remote simultaneous interpreting [S/OL]. 2020c. [2021-7-15]. https://aiic.ch/wp-content/uploads/2020/05/aiic-ch-reference-guide-to-rsi.pdf.

[12] Albl-Mikasa, M. The importance of being not too earnest: A process- and experience-based model of interpreter competence [A]. In Ahrens, B., Albl-Mikasa, M. & Sasse, C. (eds.). Dolmetschqualität in Praxis, Lehre und Forschung. Festschrift für Sylvia Kalina [C]. Tübingen: Narr, 2012.

[13] Amato, A., Bertozzi, M., Braun, S., *et al.* Handbook of remote interpreting-SHIFT in orality [M]. 2018. https://doi.org/10.6092/unibo/amsacta/5955

[14] Braun, S. Multimedia communication technologies and their impact on interpreting [A/OL]. In Carroll, M., Gerzymisch-Arbogast, H. & Nauert, S. (eds.). Proceedings of the Marie Curie Euroconferences MuTra: Audiovisual Translation Scenarios Copenhagen, 2006. [2022-3-30]. https://www.euroconferences.info/proceedings/2006_Proceedings/2006_Braun_Sabine.pdf.

[15] Braun, S. The European AVIDICUS projects: Collaborating to assess the viability of video-mediated interpreting in legal proceedings [J/OL]. European Journal of Applied Linguistics, 2016(1): 173-180. https://doi.org/10.1515/eujal-2016-0002

[16] Chmiel, A. Boothmates forever?-On teamwork in a simultaneous interpreting booth [J/OL]. Across languages and Cultures, 2008(2): 261-276. https://doi.org/10.1556/Acr.9.2008.2.6

[17] Davitti, E., & Braun, S. Analysing interactional phenomena in video remote interpreting in collaborative settings: Implications for interpreter education [J/OL]. The Interpreter and Translator Trainer, 2020(3): 279-302. https://doi.org/10.1080/1750399X.2020.1800364

[18] Ghinos, H. An incomplete account of the thoughts expressed last Saturday on distance conference interpreting [OL]. 2020. [2022-5-1]. https://aiic.ch/wp-content/uploads/2020/04/thoughts-on-di-040420-tfdi-aiic-canada.pdf.

[19] Gile, D. Testing the effort models' tightrope hypothesis in simultaneous interpreting — A contribution [J/OL]. Hermes, 2007(23): 153-72. https://doi.org/10.7146/hjlcb.v12i23.25553

[20] Gile, D. Basic concepts and models for interpreter and translator training [M]. Amsterdam: John Benjamins, 2009.

[21] Hale, S. & Napier, J. Research Methods in Interpreting: A Practical Resource [M]. London: Bloomsbury Academic, 2013.

[22] Han, C. Lacunae, myths and legends about conference interpreters: A diary study to explore conference interpreting practice in China [J/OL]. Perspectives, 2015(3): 440-457. https://doi.org/10.1075/intp.18.2.05han

[23] Jalón, J. B. Interpreters at the United Nations: A history [M]. Salamanca: Universidad de Salamanca, 2004.

[24] Jensen, J. B. The strategic partnership in the conference interpreting booth [A/OL]. In Annual Meeting of the American Translators Association [C]. 2006. [2021-9-10]. https://docest.com/the-strategic-partnership-in-the-conference-interpreting-booth.

[25] Jones, R. Conference Interpreting Explained (2nd Ed.)[M]. New York: Routledge, 2002.

[26] Kalina, S. Quality in interpreting and its prerequisites: A framework for a comprehensive view[A]. In Garzone, G. & Viezzi, M. Interpreting in the 21st Century [M], Amsterdam: John Benjamins, 2002.

[27] Koutsombogera, M. & Vogel, C. Speech pause patterns in collaborative dialogs [A]. In Esposito, A., Esposito, A. M. & Jain, L. C. (eds.). Innovations in Big Data Mining and Embedded Knowledge [M]. Berlin: Springer, 2019.

[28] Kurz, I. Physiological stress responses during media and conference interpreting [A]. In Garzone, G. & Viezzi, M. (eds.). Interpreting in the 21st Century [M]. Amsterdam: John Benjamins, 2002.

[29] Monacelli, C. Self-preservation in Simultaneous Interpreting[M]. Amsterdam: John Benjamins, 2009.

[30] Moser-Mercer, B. Remote interpreting: Assessment of human factors and performance parameters [OL]. The AIIC webzine. 2003. [2021-9-10]. https://aiic.org/document/516/AIICWebzine_Summer2003_3_MOSER-MERCER_Remote_interpreting_Assessment_of_human_factors_and_performance_parameters_Original.pdf.

[31] Moser-Mercer, B. Remote interpreting: Issues of multi-sensory integration in a multilingual task [J/OL]. Meta: Translators' Journal, 2005(2): 727-738. https://doi.org/10.7202/011014ar

[32] Mouzourakis, P. Videoconferencing: Techniques and challenges [J/OL]. Interpreting, 1996(1): 21-38. https://doi.org/10.1075/intp.1.1.03mou

[33] Mouzourakis, P. That feeling of being there: vision and presence in remote interpreting. The AIIC webzine [OL]. 2003. [2021-11-13]. http://www.aiic.net/ViewPage.cfm/page1173.

[34] Pradas Macías, P. Probing quality criteria in simultaneous interpreting: The role of silent pauses in fluency [J/OL]. Interpreting, 2006(1): 25-43. https://doi.org/10.1075/intp.8.1.03pra

[35] Ren, W., & Yin, M. Conference interpreter ethics [A]. InKoskinen, K. & Pokorn, N. K. (eds.). The Routledge Handbook of translation And Ethics [M]. New York: Routledge, 2020.

[36 Robertson, T. Building bridges: Negotiating the gap between work practice and technology design [J/OL]. International Journal of Human-Computer Studies, 2000(1): 121-146. https://doi.org/10.1006/ijhc.2000.0373

[37] Roziner, I. & Shlesinger, M. Much ado about something remote: Stress and performance in remote interpreting [J/OL]. Interpreting, 2010(2): 214-247. https://doi.org/10.1075/intp.12.2.05roz

[38] Seeber, K. G., Keller, L., Amos, R. & Hengl, S. Expectations vs. experience: Attitudes towards video remote conference interpreting [J/OL]. Interpreting, 2019(2): 270-304. https://doi.org/10.1075/intp.00030.see

[39] Setton, R. & Dawrant, A. Conference Interpreting — A Trainer's Guide [M]. Amsterdam: John Benjamins. 2016.

[40] Shreve, G. M. The deliberate practice: Translation and expertise[J]. Journal of Translation Studies, 2006(1): 27-42.

[41] Symphonie Experiment Study Group. A UNESCO experiment [J/OL]. Journal of Communication, 1978(3): 149-156. https://doi.org/10.1111/j.1460-2466.1978.tb01642.x

[42] Wang, J. "Telephone interpreting should be used only as a last resort." Interpreters' perceptions of the suitability, remuneration and quality of telephone interpreting [J/OL]. Perspectives, 2018(1): 100-116. https://doi.org/100-116. 10.1080/0907676X.2017.1321025

附　录

第 I 部分：编码缩写表

缩写	指代内容
CN°-1	中文组组长
CN°-2	中文组组员（笔者）
JP°-1	日语组组长
KN°	韩语口译员
Matl-Pre	获取材料–任务前期
Cond-Pre	协商工作条件–任务前期
Matl-Peri	获取材料–任务临近
Prep-Peri	准备工作–任务临近
Cond-Peri	协商工作条件–任务临近
Info-In	信息抓取–任务中
Cont-In	处置突发状况–任务中
Equip-In	设备监控–任务中

（待续）

（续表）

缩写	指代内容
H/O-In	交接棒–任务中
Cns-In	一致性–任务中
Rflt-Post	反思–任务后
Rapp-Post	建立融洽关系–任务后

第Ⅱ部分：与本研究相关的问卷题目

2. 口译工作年限？

（1）1—2 年　（2）2—5 年　（3）5—10 年　（4）10 年以上

5. 第一次承担远程口译是在什么时候？

（1）2019 年之前　（2）2019 年至 2020 年之间

7. 过去一年，远程口译占您个人口译服务的比例大约是多少？（0—100%）

（1）0—10%　（2）10%—20%　（3）20%—30%　（4）30%—40%
（5）40%—50%　（6）50%—60%　（7）60%—70%　（8）70%—80%
（9）80%—90%　（10）90% 以上

8. 新冠疫情之前，远程口译占您个人口译服务的比例大约是多少？（0—100%）

（1）0—10%　（2）10%—20%　（3）20%—30%　（4）30%—40%
（5）40%—50%　（6）50%—60%　（7）60%—70%　（8）70%—80%
（9）80%—90%　（10）90% 以上

9. 您曾经在哪些会议平台上做过口译（包括交传和同传）？

（1）ZOOM　（2）腾讯会议　（3）钉钉　（4）KUDO
（5）Interprefy　（6）Webex　（7）其他（请注明）

19. 我曾经和身在其他城市的译员一起在线做过远程口译。

（1）总是　（2）经常　（3）偶尔　（4）极少
（5）从不

23. 远程口译需要译员拿出更多时间参与技术测试。
（1）是　　（2）否
29. 远程口译时，我遇到过以下问题（多选题）：
（1）发言者、搭档或自己断线
（2）音质不佳
（3）环境噪音
（4）参会者忘记静者导致干扰
（5）其他（请注明）
33. 远程同传时，我帮助搭档的积极性降低了（单选题）。
（1）非常同意　（2）同意　（3）不确定　（4）不同意
（5）非常不同意
34. 远程同传时，我并不期待搭档在休息时为我提供帮助（单选题）。
（1）非常同意　（2）同意　（3）不确定　（4）不同意
（5）非常不同意。
35. 远程同传时，我会使用第二台设备监听搭档的译文（单选题）。
（1）总是　（2）经常　（3）偶尔　（4）很少
（5）从不
36. 远程同传时，阻碍我为搭档提供帮助的原因是（多选题）。
（1）无法监听对方
（2）操作太费时，来不及
（3）看不到对方，无法确定对方是否需要帮助
（4）无法及时将对方静音，不方便讲话
（5）其他（请具体说明）
45. 总体而言，远程口译让我的工作变得更轻松了（单选题）。
（1）非常同意　（2）同意　（3）不确定　（4）不同意
（5）非常不同意
46. 总体而言，您更愿意哪种口译形式成为您的常态化工作模式（单选题）？
（1）线下口译　（2）远程口译

A Comparative Study of Student Interpreters' Performance in EC Simultaneous-Consecutive and Consecutive Interpreting Modes

Ma Zhipeng Sun Tingting
Beijing Foreign Studies University

Abstract: Simultaneous Consecutive Interpreting (Sim-Consec) is a relatively new and rarely used hybrid mode of interpreting, in which interpreters use a digital recording device to record the source speech (while taking or not taking notes), play it back into earphones and interpret it simultaneously. Often seen as an alternative for long CI for its duration (the same as CI's), Sim-Consec enjoys better interpreting quality than CI as shown in some studies. Nevertheless, this novel model is still under-researched in the Chinese-English language combination. This study seeks to compare Sim-Consec with traditional CI in a controlled experiment with student interpreters, in order to test its superiority, identify the differences in interpreting quality and explore the feasibility of applying this mode to real conferences, interpreting practice and teaching. The study reveals that Sim-Consec can overall yield better interpreting quality based on triangulation of data (subject interviews, audience response and video-and transcript-based analysis). More specifically, it can enhance interpreting performance in accuracy, information completeness, and logic clarity while reducing interpreters' memory load and stress. However, the hybrid mode seems to be a hindrance in terms of eye contact, pronunciation and intonation, and confidence perceived by the audience, with the last two contrary to some previous studies, albeit not to the extent of offsetting the

benefits and hampering the enhanced performance. The post-experiment interview shows that students are generally positive about Sim-Consec with more than 85% of subjects expressing their willingness to use this mode in real conferences, provided that they are more familiar with the mode and receive proper training. Sim-Consec is also suitable for the preliminary training of SI, which can be incorporated into the curricula of interpreter training programs.
Keywords: technology-assisted interpreting; Simultaneous Consecutive Interpreting; hybrid mode; interpreting quality assessment; interpreting practice and teaching

同交传和传统交传模式下学生译员表现的比较研究

马志鹏　孙婷婷　北京外国语大学

摘　要：同交传（Simultaneous Consecutive Interpreting，Sim-Consec）是一种新型的、使用较少的混合口译模式。该模式指的是译员在讲者发言时用任何录音设备录音（在此过程中可以适当做笔记或者不做笔记），当讲者说完轮到译员口译时，译员通过无线耳机等蓝牙设备回放讲者讲话，并根据耳机里的源语进行同声传译。这一模式所占的时间和传统交传相当，通常用于代替长交传。虽然有少数研究显示，这一模式和传统交传相比产出的译文质量更高，但是对英汉语对同交传的研究少之又少。本研究旨在通过口译实验对比学生译员同交传和传统交传的质量差异，并回答以下研究问题：1）同交传模式下的口译质量是否更高？ 2）质量差异主要体现在哪些方面？ 3）在实战、练习和教学中运用这种模式是否有可行性？视频和文本质量评分、回溯性访谈和观众问卷形成的三角互证结果显示，学生译员在同交传模式下的口译表现总体比交传更好。虽然在眼神交流、语音语调、专业和自信程度方面质量有所下滑，但是在忠实度、完整度和逻辑连贯性方面显著更好，还减轻了译员的记忆负担和心理压力，总体利大于弊。超过 85% 的学生译员表示愿意在实战中使用同交传，前提是更加熟悉这种模式和接受相应训练，此类训练可以整合到口译课程中。
关键词：技术辅助口译；同交传；混合口译；口译质量评估；口译练习和教学

1. Introduction

Consecutive and simultaneous interpreting have long been the common modes of interpreting which are also "the basic techniques that each conference interpreter should master" (Štefčík, 2018: 407). For most of its history, consecutive interpreting has dominated with its simplistic form of rotation between the speaker and the interpreter who renders the content, with or without a pen and paper. Then came simultaneous interpreting, the more technically and technologically demanding, parallel and real-time interpretation of the speech that was enabled by the use of electro-acoustic transmission systems dating back to the mid-1920's (Baigorri-Jalón, 1999). This mode of interpreting has gained momentum since its initial public success at Nuremberg trials (1945–1946) and now are on a par, if not more popular, with its simpler yet older counterpart.

In the context of breakneck development of technologies, language service providers in this new era face new challenges and opportunities when using different kinds of technologies. As a consequence, the technology-assisted interpreting has long been of particular interest to trainers, practitioners and students who seek to find ways of integrating these technologies into their everyday professional life (Orlando, 2014: 39). More recently, thanks to the immediate recording and play-back functions, Simultaneous-Consecutive Interpreting emerged. This hybrid mode of interpreting, the one that integrates both attributes of consecutive interpreting (CI) and simultaneous interpreting (SI), provides yet another eloquent example of how technologies have revolutionized the practice of interpreting.

Despite many claims laid to the invention of this new technique, Sim-Consec is generally credited to the former EU interpreter Michele Ferrari, who first used it at a press conference in Rome in early 2000 (Pöchhacker, 2015). As he explained, he adopted this "unorthodox mode" (Orlando, 2020: 2) for the sake of accuracy because he was assigned at very short notice to interpret for a speaker noted for his dense, fast and witty speeches (Gomes,

2002). On account of its novelty, no agreement has been reached on the term used to refer to this technique. Different designations have been employed in academic works under the following names: "digitally remastered consecutive" or "technology assisted consecutive" (Ferrari, 2002), "DRAC-digital recorder assisted consecutive" (Lombardi, 2003), "digital voice recorder assisted CI" (Camayd-Frexas, 2005), "SimConsec" (Hamidi & Pöchhacker, 2007; Pöchhacker, 2016; Barttomiejczyk *et al.*, 2022), "consec-simul with notes" (Orlando, 2014), "Sim-cons" (Štefčík, 2018), "consecutive simultaneous" (Barttomiejczyk *et al.*, 2022), and "simultaneous (-) consecutive" (Hiebl, 2011; Setton & Dawrant 2016a, 2016b; Barttomiejczyk *et al.*, 2022). In this study, the most common name is used: Simultaneous-Consecutive (interpreting), or the abbreviation Sim-Consec.

In Sim-Consec, while recording the speech, the interpreter first listens, understands, and analyses what the speaker is saying and possibly takes notes, as for any consecutive interpretation (Orlando & Hlavac, 2020: 3). The main difference is the presentation or production phase when the interpreter plays back the recording, listens to the speech a second time and interprets it simultaneously.

This hybrid and innovative mode came from purely practical motivations, away from any academic intention (Štefčík, 2018) and has intrigued researchers, trainers and practitioners over the last two decades.

2. Previous research on Sim-Consec

Simultaneous consecutive, or Sim-Consec, is a technology-assisted hybrid mode of interpreting in which interpreters use a digital voice recorder to record the original speech, and then interpret it in simultaneous mode from the playback of the recording (Pöchhacker, 2015: 381).

Sim-Consec-related studies fall inadequate in contrast to those of the two conventional modes (consecutive and simultaneous interpreting), although the inviting and tech-enabled features of this mode are considered by some as "radical innovation" (Pöchhacker, 2016: 183) and should have kept in step with the technological advances. The full potential of Sim-Consec is still comparatively under-studied (Orlando & Hlavac, 2020: 15).

Ferrari, both the inventor and pioneer of the research on Sim-Consec, carried out a series of informal test within the DG Interpretation in the early 2000s (Ferrari, 2001) to test the efficiency of this hybrid mode and different devices used such as a handheld PC and a digital voice recorder, which already yielded results that Sim-Consec was objectively more complete and precise (*ibid.*). Other initial studies included trials on Sim-Consec in a court setting conducted by court interpreters Lombardi (2003) and Camayd-Freixas (2005), and a small-scale study at the University of Vienna that compared the conventional CI and the hybrid mode (Hamidi & Pöchhacker, 2007). These trials all generated positive feedback with Hamidi and Pöchhacker's success in finding out the superiority of Sim-Consec both perceived by the subjects and reflected in better fluency, closer source-target correspondence and fewer prosodic deviations (*ibid.*). Similar findings were echoed by other comparison studies done in the same institution (Hawel, 2010; Sienkiewicz, 2010; Hiebl, 2011).

2.1 Merits of Sim-Consec

The functions of this hybrid mode transcend the confines of both modes (Orlando & Hlavac, 2020: 3). The basic claim of Sim-Consec beating traditional CI centers on superior accuracy and completeness (Pöchhacker, 2015: 381). As most attempts have shown, Sim-Consec indeed enables a higher interpreting quality especially with regard to accuracy and completeness (Ferrari, 2001; Camayd-Freixas, 2003; Hamidi & Pöchhacker, 2007; Hawel, 2010; Orlando, 2014; Orlando & Hlavac, 2020). One study even showed this hybrid mode helped consecutive interpreters to improve their accuracy by an average of 35% with few or no errors, regardless of the length of the statements interpreted (Camayd-Freixas, 2005: 40), whereas the accuracy of CI declined as the statement length increased (*ibid.*: 43). This finding echoed Orlando's

(2014: 13) survey-based study that showed self-perceived better accuracy by the informants.

Other benefits include increased fluency (Orlando, 2014), better and more faithful style of delivery including paralinguistic features such as tone and rhythm (Hamidi & Pöchhacker, 2007; Pöchhacker, 2015), more confidence or less pressure (Hamidi & Pöchhacker, 2007; Orlando, 2014; Orlando & Hlavac, 2020), diminished interpreter fatigue and increased endurance (Lombardi, 2003: 8; Caymad-Freireixas, 2005), memory support and notation economy, meaning that a limited number of note-taking symbols already suffice (Štefčík, 2018; Orlando & Hlavac, 2020).

All the benefits seem to be accounted for by hearing the source language twice, which enables deeper understanding, greater fidelity and less pressure due to the reduced memory load.

2.2 Demerits of Sim-Consec

In terms of shortcomings, caveats were noted as follows. First, poor communication with the public (Hiebl, 2011; Orlando & Hlavac, 2020; Svoboda, 2020), which can be overcome if interpreters are made aware of this risk and properly trained (Orlando, 2014: 48). Second, extra coordination efforts during the simultaneous part (Orlando & Hlavac, 2020). Third, external uncertainties such as technical failure, misoperation and possibly less control of the delivery (Orlando, 2014: 13). An experimental study employing a smartpen (Hiebl, 2011) in which participants were given the choice to choose CI or Sim-Consec, yielded a clear preference for Sim-Consec when the source speech was fast and dense, whereas a more redundant, impromptu-style input speech was preferably rendered in conventional CI (Pöchhacker, 2015: 382). Fourth, limited applicable scenarios because of confidentiality issues. Interpreters should get the consent in advance and if necessary, delete recordings as required, as was described in the courting interpreting setting where the interpreter must explain to all parties that the recorder will be used only as an interpreting aid, and that it will be completely erased at the end of the proceeding (Camayd-Freixas, 2005: 44).

Despite a new research topic for some researchers in the international interpreting community, Sim-Consec studies, surprisingly, are very rare in China. Only two studies explored the viability and superiority of the smart pen technology used in traditional CI to facilitate note-taking and production. Yang's (2017) research showed that a digital pen lends itself to CI because it provides three dimensions for review both during the production phase and after CI: audio, video (of the note-taking process) and text. She contends that such a digital technology empowers the study on interpreting process by displaying the dynamics of note-taking in CI. The similar results were echoed by Sun's (2020) study that demonstrated the superiority of a digital pen adopted in CI compared to a traditional one. However, both studies were carried out in the traditional CI mode and failed to employ smart pens in the context of Sim-Consec.

2.3 Interpreting quality assessment in Sim-Consec

As regards interpreting quality, early Sim-Consec studies mostly focused on accuracy and completeness of the interpreting performance with the hypothesis that this hybrid mode could enhance interpreters' performance. However, it is worth noting that since the very beginning of the Sim-Consec experiments, multi-faceted assessment criteria had already been adopted which involved different actors: the audience, the interpreters themselves and the original speech. When trialing his invention (Sim-Consec) in a real interpreting assignment, Ferrari (2001) paid much attention to the source-target correspondence or accuracy as expected, but he also documented his own impression of and reflection on this hybrid mode as the subject. Haimdi and Pöchhacker (2007) measured transcript- and video-based output, audience response and the interpreters' own assessment for overall quality evaluation, thus creating triangulation of data. After a lack of visual engagement was identified as a major shortcoming by Ferrari in his initial trials, the following studies incorporated this specific criterion and gave it a special mention or sometimes an equal footing with accuracy or delivery. The similar yardsticks were employed by the following studies (Hawel 2010; Sienkiewicz 2010; Orlando 2014).

The quality assessment standards of this study are primarily modelled after Haimdi and Pochhacker's (2007) criteria: fluency, clarity and cohesion, quality of expression (language), intonation and emphasis, level of communication with the audience and confidence and professionalism. In order to make the assessment more valid, audience comprehension as a yardstick (Reithofer, 2013) is also leveraged in the study as was in Haimdi and Pochhacker's (2007).

The research later on laid much emphasis on the demerits of Sim-Consec with a focus on yardsticks often found with poorer performance, such as eye contact (Hamidi & Pöchhacker, 2007; Orlando, 2014; Orlando & Hlavac, 2020), with a view to improving the quality in these aspects.

To recapitulate, previous research focused more on the responses of practicing interpreters, namely freelancers on the private market or staff interpreters in institutions (Hamidi & Pöchhacker, 2007; Orlando, 2014) and the language pairs studies are limited in languages that belong to the same language family such as English-French (Orlando, 2014), French-German (Hamidi & Pöchhacker, 2007), German-Italian (Hawel, 2010). Moreover, among previous studies where experiments were employed, the number of subjects tend to be small given difficulty to find practicing interpreters and analyze a large volume of data.

Given that Sim-Consec studies are also very rare in China, a gap is thus found in the Chinese-English pair that is deemed more linguistically distinctive with the focus on novice interpreters. Built on the previous work in this field, this study seeks to investigate the impact of Sim-Consec on the performance of Chinese-English student interpreters by putting both the conventional CI and Sim-Consec to the test.

3. Research objectives

Built on the pioneering research, the present study seeks to test the viability or even superiority (if any) of Sim-Consec. An experiment is devised with English source texts for trainee interpreters to interpret into Chinese with a view to comparing the hybrid mode and the conventional CI. Supplied with an experiment, a questionnaire for the audience and a post-test interview with the subjects, the study mainly focuses on the three dimensions: impacts of the Sim-Consec mode on the interpreting performance, audience feedback, and the interpreters' response. Hence, the performance will be assessed based on accuracy, fluency, and level of communication with the audience. More specifically, the research seeks to answer the following questions:

1) Does Sim-Consec yield better interpreting performance than the conventional CI in EC interpretation?

2) What are the differences of the two modes in interpreting performance?

3) Is Sim-Consec likely to be adopted by interpreters for self-directed practices or real-life assignments?

4. Research design

To answer the research questions, an experimental comparison of CI and Sim-Consec is required. Subjects' interpreting performances in the two modes will be compared within group (namely the two speeches of the same subject will be compared), mainly from three perspectives: the interpreters, audience and graders/professionals. For that to happen, three methods are adopted to collect and analyze data: an interpreting experiment in which subjects' performances are video-recorded (for video-and transcript-based grading and analysis), post-experiment interviews of subjects (for interpreter self-assessment), and audience questionnaire (for audience response study). As is shown in Figure 1, research procedures can be divided into the following steps.

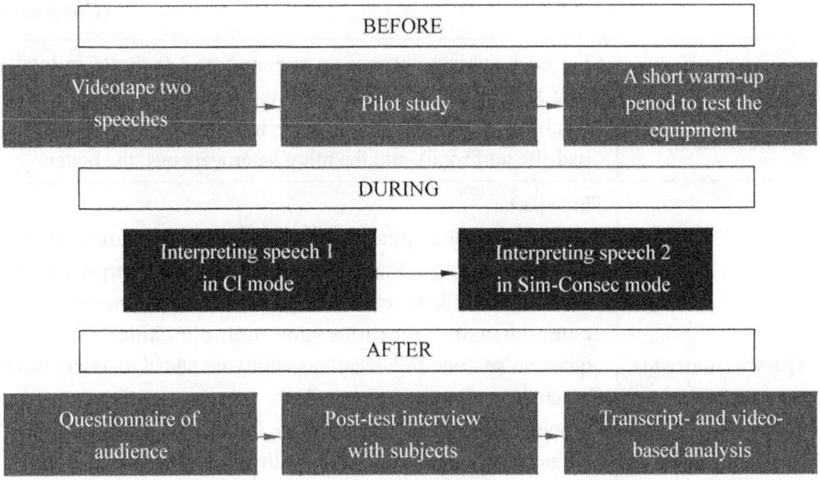

Figure 1 Research procedures

4.1 Experimental design

The key elements of the experiment are summed up in the table 1.

Table 1 Summary of the experimental design

Subjects	• 8 student interpreters in the Chinese/English language pair (with Chinese as A language and English as B language) who have received at least one year of training in both CI and SI. • These subjects have not been exposed to Sim-Consec before.
Materials (2 speeches with)	• 2 English speeches with the approximate length of 5 minute per speech. • Both speeches are comparable in terms of content and level of language use, such as the comparable number of proper names, dates and figures. • Authentic materials. If necessary, these materials can be scripted for the purpose of the experiment, and delivered either by a native speaker (recorded) or TTS (Text To Speech) software. • See to it that the articulation rate of the two speeches are similar.

(To be continued)

(Continued)

Audience (3 for each subject, 24 in total)	• For each subject, there is an audience of 3 (8*3=24 in total) The audience should have limited or no knowledge about English so that they rely on the interpreting (simulation of real-life audience), and the more heterogeneous, the better.
Questionnaire for Audience	Three parts: • Questions about general impression of the interpreter's performance (e.g., How well do you follow the interpretation?) with 7-point Likert scales and space to add comments. Three comprehension questions (one multiple choice, one T/F question and one free recall question) are added to assess how much the audience understands the speech. • 7-point Likert scales for rating the following 6 quality criteria: fluency, clarity and cohesion, quality of expression (language), intonation and emphasis, level of communication with the audience and confidence and professionalism. • Choose the interpretations they like better, and answer why.
Electronic Device	• Traditional CI tools: a pen and paper. • A smartphone with an advanced recording application (play-back, slow-down or acceleration, marking a specific point in time, fast forward or rewind with 3 seconds). • Bluetooth earbuds connected to the smartphone.
Post-test Interview for Subjects	• Focus on preferred working mode and reasons, and assessment of the two performances and the Sim-Consec mode.
Output Analysis	• transcription- and video-based grading and analysis. • post-test interviews for the subjects. • Questionnaire for the audience.

The experimental setup was tested in a pilot study with a focus to test the comparability of the two speeches and the feasibility of the devices. It involved four student interpreters who meet the subject selection criteria in the main study. All of them gave positive feedback recognizing the comparable features of the two speeches and viability of these devices. However, two of them commented that although the devices involved were quite common and used on a daily basis, they were not familiar with the Sim-Consec mode. Thus, a warm-up session was added to the experiment to better prepare subjects for the mixed mode.

4.2 Post-experiment interview

A retrospective interview is conducted to obtain feedback from each subject on the two modes. It is a semi-constructed interviews where questions within a predetermined thematic framework are asked but not set in order or in phrasing. Such an open and flexible style allows new ideas to be brought up by the interviewees and customized follow-up questions can be added to gain more insights.

Basically, the subjects are asked about their perception of the difficulty level of the two speeches, their own evaluation of the performances, preferred interpreting mode (interpreting quality-wise and effort-wise), perspectives on and willingness to use Sim-Consec, with possible follow-up questions. The interviews are recorded for later analysis.

4.3 Audience questionnaire

To study audience response, a questionnaire was devised according to the design in Hamidi and Pöchhacker's (2007: 280) study and sent to three experts for their advice (three lecturers teaching translation and interpreting in universities and one of them also taught research methodology). Adjustments were thus made based on the experts' feedback for a better questionnaire design.

The Likert scale-based questionnaire starts with basic background checks, followed by general impression questions, comprehension questions and evaluation questions. After listening to the interpreter's performance (subjects' videos were inserted into online questionnaires), listeners are asked to detail their general impression (blank filling with no less than 15 words) and indicate how well they are able to follow the interpretation on a 7-point Likert scale. A few comprehension questions are designed to corroborate their ability to follow, including one multiple choice, one true or false question, and one free recall. Then the audience are invited to assess the performance on a 7-point Likert scale based on the following aspects: 1) pronunciation and intonation; 2) fluency of delivery; 3) clarity and cohesion; 4) quality of expression; 5) eye contact; and 6) confidence and professionalism. Since these indicators do not involve any expertise in interpreting, the audience is capable of giving credible feedback. Having evaluated the two performances, listeners are also asked to pick a better one and state why (no less than 15 words).

4.4 Output analysis

To begin with, subjects' interpreting videos were transcribed through the Sougou transcription website (with claimed 98% of accuracy) and proofread by the researcher. Two third-year postgraduates, both translation and interpreting majors in undergraduate and postgraduate study with three years of part-time interpreting experience, watched subjects' interpreting videos and grade their performances in accordance with the translations for reference. Both videos and transcripts were provided for the two raters. Spearman's rank correlation coefficient was used for the inter-rater reliability test (See Table 2). The inter-rater coefficient of the overall score was 0.881 (Speech 1, $p<0.01$) and 0.922 (Speech 2, $p<0.01$), meaning the scores given were highly correlated and reliable.

Table 2 Inter-rater reliability

Inter-Rater Reliability by Spearman's Rank Correlation Coefficient		
Scoring Criteria	Speech 1	Speech 2
	Correlation Coefficient (R value)	Correlation Coefficient (R value)
(1) Sense Consistency	0.937**	0.955**
(2) Information Completeness	0.892**	0.889**
(3) Correct Terminology	1.000**	1.000**
(4) Pronunciation and Intonation	0.775*	0.679
(5) Fluency of Delivery	0.764*	0.785*
(6) Logic Clarity and Cohesion	0.799*	0.835**

(To be continued)

(Continued)

Inter-Rater Reliability by Spearman's Rank Correlation Coefficient		
Scoring Criteria	**Speech 1**	**Speech 2**
	Correlation Coefficient (R value)	**Correlation Coefficient (R value)**
(7) Quality of Expression/Language	0.819*	0.741*
(8) Language Style/Register	0.873**	0.795*
(9) Eye Contact	1.000**	1.000**
(10) Confidence and Professionalism	0.675	0.943**
Overall Score	0.881**	0.922**

Notes: ** Correlation is significant at the 0.01 level (2-tailed).
* Correlation is significant at the 0.05 level (2-tailed).

Interviews were also transcribed the same way as subjects' videos and key points were summarized by the researcher based on transcripts and notes taken amid interviews.

In terms of audience response analysis, firstly, the profile of the audience was sketched out, including their age, educational level (including both degree holders and candidates) and majors to ensure the diverse make-up.

Secondly, both quantitative and qualitative data generated by questionnaires were examined carefully. Quantitative data, mainly the 7-point scores that denote interpreting quality, went through reliability tests first. The results are very good (see Table 3). Additionally, the data created by comprehension questions were used to corroborate the quality of the interpreting as well.

The qualitative data, mainly comments from the audience, were checked manually by the researcher and the keywords extracted were analysed and used to generate the word cloud.

Table 3 Audience questionnaire reliability

Questionnaire	Cronbach α Coefficient	
	Speech 1	Speech 2
Subject 1	0.889	0.904
Subject 2	0.993	0.995
Subject 3	0.856	0.940
Subject 4	0.982	0.915
Subject 5	0.935	0.702
Subject 6	0.938	0.874
Subject 7	0.911	0.974
Subject 8	0.895	0.665

Notes: $\alpha > 0.8$, very good reliability.
$0.7 \leqslant \alpha \leqslant 0.8$, good reliability.
$0.6 \leqslant \alpha \leqslant 0.7$, acceptable reliability.
$\alpha < 0.6$, poor reliability.

5. Results

5.1 The better mode

Based on audience response, video- and transcript-based grading and interviews with subjects, Speech 2 done in Sim-Consec was found with better quality.

Sim-Consec enables better performance in semantic and language aspects mainly, with improved sense consistency and logic clarity and cohesion. Subjects also reported less strain in doing Sim-Consec. Nevertheless, Sim-Consec witnessed a drop of scores in some indicators — mainly eye contact and confidence and professionalism and in some cases, pronunciation and intonation. On the whole, Sim-Consec yielded better interpreting performance as evidenced by triangulation of data.

To be more specific, according to the overall scores of the two performances (the average of the two graders'), Speech 2 was rated much higher, which was the case for 7 in 8 subjects (see Figure 2). 5 in 7 subjects thought Speech 2 rendered in Sim-Consec was better (see Figure 3) based on the self-assessment done in the post-experiment interviews with subjects. The same number (and proportion) of subjects reported more comfort and less strain (see Figure 4). The audience also liked Sim-Consec better with 5 in 8 subjects were given better scores in Speech 2 (see Figure 5), a result based on the average scores of 3 listeners against 6 criteria.

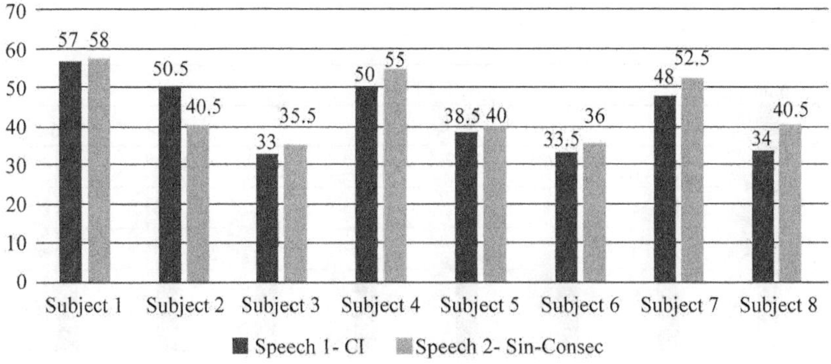

Figure 2 Video- and transcript-based grading

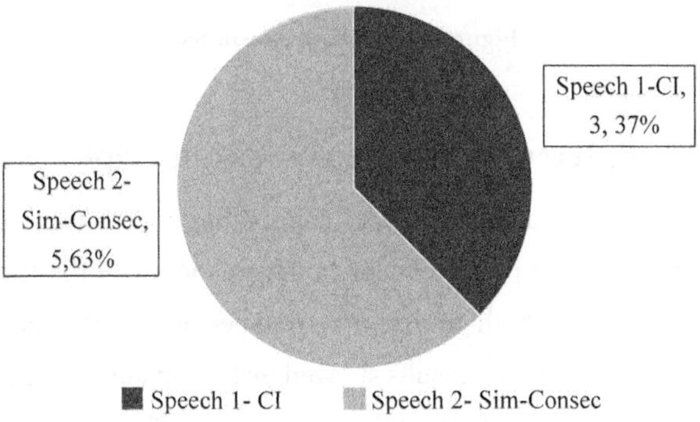

Figure 3 Better quality perceived by subjects

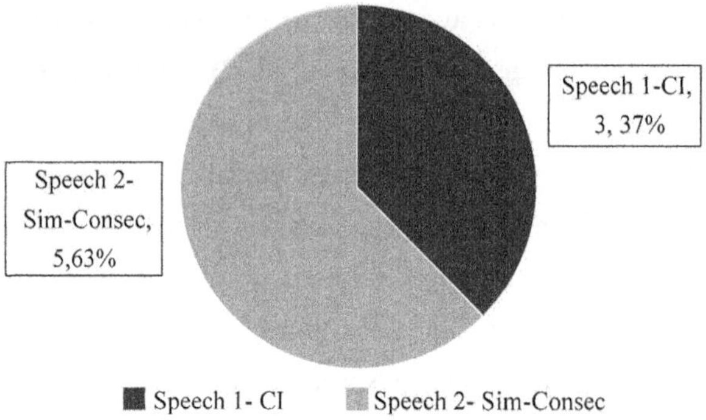

Figure 4 Less strain reported by subjects

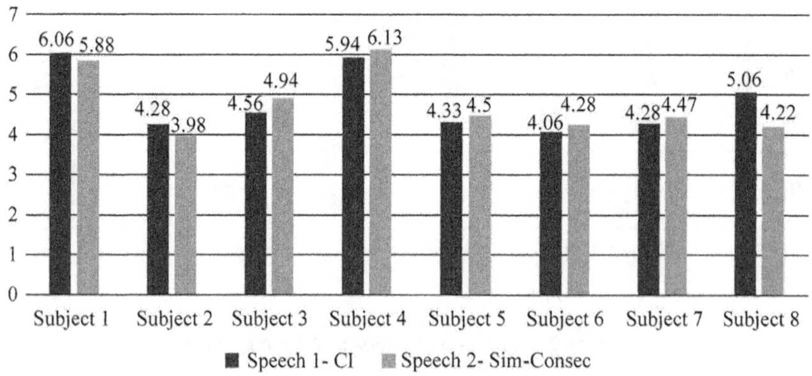

Figure 5 Audience response

5.2 Quality differences by video- and transcript-based analysis

The two graders watched subjects' interpreting videos (with transcripts in hand) and assessed their performances in accordance with the translations for reference. On the whole, both graders preferred performances in the Sim-Consec mode for higher quality as the results showed that the majority of subjects earned higher scores for their second speech in Sim-Consec with 7 among 8 rated higher by Rater 1 and 6 in 8 by Rater 2.

Except for Subject 1, both graders prefer Speech 2 of Subjects 3, 4, 5, 6, 7, 8 and Speech 1 of only Subject 2. Given the small scale of this experiment, such results already provided a telling argument that Sim-Consec can yield better interpreting performance than the conventional CI from the perspective of graders/professionals.

With a difference of 3 points (± 3) as the threshold for significance (30% of 10 criteria measured in 1 point), the two performances of Subjects 1, 2, 4, 7, 8 (based on Rater 1's evaluation) and Subjects 2, 3, 4, 6, 7, 8 (based on Rater 2's) appeared significantly different. A match was thus found that Speech 2 of Subjects 4, 7, 8 were significantly better than their Speech 1 done in the CI mode, reinforcing the argument by showing that Sim-Consec is not only able to produce interpretation with higher quality, but also significantly improve the quality in some cases.

To be more specific, the paired samples test demonstrated that significant difference was found in the following criteria based on Rater 1 and 2's grading: 1) sense consistency; 4) pronunciation and intonation; 6) logic clarity and cohesion; 7) quality of expression (only significantly different in Rater 1's assessment), and 9) eye contact (see Table 4).

Table 4 Criteria with significant difference

Criteria with Significant Difference (Paired Samples Test)		
Rater	**Criteria with Significant Difference**	**Significance**
Rater 1	1) sense consistency	0.009**
	4) pronunciation and intonation	0.000**
	6) logic clarity and cohesion	0.008**
	7) quality of expression	0.021*
	9) eye contact	0.042*
Rater 2	1) sense consistency	0.028*
	4) pronunciation and intonation	0.011*

(To be continued)

(Continued)

Criteria with Significant Difference (Paired Samples Test)		
Rater	**Criteria with Significant Difference**	**Significance**
Rater 2	6) logic clarity and cohesion	0.005**
	9) eye contact	0.042*

Notes: ** Correlation is significant at the 0.01 level (2-tailed).
* Correlation is significant at the 0.05 level (2-tailed).

More in-depth analysis was made into the considerable overlapping criteria found significantly discrepant: 1) sense consistency; 4) pronunciation and intonation; 6) logic clarity and cohesion; and 9) eye contact.

5.2.1 Sense consistency

Better sense consistency (or accuracy) appeared in Sim-Consec with fewer meaning-relevant departures from the original and substantial additions and substitutions.

Almost every subject interpreted Speech 2 more accurately with the exception being Subject 2 whose Speech 2 was found with more deviations, especially more meaning-relevant substitutions and omissions. The increase in scores varied from 1 to 3 by Rater 1's standards and 1 to 4 by Rater 2's with a consensus on choosing Subject 8 as the one who benefited most from Sim-Consec in terms of sense consistency. Both Rater 1 and Rater 2 accorded only 1 point (in a 7-point scale) for Subject 8's Speech 1 but significantly higher scores (4 by Rater 1 and 5 by Rater 2) for Speech 2. The performances of some subjects even hit 7, the highest point, in sense consistency in the Sim-Consec mode (Subject 4 by Rater 1 and Subject 4 and 1 by Rater 2).

In addition, higher accuracy can be reflected in better rendition of terms (see Figure 6). 5 in 8 subjects interpreted more proper nouns accurately in Speech 2 than Speech 1 with tremendous progress seen in the performances of Subject 4 and Subject 8 (an increase of 3 terms). Subject 1 and Subject 6 also fared better in Speech 2 with one more term correctly interpreted, a slight improvement. While the number of terms correctly interpreted remained the same for Subject 5, two outliners were found with deteriorating performance terminology-wise: Subject 7 rendered one term less in Speech 2 and Subject 2 even four less, a great slump. Notwithstanding, on the whole interpreters still did a better job in Sim-Consec as far as terms are concerned.

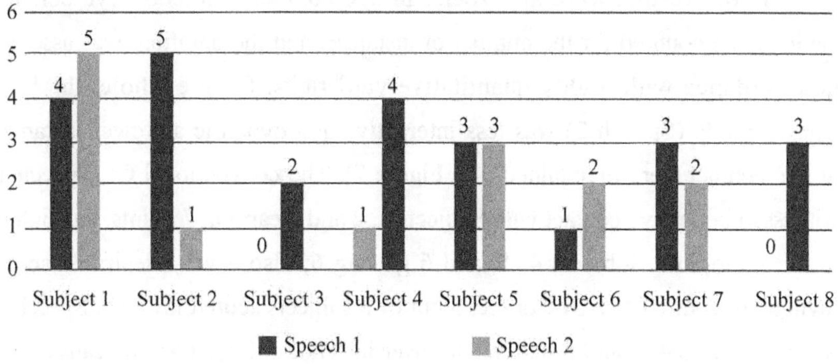

Figure 6 Number of terms accurately interpreted

5.2.2 Logic clarity and cohesion

Better performance was also found in (6) logic clarity and cohesion. Rendition in the Sim-Consec mode was more logical and coherent, as evidenced by higher scores for Speech 2 interpreted by the majority of subjects. Rater 1 preferred the second speech of all subjects except Subject 2, whose score was 1 point down compared to Speech 1. Rater 2, on the other hand, held that there was not much change in Speech 2 of Subject 2 and 5 compared to their Speech 1 when it comes to logic clarity and cohesion, though the rest did perform better in Sim-Consec. It is also worth noting that the score of this criterion was two degrees/points higher for half (4 by Rater 2's grading) or more than half (5 by Rater 1's grading) of the subjects when they worked in the Sim-Consec mode.

5.2.3 Pronunciation and intonation

Despite a boost to overall performance, Sim-Consec was less of a helper judged from some criteria: pronunciation and intonation, and eye contact. Compare with Speech 1, the scores of pronunciation and intonation changed little or even fell in Speech 2, albeit to a small extent. More precisely, Rater 1 dialed down the score for all subjects by 1 degree whereas Rater 2 gave Subjects 1, 5, 6, 7, 8 one point lower.

5.2.4 Eye contact

Similar results were also found in eye contact. Subjects' eye contact, having been counted for the number of instances and the duration, was assessed in accordance with highly quantitative yardsticks. On the whole, the Sim-Consec mode (Speech 2) was less interactive and dynamic as fewer instances of eye contact were maintained (see Figure 7). The conventional CI (Speech 1) witnessed better eye contact with Subjects 1, 2 and 7 earning 7 points, the highest in the scale, and Subjects 4, 5, and 6 getting 6, also a very desirable score. Switching from CI to Sim-Consec, 5 out of 8 subjects scored lower in Speech 2, where Subjects 4, 5 and 6 had much fewer instances of eye contact, causing the score to plummet from 6 to 3 (Subjects 5 and 6) and 6 to a meagre 1 (Subject 4).

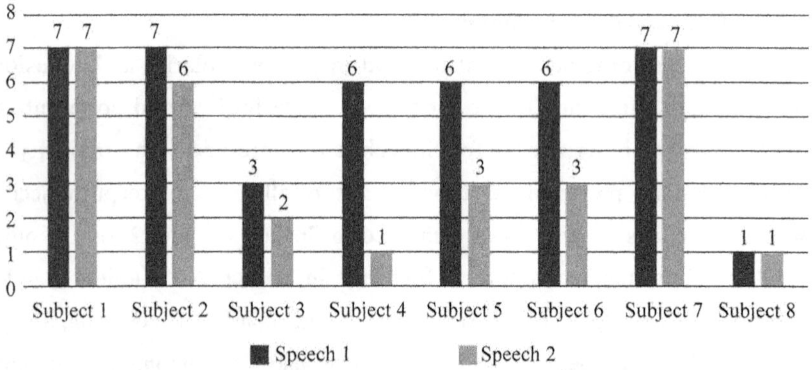

Figure 7 Eye contact scores of subjects

The number of instances and the duration can better reflect such a downward trajectory (see Figure 8). Despite the above-mentioned cases, there were outliers. Subject 1, whose eye contact instances surged from 24 to 47. Another encouraging example was Subject 7, who maintained extraordinary eye contact in both speeches. Interestingly, some subjects were less inclined to interact with the audience through eye contact, for example, Subject 8 who had no eye contact with listeners at all in both Speech 1 and Speech 2. Such a consistent result may demonstrate that she belongs to the less interactive type of interpreters who concentrate on doing interpreting more.

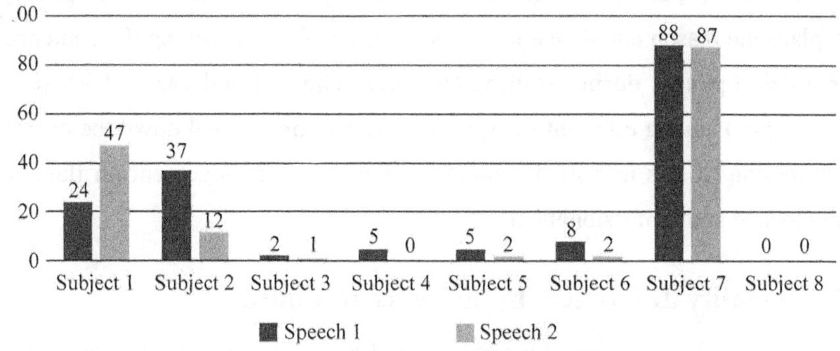

Figure 8 Total eye contact instances of subjects

5.2.5 Confidence and professionalism

Confidence and professionalism evaluation in this study, different from Hamidi and Pöchhacker's (2007: 287), was more aligned with laymen's perspective, focusing more on overall impression. In other words, the criterion whether an interpreter generally looks confident and professional was employed to assess confidence and professionalism.

It is noteworthy that no correlation was identified between eye contact and confidence and professionalism. Contrary to Hamidi and Pöchhacker's (2007: 287) practice of adopting eye contact and body language as indicators for confidence and professionalism, it is the present author's view that keeping eye contact with audience has a lot to do with an interpreter's personality or interpreting style, so it is with body language. Less or simply no eye contact is likely to be a result of more introverted personality, but not necessarily confidence and professionalism. An interpreter can be the least interactive but found composed, confident and professional at the same time for his or her voice, language quality, accurate translation of terms, etc.

Interestingly, contrary to some previous findings that Sim-Consec can boost interpreters' confidence (Hamidi & Pöchhacker, 2007), the present study found that enhanced confidence was self-claimed by interpreters and not backed by audience response and grading in which scores of confidence and professionalism dropped in the hybrid mode (especially in audience response). A plausible reason could be a lack of knowledge about SI among the audience. Inevitable pauses during waiting (for more chunks) and varied EVS (ear-voice span) among different interpreters may conspire to dial down the overall impression of less informed audience, affecting their judgement on fluency, confidence and professionalism.

5.3 Quality differences by audience response

Generally speaking, the experimental audience gave a more favorable assessment to Speech 2 done in the Sim-Consec mode (5 out of 8 subjects), though subject-by-subject scores varied. For Subject 3, a unanimous result was found with all three listeners rating Speech 2 higher. When it comes to the performances of Subjects 4, 5, 6, and 7, the majority of listeners (2 in 3) liked Speech 2 better, saying that they could follow Speech 2 more easily, a strong observation supported by better results in listening comprehension questions. The primary reasons accounting for the superiority of Sim-Consec include "clear logic", "more substantial content delivered (referring to better accuracy and information completeness)", "more pleasant to ears" and "more fluent delivery".

One prominent example (Subject 3) is singled out for case study. It is worth noting that a landslide win for Sim-Consec was found in Subject 3's two performances with all 3 listeners preferred Speech 2 by giving it higher scores (see Figure 9). The audience indicated that they were able to follow Speech 2 better with 5 in 7-point scale on average compared to 4.67, an impression corroborated by the results of the comprehension tests. More concretely, for the criteria under study, all 3 listeners rated Speech 2 higher, except for (5) eye contact by which the scores tied and (1) pronunciation and intonation by which Speech 1 was better. As a result, they preferred Speech 2 done by Subject 3 for its "higher level of fluency" (raised by all listeners), "better logic" (1 listener) and "less changeable tone of voice" (1 listener).

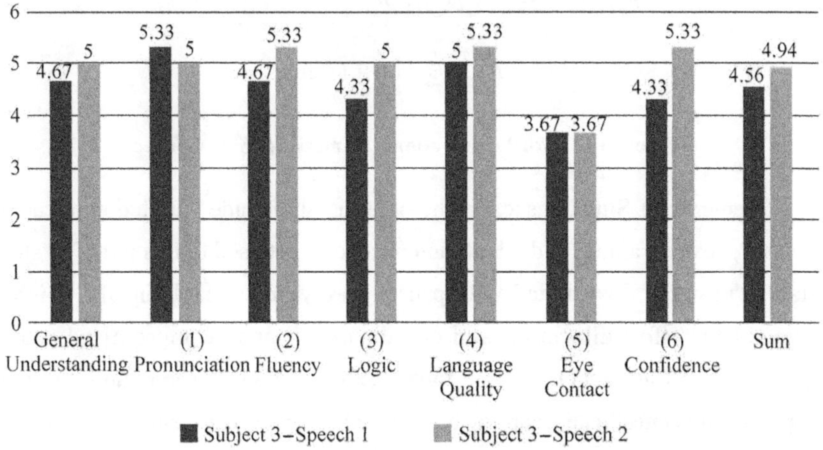

Figure 9 Subject 3's performances in comparison

5.4 Quality differences by interpreter interviews

Overall, interpreters though they did a better job in Speech 2 than Speech 1. More than half (5 in 8 subjects) chose Speech 2 when asked which one they thought was better in quality. According to the word cloud based on the keywords extracted from the interviews (see Figure 10), the main reason was the opportunity to "listen twice", which generated many benefits, including "reduced memory load in a long speech", "more complete and logical rendition", "chance to grasp the full picture of the speech and better listening comprehension", "opportunity to finish transformation from source language to target language beforehand in the mind" and "stronger confidence".

Figure 10　Word cloud about the merits of Sim-Consec

Demerits of Sim-Consec, on the other hand, include "limited application scenes", "extra training and adaptation needed to get used to this mode", "slow start", "unstable flow dotted with pauses hardly unavoidable in SI", "higher demand for effort allocation and coordination", and "compromised sound quality" (see Figure 11). Among them "extra training needed" and "limited application scenes" (i.e., cannot be used when speeches cannot be recorded for confidentiality requirements or technical reasons) were considered the main disadvantages. Some interviewees pointed out that unfamiliarity with Sim-Consec, despite a warm-up session in this mode, may result in the higher demand for effort allocation and coordination, and extra training and adaptation can solve this problem just as for SI and CI.

Figure 11　Word cloud about the demerits of Sim-Consec

5.5 Willingness to adopt Sim-Consec

Remarkably, the interview-based analysis revealed that the majority (7 out of 8 subjects) expressed their willingness to adopt the Sim-Consec mode in the future at least in one scenario. According to them, the main merit of Sim-Consec is "less strenuous" with 5 in 8 think that it can reduce short-term memory load. To be more specific, 3 interpreters reported that they would consider using it in both self-directed practices and real-life interpreting. More were apt to employ this mode in real conferences (7 in 8) than in practices (4 in 8) with Subject 4 showing strong inclination for such adoption in real conferences, extolling this mode as a preferable burden-easing attempt that can "make interpreters life much easier and improve the interpreting quality in the meantime". The most common combination, though, was "No" in practices and "Yes" in real interpreting tasks with 4 out of 8 giving such answers, because they harboured doubts about practicing in this mode. A second listening of the original speech, they believe, "may hamper the effect of interpreting practices" for detailed reasons such as "time-consuming", "unable to reflect the real active listening competence", "diluting difficulty of an interpreting practice" and "less cost-effective". However, 3 subjects did find a place for Sim-Consec to fit in — used in the preliminary stage of SI training where rookie interpreters can practice effort allocation and coordination, active listening skills and delivery (especially language quality) in a novice-friendly environment with opportunities of listening twice with the aid of notes), gradually moving to real SI.

6. Discussion

According to the results, Sim-Consec enables enhanced interpreting performance reflected mainly in accuracy (sense consistency or source-target correspondence) and logic clarity and cohesion (with statistical significance and supported by triangulation of data). Other benefits include better quality in information completeness (though not significant), confidence (proposed by subjects but not corroborated by audience response and grading) and reduced stress and increased mental stamina (raised by subjects).

Enhancement in accuracy and information completeness were echoed by many previous studies done in different language pairs. As was concluded by Orlando (2020: 5), all the following studies have compared performances of interpreters working in traditional consecutive interpreting and in the hybrid mode, using various indicators and recording devices, and with samples ranging from 2 interpreters to 24 (Chitrakar, 2016; Svoboda, 2020), and all have found an enhanced accuracy and completeness in the interpretations in the new mode (Ferrari, 2002; Camayd-Freixas, 2005; Hamidi, 2006; Hamidi & Pöchhacker, 2007; Gomes, 2002; Hawel, 2010; Orlando, 2014; Chitrakar, 2016; Mielcarek, 2017; Özkan, 2020; Svoboda, 2020). As for why interpretation in Sim-Consec was overall more complete but without statistical significance, a plausible explanation could be some subjects, being student interpreters with limited experience, were not very adept at SI and sometimes failed to catch up with some segments, which may lead to loss in completeness despite higher accuracy for what they had interpreted.

In addition, positive feedback from interpreters on comfort in interpreting was also in line with other research results (Lombardi, 2003: 8; Özkan, 2020: 58), such as "less strenuous", "reduced stress" and "having the recording as a backup" reported by subjects.

In regard to the underlying reasons for improved accuracy and completeness, Gile (2009) maintained that overall accuracy in simultaneous is clearly superior to consecutive. In accordance with this claim, Sim-Consec, a quasi-SI mod (Kalina & Ahrens, 2010: 148), certainly has an edge over CI when it comes to accuracy and completeness. In addition to this cause, a second listening to the source speech is commonly thought to be the main reason for improved accuracy and completeness (Hamidi & Pöchhacker, 2007; Orlando, 2014; Orlando & Hlavac, 2020). To be more precise, the reasons can be explained through refined Gile's effort model (see Table 5).

Table 5 Effort model for Sim-Consec based on Orlando (2014) and Gile (2009)

Phase 1 CI	Interpreting = L + (N) + M ↓ + C ↓ L Listening 1 and analysis 1 (N) (Note-taking, optional and the number of elements written is often reduced) M Short-term memory operations (↓ less effort) C Coordination (operate the device and press the <Record> button when the speaker starts) (↓ less effort amid the process)
Phase 2 SI	Interpreting = L ↓ + P + M ↓ + C ↑ L Listening 2 and analysis 2 M Short term memory operations Long term memory operations (reconstructing the speech) C Coordination Possible Coordination Components: *(Note-reading-optional) (could be a new component compared to traditional SI) Retrieving information Anticipation *(Operating the recorder (playback) if necessary) (could be a new component compared to traditional SI) *Eye contact with the audience (a new component compared to traditional SI) Self-Monitoring P Production *means the component is optional

During Phase 1, the Effort components are identical to those involved in traditional CI albeit with different weighting. The key is that the interpreter knows that s/he will hear the speech a second time and interpret it simultaneously. Note-taking is thus made optional or can be done in a more economical way with a focus on the macro-linguistic and structural elements of the speech (Orlando & Hlavac, 2020). The notes written down can also serve as a backup and used for anticipation later on. Since note-taking is not compulsory, the Memory Effort is reduced, namely short-term memory operations in which a speech segment is heard and then either written down or processed mentally before sending on to long-term memory. Meanwhile, the requirement for long-term memory to function is also dialled down as the interpreters does not need to rely that much on notes and long-term memory in traditional CI. As a consequence, Efforts of short-term memory operations, coordination and note-taking (if any), in theory, should be reduced in the hope that listening and analysis can be much easier with more effort or energy devoted to it.

During Phase 2, the Efforts usually required and coordinated in SI are supposedly facilitated by the fact that the interpreter hears the content of the speech for a second time, despite a rise in the coordination effort. Better understanding of the content, coupled with specific notes the interpreter may have taken, should be able to offset, if not outweigh, the extra load added by diversified coordination efforts such as operating the recorder (playback) in the beginning and eye contact with the audience (a special mention by many previous studies).

Knowing that they have a second-time listening to fall back on, interpreters in Phase 1 may devote more effort to listening and analysis with a focus on logic, "macro-linguistic and structural elements" of the speech (Orlando & Hlavac, 2022), and find it easier to cope with short-term memory load and coordination load (in cases of fewer or no notes). Such an observation was corroborated by the interviews with the subjects who applauded Sim-Consec for its listening benefits such as "opportunity to grasp the full picture of the speech in a more comfortable way" (with no or fewer notes) and "ability to focus on the logic and structure in the first listening". During Phase 2, interpreters face higher loads in coordination but can possibly spare some effort in listening 2 and analysis 2, built on the first listening experience.

For subjects who found Sim-Consec better, despite more loads introduced and thus a higher demand for effort allocation, familiarity with the content, coupled with specific notes the interpreter may have taken, should facilitate management of the extra load (e.g., anticipation, re-reading notes from the first hearing, using functions of the recorder) (*ibid.*). With more effort dedicated to listening comprehension and grasping macro and structural information, interpreting quality improves especially in accuracy, completeness and logic.

Another take on better logic could be that Chinese is an implicit language which tends to hide or understate the logic whereas English or other western languages are the opposite. Hence, it may be easier for interpreters to follow the already-explicit logic and cohesion devices (such as conjunction and conjunctive adverbs) in Sim-Consec since the production phase is quasi-simultaneous. CI, on the contrary, gives freer rein to interpreters during the production phase, resulting in less explicit logic and poorer coherence.

Interestingly, contrary to some previous findings that Sim-Consec can boost interpreters' confidence (Hamidi & Pöchhacker, 2007), the present study found that enhanced confidence was self-claimed by interpreters and not backed by audience response and grading in which scores of confidence and professionalism dropped in the hybrid mode (especially in audience response). A plausible reason could be a lack of knowledge about SI among the audience. Inevitable pauses during waiting (for more chunks) and varied EVS (ear-voice span) among different interpreters may conspire to dial down the overall impression of less informed audience, affecting their judgement on fluency, confidence and professionalism.

Moreover, the quality of pronunciation and intonation deteriorated in Sim-Consec, another interesting finding different from several previous studies that reported better prosody (Hamidi & Pöchhacker, 2007: 288) and "more faithful intonation and liveliness" (Camayd-Freixas, 2005: 42). Hamidi and Pöchhacker's small-sized experiment, which the present study was mainly modelled after, came up with the result that fewer prosodic deviations were found such as pauses and acceleration in this novel mode.

Different prosodic features of the two modes and interpreting experience may offer a clue. Compared to CI, interpreters are more prone to stutter, a slip of tongue and conscious or unconscious mispronunciation of words when working in SI. Working in such a quasi-simultaneous mode (as far as strategies and presentation are concerned), despite a second-time listening to the original speech, interpreters, especially novice interpreters, may still find it hard to beat pronunciation or intonation errors. More subjects did finish Speech 2 with a lower volume and less changeable tone of voice compared to the results of Hamidi and Pöchhacker's (2007: 286) study with veteran interpreters.

Based on Gile's effort model and tight rope hypothesis, while other effort changed little, the much reduced second-time listening and analysis load, coupled with likely more coordination effort to keep eye contact, could still affect production when it comes to pronunciation and intonation, a relatively less-weighted criterion (Bühler, 1986). Nevertheless, it is still a good trade-off when pronunciation and intonation is slightly compromised for a better interpreting quality overall.

Given Gile's theory, poorer performance in pronunciation and intonation and eye contact is plausible and understandable. In particular, reduced or even no eye contact was generally thought to be a major drawback of this hybrid mode evidenced by many studies because in general, interpreters performing in the simultaneous mode, often from booths, do not try to establish eye contact or rapport with an audience (Orlando & Hlavac, 2020: 6). However, out of particular note is that well reminded of this risk, subjects could actually pay more heed to eye contact and poorer interaction with the audience could be overcome to some extent, a finding echoed by Orlando's (2014: 48). In this study, nearly all subjects managed to still keep several instances of eye contact with the audience with several (Subjects 1 and 7) even maintaining their prosody and eye contact performance at the same level while producing a more accurate, logical and complete interpretation overall.

7. Conclusion

Based on triangulation of data (subject interview, audience response and grading), the present research found that Sim-Consec, compared with traditional CI, could yield better interpreting quality overall. More specifically, it can enhance interpreting performance in accuracy (sense consistency), information completeness, and logic clarity while greatly reducing interpreters' stress. Nonetheless, disadvantages also exist. The hybrid mode was found to be a hindrance in terms of eye contact, pronunciation and intonation, and confidence perceived by the audience (with the last two contrary to some previous studies), albeit not to the extent of offsetting its benefits and affecting the enhanced performance.

Such results can be explained through refined Gile's effort model. With more effort dedicated to listening comprehension and grasping macro and structural information, overall interpreting quality improves with enhanced performance in accuracy, completeness and logic in particular.

Interviewed subjects were also positive about Sim-Consec with 7 in 8 subjects expressing their willingness to use this mode in real conferences mainly for its boost to accuracy and completeness with more comfort in interpreting. As a quasi-simultaneous mode (Kalina & Ahrens, 2010: 148) or a "tamed" SI, Sim-Consec is novice-friendly in that it can reduce the listening and analysis load by offering two chances of listening and thus help rookie interpreters practice effort allocation with more focus on production quality.

Despite an elaborate design, a well-conducted experiment and other efforts made to increase the reliability and validity of the study, limitations still exist such as a small-sized sample with a limited focus on only student interpreters, employment of the simplest devices which is feasible but not optimal, and room for improvement in quality assessment of Sim-Consec.

The future research can improve the methodology of Sim-Consec studies and dive deeper into the following aspects: 1) factors affecting Sim-Consec, such as the necessity and amount of note taking in Sim-Consec (Phase 1) and the necessity and viability of acceleration function of recording devices; 2) how this mode can contribute in self-directed interpreting practices; and 3) how Sim-Consec fits into interpreter training, such as the timing of introducing this mode in the curricula.

References

[1] Baigorri-Jalón, J. Conference interpreting: From modern times to space technology [J]. Interpreting, 1999, 4 (1): 29-40.

[2] Barttomiejczyk, *et al.* Modes of conference interpreting: Simultaneous and consecutive [A]. In Albl-Mikasa, M. & Tiselius, E. (eds.). The Routledge Handbook of Conference Interpreting [C]. London and New York: Routledge, 2022.

[3] Bühler, H. Linguistic (semantic) and extra-linguistic (pragmatic) criteria for the evaluation of conference interpretation and interpreters [J]. Multilingua, 1986, 5(4): 231-235.

[4] Chitrakar, R. Tehnološko podprto konsekutivno tolmačenje (Technologically Supported Consecutive Interpreting) [D]. Slovene: University of Ljubljana, 2016.

[5] Camayd-Freixas, E. A revolution in consecutive interpretation: Digital Voice-Recorder-Assisted CI [J]. The ATA Chronicle, 2005 (3): 40-46.

[6] Ferrari, M. "Consecutive Simultaneous?" (undated) [EB/OL]. [28-09-2006]. http://scic.cec.eu.int/scicnews/2001/011121/default?26.htm.

[7] Gile, D. Basic Concepts and Models for Interpreter and Translator Training [M]. Amsterdam: John Benjamins, 2009.

[8] Gomes, M. "Digitally mastered consecutive. An interview with MicheleFerrari" [EB/OL]. 2002. (09-09-2008) [07-08-2021]. http://www.bootheando.com/2008/09/09/consecutiva-simultanea-una-nueva-modalidad-de-interpretacion/.

[9] Haimidi, M. & Pöchhacker, F. Simultaneous consecutive interpreting: A new technique put to the test [J]. Meta, 2007, 52 (2): 276-289.

[10] Hawel, K. Simultanes versus klassisches Konsekutivdolmetschen: Eine vergleichende textuelle Analyse (Simultaneous versus classic consecutive interpreting: A comparative textual analysis) [D]. Vienna: University of Vienna, 2010.

[11] Hiebl, B. Simultanes Konsekutivdolmetschen mit dem LivescribeTM EchoTM Smartpen (Simultaneous consecutive interpreting with the LivescribeTM EchoTM Smartpen) [D]. Vienna: University of Vienna, 2011.

[12] Kalina, S. & Ahrens, B. Consecutive: A skill out of fashion or a mode with a new profile? — Implications for teaching [A]. In CRATIL (ed.). Les pratiques de l'interprétation et l'oralité dans la communication interculturelle [C]. Lausanne: L'âge d'homme, 2010.

[13] Lombardi, J. "DRAC Interpreting: Coming soon to a courthouse near you?" [EB/OL] . 2003. [28-09-2006]. http://www.najit.org/proteus/0$&6ersions/0roteus?3pr03%20web.pdf.

[14] Mielcarek, M. Das simultane Konsekutivdolmetschen (Simultaneous consecutive interpreting) [D]. Vienna: University of Vienna, 2017.

[15] Orlando, M. A study on the amenability of digital pen technology in a hybrid mode of interpreting: Consec-simul with notes [J]. Translation & Interpreting, 2014, 6(2): 39-54.

[16] Orlando, M. & Hlavac, J. Simultaneous-consecutive in interpreter training and interpreting practice: Use and perceptions of a hybrid mode [J]. The Interpreters' Newsletter, 2020(25): 1-17.

[17] Özkan, C. E. To use or not to use a smartpen: That is the question. An empirical study on the role of Smartpen in the viability of simultaneous-consecutive interpreting [D]. Ghent: Ghent University, 2020.

[18] Pöchhacker, F. (ed.). Routledge Encyclopedia of Interpreting Studies [M]. New York: Routledge, 2015.

[19] Pöchhacker, F. Introducing Interpreting Studies (2nd Ed.) [M]. London: Routledge, 2016.

[20] Reithofer, K. Comparing modes of communication: The effect of English as a lingua franca vs. interpreting [J]. Interpreting, 2013, 15 (1): 48-73.

[21] Svoboda, S. SimConsec: The technology of a Smartpen in interpreting [D]. Olomouc: Palacký University Olomouc, 2020.

[22] Setton R. & Dawrant, A. Conference Interpreting: A Complete Course [M]. Amsterdam: John Benjamins, 2016a.

[23] Setton R. & Dawrant, A. Conference Interpreting: A Trainer's Guide [M]. Amsterdam: John Benjamins, 2016b.

[24] Sienkiewicz B. Das Konsekutivdolmetschen der Zukunft: Mit Notizblock oder Aufnahmegerät (Consecutive interpreting of the future: With Notepad or recording device) [D]. Vienna: University of Vienna, 2010.

[25] Štefčík, J. Sim-Cons as a new way of interpreting and didactic means [J]. Годишник на департамент „Чужди езици и култури", 2018(1) : 406-419.

[26] 孙杰. 基于云端的智能笔辅助交传笔记教学探究 [J]. 现代英语，2020（12）：103-108.

[27] 杨柳燕. 数字技术辅助下的交传笔记研究 [J]. 外语教学理论与实践，2017（3）：91-97.

八、翻译中的校企合作

MTI 学位教育与职业发展中的翻译实践层次研究

——以 RWS 专利翻译领域校企合作为例[1]

郑金凤　RWS 中国公司
许家绍　曲阜师范大学

摘　要：语言服务行业呼唤一种全新的校企直通模式，在语言服务行业构建高校与企业之间的直连通道，有效运用市场机制，实现高校学位教育与企业实际需求之间的精准对接。本文基于 RWS 的思考与实践，结合专利领域的具体翻译实践，重点围绕“翻译实践”的层次，从立足于高校的外围辅助层、定制开发层，到立足于企业的融合应用层、全面扩展层展开具体论证，探讨了 MTI 学生从高校到企业、从理论到实践，最终成长为行业栋梁的完整历程，期冀对高校与企业之间如何进行深层次协同提供一定的借鉴。

关键词：校企合作；MTI 教育；专利翻译；校企直通；RWS

A Study on the Levels of Translation Practice in MTI Education and Career Development — A Case Study of School-enterprise Cooperation in RWS Patent Translation

Zhen Jinfeng　RWS Co., China
Xu Jiashao　Qufu Normal University

Abstract: The teaching practice mode in which staff from the language service industry enter universities to teach Master of Translation and Interpreting (MTI)

1　本文系山东省研究生教育联合培养基地“曲阜师范大学与 RWS 研究生教育联合培养基地”建设项目（项目编号：SDYJD17068）的阶段性成果。

courses has been widely adopted. However, this approach has not effectively bridged the gap between university education and the needs of the industry. To establish a direct link between universities and enterprises, a new school-enterprise through mode is necessary. This mode should leverage market mechanisms to ensure that both universities and enterprises have a wide range of options and facilitate a precise alignment between degree education and the actual talent requirements of the industry. This article focuses on the level of “translation practice” and presents a specific case study in the field of patent translation. It demonstrates different forms and connotations of MTI, from the peripheral auxiliary layer and customized development layer based on universities, to the integrated application layer and comprehensive expansion layer based on enterprises. The article discusses the complete journey of MTI students’ growth from university to enterprise, from theory to practice, and ultimately to becoming pillars of the industry. This study provides valuable insights on how to deepen collaboration between universities and enterprises, and serves as a useful reference for stakeholders in the language service industry.

Keywords: university-enterprise cooperation; MTI education; translation practice; university-enterprise direct link; RWS

1. 引言

全球化进程日益加快，我国综合国力不断提高，“走出去”战略稳步实施，语言服务行业蓬勃发展，语言服务人才需求逐渐扩大的宏观时代背景，对开展专门翻译人才培养提出了现实迫切需求，2007年翻译硕士专业学位（MTI）应运而生（李军等，2007：6）。翻译硕士专业学位的设置是近年来我国翻译学科发展成果的里程碑和发展方向的指路灯（仲伟合，2017：7）。翻译专业硕士学位旨在培养高层次、应用型、专业性高级翻译专门人才，其特色就是针对日趋显著的翻译行业产业化和职业化特征，面向我国高层次、职业化、应用型翻译人才的巨大缺口（郭晓勇，

2012：34），增强翻译教学的市场针对性和适应性，创新专业翻译人才培养模式，提高专门翻译人才培养质量（穆雷，2020：87）。因而，翻译专业硕士学位具有紧密联系翻译产业，满足行业实际翻译需求，突出培养职业能力，瞄准就业目标训练，强调实际应用能力，具有明确实践要求等显明特点，并由此使得重点培养实践能力、强化职业能力导向、注重产学结合途径、加大校企合作力度成为业界共识和必然趋势（黄忠廉，2010；蔡辉，2013：51）。

2. MTI 学位教育与职业发展中翻译实践的现状与问题

2018 年《中国语言服务行业发展报告》指出，翻译专业教育与语言服务需求方和语言服务提供方的专业人才需求相比还有一些差距，与培养高层次、应用型、专业化的翻译人才的目标还有不少差距，特别在特色化、国际化、复合型人才培养方面差距明显（中国翻译协会，2018）。党中央、国务院、专门机构、地方各级政府等出台了具体指导思想和实施意见，相关语言服务企业和高等学校积极参与，产学研政各方积极联动，改进或创新语言服务人才培养机制，确保语言服务人才培养数量和质量。

《国务院办公厅关于深化产教融合的若干意见》（国办发〔2017〕95 号）中提出构建教育和产业统筹融合发展格局，推进产教融合人才培养改革，加强产教融合师资队伍建设，全面推行校企协同育人，构建校企合作长效机制。具体提出“用 10 年左右时间，教育和产业统筹融合、良性互动的发展格局总体形成，需求导向的人才培养模式健全完善，人才教育供给与产业需求重大结构性矛盾基本解决”。

全国翻译专业学位研究生教育指导委员会先后发布或修订了《翻译硕士专业学位研究生指导性培养方案》《翻译硕士专业学位基本要求》《翻译硕士专业学位培养单位评估指标体系》《增列硕士专业学位授权点基本条件》等文件，就人才培养目标、培养方案和培养模式等相关问题做出了具体要求和部署。全国翻译专业学位研究生教育指导委员会与中国翻译协会共同组织制定了《全国翻译专业学位研究生教育实习基地(企业)认证规范》和《全国翻译专业学位研究生教育兼职教师认证规范》及其相关认证活动，为推动解决实践教学基地及兼职教师队伍规范性问题提供了很好示范作用。

在上述政策的指导下，部分高校和企业努力寻求将校企合作全面融入翻译硕士教育招生、培养、学位论文及就业等全过程，也初步探索出一条翻译硕士教育中的校企合作全覆盖模式，并在招生、职业认同教育、培养方案制定/修订、课程建设、师资队伍建设（含专任“双师型”教师培养及兼职教师聘任）、翻译技术实验室和工作室建设、资源库建设、实习基地建设、联合培养基地建设、科研或教学论文发表、著作或教材出版、会议、培训、竞赛、毕业论文选题、就业及毕业生跟踪反馈等方面，实现了校企合作的有效切入（王传英，2010；丁素萍，2012；冯曼，2012；杨朝军，2012；赵军峰，2013；穆雷等，2013；滕梅、张馨元，2013；董洪学、张晴，2015；穆雷等，2018）。

在各级政策的要求引导下，在各高校的努力下，MTI学位教育与职业发展中翻译实践取得了长足进展，技术发展带来的行业变革，行业要求多样化。翻译实践中的新问题也频频发生，例如，翻译实践形式较为模式化，翻译实践评价标准单一，职业引领导向乏力等。这些问题具体可以归纳为以下四个方面。

2.1 普适性教育路线难以有效应对特定领域翻译的能力需求

社会分工造就了不同领域多样化的人才需求。作为人才供给侧的高校也在努力调整培养方案，培养各行各业所需的高素质人才。不少专业院校结合学校整体专业定位开展MTI学位教育，有鲜明的专业特色，但大多数高校遵循的是普适性教育路线，培养方案鲜有特色性课程，也不特别限定学生个人对特定领域的探索与研究。固然，这在MTI的第一阶段教育中是必要的，但是随着基础课程的学习和基本能力的习得，MTI学生必然面临将其基本能力与特定领域结合的要求与挑战（周恩、丁年青，2017：58）。特定领域有自身的行业规范和需求，高校自身力量无法充分接触到，亟须行业资源介入，同时也需要采取有效措施激发学生对特定领域的兴趣。

2.2 校外实训基地运行存在不同程度的问题，学生对特定领域的兴趣难以在更深层次得到发展

MTI 学生已经表现出了对于特定领域的强烈兴趣，并有意愿在该领域进行更深层次的探索发展。高校也都建立各种校内和校外翻译实训平台或基地。目前很多优秀的企业借助教育部产学合作协同育人平台提供了很多优质的实习基地建设项目与高校建立了良好的合作。所谓校外实训基地是指与学校对口进行校企合作的一些企业平台，后者是越来越多高校和企业较为追捧的主体形式（肖红，2005：139；李明、仲伟合，2010：32；吕亮球，2014：48）。在这些校外实训基地的实际运作中，一些典型的问题也随之出现。一方面，校外实训基地制度不完善，管理与评价体系不规范；另一方面，部分校外实训基地利用率不高，校企合作不稳定。校外实训是学生全面真实感受职场的最为重要的途径，但在实际操作过程中，部分企业由于缺乏对实训课程的清晰设置，缺乏对实训计划的缜密安排，一些实训沦为对学生的廉价使用，没有起到构建学生职业发展能力的根本目的。与此同时，部分高校也存在师资队伍和学科优势与实训基地“脱节”的现象，导致实训基地无法得到充分利用。

2.3 学生经翻译实践平台初步历练仍然无法充分就业，也难以在行业实现长足发展

当前高校毕业生就业压力大，既有客观原因，也有学生自身认知等主观原因。关于 MTI 学生的就业前景及职业发展的讨论一直不绝于耳（吴启金，2002；平洪，2014；任文，2018；穆雷，2020）。相当一段时间以来，人们普遍围绕翻译作为一种职业本身来看待这一问题，从一定程度上来说这无可厚非，但它实际上也对 MTI 广阔的就业前景进行了人为设限。事实上，当我们在谈论职业发展的时候，必须意识到它主要是基于一种行业或者领域的概念而言的，社会需要的是一种专业化的人才分工体系，个体需要在这一体系里找到适合自己的位置，并通过持续锤炼职业技巧来实现在职业阶梯上的纵深发展。理解了这一点，MTI 学生就会明白，翻译本身只是一种技能，它只有跟特定行业实现深度融合与应

用之后，才能发挥更大的价值。任何脱离了行业融合与应用的技能，都会不可避免地浮于表面，无法实现价值叠加。

2.4 全面系统翻译实践难以一以贯之，学生不具备拥抱行业发展机遇的充足条件，无法充分把握未来职业发展空间

高校和企业是两种性质不同的机构，合作观念和利益追求方面有较大差异：高校是提供社会公共服务的教育机构，关注社会效益；企业是提供商品或服务的商业机构，关注经济效益（杨桂玲，2016：97）。另外一方面，高校着眼通识教育，企业着眼专业技能，两者在合作过程中多少会遇到一些问题。究其根本，合作过程中诸多问题的表象最终都指向一个深层次的问题，即高校和企业缺乏对 MTI 学位教育与职业发展的一致性认知。学校教育具有公益性，主要还是致力于教书育人，高校教师普遍缺乏具体的企业实践，无法形成关于学生就业之后职业发展的直观感受；企业具有社会性，主要关注其招聘的人才对社会和职业的认同度，尤其是关于职业发展路径的认知程度。校企双方在合作的过程中，不仅要注重 MTI 学生在校三年的知识摄取与初步实践，更要关心就业三年内是否构建起了助力其长期职业发展的坚实基础，只有这样综合培养出来的人才才能切实担当起社会发展的重任，而这要求高校和企业能够寻求一个双方都能满意的切合点，以一种全新的视角来看待校企直通的人才培养模式，并开展全方位、宽领域、深层次的合作（杨桂玲，2016：97），从而最终实现高校、学生（人才）和公司发展的共赢。

3. 校企合作视阈下 MTI 学位教育与职业发展中的专利翻译实践层次

《教育部　人力资源社会保障部关于深入推进专业学位研究生培养模式改革的意见》（教研〔2013〕3 号）指出，专业学位研究生培养模式改革的目标是“以职业需求为导向，以实践能力培养为重点，以产学结合为途径，建立与经济社会发展相适应、具有中国特色的专业学位研究生培养模式”。明确的目标还需要切实的手段支撑实现。具体到 MTI 学位

教育来看，结合“以职业需求为导向，以实践能力培养为重点”的要求，无论 MTI 学生的职业路径如何发展，都离不开关于翻译实践能力的培养。可以说，翻译实践能力是 MTI 学生叩开其职业发展大门的最为根本的基础性能力，这项能力的培养是否扎实到位，决定了 MTI 学生未来的职业生涯能够走多高。在这一点上，高校和企业之间是有一致共识的。

针对 MTI 校企联合培养面临的上述四个层面的问题，我们选择“翻译实践”这一抓手，将“翻译实践”这一核心拆分为 MTI 学位教育以及 MTI 职业发展两个阶段，相应构建翻译实践的四个层次，即 MTI 学位教育中的外围辅助层和定制开发层以及 MTI 职业发展过程中的融合应用层和全面拓展层。这四个层次按照学校和高校分成两个大的层次，前后相互衔接，其关系如图 1 所示。

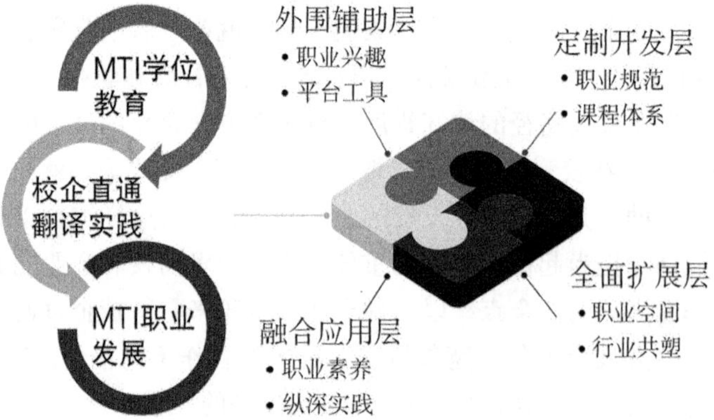

图 1　翻译实践的四个层次

通过在每个阶段进行不同的培养计划和措施，来实现贯通 MTI 学位教育和职业发展全过程中的能力培养。寻求在最大程度上有效贯通 MTI 学位教育和职业发展全过程中的能力培养，企业也能够更有针对性地将 MTI 学生的基础素质与企业的实际需求进行对接。

3.1 MTI 学位教育中翻译实践的外围辅助层

所谓外围辅助层，指的是为应对前述第一个问题普适性教育路线难以有效应对特定领域翻译的能力需求而设立的外围辅助手段。在高校人才培养供给侧，越来越多的 MTI 高校也意识到了普适性教育路线难以有效应对特定领域翻译的能力需求则这一问题，并开始在 MTI 招生阶段就有意识地关注学生的既有知识结构及背景能力，以便为后续向社会做针对性的人才输出打造坚实的基础，后续在培养全过程中，也在努力寻求企业资源融入结合。在这一层次上，企业作为外围辅助介入翻译实践，对弥补高校资源不足具有重要意义。就实施方法而言，企业在协助高校构建 MTI 学位教育中翻译实践的外围辅助层时，主要围绕如何有效延展学校常规课程教学与实践，激发 MTI 学生的职业兴趣，发挥企业的行业优势，应用通用信息技术工具或通用技术教育工具，在局部环节和要素辅助翻译实践。具体可以在先期已经参与高校培养方案制订和实施的基础上，进一步打造在线辅助教育课程，配合学校常规课程实施。

3.2 MTI 学位教育中翻译实践的定制开发层

所谓定制开发层，指的是为应对前述第二个问题学生对特定领域的兴趣难以在更深层次发展进行定制开发的一个延展层次。针对校外实训基地难以满足学生个性化需求的问题，企业在协助高校构建 MTI 学位教育中翻译实践的定制开发层时，一个基本的前提是，MTI 学生已经表现出了对特定领域的强烈兴趣，并有意愿在该领域进行更深层次的发展与探索。因此，这一层级的特征是以专门化翻译实践的定制开发为主要表现形式，应用范围涉及翻译实践的一个或多个方面。培养市场所需的职业翻译人员，需要在教学模式中以翻译能力发展为核心，而全面快速提升 MTI 学生翻译能力与职业素养，参加真实翻译项目的实习实训则是其重要途径（刘和平，2011；张政、张少哲，2012；张政、王赟，2020）。

3.3 MTI 职业发展中翻译实践的融合应用层

所谓融合应用层，指的是针对前述第三个问题学生经翻译实践平台初步历练仍然无法充分就业，也难以在行业实现长足发展而进行的融合应用尝试。MTI 学生在高校完成了“翻译实践”的外围辅助层和定制开发层的系统历练之后，本身已经形成了对特定行业的高度认同，并具备了在该行业发展自身职业生涯的基本意愿，同时也具备了进入行业中特定企业的基础条件，可以说已经完成了校企直通的初步耦合。但是，这是否意味着翻译实践已经没有必要了呢？或者说，翻译能力之于MTI学生的职业发展已经不重要了？从企业的角度来说，MTI学生在校翻译实践能力的培养，是其在特定行业发展的最为重要的基础能力之一，但要实现在行业纵深的长足发展，在校翻译实践能力的训练仍然是不够的。事实上，翻译能力只有与行业的丰富实践进行深度融合与应用之后，它对职业生涯长期发展的支撑才能真正落到实处，这样的人才也就真正能够做到游刃有余，并无限扩展自己的职业空间。在这一层次，企业可职场新晋MTI学生进一步设计更长一段时间的职场成长计划，沿袭MTI学生在校期间的“翻译实践”主题，寻求将翻译能力与行业知识进行深度融合与应用。

3.4 MTI职业发展中翻译实践的全面扩展层

所谓全面扩展层，指的是为应对前述不具备拥抱行业发展机遇充足条件的学生，无法充分把握未来职业发展空间的问题进一步设立的全面扩展学生认知和技能，全面拓展自身未来职业发展空间的一个实践层次。企业可以为MTI毕业生展现出一个全然不同的职业空间，使得所有高价值的职业通道纷纷对他们敞开大门。在这一阶段，翻译实践已经全面扩展到日常工作的方方面面，过去的所有努力都在这一阶段开花结果，个体得以在职业生涯上取得长足发展，而所有成绩的取得又进一步佐证了翻译实践的重要，它成就了个体，个体又成就了世界，正是在这样的正向循环中，人类达成了对集体命运的塑造。

4. RWS与中国高校联合构建翻译实践四个层次的实践

以下结合RWS公司与高校开展校企合作的长期实践，从企业的角度系统阐述如何将职业发展与高校MTI学位教育进行精准对接，尤其是围绕“翻译实践”这一核心主题，我们将系统探讨如何助力MTI学生逐步构建起其长期职业发展的能力体系，以实现莘莘学子在职场中乘风破浪的梦想。我们将从翻译实践的层次方面展开探讨，分享 RWS 与曲阜师范大学等高校在这方面的经验与积累，以期就教于方家。

4.1 RWS 构建的 MTI 学位教育中翻译实践的外围辅助层实践

以知识产权这一领域为例，在构建 MTI 学位教育中翻译实践的外围辅助层时，专利语言服务行业的积极参与是培育和顺利实施的关键。在专利语言服务相关的学校教育和行业培训领域，国际及国家知识产权监管服务机构以及国内外企业的积极参与是重要条件。像世界知识产权组织网站本身就提供了包括五大局在内的语言网页，提供了以英文为主的法律条文和申请服务，另外还提供了 Patentscope 检索服务，以及 WIPO Academy 提供培训服务，网站本身就是一个完备的专利语言服务及培训平台。中国国家知识产权局也提供了类似完备的服务和培训内容。

RWS 中国公司基于过去十年校企共建课程实施和学生实习实践经验，在 2017 年与曲阜师范大学联合申报并获批“山东省研究生教育质量提升计划”中研究生联合培养基地建设项目的基础上，进一步合作推出了面向 MTI 专利语言服务教育的行业专著《专利语言服务实务》，既是对以往校企合作在知识产权和专利翻译教育领域的一次阶段性总结，也是对后续校企联合培养知识产权人才的一次系统性探索。

目前，以《专利语言服务实务》的架构体系为依托，为进一步丰富教学内容与教学形式，RWS 与曲阜师范大学等高校联手，采用目前在高校教育中喜闻乐见的慕课形式，推出了面向全国 MTI 高校学生的公益课程“专利翻译实践”，将知识产权翻译实践所需具备的基础能力分解为 20 个左右的具体知识点，以视频教学的形式呈现给全国的 MTI 高校学生，如表 1 所示。学生每天只需花上 15—20 分钟的时间，坚持学习一个月，便可掌握有关知识产权领域“翻译实践”的基础知识，非常便于学生了解知识产权行业，并思考未来自己是否需要投身知识产权这一领域，并最终成就自己。

表 1 专利翻译实践课程教学计划

周	课次	课程	名师精讲
第 1 周	1	知识产权行业介绍	企业资深译审
	2	专利文件的组成	企业资深译审
	3	专利全文理解的思路	企业资深译审
	4	摘要 / 背景技术翻译特点精讲	企业资深译审
	5	具体实施方式翻译特点精讲	企业资深译审
第 2 周	6	专利申请的基本程序	企业资深译审
	7	权利要求的分类及结构	企业资深译审
	8	权利要求的相关法律规定	企业资深译审
	9	权利要求的常见问题分析	企业资深译审
	10	专利翻译的基本原则	高校教师
第 3 周	11	专利文献通用翻译规范——冠词	企业资深译审
	12	专利文献通用翻译规范——数词	企业资深译审
	13	专利审查的具体内容	企业资深译审
	14	术语选择——一致性与差异性	企业资深译审
	15	术语选择——准确性与专业性	企业资深译审
第 4 周	16	专利文献通用翻译规范——介词	企业资深译审
	17	专利文献通用翻译规范——从句	企业资深译审
	18	各技术领域专利文件的特点及翻译技巧	企业资深译审
	19	专利文献法律段落解读	高校教师
	20	专利文献附属文件翻译及对原文疑问的处理	企业资深译审

在有效学习“1 个月精品慕课”的基础之上，MTI 学生如果就此产生了对知识产权行业的浓厚兴趣，在完成相关课后测验并通过期末考试

的基础之上，可以申请进入“翻译实践”的下一层级，即我们所指的定制开发层。

4.2 RWS构建的MTI学位教育中翻译实践的定制开发层实践

RWS公司针对这些问题进行了有效的研究，并特别注意进行提前规避，对于申请进入这一层级的受训学生，RWS结合长期经验进行了定制开发，并设计了长达半年的实训体系，全部实训以职场能力养成为目标，同时紧扣“翻译实践”的核心主题，将日常的管理与评价细化到每个月以及每个月的每一周，通过制定清晰明确的实训内容、实训目标和实训评估标准，加强过程管理和评估考核，将各个环节落到实处。如表2、表3、表4所示。

表2 第1个月“职场素质养成”

周	主　题	收　获	细　节
第1周	语言服务行业	了解语言服务行业的历史与现状、内在运作机制与宏观发展格局	•语言服务行业的价值与基本运营方式 •语言与语系 •字符与字体 •计算机使用及网络常识 •信息安全教育与行为 •机翻适用场景和禁忌 •OA系统入门与知识库 •TMS翻译管理系统使用入门
第2周	CAT工具与翻译技术	掌握语言服务行业的必备基本技能与实用技术工具	•文件预处理（术语提取） •新建项目 •调用句库与术语库 •预翻译（术语预灌） •锁定与匹配 •审校与核准模式 •部分案例库的拆分与合并

（待续）

（续表）

周	主　题	收　获	细　节
第 3 周	语言服务行业职业素养	实现对语言服务行业基本规则的理解与运用、职业能力与素养的养成	• 保密意识 • 质量责任意识 • 守时性 • 团队协作 • 服务主动性 • 快速响应
第 4 周	语言服务公司生产流程与质量标准	实现语言服务行业理论知识学习与真实世界语言服务实践动手能力的衔接与融合	• 一般生产流程 • 各流程的操作规范及质量要求 • 质量评估标准 • 质量评估插件 • 质量管理体系

表 3　第 2、3 个月"分项强化实训"

周	专利翻译		语言工程
	内　容	形　式	
第 5 周	医药、化工、机械、电子领域主要申请人的专利内容概览	• 范文解读 • 错题培训 • 段落练习	• 语言工程内容 • 文件对比
第 6 周	专利文件中惯用段落、表达、术语解读		• Trados Log 分析，入库，锁重
第 7 周	翻译中的正则表达式使用		• Trados 双语转繁体（PTW） • 术语替换
第 8 周	RWS 工具集在翻译流程中的整合		• NMR RTE 非译元素处理 • 文中图和公式提取
第 9 周	语言规范——冠词及标点符号	• 2 万字全文翻译任务 • 导师全文修改及讲解 • RWS 案例库-语言规范专题培训	• 工程预处理（PRE）流程及内容介绍 • 目标要求确认

（待续）

（续表）

周	专利翻译		语言工程
	内　容	形　式	
第 10 周	语言规范——长句拆分与短句合并	• 2 万字全文翻译任务 • 导师全文修改及讲解 • RWS 案例库-语言规范专题培训	• Word 编辑器、ABBY 的使用 • Word 基本设置与 RWS Toolset
第 11 周	语言规范——表达一致性		• PDF 编辑器使用 • 数据库网站
第 12 周	语言规范——表达准确性		• PRE 格式要求 • PRE 提交文件要求

表 4　第 4—6 个月“个人进阶实训”

周	专利翻译		语言工程
	内　容	形　式	
第 13 周	技术理解——如何提炼全文技术方案	• 4 万字全文翻译任务 • 导师全文修改及讲解 • RWS 案例库-技术理解专题培训	• ENG 错误案例分析
第 14 周	技术理解——权利要求技术方案的语言结构分析		• PRE 错误案例分析
第 15 周	技术理解——如何选择术语的上下位概念		• 译后排版（LAY）流程及内容介绍
第 16 周	技术理解——术语词性处理		• Xbench 质检方法 • Word、Trados 质检方法
第 17 周	句型分析——介词用法	• 4 万字全文翻译任务 • 导师全文修改及讲解 • RWS 案例库-句型分析专题培训	• LAY 通用模板介绍
第 18 周	句型分析——修饰关系		• LAY 特殊模板处理
第 19 周	句型分析——长句逻辑		• 德语、韩语、日语 LAY 方法 • 繁体专利 LAY 方法
第 20 周	句型分析——句意合理		• LAY 格式要求 • LAY 提交文件要求

（待续）

（续表）

<table>
<tr><th rowspan="2">周</th><th colspan="2">专利翻译</th><th rowspan="2">语言工程</th></tr>
<tr><th>内　容</th><th>形　式</th></tr>
<tr><td>第 21 周</td><td>能力扩展——语言对双向互译技巧</td><td rowspan="4">• 5 万字全文翻译任务
• 导师全文修改及讲解
• 多流程、多语言对、多文件类型翻译方法培训</td><td>• 专利制图（DRW）流程及内容介绍
• 专利 DRW 基本类型</td></tr>
<tr><td>第 22 周</td><td>能力扩展——译文校读环节的要求和方法</td><td>• PDF 编辑器、Word、PS 软件使用</td></tr>
<tr><td>第 23 周</td><td>能力扩展——专利审查文件解读</td><td>• 专利文件说明书附图的 DRW 方法
• 专利文件摘要的 DRW 方法</td></tr>
<tr><td>第 24 周</td><td>能力扩展——各类质检工具的应用</td><td>• 繁体专利 DRW 方法
• 其他特殊文件的 DRW 方法</td></tr>
</table>

经过上述实训体系淬炼之后的 MTI 学生，可以说基本达到了培养“强基础、重实践、高素质”的职业化、创新型高水平人才的目的，也充分满足了 MTI 学位教育的要求，为学生顺利完成学位教育并做好职业发展长远考虑打下了坚实的基础。下一步，MTI 学生也具备了顺利跨入职场的基本素质，并可结合未来职业发展进一步锤炼自己的“翻译实践”能力。

4.3 RWS 构建的 MTI 职业发展中翻译实践的融合应用层实践

在定制融合应用层过程中，RWS 对于职场新晋 MTI 学生进一步设计了三年的职场成长计划，如表 5、表 6、表 7 所示。该计划沿袭 MTI 学生在校期间的“翻译实践”主题，着眼于如何将翻译能力与行业知识进行深度融合与应用，培养新晋人才对于职场的纵深能力。

表 5 第 1 年成长计划“用翻译说话，奠定投身知识产权的深厚根基”

年	专利翻译		语言工程	
	培养内容	目标达成	培养内容	目标达成
第 1 年	1. 全面参与特定技术领域的多语言方向、多文件类型的翻译实践； 2. 全面接触特定技术领域的全球专利申请量前列客户的专利文件，提供合格水平的翻译； 3. 专攻某个客户或某一具体领域的专利翻译。	1. 熟练掌握基本的翻译风格和翻译技巧； 2. 对于特定技术领域能提供总体稳定的翻译质量，具体为质量罚分低于每千字 7 分； 3. 积累 100 万字的翻译实践经验； 4. 针对某个客户或某一具体领域的翻译能力优异，具体为质量罚分低于每千字 4 分。	1. 参与专利全领域的 ENG、PRE 和 LAY，能够独立、且高质量完成语言工程任务； 2. 按照语言工程小组的质量、时效、工作量、态度等全方位满足岗位工作要求，及时提交规范的日报和总结； 3. 能够在某一到两个专利领域，独立承担 ENG、PRE 和 LAY 全流程。	1. 掌握 PRE、ENG 和 LAY 技能与质量要求，每月低级错误不超过 3 处及以上； 2. 6 个月内工程工作量折合成排版后的字数稳定达到 50 万字 / 月，第 12 个月达到 70 万字 / 月； 3. 日报及时、规范提交率达到95%； 4. 综合绩效考核达到公司的及格线为最低要求。

表 6 第 2 年成长计划“与行业接触，从业务体系上全面理解知识产权”

年	专利翻译		语言工程	
	培养内容	目标达成	培养内容	目标达成
第 2 年	1. 全面强化特定技术领域的多语言方向、多文件类型的翻译，专注翻译效率；	1. 对于特定技术领域能提供总体优异的翻译质量，具体为质量罚分低于每千字 4 分；	1. 全面独立承担专利全领域的 ENG、PRE、LAY 和其他工程 Job，能够独立、且高质量完成语言工程任务，承担本小组质量控制责任；	1. 熟练掌握 PRE、ENG 和 LAY，每月低级错误能够不超过 2 处及以上；

（待续）

（续表）

年	专利翻译		语言工程	
	培养内容	目标达成	培养内容	目标达成
第2年	2. 全面参与专属客户或领域的专利译文审校工作，专注独立出稿质量； 3. 参与新译员培养，进一步巩固个人的翻译知识体系。	2. 累计积累200万字的翻译实践经验，包含至少30万字的审校经验； 3. 针对某个客户或某一具体领域的审校能力稳定且优异，具体为质量罚分低于每千字2分； 4. 能对新译员开展培训。	2. 按照语言工程小组的质量、时效、工作量、态度等全方位满足岗位工作要求，及时提交规范的日报和总结； 3. 及时总结新客户、新业务的工程规范与Checklist，辅导实习生按时、高质量达标。	2. 工作量折合成排版后的字数稳定在100万字/月以上； 3. 日报及时、规范提交率达到95%； 4. 能够对当前承担工作及时总结工作规范，并外延到部分新客户、新业务。

表7 第3年成长计划“展翅欲高飞，为进入五百强中高端职位做准备”

年	专利翻译		语言工程	
	培养内容	目标达成	培养内容	目标达成
第3年	1. 全面参与特定技术领域的多语言方向、多文件类型的定稿工作； 2. 全面参与专属客户或领域的专利译文的质量控制工作；	1. 对于特定技术领域能提供总体优异的定稿质量，具体为内部质检不合格率低于5%； 2. 累计积累400万字的翻译实践经验，包含至少80万字的定稿经验；	1. 基于现有成熟业务，为新业务制定新的工程规范与新技术研发和攻关能力； 2. 按照语言工程小组的质量、时效、工作量、态度等全方位满足岗位工作要求，及时提交规范的日报和总结；	1. 成为内部同岗位的质量标杆和合格讲师； 2. 具备全面的语言工程与技术体系知识，并具备新业务开拓需要的技术研究与拓展能力；

（待续）

（续表）

年	专利翻译		语言工程	
	培养内容	目标达成	培养内容	目标达成
第 3 年	3. 参与部门译员培养、以及部门客户维护。	3. 成为某个客户或某一具体领域的质控专家，能够开展专业性培训； 4. 能与客户就专业问题独立沟通。	3. 全面承担质量管理与培训，协助上司对内外部资源的生产提交进行质控与培训。	3. 日报及时、规范提交率达到 95% 4. 能够协助上司达成团队的质量管理和培训目标。

对于大多数职场新人来说，前三年的融合与应用都会在极大程度上决定未来职场生涯能够走得多高、多远。自觉而主动地将自己的个人意愿与大的时代方向、大的行业趋势加以契合，是个体能够在一定程度上超越自我的最为有效的方式。也只有将个人的基础素质和特定行业实现了深度融合与应用之后，个体才能够在融入行业的基础上，进一步驾驭行业，并最终实现职业生涯的长足发展。“翻译实践”在这其中成为贯穿学位教育与职业发展的主线，是始终不能忽视的基础能力培养。

4.4 RWS 构建的 MTI 职业发展中翻译实践的全面扩展层实践

我们通常理解的职业发展，就是在自己选定的领域里，在自己能力所及的范围内，成为最好的专家。而职业发展规划则是企业和员工长期利益的统一，每一家具有高度责任感的企业都有义务为其员工指明职业发展方向，设计职业发展通道，使员工看见个人发展的希望，实现人才的长期稳定性（姚裕群，2003）。

科学技术发展引发翻译业务与管理方式的变革，翻译对象、方式、工具和手段，翻译研究对象和翻译研究队伍均已发生重大变化，随着其职业化进程逐步加快，翻译业已进入职业化时代（谢天振，2013）。MTI学生在校学习三年，积累了基础知识，掌握了基本技能，对行业有了初步认知和经验。一方面 MTI 毕业生步入职场三年后，还需要持续学习，与时俱进，形成关于职业发展的全面认知。具体到特定的行业中，也应该形成关于在该行业中如何进行长远职业发展的完整理解。另一方面，MTI 毕业生将在这一阶段完成关于翻译实践的实质性切换，即从过去主要着眼于通过翻译实践打造基础翻译能力与素质，切换到未来主要以行业实际业务为工作内容，翻译实践则内化为一种基础工作能力。那些围绕"翻译实践"主题出发并充分利用了三年 MTI 教育、三年企业实践的人会发现，他们面前已经展现出了一个全然不同的职业空间，所有高价值的职业通道纷纷对他们敞开了大门，他们也具备了拥抱行业发展机遇的充足条件。

以知识产权行业为例，MTI 毕业生经过三年关于专利"翻译实践"的针对性训练之后，所面对的职业前景将远远不再局限于专利翻译工作本身，而是知识产权行业中所有需要以翻译能力为基础的职位，如事务所的涉外代理、知识产权机构的涉外专利审查、企业的全球专利运营、全球专利布局等，这些职位一方面需要具备深厚的语言功底，另一方面还要有扎实的行业知识。如图 2 所示。

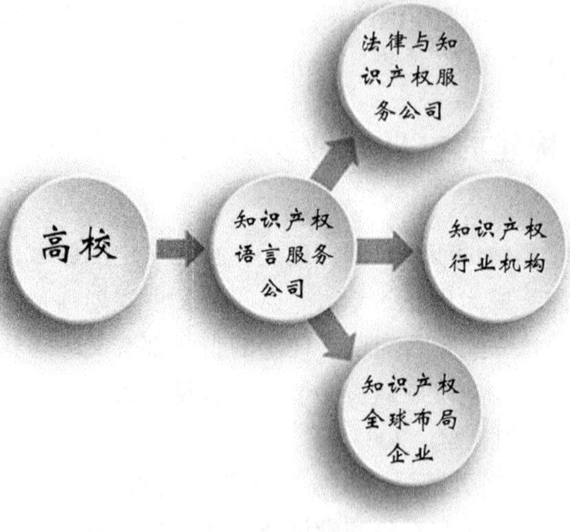

图 2 "知识产权"校企直通全景图

5. 结语

校企合作虽然在形式上为高校与企业之间的协作打开了大门，但实际操作过程中无论出于企业还是高校的原因，还是存在一些无法避讳的痼疾，从而导致学位教育与企业需求之间事实上的某种“脱节”。如何寻找到有效抓手，构建起校企直连通道，是摆在 MTI 教育中的现实问题。

“翻译实践”的层次，从立足于高校的外围辅助层、定制开发层，到立足于企业的融合应用层、全面扩展层，不同层级体现出不同的形式及内涵。RWS 结合与多所高校的 MTI 教学合作与实践，创新性地提出“校企直通”模式，以翻译实践为抓手，系统探讨了 MTI 学生从高校到企业、从理论到实践，最终成长为行业栋梁的完整历程，对启迪校企之间如何进行更深层面协同提供了有益借鉴。

未来，只有经由“翻译实践”武装起来的行业人才，才是真正强大的专业人才，也是顺应时代要求、能够创造更大价值的人才，而这正是校企直通模式的核心与要旨，是学位教育与职业发展相融合的方向与进路。

参考文献

[1] 蔡辉. 论翻译专业硕士培养中的校企合作 [J]. 中国翻译，2013（3）：51-55.

[2] 丁素萍. 建立翻译硕士专业学位（MTI）双导师制可持续发展的合作机制 [J]. 教育与职业，2012（32）：181-182.

[3] 董洪学，张晴. 翻译硕士（MTI）专业学位实习基地建设模式创新思考 [J]. 外语电化教学，2015（2）：30-34.

[4] 郭晓勇. 中国语言服务行业发展状况、问题及对策——在 2010 中国国际语言服务行业大会上的主旨发言 [J]. 中国翻译，2010（6）：34-37.

[5] 国务院办公厅. 国务院办公厅关于深化产教融合的若干意见 . 国办发〔2017〕95 号 [EB/OL].（2017-12-19）[2020-09-19]. http://www.gov.cn/zhengce/content/2017-12/19/content_5248564.htm.

[6] 国务院学位委员会. 关于开展增列硕士专业学位授权点审核工作的通知. 学位〔2013〕37 号 . 增列硕士专业学位授权点基本条件 [EB/OL].（2013-11-18）[2020-09-26]. http://old.moe.gov.cn/publicfiles/business/htmlfiles/moe/moe_820/201311/159668.html.

[7] 冯曼. 以职业化为导向的 MTI 实践教学体系的构建 [J]. 广西大学学报（哲学社会科学版），2012（8）：128-132.

[8] 黄忠廉. "翻译硕士专业学位"更应突出应用性和实践性 [N]. 中国社会科学报，2010-6-15.

[9] 教育部，人力资源社会保障部 . 教育部　人力资源社会保障部关于深入推进专业学位研究生培养模式改革的意见. 教研〔2013〕3 号 [EB/OL].（2013-11-13）[2020-09-16]. http://www.moe.gov.cn/srcsite/A22/moe_826/201311/t20131113_159870.html.

[10] 李军，黄宝印，朱瑞. 改善和完善外语专业研究生培养模式，培养翻译硕士专业学位人才 [J]. 中国翻译，2007（4）：6-7.

[11] 李明，仲伟合. 翻译工作坊教学探微 [J]. 中国翻译，2010（4）：32-36.

[12] 刘和平. 翻译能力发展的阶段性及其教学法研究 [J]. 中国翻译，2011（1）：37-45.

[13] 吕亮球. 翻译工作坊教学模式探究 [J]. 上海翻译，2014（4）：48-51.

[14] 穆雷，仲伟合，王巍巍. 从职业化角度看专业翻译人才培养机制的完善 [J]. 中国外语，2013（1）：89-95.

[15] 穆雷，李雯，蔡耿超. MTI 实践能力培养考核制度的改革设想——来自临床医学专业硕士的启示 [J]. 上海翻译，2018（4）：56-62.

[16] 穆雷. 我国翻译硕士专业学位现状与问题——基于《翻译硕士专业学位发展报告》的分析研究 [J]. 中国翻译，2020（1）：87-96.

[17] 平洪. 主动服务社会需求，全面提高 MTI 教育质量——全国翻译专业学位研究生教育 2014 年年会综述 [J]. 中国翻译，2014（3）：57-59.

[18] 全国翻译专业学位研究生教育指导委员会. 翻译硕士专业学位基本要求 [EB/OL].（2018-09-09）[2020-09-19]. https://cnti.gdufs.edu.cn/info/1006/2029.htm.

[19] 全国翻译专业学位研究生教育指导委员会. 翻译硕士专业学位培养单位评估指标体系 [EB/OL].（2013-05-09）[2020-09-19]. https://cnti.gdufs.edu.cn/info/1015/1029.htm.
[20] 全国翻译专业学位研究生教育指导委员会. 翻译硕士专业学位研究生教育指导性培养方案（2011 年 8 月修订）[EB/OL]（2013-12-27）[2020-09-26]. https://cnti.gdufs.edu.cn/info/1006/1094.htm.
[21] 全国翻译专业学位研究生教育指导委员会. 全国翻译专业学位研究生教育兼职教师认证规范 [EB/OL].（2015-09-16）[2019-09-26]. https://cnti.gdufs.edu.cn/info/1015/1411.htm.
[22] 全国翻译专业学位研究生教育指导委员会. 全国翻译专业学位研究生教育实习基地（企业）认证规范 [EB/OL].（2015-09-16）[2020-09-20]. https://cnti.gdufs.edu.cn/info/1015/1410.htm.
[23] 任文. 新时代语境下翻译人才培养模式再探究：问题与出路 [J]. 当代外语研究，2018（6）：96-102.
[24] 滕梅，张馨元. 翻译行业产业化和职业化背景下的翻译硕士（MTI）专业课程设置 [J]. 山东外语教学，2013（4）：96-101.
[25] 王传英. 本地化行业发展与 MTI 课程体系创新 [J]. 外语教学，2010（4）：110-113.
[26] 吴启金. 翻译教育要进一步与市场需求相衔接 [J]. 外语与外语教学，2002（9）：45-48.
[27] 肖红. "翻译作坊"在翻译教学中的运用 [J]. 四川外语学院学报，2005（1）：139-142.
[28] 谢天振. 从翻译服务到语言服务——翻译的职业化时代的理念与行为 [J]. 东方翻译，2013（3）：4-8.
[29] 杨朝军. 产业化视域下的翻译硕士培养模式 [J]. 中国翻译,2012（1）：24-28.
[30] 杨桂玲. 理工科院校 MTI 实训基地建设研究 [J]. 中国成人教育，2016（2）：95-97.
[31] 姚裕群. 职业生涯规划与发展 [M]. 首都经济贸易大学出版社，2003.
[32] 张政，王赟. MTI 项目化翻译教学与翻译能力培养：理论与实践 [J]. 外语界，2020（2）：65-72.

[33] 张政，张少哲. 真项目，真实践，真环境，真体验——基于北京 师范大学 MTI CAT 案例教学的探索与实践 [J]. 中国翻译，2012（2）：43-46.

[34] 赵军峰. MTI 教学的创新与实践：以广外高翻学院为例 [J]. 外文研究，2013（6）：78-85.

[35] 郑金凤，王凤，王蒙，王华伟. 专利语言服务实务 [M]. 北京：知识产权出版社，2019.

[36] 中国翻译协会 . 2018 中国语言服务行业发展报告 [R]. 2018.

[37] 仲伟合. 十年扬帆，蓄势远航：MTI 教育十年回顾与展望 [J]. 中国翻译，2017（3）：7-9.

[38] 周恩，丁年青. 西方翻译能力模式研究及对我国 MTI 翻译能力培养的启示 [J]. 外语界，2017（4）：51-60.

[39] Bond, E. Record number of patent applications drive translation demand [EB/OL]. (01-04-2019) [01-06-2019]. https://slator.com/demand-drivers/record-number-of-patent-applications-drive-translation-demand/.

[40] TAUS. DQF: Quality benchmark for our industry [EB/OL]. [01-06-2019]. https://www.taus.net/evaluate/dqf-background.

九、翻译合作及其他

Status Quo of Medical Interpreters and Their Expectations in Professionalization of Medical Interpreting: Evidence from Two Surveys in Five Years in China[1]

Mayinuer Yusufu University of Melbourne
Zhang Xuxi Peking University
Zhou Ling University of International Business and Economics
Dai Yitong Li Jun (correspondence author) Peking University

Abstract: Medical interpreting has attracted more attention as service demand increased in recent years in China. However, the development of the profession is largely unknown. Thus, the authors conducted surveys, to elucidate the current situation, dilemma, and prospect of the medical interpreting profession in China. Two surveys were carried out between March and April 2015 and between February and March 2020, respectively, with 34 and 196 responses received, respectively. According to the results of the two surveys, the remuneration was barely acceptable by half of the interpreters. Unstable income due to fluctuating market demands was considered as the leading barrier to a career as a freelance interpreter. Furthermore, comparing with the results in the 2015 survey, though the market scale expanded greatly in the 2020 survey, the values of interpreters were still under-recognized, with only one-third of participants satisfied with the remuneration. The participants reported the necessity of establishing an accreditation system and professional

1 The authors thank all the friends and colleagues who helped to circulate the online survey and are grateful to all the participants for taking time out of their busy schedule to participate in this survey.

society for medical interpreting. The findings suggest that the high-difficulty, lower-than-expectation remuneration and ad-hoc nature of medical interpreting in China call for the professionalization of the practice, which might start with the establishment of an accreditation system and professional association and opening of training programs.

Keywords: Medical interpreting profession; Job satisfaction; Qualification; Interpreting for special purposes; Accreditation system

中国医学译员的现状及其对医学口译职业化的期待：基于五年两次调查结果的实证研究

玛依努尔·于苏甫　墨尔本大学

张旭熙　北京大学

周　玲　对外经济贸易大学

代翊彤　李　俊（通讯作者）　北京大学

摘　要： 近年来，随着服务需求的增加，医学口译在我国逐渐受到关注，但人们对该职业的发展情况所知甚少。本研究开展问卷调查以阐明医学口译职业在中国的现状、困境和前景。于 2015 年 3 月至 4 月和 2020 年 2 月至 3 月之间进行了两次调查，分别收到 34 和 196 份回复。调查结果显示，一半的译员认为薪酬勉强可以接受；市场需求波动导致的收入不稳定是选择自由译员作为职业的主要障碍。此外，与 2015 年的研究结果相比，尽管 2020 年调查发现医学口译市场规模大幅扩大，但译员价值仍未得到充分认可，仅三分之一的受访者对薪酬感到满意。参与调查的译员认为有必要建立医学口译认证体系和专业协会。研究结果表明，医学口译在中国具有高难度、低薪酬和临时性的特点，职业化程度仍需提高。职业化发展的第一步可以考虑建立认证体系和专业协会并开设培训课程。

关键词： 医学口译职业；职业满意度；从业资质；专门用途口译；认证体系

1. Introduction

Medical interpreting refers to interpreting in any medical setting, especially in hospitals for conversation doctors and patients in the US (Liu & Zhu, 2015) and for attendees of international conferences and lectures in China. In international sports events and medical tourism, medical interpreting also helps remove the barrier to accessing health care and helps foreigners in communicating with medical professionals (Ono, 2020).

In the context of globalization, there is an increasing need for interpretation in academic, business and other settings, in order to provide a platform for communication for healthcare professionals and allied healthcare professionals from different countries or cultures. With the implementation of the Belt and Road Initiative, medical interpreting became even more important, serving both China and its collaborators (Yang, 2021). International medical aid from China has reached a scale of over 3 billion dollars per year (Wang, Jin & Fan, 2017). Although non-professional interpreters could work as volunteers during the COVID-19 pandemic (Gong, 2022), any kind of training in medical interpreting could improve the quality of medical service for Low-English-proficient (LEP) patients (Schlange, 2022). The response to the pandemic also highlights the importance of training and pooling medical interpreters (Wang, 2020). These findings highlight the necessity of professionalization of medical interpreting and interpreters.

According to the *Report on Development of Language Services Industry 2022*[1], the market scale has been expanding, and standardization of the industry is in progress, translation (and interpretation) of languages used in countries along "the Belt and Road" saw a rapid increase, especially Arabic,

---

1 There were 423,547 enterprises offering language services in 2021 with a total output of 55.448 billion yuan, an 11.1% increase compared with that in 2019. There were 316 colleges and universities offering Master of Translation and Interpreting nationwide, with a total enrollment of about 97,000 students, and 5.38 million people worked in translation (and interpretation) service, a 40% increase compared with that of 10 years ago.

Russian, German, English, and Belarusian. Besides, artificial technology was drawing increasing attention. However, the lack of high-quality, professional, and Chinese-English translation talents and talents specialized in "smaller languages" remain. Nevertheless, the *Report* lacks detailed data on the medical interpreting profession. It is necessary to learn about the current situation of the medical interpreting profession, the qualification of medical interpreters and their perception of the profession (Wang, 2005).

While Zhan and Yan (2013) and Zhu and Liu (2015) have investigated the profession, their data were dated. Thus, the authors conducted surveys, to elucidate the current situation, dilemma, and prospect of the medical interpreting profession in China. Two surveys were carried out between March and April 2015 and between February and March 2020, respectively, with 34 and 196 responses received, respectively.

2. Literature review

Medical interpreter is a very hot research topic in academia. As many as 680 results were retrieved after searching with the theme of "medical interpreter" in one year in PKU library search engine.

Research focused on who should be medical interpreters (family members or professionals) (Quesada., Solis & Levi, 2020; Pines, Jones & Sheeran, 2020; Iftikhar, 2022), how to train medical interpreters (Sabar & Tenenboim, 2018), how they work (Kamara *et al.*, 2018; Sleptsova *et al.*, 2017; Rhodes *et al.*, 2021), their role in service (Li *et al.*, 2017; Wu & Rawal, 2017; Zhan & Zeng, 2017; Álvaro Aranda, Gutiérrez & Li, 2021; Martin, Philip & McLachlan, 2022), advocating enhancing medical communication and care through professional medical interpreters (Iftikhar, 2022). Most study settings were in healthcare facilities overseas, with a few happened in Chinese hospitals (Zhan & Zeng, 2017). The demographic features, satisfaction towards job, income and financial stability of medical interpreters were largely under-examined. Only one study looked at the well-being of medical interpreters (Geiling *et al.*, 2022).

The importance of using professional medical interpreters has been emphasized once and again in literature, arguments include that "professional medical interpreters have the knowledge and skills for interpretation and have a basic understanding of medical terminology and diseases and that they abide by a professional code of ethics that includes confidentiality, impartiality, accuracy, and completeness, and they know their role, limitations, and responsibilities" (Iftikhar, 2022). The inadequacy and inappropriateness, such as inaccuracy and omission, lack of cross-cultural communicative skills, and challenges in multi-tasking (acting concurrently as student and interpreter) of ad hoc medical interpreters, such as relatives or medical students have been pointed out (Wu & Rawal, 2017; Quesada, Solis & Levi, 2020; Iftikhar, 2022)

Furthermore, in these studies, medical interpreters often, if not always, refer to those interpreting conversations between healthcare providers and patients. This is due to the difference in the demand for medical interpreting. In China, the mainstay job of medical interpreters is not for health care interpreting, though that does exist (Zhan & Zeng, 2017). Medical interpreters in China also work for medical conferences, who could be further profiled as those working for business, academic or clinical settings related to healthcare or the healthcare industry (Yusufu, 2016).

In recent years, Chinese scholars, including the authors of this article, have proposed the professionalization for medical interpreters in China, both for healthcare interpreting and for conference interpreting (Zhu & Liu, 2015; Yusufu, 2016; Li, Yusufu, & Zhou, 2021). Did such advocacy bring any changes in the landscape of medical interpreting in China? To find out that, we set out for questionnaire surveys. In 2015, we conducted a small-sized one, and with the expansion of our professional networks, we were able to send out the questionnaire to more participants in 2020. In this article, we present the survey results and analysis we conducted in 2015 and 2020.

3. Materials and methods

A questionnaire was developed based on literature review and was further revised after in-depth discussions with two experts who have engaged in medical interpreting for over five years. The questionnaire contains 33 questions covering three aspects: basic information of interpreters, interpreters' experience, and interpreters' perception of the medical interpreting profession. The detailed description of the development of the questionnaire was published elsewhere (Yusufu, 2016).

Medical interpreting was further divided into three categories based on the purpose of the interpreting: medical interpreting for academic purposes (for academic exchanges, such as lectures or medical conferences), medical interpreting for business purposes (for business cooperation in the medical field, such as acquisition and merger of pharmaceutical companies, or purchase of medical devices), medical interpreting for clinical purposes (for communications during clinical activities, such as interpreting for patients and doctors during the hospital visit). Based on the purpose and the most three common types of interpreting (simultaneous interpreting, consecutive interpreting and liaison interpreting), in this study, medical interpreting was further divided into 7 subtypes: simultaneous medical interpreting for academic purposes, consecutive medical interpreting for academic purposes, liaison medical interpreting for academic purpose, simultaneous medical interpreting for business purpose, consecutive medical interpreting for business purpose, liaison medical interpreting for business purpose, and liaison medical interpreting for clinical purpose. The participants were invited to report the difficulty level, remuneration satisfaction and difficulties they encountered during interpreting.

The questionnaire was distributed online through an online survey platform Wenjuanxing. Associates of the investigators help to disseminate the survey online and through their professional circles, and responses were collected between March and April 2015 and between February and March

2020, respectively, with 196 and 34 valid responses obtained, respectively. The data were analyzed with SPSS 19.0.

4. Results

4.1 Basic information

4.1.1 Sex and age

In 2020, a total of 196 interpreters participated in the survey, with males accounting for 26.53% (n=52) and females accounting for 73.47% (n=114). As for the age groups, 29.08% of participants were under 25 years, 33.67% were between 26-35 years, 26.53% were between 36-45 years, and 10.71% were over 45 years. In both surveys, the majority of the participants were aged between 26 to 35 years (58.82% in 2015 and 33.67% in 2020). The details of the sex and age of the participants are shown in Table 1. These data suggest that medical interpreters are mainly females in their mid-20s to 30s.

Table 1 Age and sex of participants in 2015 and 2020

Age groups (years)	Participants in 2015			Participants in 2020		
	Male (n=13)	Female (n=21)	Total (n=34)	Male (n=52)	Female (n=144)	Total (n=196)
<25	3 (23.08%)	11 (52.38%)	14 (41.18%)	9 (17.31%)	48 (33.33%)	57 (29.08%)
26-35	10 (76.92%)	10 (47.62%)	20 (58.82%)	13 (25.00%)	53 (36.81%)	66 (33.67%)
36-45	0	0	0	21 (40.38%)	31 (21.53%)	52 (26.53%)
>45	0	0	0	9 (17.31%)	12 (8.33%)	21 (10.71%)

4.1.2 Occupation

In 2020, 191 effective answers on occupation were collected from 66 (34.55%) teachers, 61 (31.94%) students, 31 (16.23%) participants working in medical facilities (including 19 doctors) and 28 (14.66%) full-time interpreters, 3 (1.57%) administrative staff and 2 (1.05%) editors. The proportion of teachers increased by 12.67% in 2020 (34.55%) compared with that in 2015 (21.88%). However, the proportion of students and full-time interpreters decreased by 14.94% (31.94% in 2020 vs. 46.88% in 2015) and 4.09% (14.66% vs. 18.75%) respectively. The profession of participants was mainly teachers and students.

4.1.3 Education background

In 2020, for undergraduate study, 145 out of 193 (75.13%) went to first-tier universities in China, such as Peking or Tsinghua Universities. As for the major, 81 (41.97%) studied in English related programs, while 68 (30.43%) medicine related programs, and 32 (16.58%) English and medicine related programs.

For postgraduate study, 115 out of 138 (83.33%) went to first-tier universities, and as for the program, 72 (52.17%) studied English related programs, 42 (30.43%) medicine related programs, 7 (5.07%) English and medicine related programs.

For the doctoral study, 42 out of 52 (80.77%) went to first-tier universities, and as for the program, 14 (26.92%) studied English related programs, 27 27 (51.92%) medicine related programs, 3 (5.77%) English and medicine related programs.

In the 2020 Survey, there were 3 participants reporting high school or lower education as their highest education qualification. A total of 53 participants had an education background in both English and medicine in 2020, and in 2015, that figure was 15 out of 34. The details of the graduation universities and programs of participants are shown in Table 2.

Table 2 Programs and graduation universities of participants in 2015 and 2020

Programs and graduation universities	Participants in 2015			Participants in 2020		
	Bachelor's degree (n=34)	Master's degree (n=29)	Doctor's degree (n=8)	Bachelor's degree (n=193)	Master's degree (n=138)	Doctor's degree (n=52)
First-tier universities	29 (85.29%)	23 (79.31%)	4 (50%)	145 (75.13%)	115 (83.33%)	42 (80.77%)
Second-tier universities	4 (11.76%)	2 (6.9%)	0	44 (22.8%)	17 (12.32%)	5 (9.62%)
Third-tier universities	0	0	0	2 (1.04%)	0	0
Other universities	1 (2.94%)	4 (13.79%)	4 (50%)	2 (1.04%)	6 (4.35%)	5 (9.62%)
English-related programs	13 (38.24%)	16 (55.17%)	0	81 (41.97%)	72 (52.17%)	14 (26.92%)
Medicine-related programs	8 (23.53%)	11 (37.93%)	8 (100%)	68 (35.23%)	42 (30.43%)	27 (51.92%)
Medical English-related programs	12 (35.29%)	1 (3.45%)	0	32 (16.58%)	7 (5.07%)	3 (5.77%)
Other programs	1 (2.94%)	1 (3.45%)	0	12 (6.22%)	17 (12.32%)	8 (15.38%)

These data suggested that the investigated medical interpreters were well-educated. In the 2015 survey, most participants majored in English or Medicine, whereas in the 2020 survey, half of the participants majored in both English and medicine related programs.

4.1.4 Qualifications/Certificates

In 2020, 82 (41.84%) and 54 (27.55%) of the participants responded that they obtained Test for English Majors-Band 8 (TEM-8) and Test for English Majors-Band 4 (TEM-4) certificates respectively. The proportion of participants holding TEM-4, TEM-8 and CATTI-1 for interpreters all decreased by 13.63% (27.55% in 2020 vs. 41.18% in 2015), 31.69% (41.84% vs. 73.53%), and 1.41% (1.53% vs. 2.94%), respectively. However, the proportion of participants holding CATTI-2 for interpreters increased by 0.6% (15.31% vs. 14.71%).

One participant reported having all 6 certificates, one participant had 5 certificates, 6 had 4, 16 had 3, 37 had 2 and 98 had only one. The proportion of participants with over 4 certificates and with over 2 certificates decreased by 10.62% (4.08% vs. 14.7%) and 18.88% (31.12% vs. 50%) respectively. The details of the certificates held by participants are shown in Table 3.

The data from two surveys suggested that most participants have at least one English language proficiency certificate, and some even have high-level certificates, but few had certificates of translation.

Table 3 Certificates held by participants in 2015 and 2020

Certificates	Participants in 2015 (n=34)	Participants in 2020 (n=196)
TEM-4	14 (41.18%)	54 (27.55%)
TEM-8	25 (73.53%)	82 (41.84%)
CATTI-1 for interpreters	1 (2.94%)	3 (1.53%)
CATTI-1 for translators	1 (2.94%)	4 (2.04%)
CATTI-2 for interpreters	5 (14.71%)	30 (15.31%)
CATTI-2 for translators	8 (23.53%)	26 (13.27%)
Other	5 (14.71%)	55 (28.06%)

4.2 Interpreters' experience

4.2.1 Job seniority and frequency

With regard to job seniority, 42 (26.42%) engaged in medical interpreting for over 5 years, while 53 (33.33%) for less than 6 months. The proportion of participants with work experience of over 5 years was over 3 times higher than that in 2015, while the proportion of participants with work experience of less than 6 months was over one-third times lower. The details of the job seniority of interpreters are shown in Table 4. These data suggested that participants of the 2015 survey were mostly novice, and those in the 2020 survey were more experienced.

Table 4 Job seniority of interpreters in 2015 and 2020[1]

Frequency	Participants in 2015 (n=32#)	Participants in 2020 (n=159*)
< 6 months	17 (53.13%)	53 (33.33%)
6-12 months	2 (6.25%)	19 (11.95%)
1-2 years	3 (9.38%)	16 (10.06%)
2-3 years	4 (12.5%)	12 (7.55%)
3-5 years	4 (12.5%)	17 (10.69%)
> 5 years	2 (6.25%)	42 (26.42%)

As for the frequency of interpreting, 23 (11.73%) did 1-2 interpreting sessions every week, 19 (9.69%) 1-2 interpreting sessions every month, and 54 (27.55%) every half year. The proportion of interpreters doing 1-2 interpreting sessions every week increased by 5.49% compared with that in 2015. The details of the frequency of medical interpreting sessions are shown in Table 5. The data here indicates that medical interpreting is inadequate to support an interpreter to make a living. As shown here, if only 30% of participants could work 1-2 sessions per week/month, according to the market price, their income would be 5000-10000 RMB per week/month. Such a salary is barely enough for an interpreter to live in tier-one cities such as Beijing or Shanghai. The monthly rent for an apartment with one living room is 5000 RMB per month. Given that medical interpreting is challenging, few might consider it as their only job. They might consider it as a part-time job, which is proved by the data in Table 6. As is shown in Table 6, Full-time interpreters in translation companies accounted for about only 10%.

1 # 2 participants did not respond.
* 37 participants did not respond.

Table 5 Frequency of medical interpreting sessions in 2015 and 2020[1]

Frequency	Participants in 2015 (n=34)	Participants in 2020 (n=133*)
1-2 sessions per week	4 (11.80%)	23 (17.29%)
1-2 sessions per month	6 (17.60%)	19 (14.29%)
1-2 sessions per quarter	6 (17.60%)	16 (12.03%)
1-2 sessions per half-year	13 (38.20%)	54 (40.60%)
Other	5 (14.70%)	21 (15.79%)

4.2.2 Job opportunities

The main source of job opportunities was recommendation by acquaintances, followed by part of job responsibility, translation agencies, and full-time interpreters in translation companies, and the ranking was the same as that in 2015. The details are shown in Table 6.

Table 6 Source of job opportunities[2]

Source	Participants in 2015 (n=34)	Participants in 2020 (n=145*)
Recommendation by acquaintances	22 (64.70%)	90 (62.07%)
Translation agencies	7 (20.60%)	22 (15.17%)
Part of job responsibility	10 (29.40%)	36 (24.83%)
Full-time interpreters in translation companies	3 (8.80%)	15 (10.34%)
Others	2 (5.90%)	13 (8.97%)

4.2.3 Difficulty of the task

A total of 133 participants reported that they had done medical interpreting for academic purposes, and 62 (42.62%) participants found it to be difficult,

1 * 63 participants did not respond.

2 * 51 participants did not respond.

and 27 (20.30%) thought it was extremely difficult; 123 participants reported that they had done medical interpreting for business purposes, and 26 (21.14%) participants found it to be difficult, and 7 (5.70%) thought it was extremely difficult; 124 participants reported that they had done medical interpreting for clinical purpose, and 38 (30.65%) participants found it to be difficult, and 22 (17.74%) thought it was extremely difficult. In summary, medical interpreting for academic or clinical purposes was reported most difficult. In 2015, the majority (81.25%) of participants reported that medical interpreting for academic purpose was difficult or extremely difficult. This echoes with Cheng (2010) for the reason why medical knowledge is important. As clinical or academic purposes conferences largely communicate knowledge, more often than not, the latest advances, it is extremely important and difficult for interpreters to have a mastery of medical knowledge. Many conferences tend to hire part-time temporary interpreters from healthcare professionals, although these professionals lack the skills for interpreting.

4.2.4 Remuneration satisfaction

For all 7 sub-types of medical interpreting, around half of the participants felt the remuneration was barely acceptable. The proportion of participants satisfied with the remuneration ranged from 35.51% to 36.36% for simultaneous interpreting, 35.51% to 35.71% for consecutive interpreting, and from 26.53% to 31.18% for liaison medical interpreting. The details for satisfaction towards the remuneration of 7 sub-types of medical interpreting are presented in Table 7. In 2015, the proportion of participants satisfied with remuneration was also the highest for simultaneous interpreting, ranging from 26.32% to 46.15%, the lowest for liaison interpreting, ranging from 16.67% to 28%, with around half of participants reporting the remuneration to be barely acceptable. In summary, satisfaction towards remuneration from medical interpreting, in general, was low, and that towards simultaneous interpreting is slightly better.

Table 7 Satisfaction towards remuneration

Sub-types of medical interpreting	Total response	Extremely discontent	Discontent	Acceptable	Content	Extremely content
SMI for AP	107	9 (8.41%)	12 (11.21%)	48 (44.86%)	33 (30.84%)	5 (4.67%)
CMI for AP	107	7 (6.54%)	15 (14.02%)	47 (43.93%)	34 (31.78%)	4 (3.74%)
LMI for AP	98	8 (8.16%)	10 (10.20%)	54 (55.10%)	23 (23.47%)	3 (3.06%)
SMI for BP	99	6 (6.06%)	7 (7.07%)	50 (50.51%)	31 (31.31%)	5 (5.05%)
CMI for BP	98	6 (6.12%)	5 (5.10%)	52 (53.06%)	29 (29.59%)	6 (6.12%)
LMI for BP	93	5 (5.38%)	8 (8.60%)	51 (54.84%)	25 (26.88%)	4 (4.30%)
LMI for CP	98	8 (8.16%)	13 (13.27%)	49 (50.00%)	25 (25.51%)	3 (3.06%)

Note: SMI=simultaneous medical interpreting, CMI=consecutive medical interpreting, LMI=liaison medical interpreting, AP=academic purpose, BP=business purpose, CP=clinical purpose.

The dissatisfaction towards remuneration influences the enthusiasm for in-depth involvement and professional development. They might also speak low of the profession for the people considering joining this profession. Their income should be raised. As medical interpreters, the preparation for translation, mainly the ad hoc acquisition of medical knowledge is time-consuming and effortful and should be better recognized. Although they might work on-site for interpreting for one or two presentations, the time for preparation might be hours and even days.

4.3 Interpreters' perceptions of the medical interpreting profession

4.3.1 Intensity of competition

Among 165 interpreters who responded to this question, 90 (54.55%) participants thought there were insufficient interpreters in the market and more interpreters should be trained for medical interpreting, 14 (8.48%) participants thought the supply and demand were balanced, and 15 (9.09%) thought there were more interpreters than needed and the competition was intense. Comparing the response to this question in the 2015 and 2020 surveys, the proportion of participants thinking there was an undersupply and oversupply increased by 7.45% (54.55% vs. 47.10%) and 3.19% (9.09% vs. 5.90%) respectively, while the proportion of participants believing the supply was balanced with the demand decreased (8.48% vs. 5.90%). In summary, half of the participants believed there was inadequate supply in the medical interpreting market.

4.3.2 Types of interpreters

We asked the participant, "who were working in medical interpreting?" Among the 139 participants who responded to this question, 111 (79.86%) participants reported medical staff with proficient English language ability; 82 (58.99%) reported interpreters who had been trained in translation and interpreting and work in medicine related agencies/facilities after graduation; 70 (50.36%) reported interpreters who had been trained in translation and interpreting but have interest in medicine; 63 (45.32%) reported medical students who later studied translation and interpreting; 47 (33.81%) reported interpreters majored in Master of Translation and Interpreting for medical purpose; 3 (2.16%) reported others.

In the 2015 survey, the participants believed the largest proportion of medical interpreters were staff working in medical institutions after graduation from translation programs, with medical personnel with good English skills accounting for the second largest proportion. The order of the two types switched in 2020, with the order of the other types staying the same.

These data prove that medical staff were actually working as the mainstay of medical interpreters. The difficulty and high learning curve might be the reason. However, we might ask the question, are they qualified for the job? This remains unknown and needs to be verified. Previous studies have demonstrated that medical staff have difficulties dealing with complex, long sentences in written medical translation (Fu, 2019). Whether this holds true for medical interpreting, research is needed.

4.3.3 Barriers to and risks of freelancing

For the barriers to and risks of being a freelance interpreter, 89 (65.44%) out of 136 participants who responded to this question thought that the difficulty to ensure a stable income as there are low and peak seasons in the interpreting market is one major obstacle; 76 (55.88%) are concerned about the risk of self-employment (such as risks that might occur due to their own physical conditions or performance status), 60 (44.12%) regarded having to pay their social security (social and medical insurance) contributions as a major obstacle, and other barriers and risks reported include the lack of proper pricing system, development of machine translation as a substitute, lack of job opportunities at the beginning of the career, and the tapering down of the demand with people getting better at English, etc. In both 2015 and 2020, the unstable income due to fluctuating market demand was considered the leading obstacle. In 2015, having to pay contributions to social security was considered the second major obstacle followed by the risk of self-employment, and the order of the two switched in 2020. These findings revealed that the financial instability and burden of working as a freelance prohibit professionalized freelancing.

4.3.4 The necessity of establishing a qualification accreditation system

With regard to the necessity to establish an accreditation mechanism for medical interpreters, 138 participants responded, with 75 (54.35%) thought it is absolutely necessary, 27 (19.57%) thought it is necessary, 13 (9.42%) thought "it does not matter", 12 (8.70%) thought it is unnecessary, and 11 (7.97%) thought it is absolutely unnecessary. In 2015, 38.2% thought it is necessary, 20.6% thought it doesn't matter, and only 17.6% thought it's absolutely necessary. However, in 2020, over half (54.35%) of the participants thought it's absolutely necessary, and 19.57% thought it's necessary. These data prove the necessity of establishing a qualification accreditation system.

4.3.5 The necessity of establishing an association for medical interpreters

In the 2020 survey, a total of 139 participants responded, and 42 (30.22%) thought it was necessary, 53 (38.13%) thought it was extremely necessary, 27 (19.42%) thought it doesn't matter, 14 (10.07%) thought unnecessary and 3 (2.16%) thought absolutely unnecessary. Compared that of the 2015 survey, the proportion of participants believing that it was necessary or very necessary to set up a special medical interpreting association increased by 9.45% (68.35% vs. 58.9%). These data prove the necessity of establishing an association for medical interpreters.

5. Discussion

Here are the main findings of the current study. According to the two surveys, the responded medical interpreter were mainly females in their mid 20s and 30s, who are teachers or students. In the 2015 survey, most participants majored in English or Medicine, whereas in the 2020 survey, half of the participants major in both English and medicine related programs. Most of them hold TEM-8 certificate, indicating that mostly they major in English. Our participants of the 2015 survey were mostly novice, and those in the 2020 survey were more experienced.

In two rounds of survey, the data indicated that medical interpreting is inadequate to support an interpreter to make a living and the main source of job opportunities was recommendation by acquaintances. Medical interpreting for academic or clinical purposes was reported most difficult. Satisfaction towards remuneration from medical interpreting, in general, was low, and that towards simultaneous interpreting is slightly better.

Half of the participants believed there was inadequate supply in the medical interpreting market. Medical staff were actually working as the mainstay of medical interpreters. The financial instability and burden of working as a freelancer prohibit professionalized freelancing. The participants believed in the necessity of establishing a qualification accreditation system and an association for medical interpreters.

Following are the discussion and explanation of the selected findings.

5.1 Further improvement of professionalization

5.1.1 Lack of professionalization due to a late start

With the increasingly frequent international medical exchanges since 1979, the demand for medical interpreting is also expanding. However, the practice of medical interpreting was introduced in China at a relatively late stage (Chen, 2020: 5-79). Both the 2020 survey and the 2015 survey showed that the interpreters engaged in medical interpreting were relatively young, and the vast majority were under 45 years old, which fits the fact that after China joined the World Trade Organization at the beginning of the 21st century, the trend of globalization really kicked in in China and the exchange in the medical field became more and more common (Sun, Zhang & Tao, 2005: 96-100) and the fact that interpreting was included as a compulsory course in undergraduate English courses since 2000 (Zhang, 2004). Due to the late start, medical interpreting as a profession was not well developed yet, as revealed by the current study, the proportion of full-time interpreters was low in both the 2020 survey and the 2015 survey, and even though the proportion of student interpreters dropped by about 15% in the 2020 survey, the proportion of full-time interpreters was still low, less than 15%.

5.1.2 Lack of professional medical interpreters

As a typical example of interpreting for special purposes (ISP), medical interpreting not only requires interpreters to have solid bilingual interpreting skills, but more importantly, interpreters need to master at least basic medical knowledge and terminology (Cheng, 2010; Ye, Yue & Feng, 2014: 65-67). Therefore, students studying English majors are not qualified to perform medical interpreting unless they receive training on medical knowledge. Although with colleges and universities gradually realizing the need to carry out ISP courses focusing on fields that require highly specialized training, many English programs or translation programs have set up ISP courses, such as business interpreting, legal interpreting, and medical interpreting courses, the gap between supply and demand is still large considering the current large demand of medical interpreters (Chen, 2020: 75-79). The 2020 survey showed that the interpreters who studied medical English-related majors (English for Specific Purposes) at the undergraduate level accounted for only 16.58%, and the proportion was as low as about 5% at the master's and doctoral levels. The difficulty of setting up such multidisciplinary programs might be attributable to the highly specialized management of disciplines, which are mostly mono-discipline.

5.1.3 Training programs

ISP programs in colleges and universities are of crucial importance if the country wishes to facilitate the professionalization of interpreting in China, and the special field knowledge must be taken into consideration at the beginning of the training, so as to ensure that the trained interpreters are qualified to provide service in a very specialized field. In addition, the training focusing on different professional fields will not only contribute to the professionalization of interpreting but also ensure the professional competence of interpreters. As reported by Zhang (Zhang, 2017: 102-105), most graduates studying translation/interpreting are unable to obtain jobs related to translation/interpreting, as such positions often require professional knowledge in a certain field, such as pharmacy or law. The professionalization of ISP helps to ensure high-quality interpreting services, which is beneficial for both the clients and the interpreter's reputation. In the long run, it will help interpreters to create their professional image, thereby further consolidating the social status of interpreting as a profession.

The current study showed that in terms of accreditation, the proportion of interpreters holding TEM-4 and TEM-8 was the highest, and as for the major, the proportion of interpreters studying English majors at the undergraduate and master levels was also the highest. Therefore, incorporating medical interpreting courses into English or translation/interpreting majors would constitute a very efficient solution to the current personnel shortage in the medical interpreting market and a potential approach to ensure high-quality services. Many researchers also believe that English for Specific Purposes should be the next step for English programs in colleges and universities in China (Li, 2012: 85-91). A study aimed at understanding the needs of English major students for medical interpreting courses showed that 89.2% of the students believed that it was necessary to set up a medical interpreting course or a medical interpreting module within the interpreting course. At the same time, 78.8% of the students indicated that they needed professional medical interpreting textbooks (Chen, 2020: 75-79).

In addition, some researchers proposed a different solution: to set up medical English interpreting courses in medical schools. They believe that this would give full play to the advantages of medical students' professional knowledge (Sun, 2019: 89-09). A questionnaire survey among medical students showed that 78% of the students were "very interested" in the interpreting courses, and 80% believed that "the mastery of interpreting skills will be helpful in their career or further education" (Sun, 2021: 229-230). However, the motivation of mastering interpreting skills needs closer examination.

A variety of viable models could be adopted for the cultivation of medical interpreting talents. In higher education, corresponding courses can be set up, factoring in the features and strengths of the school itself. It might be feasible to set up medical knowledge training courses in a foreign language program or interpreting training courses in medical schools. A Danish survey on the medical training course for interpreters showed that the majority of participants (83%–95%) found such courses to be useful in their subsequent interpreting work (Saud, 2021: 109-116). At the same time, various forms of training should be developed. For instance, colleges or universities could consider providing training courses for professionals, such as offering English interpreting courses for medical practitioners. All of the aforementioned approaches serve the same goal, namely, the cultivation of talents who master both bilingual translation ability and professional knowledge to address the shortage of medical interpreting talents.

5.2 Establishment of an accreditation system

5.2.1 Recognition of professional value

The 2020 survey showed that the proportions of interpreters graduating from first-tier universities and having education background in both medicine and English were higher. In addition, more than 80% of the interpreters hold at least one form of qualification certificate in English language proficiency. However, most of the participants reported that they were not satisfied with the remuneration, with only one-third of the participants satisfied with the remuneration. It is worth noting that the 2015 survey also showed that medical interpreters were not very satisfied with their remuneration, which indicated that in the past 5 years, medical interpreters remain undervalued.

Another evidence that the undervaluation of professional interpreters is that the professional title of the interpreter is not recognized in many facilities and institutions, including hospitals and universities. The current study showed that the full-time occupation of a significant percentage of medical interpreters was lecturer/professor or doctors. However, since universities or hospitals do not recognize academic or professional titles related to interpreting, when it comes to the appraisal of their work, the contributions or achievements they made in the field of translation/interpreting will not be considered, which could be discouraging.

It's needless to stress the importance of the accuracy of the medical interpreting and the professionalism of the medical interpreters, as it could be a matter of life and death. For example, there have been case reports (Zhan & Yan, 2013: 47-50) on "temporary" interpreters mistakenly interpreting rectal suppositories as pills, causing patients to take rectal suppositories orally. There are also cases reported abroad. In a case, the patient ended up progressing into quadriplegia due to translation errors, and the hospital faced a compensation fee of US$ 71 million (Arocha, 2013: 127-142). Furthermore, although more than 80% of the participants in the Survey 2020 held at least one certificate in English, many still found medical interpreting hard, especially for academic purposes. In addition, according to the results of the Survey 2020, in most cases, medical interpreters hear about medical interpreting service demand from acquaintances and get recommended for the job, which also reflects the phenomenon that the medical interpreters on the market do not need qualification accreditation to get jobs and there is also no clear standard for the assessment of the medical interpreting ability of interpreters. In view of the importance and difficulty of medical interpreting, it is in the interest of the service provider (medical interpreters), the service recipients (the clients and audience), and the development of the medical interpreting profession to establish qualification accreditation system, as it serves the aim of ensuring the quality of interpreting services, improving the client and audience experience, and in the long run, helping interpreters to establish their professional image, which is conducive to consolidating interpreting as a profession, promoting the social recognition of the value of interpreters, and enhancing the social status of interpreters.

5.2.2 Necessity of professional accreditation system

Medical interpreting has developed into a relatively mature stage in some European and American countries with multi-ethnic population groups, diverse cultures, and relatively large immigration populations. Given the important and challenging nature of medical interpreting, in those countries, a series of national standards, legislation and professional qualification accreditation systems for the medical interpreting profession have been set up (Mara, 2013: 114-126; Zhu, Liu & Feng, 2015: 111-114), such as the National Council on Interpreting in Health Care in the United States and the National Accreditation Authority for Translators and Interpreters in Australia, although these standards are mainly designed for medical interpreting for health care purposes, or liaison medical interpreting for clinical purpose as classified in the current study. In China, the most authoritative accreditation on translation and interpreting, the China Accreditation Test for Translators and Interpreters (CATTI), mostly focuses on the ability to convey conference interpreting service, with most of the tested content relating to general knowledge and foreign affairs.

In both the 2015 survey and the 2020 survey, the majority of participants felt it is necessary to establish an accreditation system for medical interpreters. The establishment of an accreditation system for medical interpreters will play a positive role in improved regulation of the market. First, the accreditation system ensures that clients are able to find qualified interpreters whose certifications serve as reliable evidence that they are qualified to provide medical interpreting services. And vice versa, certification can also reflect the interpreter's professional competence when looking for job opportunities. It should be noted that the proposed accreditation system differs from the current CATTI and other English-language certificates as it requires interpreters to have solid medical knowledge and clinical communication skills. At present, the professionalization of medical interpreting in China still has a long way to go. Only Zhan Cheng *et al*. (2013: 47-50) reported that the "Medical Interpretation Center" affiliated to Guangzhou Qifu Hospital arranges professional knowledge and interpreting skills tests every year, while in the United States, the National Council on Interpreting in Health Care was established as early as in 1998 (Hsieh, 2009: 135-160), and obtaining qualification certification is a basic requirement for engaging in the medical interpreting profession (Zhu, Liu & Feng, 2015: 111-114).

In China, many universities have opened medical translation and interpreting programs at the master level and still many universities have opened medical English programs which involve intensive translation and interpreting training and medical knowledge teaching. However, there is only the general CATTI accreditation that doesn't assess their medical interpreting expertise. These provide a basis for the attendees of the accreditation system.

5.3 Establishment of medical interpreting association

5.3.1 The necessity of medical interpreting association

Both the 2015 survey and the 2020 survey showed that most interpreters thought it's necessary to establish a medical interpreting association. However, when it comes to choosing to be a professional freelance interpreter, concerns over unstable income due to fluctuating market demand, social security, the risk of self-employment, the lack of a proper pricing system, the development of machine translation as a substitute, and the tapering down of the demand with people getting better at English, etc. were reported in the current study. The fact that the surveyed interpreters actively reporting various risks showed that the value of interpreting service is not adequately recognized though it's a very demanding job.

The establishment of medical interpreting association can protect interpreters from the risk of self-employment and provide them with career development opportunities. The association could serve multiple purposes, such as formulation of relevant professional standards, ethics and training standards, organization of seminars, and publication of journals and newsletters, etc., and most importantly, the association should commit to improving the social status of medical interpreters and ensuring proper working conditions and reasonable remuneration of interpreters (Zhu, Liu & Feng, 2015: 111-114). In some countries, there are professional associations, such as the International Medical Interpreters Association, that allow members to apply for subsidies when necessary, providing that the members paid their membership fees regularly.

At present, there is no such association for medical interpreting in China. In addition, there is a lack of platform connecting interpreters with customers. While customers are having a hard time finding qualified medical interpreters, medical interpreters are also having a hard time finding suitable job opportunities. The establishment of medical interpreting association might solve this issue, as it might serve as an official platform for regular assessment and training of medical interpreters and the post of appropriate job opportunities. German Association of Freelance Interpreters and Translators, or Deutscher Verband der freien Übersetzer und Dolmetscher, has a website[1] that publicized the translator and interpreter qualifications and whether they could perform bio-medical conference interpreting, their source language and target language, working locations, etc.).

5.3.2 The feasibility of medical interpreting association

According to the notice of the Ministry of Civil Affairs on printing and distributing "the 14th Five-Year Plan for the Development of Social Organizations", in order to further improve the supervision and service system for social organizations, the establishment of social organization should shift focus from "the number" and "the increase rate" to its "stable development" and "quality". Therefore, for the establishment of the medical interpreting association, the authors believe that the association can be established in the form of a professional committee under national society or national associations, such as the Translators Association of China (TAC).

Up to now, there are 15 professional committees including ethnic languages, foreign communication, translation theory and translation teaching, legal translation, interpreting, and cross-cultural communication research. In addition, the TAC is committed to promoting the formulation and implementation of national and industrial standards of translation. It has released the "China Language Service Industry Development Report" for five consecutive years and has participated in the formulation of 19 national and industrial standards. The establishment of a professional medical interpreting committee under the TAC might provide guidance to the medical interpreting profession, better the regulation of the medical interpreting market, safeguard

1 https://sprachdienstleister.dvud.de/

the rights and interests of medical interpreters, and promote the healthy, sustainable and high-quality development of the profession.

5.4 Limitations

There are some limitations to this study. First, this survey focuses on the medical interpreters and their perception of the current situation of the medical interpreting profession, namely, it was from the perspective of the service supplier, without the perspective of the service demand side. Second, the sampling method of both the two rounds of survey was non-probability sampling due to the consideration of time and cost, which may limit the generalization of our findings to the entire population of medical interpreters. Meanwhile, due to the online distribution method of questionnaire of both rounds of surveys, people who were more engaged/active online may dominate the respondent mix of the study, which potentially caused selection bias. However, the population of medical interpreters is relatively small and highly-educated, and we believe the online questionnaire has a good accessibility to most of them. Third, the differences between the two rounds of surveys may be partly due to the sample size and random differences, which should be taken into consideration when interpreting the results. However, since the methods of sampling and questionnaire distribution are the same in both rounds of surveys, the comparison between the results of the two rounds can indicate the trends and differences between 2015 and 2020 to some extent. Further studies should be carried out to confirm the findings of the current study.

6. Conclusion

Currently, in China, most medical interpreters are relatively young and have a high education level and education background in both English and medicine. However, with a low proportion of full-time interpreters, barely acceptable remuneration, acquaintances' recommendation dominance in source of job opportunities, and the high risk of freelancing, the professionalization of medical interpreting in China still has a long way ahead, and the regulation of the medical interpreting profession should be attempted. Moreover, the comparison of the survey results between the two rounds of survey showed that over the five years the value of interpreters was still not fully recognized, social status of interpreters remained low. Therefore, the establishment of an accreditation system for medical interpreters and associations of medical interpreting might be the solution. To our best knowledge, this is the first study in the English language that examined the status of medical interpreters and their perception of the market and the profession that includes conference interpreters in China. Future research should explore the feasibility of the establishment of a medical interpreter accreditation system and medical interpreting association and the appropriate training model for medical interpreters.

References

[1] Álvaro Aranda, C., Gutiérrez, R. L. & Li, S. Towards a collaborative structure of interpreter-mediated medical consultations: Complementing functions between healthcare interpreters and providers [J/OL]. Social Science & Medicine (1982), 2021, 269: 113529-113529. https://doi.org/10.1016/j.socscimed.2020.113529

[2] Arocha, I. S. & Joyce, L. Patient safety, professionalization, and reimbursement as primary drivers for National Medical Interpreter Certification in the United States [J]. The International Journal of Translation and Interpreting Research, 2013, 5(1):127-142.

[3] Benda, N. C., Bisantz, A. M., Butler, R. L., Fairbanks, R. J. & Higginbotham, J. The active role of interpreters in medical discourse — An observational study in emergency medicine [J/OL]. Patient Education and Counseling, 2022, 105(1): 62-73. https://doi.org/10.1016/j.pec.2021.05.029

[4] Chen, Y. Research on situational construction based medical interpretation teaching [J]. Journal of Fujian Medical University: Social Science Edition, 2020, 21 (4): 5.

[5] Cheng, Y. The conception and exploration of offering elective course of medical interpretation in medical colleges and universities [J]. Exploration of Medical Education, 2010(6): 4.

[6] Fu, S. Analysis of the characteristics of medical translation of medical personnel from the perspective of habituation — Take the translation of Live Translation as an example [J]. Medical Education Management, 2019(S1): 70-74.

[7] Geiling, A., Böttche, M., Knaevelsrud, C. & Stammel, N. A comparison of interpreters' wellbeing and work-related characteristics in the care of refugees across different work settings [J/OL]. BMC Public Health, 2022, 22(1): 1-1635. https://doi.org/10.1186/s12889-022-14034-7.

[8] Gong, H., Liu, X., Xiong, H. & Yang, Y. Non-professional medical interpreting as a contextualized practice: Chinese volunteer interpreters' role-spaces in mediating provider-patient conflicts amid the pandemic [J]. Health Communication, 2022:1-10.

[9] Hsieh, E. Bilingual health communication: Medical interpreters' construction of a mediator role [A]. In Brashers, D. & Goldsmith, D. (eds.). Communicating to Manage Health and Illness (pp.135-160) [C]. New York: Routledge, 2009.

[10] Iftikhar, S. Enhancing medical communication and care through professional medical interpreters [J/OL]. Mayo Clinic Proceedings, 2022, 97(5): 820-825. https://doi.org/10.1016/j.mayocp.2022.01.013

[11] Kamara, D., Weil, J., Youngblom, J., Guerra, C. & Joseph, G. Cancer counseling of low-income limited english proficient latina women using medical interpreters: Implications for shared decision-making [J/OL]. Journal of Genetic Counseling, 2018, 27(1): 155-168. https://doi.org/10.1007/s10897-017-0132-5

[12] Li, J., Yusufu, M. & Zhou, L. The predicament and outlet of the specialization of special purpose interpretation — Based on the survey of the current situation of medical interpretation in Beijing [A]. Medical

Language and Culture Studies (Volume III) [M]. Shanghai: Shanghai Fudan University Electronic Audio Video Press, 2021.

[13] Li, L. The obstacles and countermeasures of college public English teachers' transition to medical English [J]. Chinese Journal of ESP, 2012, 3 (2): 85-91.

[14] Li, S., Gerwing, J., Krystallidou, D., Rowlands, A., Cox, A. & Pype, P. Interaction — A missing piece of the jigsaw in interpreter-mediated medical consultation models [J/OL]. Patient Education and Counseling, 2017, 100(9): 1769-1771. https://doi.org/10.1016/j.pec.2017.04.021

[15] Mara, Y. The development of certification for healthcare interpreters in the United States [J]. The International Journal of Translation and Interpreting Research, 2013, 5(1): 114-126.

[16] Martin, F. C., Philip, J. & McLachlan, S. Healthcare professionals' views of working with medical interpreters in a cancer setting: An exploratory study [J/OL]. Journal of Cancer Education, 2022, 37(4): 1115-1121. https://doi.org/10.1007/s13187-020-01927-7

[17] Ono, N. Medical interpreting at the Tokyo 2020 Olympic and Paralympic Games [J]. Juntendo Medical Journal, 2020.

[18] Pines, R. L., Jones, L. & Sheeran, N. Using family members as medical interpreters: An explanation of healthcare practitioners' normative practices in pediatric and neonatal departments in Australia [J/OL]. Health Communication, 2020, 35(7): 902-909. https://doi.org/10.1080/10410236.2019.1598740

[19] Quesada, P. R., Solis, R. N. & Levi, J. R. Student medical interpreters: A double-edged sword [J/OL]. Otolaryngology-Head and Neck Surgery, 2020, 162(4): 476-478. https://doi.org/10.1177/0194599820909083

[20] Rhodes, M. G., Fletcher, K. E., Blumenfeld-Kouchner, F. & Jacobs, E. A. Spanish medical interpreters' management of challenges in end-of-life discussions [J/OL]. Patient Education and Counseling, 2021, 104(8): 1978-1984. https://doi.org/10.1016/j.pec.2021.01.018

[21] Sabar, G. & Tenenboim, S. "We must do something instead of just watch": The first medical interpreter training course for Eritrean asylum seekers in Israel [J/OL]. The European Legacy, Toward New Paradigms, 2018, 23(7-8): 804-820. https://doi.org/10.1080/10848770. 2018.1499206

[22] Saud, A., Morten, S., Claire, G., *et al.* The impact of a health introduction course for medical interpreters in the healthcare sector [J]. Nordic Journal of Nursing Research, 2021, 41(2): 109-116.

[23] Schlange, S. A., Palmer-Wackerly, A. L. & Chaidez, V. A narrative review of medical interpretation services and their effect on the quality of health care [J]. Southern Medical Journal, 2022,115(5): 317-321.

[24] Sleptsova, M., Weber, H., Schöpf, A. C., Nübling, M., Morina, N., Hofer, G. & Langewitz, W. Using interpreters in medical consultations: What is said and what is translated — A descriptive analysis using RIAS [J/OL]. Patient Education and Counseling, 2017, 100(9): 1667-1671. https://doi.org/10.1016/j.pec.2017.03.023

[25] Sun, J., Zhang, R. & Xu, T. The strategies of developing Chinese medicine industry under economy globalization [J/OL]. Commercial Research, 2005, 4(33): 96-100. http: //doi: 10.13902/j.cnki.syyj.2005.04.033

[26] Sun, J. Discussion on offering elective course of medical interpretation for medical students [J]. Theory Research, 2021(11): 2.

[27] Sun, L. Research on the cultivation model of medical interpretation based on the output-oriented approach [J]. Journal of Kaifeng Institute of Education, 2019, 39 (5): 89-90.

[28] Wang, E. Interpretation as a profession in China: A survey [J]. Chinese Translators Journal, 2005(2): 57-60.

[29] Wang, L. F., Mu, L., Liao, R. X., *et al.* Multi-dimensional thinking on emergency language service response and talent preparation in the pandemic [J]. Contemporary Foreign Languages Studies, 2020(4): 46-54.

[30] Wang, Y. P., Jin, N. & Fan, X. D. History, status quo and development trend of China's medical aid healthcare facilities [J]. China Health Policy Research, 2017(8): 60-67.

[31] Wu, M. S. & Rawal, S. "It's the difference between life and death": The views of professional medical interpreters on their role in the delivery of safe care to patients with limited English proficiency [J/OL]. PloS One, 2017, 12(10): e0185659-e0185659. https://doi.org/10.1371/journal.pone.0185659

[32] Yang, S. & Zhao, C. X. Construction of medical interpreting course and teaching mode from the ESP perspective [J/OL]. 2021. http: // doi:10.13555/j.cnki.c.m.e.2021.01.031

[33] Ye, H., Yue, F. & Feng, X. Cognition and operation: A preliminary study on the training of medical interpreters in China [J]. Journal of Jilin Normal University of Engineering Technology, 2014, 30 (7): 3.

[34] Yusufu, M. Empirical study of status quo and industry analysis of interpreting market in medical field [D]. Beijing: University of International Economics and Business, 2016.

[35] Zhan, C. & Yan, M. The status quo, problems and development of domestic medical interpretation — An empirical study on medical interpretation activities in Guangzhou [J]. Journal of Guangdong University of Foreign Studies, 2013(3): 47-50.

[36] Zhan, C. & Zeng, L. Chinese medical interpreters' visibility through text ownership: An empirical study on interpreted dialogues at a hospital in Guangzhou [J/OL]. Interpreting: International Journal of Research and Practice in Interpreting, 2017, 19(1): 97-117. https://doi.org/10.1075/intp.19.1.05zha

[37] Zhang, J. Consecutive interpretation and its teaching [D]. Wuhan: Central China Normal University, 2004.

[38] Zhang, L. The predicament and realistic path of MTI talent training [J]. Theory and Practice of Contemporary Education, 2017, 9(2): 102-105.

[39] Zhu, S., Liu, Y. & Feng, H. Current situation and practice principles of medical interpretation [J]. Chinese Translators Journal, 2015, 36 (2): 4.

中国社区口译研究动态

——基于 Citespace 的文献计量学研究

陈靖怡　北京外国语大学

摘　要：在翻译研究社会学转向的背景下，社区口译研究日益走向前沿。本文基于中国知网（CNKI）数据库的相关文献，运用可视化软件 Citespace 绘制知识图谱，从发文总体趋势、作者与期刊概况、关键词共现、关键词突变趋势五个方面入手，尝试厘清我国社区口译研究的源流与动态。通过定量与定性分析，本文发现现有研究多以实践为导向，关注具体场景社区口译，如重点聚焦手语翻译、法庭口译、远程口译、医疗口译等，辅以综述性研究；研究主题和方法较为单一，研究结论指导性仍待提升。最后，本文基于研究热点的历时性分析，预测未来研究场景将更丰富多元，实践主体将得到更多关注，技术与大数据将成为重要助力，跨学科、跨区域合作乃大势所趋。

关键词：社区口译；口译研究；可视化分析；发展动态；未来趋势

Dynamics of Community Interpreting Studies in China — A Citespace-Based Bibliometric Study

Chen Jingyi
Beijing Foreign Studies University

Abstract: Building on the sociological turn in Translation Studies, community interpreting studies is gaining traction. This paper analyzes literature in the CNKI database and utilizes Citespace, a visualization software, to present the evolution and dynamics of community interpreting studies in China from five perspectives: publication trends, author and journal profiles, keyword co-occurrence, and keyword mutation trends. Through quantitative and

qualitative analysis, this paper reveals that existing studies are mainly practice-oriented and focus on specific scenarios of community interpreting, such as sign language interpreting, courtroom interpreting, remote interpreting, and medical interpreting, supplemented by theoretical reviews. The research themes and methods are relatively homogeneous, and the research findings are not yet detailed enough for practical application. Based on the analysis of research hotspots over time, this paper predicts that future research will focus on diversified scenarios, subjects, and technology. Interdisciplinary and cross-regional cooperation will also become more prevalent.
Keywords: community interpreting; interpreting studies; visualization analysis; dynamics, trends

1. 引言

五方之民，言语不通，鞮译象寄，古已有之。论及最古老的口译形式，社区口译当仁不让。广义来讲，当不同语言民族之间产生交际时，社区口译即应运而生（Roberts，1997：7）。在现代社会语境下，社区口译特指“不同于多国代表之间的会议口译、发生在一个国家的社区内部居民之间的口译活动”（Hale，2007：30），其场合多为公共服务部门，如医疗卫生、法律、警局、移民部门等，也包括为听障人士提供的手语翻译（刘建军，2014：1），是一种即时、现场、跨语言跨文化的交际行为。

然而，相较于实践，社区口译研究兴起较晚，最早可追溯至20世纪70年代的西方学界口译研究中，主要聚焦法庭与医疗语境下的口译实践，以及以手语翻译为代表的符际翻译（Pöchhacker，2007：123-142）。1995年在加拿大渥太华召开的首届全球社区口译国际会议（First International Conference on Interpreting in Legal, Health, and Social Service Settings）标志着社区口译逐渐迈向西方研究舞台的中心。国内社区口译研究主要出现在2006—2018年这一口译研究的“蓬勃发展阶段”（任文等，2019：32），这主要得益于国内翻译研究的社会学转向，研究者的目光开始由会议口译向社区口译转移。

文献梳理表明，以中文书写、从整体把握社区口译及其研究动向的综述性研究并不多见，知网迄今仅有 4 篇核心期刊论文。其中，《社区口译在中国》一文从定义与特点入手，梳理了社区口译在中国的发展，指出其面临着职业地位低下、缺乏技能培训和科学研究短缺三个方面的问题，并从不同主体出发，尝试给出解决方案（苏伟，2009）。发表于 2012 年的《国外社区口译研究文献计量分析》是唯一一篇关于社区口译的文献计量研究，文章截取 1967—2009 年间发表的论文，论述了社区口译研究发展的进程、特征与趋势（刘建军、张福勇，2012）。《我国社区口译的现状调查及其启示》一文则采取问卷调查定量分析的方式，针对我国社区口译实践的发展提出建议（邓春、文军，2012）。《翻译教学与研究的新热点——社区口译研究述评》一文在系统介绍社区口译概念、梳理研究发展概况的基础上，指出现阶段存在研究影响力仍待提升、实用性尚不突出、方法多样性与系统化有待加强等问题，描摹研究动向（张威，2016）。上述论文中，实践导向和理论导向型研究虽平分秋色，但数量有限，定量分析不够深入，且均未囊括近六年的动向；考虑到疫情对翻译行业对深刻影响，口译行业也呈现出新动态（王小曼、王斌华，2021：105）。本文特聚焦国内社区口译研究，在全面梳理近年来最新文献的基础上，尝试梳理我国社区口译研究发展脉络，厘清研究特征与热点，总结其研究局限与不足，并尝试提出未来研究趋势与方向，为我国社区口译实践与研究提供参考。

2. 分析工具与数据来源

通过数据提取、归纳与分析，文献计量学能帮助我们以定量研究的方式窥得某一研究领域的发展脉络，洞悉热点聚焦，把握前沿走向。本研究采用由美国德雷塞尔大学（Drexel University）陈超美研发的可视化知识图谱软件 Citespace 进行数据分析。该软件基于 Java 语言，主要通过高频关键词、突现专业术语及文献关键词的共现分析等功能实现对学科概貌、研究脉络及研究热点的梳理与呈现（李红满，2014：21），广泛应用于不同主题的翻译综述性研究，如语料库翻译学、视听翻译、翻译技术、影视翻译。

自20世纪90年代中期以来，社区口译成为新兴职业。相关研究在20世纪80年代至90年代稳步上升，于21世纪初期呈迅猛发展趋势（刘建军，2014）。对于概念本身，学界尚有多重界定标准（张威，2016：21）。就名称而言，存在“社区口译”“基于社区的口译”及“联络口译”之争议。《翻译研究百科全书》将社区口译定义为“发生在公共服务场合下的一种口译形式，场合包括警察局、移民局、社会福利中心等；通常是双向交替传译，有面对面口译和电话口译两种方式”（Wadensjö，1998：33）。罗伯茨（Roda P. Roberts）则提出，按照场合，可以将社区口译分为公共服务、医疗口译和法律口译三大类（Roberts，1999：9）。就场合而言，本文采取公共服务、医疗口译和法律口译的分类；就方式而言，本文采纳现场口译和远程口译两大形式。

基于上述背景，本文选择2000年至2022年作为研究区间，依托中国知网（CNKI）文献搜索引擎进行检索，文献来源范围限定为CSSCI及北大核心期刊来源期刊。检索包括以“社区口译”“联络口译”“医疗口译”“手语翻译”“法庭口译”“远程口译”“难民口译”及“移民口译”为关键词或标题的文献，经过逐条手动数据清理，排除实践报告、新闻报道、会讯等与本研究关联较低的文本类型，最终获得有效文献102篇。经过数据导入、分析与作图，研究共总结出发文趋势、期刊分布、主要作者、关键词共现及关键词突现五大分析视角。

3. 结果呈现与分析

3.1 总体研究趋势

如图1所示，自2000年始，我国社区口译研究论文发表数量一路曲折攀升，分别于2009年（10篇）、2015—2016年（共16篇）、2019—2020年（共22篇）迎来三次发文高峰；2009年至2014年及2015年至2018年间则呈现出下滑趋势；自2019年起又呈大幅回升之势，近一年来出现回落。探究三次高峰背后之缘由，与国际译学界研究动向及国内翻译行业动态紧密相关。首先，1995年至2007年共召开五届Critical Link世界社区口译大会，每届大会伴有论文集出版，既将国际社区口译研究推至聚光灯下，也为国内学者开展相关研究奠定了基础。其次，在2007

年召开的第八批新职业信息发布会上，劳动保障部将手语翻译员增设为新职业，推动了手语翻译的发展，为理论研究提供坚实的实践支撑。最后，良好的外部环境为我国语言服务业创造了巨大的发展空间，以“一带一路”建设为首的“走出去”战略为语言服务业带来诸多发展机遇，中外交流日益频繁，来华人数激增。据中国高等教育学会外国留学生教育管理分会调查，2000 年共有来自 166 个国家和地区的 52,150 名外国留学人员来华，2015 年该数据已经上升到 202 个国家和 397,635 人，就人数而言，大约增长了 8 倍[1]。2019 年入境旅游人数为 1.45 亿人次，比同期增长 2.9%[2]。值得注意的是，2020 年出现的第三次高峰或与新冠疫情不无关联。疫情期间，应急语言服务与医疗口译需求激增，语言服务行业及从业人士纷纷投身抗疫，以提供“线上抗疫口笔译服务”“疫情相关培训服务”“海外捐赠物资的语言服务”“外籍人士咨询服务”等形式贡献力量[3]。概言之，以上的新需求与新语境滋养了新视角，社区口译研究因此焕发新生。

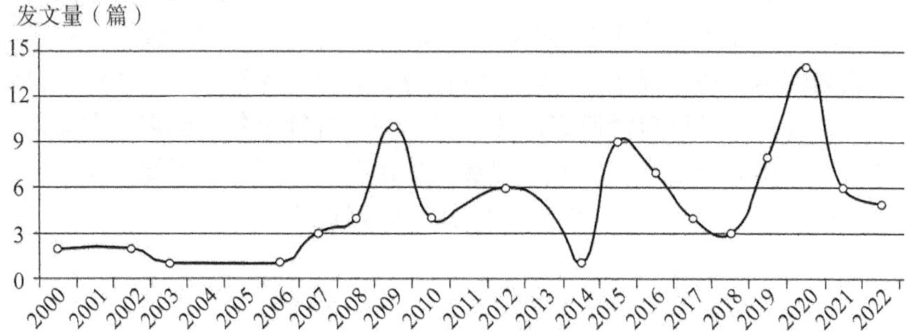

图 1　2000—2022 国内社区口译相关研究发文趋势图

2009 年至 2014 年、2015 年至 2018 年间，相关研究发文量有所减少，其原因也许能从《中国语言服务行业发展报告》中窥见一二。中国译协发布的《2018 中国语言服务行业发展报告》[4]指出，翻译技术已经进入繁荣发展阶段。2019 年的报告中更是有直观数据显示[5]，国内语言服务行业

1　详见 http://www.cafsa.org.cn/research/72/1.html（访问日期：2022-10-3）
2　详见 http://www.asean-china-center.org/travel/lvxx/2020-07/4975.html（访问日期：2022-10-3）
3　详见 https://www.sohu.com/a/465061174_378467（访问日期：2022-10-3）
4　详见 https://www.sohu.com/a/285256429_100092936（访问日期：2022-10-3）
5　详见 http://www.seetrans.net/News-info-id-111.html（访问日期：2022-10-3）

涉及的主要翻译订单领域中，信息技术以 63% 的占比高居榜首。随着口译术语管理技术、AI 机器翻译、口译语料库等技术日趋成熟，简单的口译需求已经可以由机器满足，这或许是社区口译研究跌入波谷的一大诱因。此外，社区口译行业固有痼疾，如译员职业地位模糊、行业职业化进程缓慢、缺乏培训与合理评价机制等。不破不立，实践的停滞在一定程度上限制了研究与创新，使相关研究趋于饱和。

3.2 发文情况：作者与期刊

分析某一研究领域核心作者及发文期刊，有助于了解该领域研究者与发文期刊的群体性特征（向明友，2015：38）。如图 2 所示，从主要研究者来看，累计发表相关文献两篇及两篇以上的作者共计 18 人，其中，较为高产的学者有赵军峰（6 篇）、肖晓燕（5 篇）、王斌华（4 篇）、高文（4 篇）和张威（4 篇）。赵军峰聚焦法庭口译，发文多围绕法庭口译研究综述与动态、法庭口译员角色及法庭口译立法；肖晓燕关注手语翻译教育与研究，旁涉电话口译；高文主要关注手语识别与合成领域；王斌华与张威则较为关注口译研究本体，前者侧重远程口译教学及口译跨学科研究，后者侧重社区口译研究评述。五人的深耕领域各有侧重，在知识图谱中呈现出分散之态。此外，观察主要作者的合著连接可知，相关学者在一定范围内展开合作，但数量有限，未成气候。

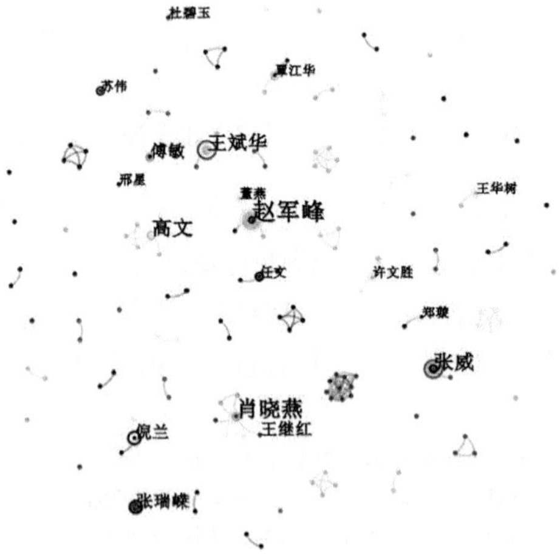

图 2 社区口译研究主要作者知识图谱

如图3所示，从主要期刊分布来看，排名前10的期刊中，语言类期刊占据7席，其余三者分别为《中国特殊教育》《残疾人研究》及《计算机学报》；发文量前三甲分别为《中国翻译》(22篇)、《上海翻译》(13篇)和《中国科技翻译》(6篇)。这说明，社区口译研究仍以翻译本体研究为重，但具有不容忽视的跨学科倾向，而且与弱势群体利益及技术发展紧密相关。

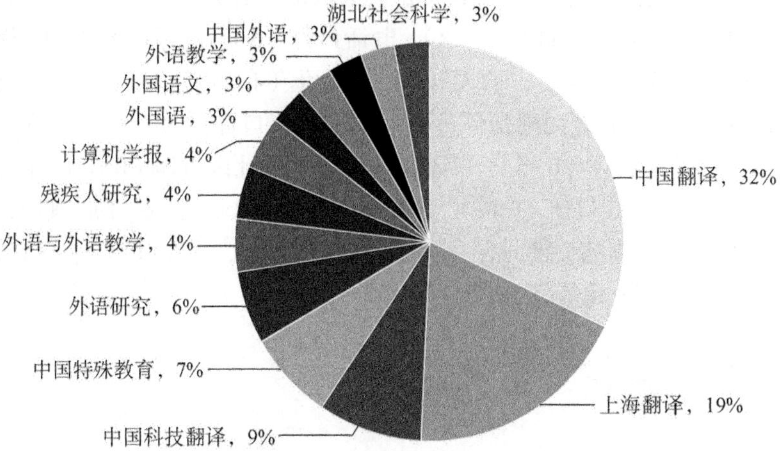

图3 主要期刊分布

纵观核心作者与发文期刊领域可发现，分散化是国内社区口译研究发表的一大特征，具体体现在核心作者产出领域各有侧重、作者合作网络不紧密、主要发表刊物多样等方面，表明虽然社区口译研究业已获得了学界一定程度的关注与认可，但尚未形成系统、连贯的学术体系与派别，影响力亟待提升。

3.3 研究热点与趋势

本研究选取关键词共现分析与突现词列表两个指标探究社区口译研究的源流、现状与前沿。共现分析则采用寻径算法，基于关键词出现频次与共现关联，以可视化的方式呈现出重点研究话题。关键词是文献内容的核心提炼与高度浓缩，知识图谱中的节点面积越大，说明其出现频次越高，是该领域的研究热点；中心度则反映关键词在研究网络中作为“媒介”的能力（张继光，2016：432），关键词中心度越高，该话题引起的学术关联就越多，文献产出量也越大。“突变检测”通过计算特定时间区间内突现词的演变，展示该领域研究兴趣的迁移与研究热点的历时变化。

3.3.1 关键词共现分析

按降序排列，图 4 中关键词出现频次前十者分别为手语翻译（18）、法庭口译（17）、社区口译（8）、电话口译（5）、口译研究（5）、译员角色（4）、口译（4）、口译员（4）、职业化（4）和手语（3）；中心度排名靠前的十个关键词则是译员角色（0.83）、口译员（0.54）、法庭口译（0.47）、手语翻译（0.45）、口译研究（0.44）、社区口译（0.28）、中国手语（0.17）、医疗口译（0.17）、口译（0.13）和职业化（0.13）。其中，频次与中心度双高的关键词有手语翻译、译员角色、法庭口译、社区口译、口译研究和职业化等。

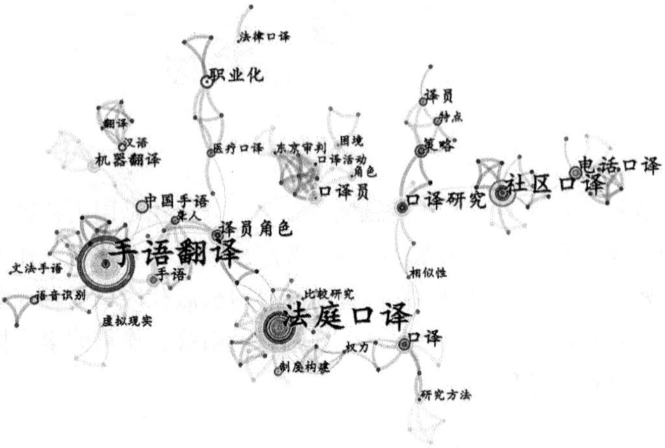

图 4 社区口译研究关键词共现知识图谱

将上述数据进行归纳整合，可大致将研究重心分为以下四类：

1）社区口译分类框架下的具体场景研究，如手语翻译、法庭口译、电话口译和医疗口译；

2）社区口译研究相关的综述性研究，如特定领域的社区口译研究回顾与展望、口译研究热点追踪、社会学视角下的口译研究等；

3）社区口译场景下的伦理研究，以译员角色与角色认知为主；

4）社区口译行业体系建设研究，如社区口译在中国的发展与回顾、社区口译职业化进程等。

在第一类中，手语翻译研究所占比重最大，研究跨度最长，跨学科趋势最为明显。在早期研究中，手语识别、手语翻译系统和手语翻译器等侧重计算机和电子技术与手语翻译实践的文章占据主流，且技术类研究贯穿了整个时间区间。该主题下发表时间最早的两篇文献发表于 2000 年，分别是《面向机器翻译的中国手语的理解与合成》和《基于 DGMM 的中国手语识别系统》，严格意义上均属于计算机领域，以技术为抓手推动手语识别和手语机器翻译。最新发表的文献是《端到端手语翻译研究》，以改善聋哑学生高等教育教学环境为目的，对语音到手语的专项翻译展开研究，提出了新型的语音到手语的翻译方法（杨淑莹等，2022：278）。手语翻译研究真正将目光投向翻译与口译，则是 2009 年《手语翻译研究——模式、内容及问题》一文首次梳理了国外手语翻译研究的历史与现状，廓清研究理论模块，指出研究现有问题（肖晓燕、王继红，2009）。同年发表的《国内外手语翻译研究：历史与现状》和《手语翻译与口译的异同》也均从手语翻译的行为本质出发，试图为确定种类归属寻求理论及实践依据（王继红，2009）。随着时间的推进，还出现了针对本土手语翻译实践的实证研究。例如，《中国大陆手语传译调查：现状、问题与前景》一文针对聋人和手语译员展开问卷调查，从译员资质、传译场合、传译困难、质量满意度、译员角色定位等方面展示了中国大陆手语传译市场的现状，为行业发展提供指引（肖晓燕等，2018）;《上海手语翻译服务需求与现状调查》也采取问卷调查和访谈的形式，针对手语翻译需求旺盛、翻译人才短缺、行业监管缺失等问题提出建议（倪兰、和子晴，2022）。此外，手语翻译教育、人才培养及课程设置等研究话题在中后期异军突起，仅 2009 年至 2020 年间，相关主题文献发表量为 8 篇，占同期发表总量的 30%。

紧随其后的是法庭口译，以对比研究和实证研究为主。对比研究层面，最早的文献发布于2006年，从FCICE资格考试制度、法庭口译语言特点及困境三方面介绍了美国法庭口译概况（刘淑颖，2006）。此后，研究者多将目光聚焦美国、中国香港、澳大利亚等国家和地区，汲取其在法庭口译立法、法庭口译制度构建等方面的经验，如赵军峰与赵安对话法庭口译专家桑德拉·黑尔（Sandra Hale），跟进澳大利亚法庭翻译立法实践等方面的最新进展（赵军峰、赵安，2016）。也不乏如宋莹、覃江华等学者，通过比较分析纽伦堡审判与东京审判在工作语言、工作设备、人员聘用、口译效果、仲裁机制等方面的异同，为当代法庭口译制度构建提供借鉴（宋莹、覃江华，2016）。在实证研究层面，多为侧重个案的规约性研究。例如，《法庭口译中的角色冲突——以Camayd-Freixas“声明”为例》一文针对化解角色冲突、提升译员职业化水平提出了建议（朱波、高虹，2015）；《法庭口译的特点及应对策略——以小额索赔案件为例》一文也就法庭专业术语、数字、长句、跨文化问题的翻译总结了技巧（牛丽霞、王跃洪，2015）。

再者是电话口译，其研究包含综述类研究与实证研究两大类别。早在2003年，刘和平（2003：5）在《职业口译新形式与口译教学》一文中就指出，随着网络与IT技术的迅猛发展，国际交流频繁，电话及电视口译日益成为国际间交往不可或缺的交际形式。随后，肖晓燕、张梅、郁锐玲陆续撰文介绍美国电话口译的职业现状，展开理论分析（肖晓燕、张梅，2009：30），并将其视为社区口译新趋势，分析了影响电话口译在中国发展的要素（肖晓燕、郁锐玲，2009：22）。《电话口译在我国的一次重要实践——广州亚运会、亚残运会多语言服务中心的电话口译》是同类研究中为数不多的实证研究，详细介绍了案例中的工作流程，在访谈的基础上呈现译员反思，归纳实践难点（詹成、索若楠，2012：107）。总体而言，现有的综述性研究多为宏观研究，从翻译研究和口译行业整体出发，厘清电话口译作为语言服务的定位与特点，尝试规范译员培训，分析市场动向；实证研究数量十分有限，未能充分探索不同地区、不同人群、不同行业内的电话口译实践。

最后，就医疗口译而言，思辨研究与实证研究兼而有之。在思辨研究类目下，研究对象最广泛的当属刘宇波与张威，他们对21世纪以来的医疗口译研究进了回顾与展望，指出医疗口译研究以实践案例分析为主，具有明显的跨学科特征，并基于对比，得出国内外相关研究在社会语境与研究方法上存在较大差异，国内医疗口译研究应更贴合实际（刘宇波、张威，2021）。邱进和廖雪汝则将研究对象收窄至包含医疗口译在内的特殊翻译领域，探究情绪智力与口译的诸多关联（邱进、廖雪汝，2020：141）。在实证研究类目下，苏伟就医疗译员角色展开个案分析，探究译员扮演的"代言人、共同医生、协调者"的多重角色，为研究、教学和医疗机构提供了启示（苏伟，2010）。此外，在医疗主题下，跨学科研究路径较为明显，从侧面印证了刘宇波、张威（2021）所述观点。例如，发表于《中国实用护理杂志》的《听障者就医沟通需求初探》一文指出，听障者就医沟通需求可归结为手语翻译、信息和知识、社会心理及情感支持三方面，并为提升手语翻译质量提供建议（臧渝梨等，2008）。

在第二类中，研究对象按时间远近，呈现出由小及大、连点成线的规律。以2010年为时间节点，在此之前发表的研究分别回顾展望了中西法庭口译的历史与现状（赵军峰、陈珊，2008：19），并梳理了手语翻译研究的发展与沿革（王继红，2009：23）。此后，随着翻译研究趋势逐渐从"文化转向"走向"社会学转向"，20世纪初期出现了社会学视角下的口译理论研究和社会学解读（任文、徐寒，2013）。《翻译教学与研究的新热点——社区口译研究述评》一文发表于2016年，是本类目中第一篇将研究对象扩大至社区口译的综述性研究，述评兼备，在廓清概念内核与分类的同时从研究背景、研究范围与主题、研究方法、研究价值与影响五个方面梳理出社区口译研究现状，指出社区口译研究效用、方法、影响层面的不足并提出解决方案，为社区口译未来发展指明了方向（张威，2016）。2020年发表的《当代国际译学研究课题与走向的知识图谱分析》一文基于文献计量学，采用数据可视化工具，分析了2000—2019年间发表的大量翻译学研究论文。数据表明，就当代国际译学文献主题聚类而言，法庭口译名列前五（胡显耀、李茂君，2022），从侧面力证法庭口译作为社区口译分支的高话题度。

第三类中的译员角色研究与社区口译的兴起密切相关（Pöchhacker, 2004），可进一步分为译员角色的概述与综述性研究和具体领域的译员角色研究两类。就译员角色的概述与综述性研究而言，《国内外译员角色研究的进展与思考》通过文献计量分析得出，由于社区口译具有交际性质，译员角色研究主要聚焦社区口译的不同场域（邢星，2015：68）。社区口译与译者角色的适配性在《口译“居间者”的角色认知》一文中也有体现，作者指出，社区口译员往往对自身的居间者认知更为清晰（王炎强，2017：92）。具体领域的译员角色研究主要涉及医疗、手语新闻和法庭三个方面。不论是探讨医疗口译员集“代言人、协调者、医者”三类角色于一身的现象（苏伟，2010），还是论述多重因素导致的手语译员角色错位（倪兰，2015），以及法庭口译员在话语权、形势和语言方面充当的“守门员角色”（赵军峰、张锦，2011），实践语境下的多方交际始终是该分类的研究重点。

第四类的研究围绕社区口译行业体系建设展开，多于近年出现，手语翻译偏向性明显。就行业整体规约而言，《中国口译服务标准探索与展望》一文基于中国翻译协会官网公布的口译标准文件，梳理了 9 部口译服务标准文件的主要内容和特征，并对比外国同期相关文件，为推动社区口译服务标准建设建言献策（邢杰、何映桦，2021）。郑璇聚焦手语翻译领域，以新冠疫情为背景，回顾发展历史，梳理手语翻译行业现状，聚焦人才培养，并从行业立法、教育革新、角色模式创新三个方面提出建议（郑璇，2020）。还有部分研究以特定城市，如 XX 城市的手语翻译服务需求为切入点，指出造成手语翻译行业职业化迟滞的因素（倪兰、和子晴，2022）。

3.3.2 突现词列表

图 5 为国内社区口译突现词列表，由“突变检测计算”得出。红色块意味着在对应时间段中该关键词处于研究核心，从上至下的排列展示了社区口译研究热点的历时变化。本研究在该图的基础上进一步梳理文献内容，发现国内社区口译研究热点历时变化具有以下特征。

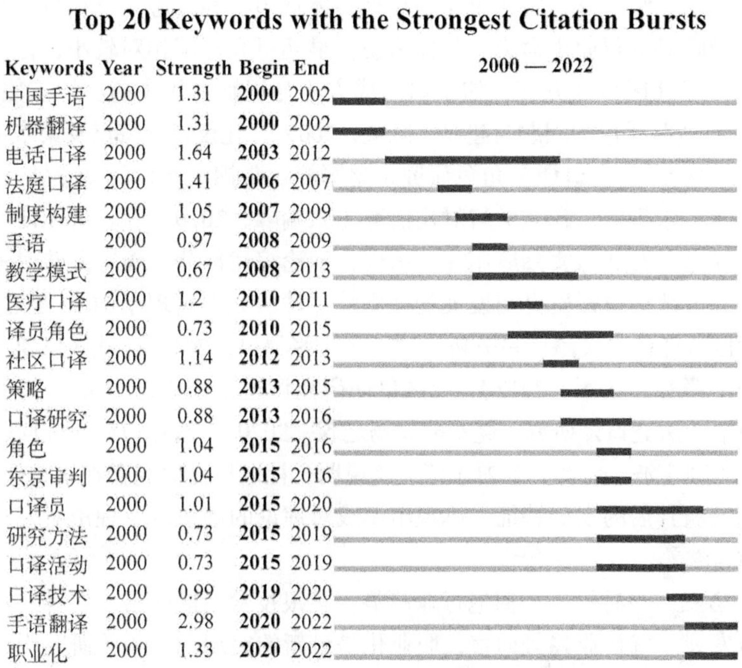

图 5 国内社区口译研究突现词列表

第一，与社会实际需求紧密结合，具有较强的实践导向性。以手语翻译为例，手语一词在列表中出现三次之多（2000—2002、2008—2009、2020—2022），跨越整个时间区间。结合关键词共现图谱可知，手语翻译的出现频次与中心度均名列前茅。三种数据互证，有力说明了手语翻译研究是我国社区口译研究的中流砥柱。究其原因，一是不容忽视的市场需求，二是行业自身的发展演进。据统计资料显示，截至 2020 年，我国听力言语残疾人数量已高达 2,057 万人，约占人口总数的 1.68%[1]，形成了庞大的需求，而且 2007 年手语翻译员正式列入第八批新职业，与第二次研究高峰出现时间相契合。此外，在学界关注社区口译的前十年，法庭口译与医疗口译在列表中均有显现，无不体现出现有研究对于场景化实践的关注。

1 详见 https://www.163.com/dy/article/GCDIGUUM0543OM0R.html（访问日期：2022-10-3）

第二，综述性研究多见于中后期，体现出学界反思、学科延续和社区口译旺盛的行业生命力。具体来说，早期研究范围相对较小，往往局限于特定社区口译分支，如手语合成方法与识别系统（高文、王兆其，2002）、新闻手语的问题与建议（陈英，2009）、礼仪口译特点及策略（宋颉，2008）、法庭口译员角色研究（赵军峰、张锦，2011）、法庭口译制度构建（张瑞嵘，2009）与对比研究（张瑞嵘，2010）等。对于社区口译的界定、发展与实际应用往往出现在理论综述部分，颇有抛砖引玉之感。关于社区口译研究与发展的独立综述性研究多出现于2012年之后，如社区口译研究文献计量分析（刘建军、张福勇，2012）、社区口译现状调查（邓春、文军，2012）、社区口译研究评述（张威，2016）、修辞学视角下的法庭口译研究（赵军峰、杨之森，2020）、医疗口译研究回顾与展望（刘宇波、张威，2021）等。这说明，社区口译研究存在实践先行，理论紧随其后的发展特征，体现出实践对理论的铺垫以及理论对实践的反哺与滋养。

第三，与时俱进，拥抱行业趋势，紧跟技术发展前沿，以科技促进自身发展。就行业趋势而言，职业化是最新的突现词。相关研究均在将职业发展与社区口译行业生态紧密结合的基础上，尝试规范健全行业发展。就技术而言，社区口译与技术的结合在研究初期就有所体现。按出现的先后顺序，相关突现词分别为机器翻译（2000—2002）、电话口译（2003—2012）和口译技术（2019—2020）。词语更迭的背后，是技术应用面的扩大和社区口译服务范围的扩大和方式的灵活。机器翻译突现时间段内，技术主要与手语识别、手语翻译系统相结合，多为应用型研究。电话口译的突现时间长达9年，为列表之最，其背后是远程口译技术的发展与革新——应用载体由电话拓展至网络在线平台，应用场景由医疗领域拓展至教学与语言服务领域。从电话口译到远程口译，研究对象的转变折射出技术发展与社会环境变化带来的新鲜血液，也反映出社区口译研究具有较强的适应性。此外，社区口译对技术的依赖也从侧面说明社区口译具有较强的临时性与灵活性，需求量大，行业覆盖面广，但译员供给量不足，需机器辅助。

4. 社区口译研究之述评与展望

基于上文分析，笔者认为，既有研究主要存在缺乏多样性、创新性及指导性三大阙如。缺乏多样性指研究主题过度聚焦手语翻译和法庭口译，对于难民及移民口译等本应是社区口译重要的实践和研究分支，数量十分有限，只有少数研究将目光投向冲突地区的口译活动（许文胜等，2019），以及政治冲突中的口译员角色（刘立胜，2013），但均以国际案例为分析对象，目前尚未有研究探讨移民口译。其原因在于中国为世界上最大的非移民国家，国内及周边环境长期保持稳定，并未形成具有"飞地意识"的外来少数族群聚居地，自然也缺少实践土壤。创新性的缺乏在于研究方法较为单一。以译者角色与意识为例，大部分研究都属于个案分析，只有极少数采用访谈与问卷调查的形式，民族志观察和问卷调查等实证研究尚处于稀缺状态。指导意义不足是因为相关研究性质以思辨为主，实证为辅，文献研究、历史研究或对比研究为多数，而实证研究结论往往也以思辨为导向，较为抽象，难以对实践产生具体和有效指导。

本研究认为，未来社区口译研究或将呈现如下趋势。第一，研究场景与语境将更丰富多元。随着疫情的暴发，加快发展和建设应急语言服务体系建设的呼声日趋高涨（王立非等，2020：28）。社区口译正是应急语言服务的重要组成部分，相关需求的增加将为理论研究提供新案例、新场景、新思路。此外，中国是统一的多民族国家，少数民族语言数目在 70 种以上，全国各地区也多有本地方言。本次检索中尚未发现涉及方言或少数民族语言的口译研究，而社区口译又高度契合跨民族沟通场景，存在较大应用空间。未来，跨民族沟通的语内社区口译或将进入研究视野。

第二，具有更强烈的人本主义倾向。社区口译自诞生伊始就以沟通公共场合下权力地位不平等的双方为主要目的，当事双方与译员在一定的社会语境中形成三向互动（任文、伊安·梅森，2011：61）。具体口译事件中的权力关系、译员角色、责任和伦理规范是社区口译绕不开的话题。近年来，出现了针对译员情绪智力这一"软技能"的研究，将目光聚焦情绪智力之于从事国家安全事务口译、医疗口译、法庭口译、手语口译和警务口译的译员的重要性（邱进、廖雪汝，2020）。社区口译的发生场景本就多容易引起情感波动，专注研究对象，深入分析实践主体以解释特定的翻译现象，未来研究或大有可为。

第三，拥抱技术与大数据浪潮。从实践来看，随着口译技术日新月异，语音识别、机器口译等技术将被广泛应用于实践中（王华树、李智，2020：54），社区口译也不例外。社区口译与技术结合的实践与研究将为未来口译质量评估、人机合作、译者主体性、翻译教学等领域带来新气象。从研究方法来看，随着数字人文转向的出现，语料库、大数据等数字技术逐渐为翻译研究者所用。建议在未来建立某一特定领域的社区口译语料库，广泛收集多模态语料，将极大地便利实证研究，使经验性描述更具说服力。

第四，进一步展开跨学科学术合作。不同领域、国家、研究主体间应相互借鉴，加强合作。社会学理论与社区口译研究的融合展现出探索跨学科研究的可能。人类学、传播学、心理学等领域将为社区口译研究提供全新的理论视角；各国不同的历史文化背景与社会状况孕育出不同的社区口译实践，为对比互鉴提供了绝佳素材；研究人员间加强交流、互通有无，也将助力社区口译研究蓬勃发展。

5. 结语

社区口译是最古老的口译形式，其光芒却远被会议口译所遮掩，直到 20 世纪 90 年代才真正走上国际译学舞台。探究社区口译，将目光从语言本身和认知过程转向社会文化语境，呼应了口译研究的社会学转向，一副立体翔实的口译研究图景就此展开。

本文采用可视化研究方法，对 2000 年至 2022 年间发表的国内相关研究进行历时归总，绘制知识图谱，从发文总体趋势、作者与期刊概况、关键词共现、关键词突变趋势四个方面回顾了我国社区口译研究发展脉络，梳理了研究进程。笔者在对文献进行定量与定性分析后，归纳总结了既有研究的特征与问题，并尝试提出社区口译研究未来发展走向。学界应持续追踪研究热点，深入挖掘各方要素，弥合研究缺口，提升社区口译主体多样性、研究方法创新性和结论的可操作性。希望本文能为后续研究的推陈出新提供借鉴与启发，助力社区口译在中华大地上开出更繁茂的花朵。

参考文献

[1] 邓春，文军. 我国社区口译的现状调查及其启示 [J]. 外国语文，2012（5）：113-117.

[2] 胡显耀，李茂君. 当代国际译学研究课题与走向的知识图谱分析 [J]. 外语与外语教学，2020（6）：131-142，151.

[3] 李红满. 国际翻译学研究热点与前沿的可视化分析 [J]. 中国翻译，2014（2）：21-26，127.

[4] 刘和平. 职业口译新形式与口译教学 [J]. 中国翻译，2003（3）：34-38.

[5] 刘建军. 全球视域下的社区口译研究 [M]. 北京：中国社会科学出版社，2014.

[6] 刘建军，张福勇. 国外社区口译研究文献计量分析 [J]. 外语教学理论与实践，2012（2）：73-81，88.

[7] 刘立胜. 政治冲突中口译员的角色研究——《口译公正：道德、政治与语言》述评 [J]. 中国翻译，2013（6）：42-45.

[8] 刘淑颖. 美国的法庭口译 [J]. 宁夏社会科学，2006（1）：43-45.

[9] 刘宇波，张威. 新世纪以来的医疗口译研究：回顾与展望 [J]. 上海翻译，2021（2）：70-75，95.

[10] 马超. 医疗口译中译员的显身性研究 [D]. 长沙：中南大学，2013.

[11] 倪兰. 论手语新闻节目中手语译员的角色定位 [J]. 上海翻译，2015（1）：46-50.

[12] 倪兰，和子晴. 上海手语翻译服务需求与现状调查 [J]. 中国翻译，2022（4）：113-119.

[13] 牛丽霞，王跃洪. 法庭口译的特点及应对策略——以小额索赔案件为例 [J]. 中国科技翻译，2015（2）：19-21.

[14] 邱进，廖雪汝. 情绪智力与口译研究——以几个特殊领域的口译为例 [J]. 外国语文，2020（1）：141-148.

[15] 任文，郭聪，黄娟. 改革开放以来中国口译研究 40 年考察 [J]. 外语教育研究前沿，2019（1）：21-37，148.
[16] 任文，徐寒. 社区口译中的场域、惯习和资本——口译研究的社会学视角 [J]. 中国翻译，2013（5）：16-22，128.
[17] 宋莹，覃江华. 纽伦堡审判与东京审判口译制度比较分析 [J]. 中国科技翻译，2016（4）：54-57.
[18] 苏伟. 从“传声筒”到“医患关系的协调者”——一项针对医疗译员角色的实证研究 [J]. 外语研究，2010（5）：84-88.
[19] 苏伟. 社区口译在中国 [J]. 上海翻译，2009（4）：42-45.
[20] 王华树，李智. 口译技术研究现状、问题与展望（1988—2019）——一项基于相关文献的计量分析 [J]. 上海翻译，2020（3）：50-55，95-96.
[21] 王继红. 国内外手语翻译研究：历史与现状 [J]. 上海翻译，2009（2）：23-28.
[22] 王继红. 手语翻译与口译的异同 [J]. 中国特殊教育，2009（8）：20-26.
[23] 王立非，任杰，孙疆卫，蒙永业. 应急语言服务的概念、研究现状与机制体制建设 [J]. 北京第二外国语学院学报，2020（1）：21-30.
[24] 王小曼，王斌华. 口译行业新动态：远程会议口译主流平台及其技术 [J]. 中国翻译，2021（5）：105-112.
[25] 王炎强. 口译“居间者”的角色认知 [J]. 上海翻译，2017（1）：90-93，95.
[26] 向明友. 语用学研究的知识图谱分析 [J]. 外国语（上海外国语大学学报），2015（6）：36-47.
[27] 肖晓燕，高昕，赵肖. 中国大陆手语传译调查：现状、问题与前景 [J]. 中国翻译，2018（6）：66-72.
[28] 肖晓燕，郁锐玲. 社区口译新趋势——电话口译 [J]. 中国翻译，2009（2）：22-27，94.
[29] 肖晓燕，王继红. 手语翻译研究——模式、内容及问题 [J]. 中国特殊教育，2009（2）：29-35.
[30] 肖晓燕，张梅. 美国电话口译的职业现状及理论分析 [J]. 上海翻译，2009（1）：30-34.

[31] 邢杰，何映桦. 中国口译服务标准探索与展望 [J]. 上海翻译，2021（5）：72-78.

[32] 邢星. 国内外译员角色研究的进展与思考（1976—2014）——一项基于相关文献的计量分析 [J]. 上海翻译，2015（3）：67-73.

[33] 许文胜，方硕瑜，叶铖. 媒体视角下冲突地区的口译活动 [J]. 外语研究，2019（2）：70-76.

[34] 杨淑莹，田迪，郭杨杨，赵敏. 端到端手语翻译研究 [J]. 系统科学学报，2022（3）：1-7.

[35] 詹成，索若楠. 电话口译在我国的一次重要实践——广州亚运会、亚残运会多语言服务中心的电话口译 [J]. 中国翻译，2012（1）：107-110.

[36] 张继光. 国内翻译研究动态的科学知识图谱分析（2005—2014）——基于 12 种外语类核心期刊的词频统计 [J]. 东北大学学报（社会科学版），2016（4）：429-435.

[37] 张威 . 中西口译研究的相似性 [J]. 中国科技翻译，2009（2）：18-21.

[38] 张威. 新世纪口译研究的热点与策略 [J]. 中国外语，2013（6）：77-82.

[39] 张威. 翻译教学与研究的新热点——社区口译研究述评 [J]. 中国外语，2016（2）：20-31.

[40] 臧渝梨，王育林，仝春兰，李晶，朱楠，沈一桥，袁魁昌，孟晓琴，程强，娄凤兰. 听障者就医沟通需求初探 [J]. 中国实用护理杂志，2008（26）：67-69.

[41] 赵军峰，陈珊. 中西法庭口译研究回顾与展望 [J]. 中国科技翻译，2008（3）：19-22，9.

[42] 赵军峰，张锦. 作为机构守门人的法庭口译员角色研究 [J]. 中国翻译，2011（1）：24-28，93.

[43] 郑璇. 加快推进中国手语翻译的职业化——基于新型冠状病毒性肺炎疫情的思考 [J]. 残疾人研究，2020（1）：24-32.

[44] 朱波，高虹. 法庭口译中的角色冲突——以 Camayd-Freixas“声明”为例 [J]. 外语与外语教学，2015（5）：75-79.

[45] Hale, S. Community Interpreting [M]. New York: Palgrave Macmillan, 2007.

[46] Pöchhacker, F. Coping with culture in media interpreting [J]. Perspectives: Studies in Translatology, 2007(2)：123-142.

[47] Pöchhacker, F. Introducing Interpreting Studies [M]. London: Routledge, 2004.

[48] Roberts, R. Overview of community interpreting [A]. In Dufour & Stein, D. (ed). The Critical Link: Interpreters in the Community [C]. Amsterdam: John Benjamins, 1997.

[49] Wadensjö, C. Interpreting as Interaction [M]. New York: Longman, 1998.

公共政策翻译规范研究

——以《抗击新冠肺炎疫情的中国行动》白皮书的英译为例[1]

王炎强　复旦大学
寿晨佳　上海中学

摘　要：中国公共政策外译是新时代讲好中国故事的理想载体，有利于国外受众从顶层设计上认识中国治理，及时、准确、全面地了解中国。因此，公共政策的翻译至关重要，需要遵守一定的翻译规范，便于译入语受众理解和接受。翻译规范是翻译活动中共同认可，在翻译过程中应该遵照的正确或恰当的行为方式，是协调译员在翻译生态系统中的行为准则。为了更好地研究影响中国当下公共政策翻译的规范，本文以《抗击新冠肺炎疫情的中国行动》白皮书的英译为例，借鉴社会学和翻译规范理论对其中的部分案例规范进行分析，以期为公共政策翻译提供理论和实践支撑。

关键词：公共政策翻译；翻译规范；产品规范；操作规范

Research on Public Policy Translation Norms — A Case Study of the English Translation of the White Paper *Fighting Covid-19: China in Action*

Wang Yanqiang　Fudan University
Shou Chenjia　Shanghai High School

Abstract: Public policies are an essential aspect of China's governance, and their

1　本文系中宣部项目“中华文化对外传播之策略研究”（项目编号：WEH3152004）的阶段性研究成果。

effective communication to foreign audiences relies heavily on the accuracy of translated laws, regulations, and other government announcements. Adequate and efficient translations play a crucial role in facilitating international communication. However, given the high stakes involved in the translation of such documents, it is essential to establish behavior regularities and norms to guide and evaluate the translation process. In this study, the authors analyze the English translation of the white paper *Fighting Covid-19: China in Action* to illustrate the product norms and operational norms that govern the translation of public policy documents. This analysis sheds light on the translation process and highlights the importance of adhering to established norms when translating documents related to public policies.
Keywords: public document translation; translation norms; product norms; operational norms

1. 引言

公共政策是指国家协调经济社会活动的一系列政策的总称。公共政策体现公共问题，需要对社会开放。特别是随着中国改革开放后经济社会的发展，希望了解和学习中国国家治国理政之道的人越来越多，而公共政策是理解中国顶层设计的窗口。这就需要我们掌握对外话语能力，主动积极开展政策沟通，增进了解（黄友义，2020）

随着中国扩大开放，更进一步融入世界舞台，需要对外翻译的公共文件和文本类型越来越多。主要包括三类文件：1）中国政府治国理政的根本性法律、法规、国家规划、政策实施方案等；2）涉及对外开放中招商引资、涉外商务等法律法规和政策指南，如外商企业投资法、自贸区管理条例等；3）中国签署批准的国际条约相关产业调整、政策法规的调整内容应提供及时的翻译，让国际社会及时了解中国的履约情况。这些公共信息都需要及时准确地向国内外发布，因此公共政策翻译就非常必要。

此外，面对百年未有之变局，我们还要与抹黑、污蔑中国的西方敌对媒体报道进行合理的舆论斗争，这也需要强化我们对外翻译和对外传播的能力和效果。一方面，中国需要更加主动地向世界发出自己的声音，让国际社会了解中国；另一方面，目前融通中外话语体系建设尚未成型，高质量、高效翻译中国国家治理方面的大政方针并不多。公共政策翻译和相关研究需要不断探索。

公共政策翻译是国家翻译实践的重要部分，无论是译者的选择、译前准备，还是翻译项目管理及出版发布，都有严格的要求。公共政策翻译需要制定详细的翻译规范，需要搞清楚先翻译什么，后翻译什么，多翻译什么，少翻译什么，外国受众最需要的是什么，如何在翻译过程中达到融通中外话语体系的效果等问题。需要在翻译操作上平衡中文话语体系和译入语受众的理解和接受，保证对外宣传效果。通过梳理剖析目前已有公共政策的翻译成果能够为公共政策规范研究提供有效样本，结合翻译规范研究总结出适合中国公共政策翻译的规范。

2. 公共政策翻译研究

习近平总书记在中共中央政治局就加强我国国际传播能力建设进行第三十次集体学习上的讲话中提道："讲好中国故事，传播好中国声音，展示真实、立体、全面的中国，是加强我国国际传播能力建设的重要任务。"公共政策翻译具有较强的外宣属性，是中国国际传播的重要组成部分，除了准确传达信息外，还要注重传播效果和受众的接受程度。然而，目前公共政策翻译还停留在照搬对内口径，对英文语境和受众接受方面考虑不足，导致传播效果不佳（王大来，2020：136）

翻译不是简单的字面转换，要了解两种语言之间的区别。翻译不仅是沟通两种语言、文化，更是沟通两种思维。公共政策的翻译需要译者充分了解两种语言体系下公共政策话语的区别，具备较强的两种语言的理解和表达能力，同时还要对翻译文本进行深入剖析，甚至需要进行译前编辑和改写，使原文文本意思更清晰，更容易翻译成外语。另外，译者还是能够辨析两种语言在结构、表达习惯、思维方式等方面的细微差异，在理解和表达上更透彻。正如 Toury 所言，翻译要"贴近国外受众的思维习惯"，翻译就要面向目标语及目标语文化体系（Toury，2001：13）。公共政策翻译需要加强对国际受众的了解，了解他们的语言习惯、思维模式、表达风格和理解能力，我们才能更加有针对性地使用他们熟悉的国际话语体系，把传播中国落到实处（黄友义，2020）。

目前，关于公共政策翻译的规范性研究较少。2017 年劳特利奇出版公司出版了 Gabriel González Núñez 和 Reine Meylaerts 合编的《翻译与公共政策——跨学科视角与案例研究》（*Translation and Public Policy: Interdisciplinary Perspectives and Case Studies*）论文集，其中部分论文涉及法律和政策文件翻译，但基本上从语言政策和宏观翻译政策角度进行案例分析，把翻译政策作为公共政策中的一部分，强调在多元文化中应该规范翻译活动，特别是从政治的角度看待翻译和语言服务。国内关于公共政策翻译规范的研究集中探讨政府文件翻译的准确性。例如，施燕华（2004）强调，在翻译外交文件时要具备高度政治敏感性，必要时需要死抠文字，以保证译文的高度忠实性。程镇球（2003）提出，翻译政治文字必须具备高度政治性，方能确保译文与原文表达效果上的对等。蔡力坚（2017）强调，准确性是公文翻译中最重要的一项要求。

北京第二外国语学院成立了中国公共政策翻译研究院，组织翻译出版了一系列公共政策的书籍，举办公共政策翻译高层论坛，产生了一批公共政策研究成果。论坛发言嘉宾主要在宏观层面梳理目前公共政策翻译的现状、探讨人才培养、提高政治话语翻译效果等问题，而并没有针对具体翻译操作总结归纳适用公共政策的翻译规范。本文从翻译规范理论视角出发，结合公共政策案例，借鉴翻译规范理论进行分析，探讨汉译英翻译的过程规范和操作规范，从宏观和微观层面认识公共政策翻译的相关规范。

3. 翻译规范

“规范”概念来自社会学，指“社会基于共同价值观念形成的行为共识，确定具体行为中什么是对，什么是错，哪些行为要被规范或禁止，哪些行为又是被容忍和许可的”（Toury, 2001：55）。按照此定义，翻译规范就是翻译活动中大家共同认可、在翻译过程中应该遵循的正确或恰当的行为方式，翻译规范是协调译员在翻译生态系统中的行为准则。译者在翻译过程中逐渐掌握一些翻译方法策略，总结归纳出一定的翻译原则，帮助解决具体翻译问题。翻译规范兼顾宏观和微观两个层面；翻译规范制约译者的具体翻译活动并影响翻译活动参与者之间的关系。

Toury 将翻译规范分为基准规范（preliminary norms）、初始规范（initial norms）和操作规范（operational norms）。基准规范指宏观的翻译政策和翻译路径，例如作品选择偏爱，以及直接翻译还是转译等。初始规范指译者的总体翻译策略，尽量靠近原文本，产出充分性（adequacy）的译本，还是偏向目标语文化，产出更具可接受性（acceptability）的译本。操作规范决定了译者具体采取的翻译方法，体现在语言的特点和风格上，如段落的划分与合并，译本内容和语言的删减或增添、句式、语法、措辞等（Toury，2001：56-61）。

在 Toury 的规范分类基础上，Chesterman（1997）也将翻译规范归纳为两大类：产品或期望规范（product norms or expectation norms）和生产或过程规范（production norms or process norms）。产品或期望规范是指翻译作品的选择和译文读者对译文的基本态度；生产或过程规范又称为专业规范（professional norms），起着对翻译具体操作过程的指导和调控作用（Chesterman，1997：67）。

两位学者的分类方法各异，但基本上都是从政策管理和操作实践宏观和微观两个层面对翻译规范进行归纳。不同语对、不同翻译方向的翻译目的、译文生产和翻译过程特点不尽相同。汉英两种语言差异明显，汉语的行文结构、表现方式和英语有很大的区别，因此翻译过程受到的源语文化和目标语文化的约束也更强，也更有必要对翻译操作过程中的词汇、句法和结构进行一定的转换和调整。本文将以《抗击新冠肺炎疫情的中国行动》白皮书的英译为例，梳理白皮书汉英翻译中的产品规范和过程规范，从规范的角度探讨具体的公共政策汉英翻译策略。

4.《抗击新冠肺炎疫情的中国行动》白皮书英译翻译规范

2020 年 6 月 7 日，国务院新闻办公室发布《抗击新冠肺炎疫情的中国行动》白皮书（以下简称“白皮书”）中英文两个版本。白皮书记录了中国人民抗击疫情的伟大历程，与国际社会分享中国抗疫的经验做法，为世界其他国家防疫提供了借鉴。白皮书的及时翻译和发布全面、完整、准确地向世界说明中国抗疫全过程，反对污名化和疫情政治化，用事实回击了抹黑中国的谣言。

4.1 白皮书翻译中的产品规范

首先，产品规范中的文本规范决定选择什么样的文本翻译。在公共政策翻译中产品规范意味着决定哪些公共政策需要翻译或者优先进行翻译。文本规范还决定了翻译产品的呈现方式，发布时间、发布平台和发布形式，在线发布还是出版读物等。白皮书记录 2020 年初中国人民抗击疫情的伟大历程，既分享中国抗疫的经验做法，说明中国抗疫全过程，又起到了反对污名化和疫情政治化的作用。因此白皮书的翻译和出版有着重大的意义。

白皮书的英文翻译和出版任务由中宣部部署。当代中国与世界研究院、中国翻译协会与外文出版社组织专家团队进行翻译。白皮书的翻译和出版时间要求急、文字量大、质量要求高。中国外文出版发行事业局启动国家重大翻译项目审定工作委员会和重点翻译任务统筹工作机制，成立专项任务领导小组，由局内外翻译专家、业务骨干及外籍专家组成的经验丰富的翻译工作组经过十余天奋战，完成 3.7 万余字的翻译、审定、编校和出版工作。

产品规范中的关系规范决定原文和译文的关系：什么样的译文是合格的译文，译文是倾向于源语的语言文化规范还是目标语的语言文化规范？如果倾向于前者，译本表现出充分性；如果倾向于后者，则体现出可接受性。白皮书中文起草组遵循的编写原则之一是：要有力量，即用明确的事实驳斥有关新冠病毒源头的谣言，也要有温度，即体现出我国人民至上、生命至上的态度。同样白皮书的翻译首先要忠实于原文的核心要义，准确传递出原文希望传达的信息。在此前提下，从融通中外、贴近国外受众思维和语言习惯出发，进行一定程度的灵活处理，以增强译文的可读性和可接受性（黄长奇，2020）。从这一原则可以看出白皮书翻译基本的原文译文关系规范是忠实于原文要义，在准确传递核心信息的前提下也要充分考虑目标语受众的可接受性。内容上力求完整体现原文，表达上要尽量贴近目标语语言规范，这对汉英两种语言结构和表达特点迥异汉英公共政策翻译提出较高的要求。

4.2 白皮书翻译中的过程规范

过程规范体现在翻译的具体实施方法和路径，过程规范对具体翻译起着指导、调控的作用。过程规范包括三个次级规范，即译者规范、管理规范和操作规范。

4.2.1 译者规范

译者规范涉及对译者的要求，什么样的译者符合要求，选择译者的过程是怎样的。随着中国国际地位的提高，中译外在整个翻译量中的占比超过外译中。按照翻译的传统逻辑，中译外应该由外语为母语的译者从事，但由于中文的特殊性，目前精通中文、能做中译外的外国人极其有限。而我们正面临讲好中国故事、加强对外传播的时代，单公共政策领域就需要大量的高水平译员，因此从现有专业队伍的状况看，在今后相当长一段时间内中译外还会是以中国人为主。

白皮书的翻译人员来自当代中国与世界研究院、外文出版社等局属单位的中译英翻译队伍，并得到外交部、《中国日报》、北京第二外国语学院等单位专家的支持，翻译项目团队从翻译水平和资源上都非常强。中国外文出版发行事业局拥有强大的外籍专家资源，参与的重大翻译项目，特别是涉及公共政策翻译都有外籍专家参与审校工作。目前国内重大的外宣翻译项目一般都是外籍专家参与审校，与中方翻译专家共同探讨相关难点重点内容的翻译，在集体讨论中确定最终翻译格式和文本。译者都是长期从事中译外对外宣传工作的资深语言专家，对白皮书等政策文件的翻译比较有经验。可以说，无论从政治素养上还是从翻译经验上应该来说都是国内最优秀的译者。中外译者的合作也是保证公共政策翻译传播效果的重要一环。通过合作翻译的模式创造了不少成功的公共政策外宣案例。例如，《习近平谈治国理政》的英文版翻译团队由 29 名多年来从事外宣工作的翻译组成，其中包括 7 名定稿人，1 名外国改稿专家，还有 2 名外国专家协助工作。

4.2.2 管理规范

管理规范包括翻译机构的要求、翻译流程控制、评估和修改机制等项目管理标准和管理机制。公共政策翻译通常由政府部门和机构主导，涉及多部门和多人参与，协调管理是公共政策翻译中的重要一环。可以说管理规范强是公共政策翻译规范的重要特征。管理规范直接影响译者实际的翻译过程，译者对具体文化、语言难点的处理，篇章、句法和选词的斟酌，段落的增删与具体翻译方法的选择都要考虑机构制定的大的翻译原则。白皮书翻译项目实际工作流程包括翻译—母语改稿—初核—复核—定稿—读方版—通读—三校—清样（11 道）等 20 余道工序。具体分工按照翻译组、术语组、核稿组、定稿组、编校组设定并组织翻译质量评估和修改。成立术语组为翻译提供支持，并给译者提供统一的参考资料。

从翻译规范的宏观层面看，类似白皮书这样的中国公共政策翻译目前主要由政府机构和国家对外出版传播单位以及合作高校完成。从翻译主体和赞助者的角度来看，一方面公共政策翻译体现出较为明显的机构赞助和多单位协作的特点，这是确保高质量及时完成翻译项目的根本保证，另一方面这些国家翻译实践项目需要协调各参与方，包括个人和不同单位之间关系的协调，除了在项目管理上设定合理的翻译审校流程，还需要有一定的翻译规范来指导和协调翻译和最终定稿过程中的语言、诗学和意识形态等因素。通常在翻译过程中通过研讨会和专家讨论等方式就某些特定的翻译问题进行探讨，最后确定合理的翻译方法。因此，公共政策翻译具有较强的翻译管理规范特点。

4.2.3 操作规范

操作规范是指译者在翻译过程中具体使用的翻译策略和方法，包括基于原文特点和译文特点的原文与译文之间的对应关系以及系统内的各类转换等。这些为实现源语与译语更高层次的对应的微观层面策略是实现高质量翻译的重要规范。下面将选取白皮书译文中在对应关系和转换处理的案例来说明操作规范在翻译中的体现。

1）原文与译文之间的对应关系

感情色彩的对应。考虑到中英文语言的差异和语境的不同，中文一些陈述客观事实的中性词译成英文时不能直接机械地对应，而要根据语境选择恰当的字词以体现原文中的感情色彩，实现超越字面对等之外的内涵意义对应。例如，在突出抗疫行动力时，选用含有积极感情色彩的字词。白皮书标题《抗击新冠肺炎疫情的中国行动》中的“中国行动”并非直接对应成含有静态意味的名词词组 China's action，而是在 China 后选用了含有动态意味的名词词组 in action，更能突出中国的行动力。

术语的翻译也要避免误用含有消极感情色彩的字词，否则会对国家形象产生负面影响。例如，“输入病例”一词的翻译就要避免使用 import，因为 import 是主动买进来、引进来的意思，将“输入病例”译为 import 会让译文读者产生中国主动引入病例的错误联想，所以白皮书翻译这个术语选用了中性词 inbound；“雷神山、火神山医院”虽是为应对新冠疫情特别建立的，但避免使用 makeshift 这个词，makeshift 使读者产生因临时拼凑而质量差的错误联想，因此白皮书选用了中性词 improvised hospitals 来表示临时规划修建的医院。

隐喻的对应。中文隐喻使用频率高，尤其是战争隐喻司空见惯，但凡表达任务艰巨、过程艰辛都会看到战争用语。“抗疫”一词本身也有战争联想。白皮书中出现多次与“战”相关的表达，不少地方都是直接翻成了 war 或 battle，全文出现 war 9 次、battle 31 次。保持了中文语言风格，凸显了中国特色。但另一方面翻译要实现有效沟通，帮助外国受众准确清晰的地理解中国。白皮书的翻译似乎也避免使用过多的战争隐喻而采取了保留本体而舍弃喻体的处理方式。下面例子中的四个“战”字并非强调隐喻本身，而更多的是一种口号，所以翻译去掉了“战”的意象，保留本体，把意思转达出去，避免在译文中过度使用战争隐喻，给外国受众留下好战的形象。

例 1：

疫情发生后，全国上下紧急行动，依托强大综合国力，开展全方位的<u>人力组织战、物资保障战、科技突击战、资源运动战</u>……

Relying on its overall national strength, China mobilized the people, enhanced R&D, procured supplies, and brought them to those in need rapidly.

抽象到具体。公共政策文本（特别是一些指导性文本）具有一定解读空间，中文表达往往偏抽象模糊，英文表达偏具象精确。翻译时需要根据实际情况在英语中明确具体的对象。例如，中文常用的动词“完善”意思常常较模糊，不具体说明应该如何完善。中文是意合语言，中文读者可以通过上下文推断理解。“完善”一词不能简单地直接对应到英文的 improve，因为英文中与 improve 的搭配一般都是有问题、有缺陷、需要改进纠正的对象，因此翻译时可以考虑使用较为具体的英文来表达。

例 2：

完善临床救治体系，全国共指定 1 万余家定点医院，对新冠肺炎患者实行定点集中治疗。

The national clinical treatment network has been expanded to include more than 10,000 hospitals dedicated to the treatment of Covid-19 patients.

公共政策类文本行文宏大，立意较高，下面例子中第一句的“重大战略成果”，如果直接译成英文比较空，没有明确具体内容。不如处理成具体成果，把这个宏大的叙事落到实处，说明成果是指 contain the spread of the virus，这样表达才清楚，上下文意思能够连贯上。

例 3：

随着本土疫情防控取得重大战略成果，……

Having succeeded in containing the spread of the virus on the mainland, ...

通过上述译例分析可以看出汉译翻译在原文与译文之间的对应关系上需要考虑的因素较多，从词汇的语体色彩到意义的抽象具象，都要根据翻译的目的和翻译的文本特点进行适当调整，超越文字字面意思的对应，在更高层次的意义层面和所表达的思想层面实现对应。

2）翻译转换策略

Catford（1965：73）提出了翻译转换（translation shifts）的概念，指“从原语出发到目标语过程中对形式对应的偏离”。由于源语和目标语在语言结构上的不对等，包括语法、句法规则、数字单位、性数搭配等差异，翻译转换是不可避免的现象。除了数字单位和语法结构的转换外，白皮书的翻译过程中句法和篇章层面上的结构转换也较多，包括词性转换、句子内部的语序调整、内容整合及篇章分段、分条列点等结构转换，还有为了增强信息的权威性和可信度把间接引语转换为直接引语。

词性转换。中文的行文强调事情发生的过程，动词使用较多；而英文需要先把结果说出来，名词使用较多。中译英时需要对多个动词进行词性转换，减少英文中的动词数量，必要时还需要对语序和内容进行整合。例如，下面的例子使用了“有”“面对”“作出”“实行”等多个动词，把采取的措施过程描述详尽。而在英文翻译中为了体现英文的结果为导向，把上述动词概念转换成名词概念，“应对机制”和“组织能力”，将几个小短句整合成一个完整的动宾结构。

例 4：

中国共产党有坚强有力的领导核心，有以人民为中心的执政理念，面对疫情危机，迅速科学作出决策，实行高效有力的危机应对。

The CPC has a strong leadership core, a people-oriented governance philosophy, and well-established organization and operation mechanisms.

段落结构转换。为了让中文的意思更明白，英文翻译将中文的一大段分成三小段，三段分别讲述起因（疫情情况）、经过（中央、国务院措施）和结果（初步成果），既避免了信息过度集中，又让逻辑更清晰，强化了信息的传播效果。

例 5：

全国新增确诊病例快速增加，防控形势异常严峻。中国采取阻断病毒传播的关键一招，坚决果断关闭离汉离鄂通道，武汉保卫战、湖北保卫战全面打响。中共中央成立应对疫情工作领导小组，并向湖北等疫情严重地区派出中央指导组。国务院先后建立联防联控机制、复工复产推进工作机制。全国集中资源和力量驰援湖北省和武汉市。各地启动重大突发公共卫生事件应急响应。最全面最严格最彻底的全国疫情防控正式展开，疫情蔓延势头初步遏制。

The situation became most pressing with the rapid increase in newly confirmed cases in China. As a crucial step to stem the spread of the virus, the Chinese government took the decisive measure to close outbound traffic from Wuhan. This marked the beginning of an all-out battle to protect Wuhan and Hubei from the epidemic.

The CPC Central Committee set up a leading group for novel coronavirus prevention and control and sent the Central Steering Group to Hubei. A joint epidemic prevention and control mechanism and in due course a mechanism to facilitate resumption of work were set up under the State Council. Resources were mobilized nationwide to assist Hubei and Wuhan. Major public health emergency responses were activated across China.

The most comprehensive, stringent and thorough epidemic prevention and control campaign was launched nationwide, and initial progress was made in curbing the spread of the virus.

最后，白皮书翻译后的内容标题与中文原文在结构上和表现形式上不对应，翻译过程中进行了调整转换。中文的动宾结构转换成英文的名词短语，让英文目录标题更吸引人，更符合英文的行文习惯。标题翻译也是在整个内容翻译完成后根据章节内容进行凝练和调整。

例 6：

二、防控和救治两个战场协同作战

（一）建立统一高效的指挥体系

（二）构建全民参与严密防控体系

（三）全力救治患者、拯救生命

（四）依法及时公开透明发布疫情信息

（五）充分发挥科技支撑作用

I. Well-Coordinated Prevention, Control and Treatment

1. Centralized and Efficient Command

2. A Tight Prevention and Control System Involving All Sectors of Society

3. An All-Out Effort to Treat Patients and Save Lives
4. China Has Released Information in an Open and Transparent Manner as Required by Law
5. Science and Technology Underpin China's Efforts

所有的翻译策略和方法，包括基于原文特点和译文特点的原文与译文之间的对应关系以及系统内的各类转换，都为提升对外传播效果服务。译者要在具体翻译操作过程中对两种语言文化和权利体系进行对比权衡，按照机构和学术界已经形成的相关公共政策翻译规范指导具体的翻译操作。虽然这些策略和原则不一定放之四海而皆准，但符合译者所从事的特定翻译领域及其所在社会文化的总体期望和要求，体现了该社会文化下的翻译职业规范。由于规范是社会群体所共有的，它的效力不是一成不变的。因此，译者的翻译实践也是在转换和优化中总结翻译经验、发现具体操作规范的过程，同时不断验证翻译规范的合理性，修正改进翻译规范。

5. 小结

公共政策翻译成果通常质量较高，尤其是国家层面主导、权威部门发布的公共政策有较强的规范性，为研究翻译规范提供的非常好的语料资源。本文以白皮书为例，描写了其中的宏观、微观翻译规范。Toury（2001：36）认为，通过对翻译的描写可以发现和确认翻译过程，通过描写源语和目标语之间的对应关系，解释其中为优化表达所做的合理调整转换，在此基础上就可以确认源语和目标语之间存在翻译关系。然后根据对应关系可以确定一些基本的翻译原则和翻译初级规范。这些原则和规范继而在其他翻译对照文本中得到验证。这样的发现和验证是科学研究的基本方法，通过扩大语料可以发现更多的翻译对应关系，在此基础上形成大多数译者认可的翻译一般规范，并在翻译学术界和翻译流派的实践中得到确认和验证。Toury 认为翻译规范是实践中发现，又在实践中得以验证的过程。

《抗击新冠肺炎疫情的中国行动》白皮书及时高质量的翻译保证了白

皮书中英文版同步对外发布，英文版白皮书是我国唯一官方讲述中国抗疫情故事的权威读物，得到了国际社会广泛关注。通过对白皮书的翻译案例分析我们看到，无论在译者的选择、翻译流程的管理和翻译中的微观操作，白皮书的翻译都为公共政策翻译提供了非常好的借鉴样本，从中发现的文本规范、产品规范以及微观的翻译操作规范都为后续类似文本的翻译传播提供了参考依据，起到了翻译规范的作用。

参考文献

[1] 黄友义. 疫情之后看外语和翻译的多与少 [J]. 中国外语，2020（6）：11-12.

[2] 黄友义. “一带一路”和中国翻译——变革指向应用的方向 [J]. 上海翻译，2017（3）：1-3.

[3] 黄友义. 中国站到了国际舞台中央，我们如何翻译 [J]. 中国翻译，2015（5）：5-7.

[4] 贾文波. 新时期政治文献对外翻译：理念更新、与时俱进才是硬道理 [J]. 上海翻译，2021（1）：18-22.

[5] 简书网. 黄长奇《〈抗击新冠肺炎疫情的中国行动〉白皮书英译有感》. (2021.01.21) [2022-02-15]. https://www.jianshu.com/p/0d12280651f5

[6] 中国网. 黄友义 2021 在“对外话语体系创新研究”分论坛上发表演 讲 [EB/OL]. (2021-09-28) [2022-02-15]. http://guoqing.china.com.cn/2021-09/28/content_77779473.htm

[7] 王大来. 翻译与文化缺省补偿策略：文学的视角 [M]. 北京：中央编译出版社，2020.

[8] Catford, J. C. A Linguistic Theory of Translation [M]. Oxford: Oxford University Press,1965.

[9] Chesterman, A. Memes of Translation: The Spread of Ideas in Translation Theory [M]. Shanghai: Shanghai Foreign Language Education Press, 2012.

[10] Toury, G. Descriptive Translation Studies and Beyond [M]. Shanghai: Shanghai Foreign Language Education Press, 2001.

二次折射新论：翻译机制及动态过程研究

赵燕凤　华中科技大学
柴　橚　兰州大学

摘　要：安德烈·勒菲弗尔借助物理学折射概念提出翻译学框架中的折射理论，但他并未对翻译的主客观机制加以细化，并且忽略了源语文本、译者、译语文本与译语文化之间的多元动态关系。而真实的译介实际涵盖了更加复杂的"二次折射"动态过程，其内部存在四种典型的二次折射译介模式。通过对这四种模式的探讨，我们不仅细化了勒菲弗尔的"折射"理论，也能够重构源语文本进入译语文化的过程与结果。

关键词：勒菲弗尔；二次折射；翻译机制与过程；译者；社会

The Concept of Double Refraction: A Study on the Translation Mechanism and Process

Zhao Yanfeng　Huazhong University of Science and Technology
Chai Su　Lanzhou University

Abstract: André Lefevere's "Refraction Theory" proposes that translation is akin to the concept of "refraction" in physics, which suggests that translation is a form of "Single Refraction" that fails to fully comprehend the overall translation process. This paper expands upon this idea by introducing the concept of "Double Refraction", which takes into account the dynamic relationships between the source text (ST), the translator, the target text (TT), and the target culture. This theory involves a subjective-objective mechanism and four translation models, and allows for a deeper understanding of the translation and reception of four Eastern and Western classics, as well as the underlying social motivations behind them.

Keywords: André Lefevere; Double Refraction; translation mechanism and process; translator; society

1. 引言

近年来，学界已经开始“跨界”借鉴其他学科理论对翻译学深入探索。翻译研究已经不仅仅汲取社会学、比较文学、传播学、心理学等人文社会科学的养料，亦涉足生物学、医学、计算机、数学、物理学等自然科学。例如，爱尔兰都柏林城市大学（Dublin City University）翻译系莎朗·奥布莱恩（Sharon O'Brien，2013）借助神经科学构建了翻译认知的理论框架；意大利博洛尼亚大学（University of Bologna）学者里卡多·穆尼奥斯·马丁（Ricardo Muñoz-Martín，2015）利用心理学研究译者的心理过程；刘满芸（2014）结合中华传统经典哲学中的“共生”思想，将生物共生学引入翻译学领域，为翻译研究提供了一种价值引导与实践示范；张璐（2019）利用计算机热门软件“Python”分析研究了中国译介文学的发展情况；邢杰等（2019）梳理拉图尔（Bruno Latour）的行动者网络理论（Actor-Network Theory）发现该理论能够为翻译研究提供宏观与微观的指导方法，等等。但事实上，早在20世纪80年代已有学者在翻译领域借助物理学相关概念进行深入探索。

2. 翻译与折射

比利时翻译理论家安德烈·勒菲弗尔（André Lefevere）曾经在1981年发表的《翻译文学：走向一种综合理论》（“Translated Literature: Towards an Integrated Theory”）一文中，将物理学“折射”概念首次引入翻译领域，推动了翻译研究的“文化转向”。尽管此后他将该理论换称为“改写”（rewriting），但是正如著名翻译理论家苏姗·巴斯奈特（Susan Bassnett, 2002：8）在《翻译研究》（*Translation Studies*）中指出的，“勒菲弗尔的翻译理论基础即为折射”。而时至今日，依然有学者借用“折射”这一概念不断探索译学中的种种现象。比如，美国哈佛大学比较文学教授大卫·丹穆若什（David Damrosch）在其专著《什么是世界文学？》（*What Is World Literature?*）中提出，世界文学是“民族文学的椭圆形折射”，并认为“世界文学是在这样一个‘双折射’情形下发生的翻译行为的自然结果”（Damrosch，2003：281）。系统功能语言学领军人物、瑞典语言学家克里斯蒂安·麦蒂森（Christian M. I. M. Matthiessen）同样将源语文本比喻为“无色”白光，将翻译视为棱镜，白光通过棱镜折射出的不同颜色光谱，分别代表译语文本中的“人际意义”“语篇意义”“逻辑意义”“经验意义”等（Matthiessen，2014：277）。中国学者张广奎等（2012）亦从反射与折射物理现象出发，探究经典译介流变的因素、发生与变革方式。王树槐（2019）提出“文化折射率”概念，对其定量分析，揭示译者的文化立场。耿强（2017）在参考西奥·赫曼斯（Theo Hermans，1994）、何绍斌（2005）两位学者对勒菲弗尔翻译思想评述的基础上，将勒菲弗尔的理论划分为元文学、折射、重写、格栅四个区块，并重点评述了折射与重写。由此可见，“折射”概念能为翻译研究提供多角度思考与启发。

1981年，勒菲弗尔认为文学中的折射是“为了某些受众（比如儿童）而加工，或根据某种诗学或意识形态而进行的改编”，它包含了“漫画、学校文集中的摘录、大学用的文集、电影、电视剧、剧情总结和批评论文等不同形式”（Lefevere，2002：72-73）。在次年发表的《大胆妈妈的黄瓜：文学理论中的文本、系统和折射》（“Mother Courage’s Cucumbers: Text, System and Refraction in a Theory of Literature”）一文中，勒菲弗尔继续对折射概念细化，指出“翻译是明显的折射形式”，并将折射重新定义为“针对不同读者所进行的改编，其意图是对读者阅读这部作品的方式产生影响，它在文学中是始终存在的”（1982：4），凸显了“读者”在折射中所起的作用，将翻译研究视角置于更加宏大、更为系统的文化领域之内。

不过，东西方学者并未对勒菲弗尔的折射概念展开具体、深入的研究，而是从经验主义的角度出发，且以非实证的方式，论述了影响折射现象的宏观因素（如意识形态、诗学、赞助人）。基于此，本文在廓清翻译学折射概念的基础上，围绕翻译过程必然涉及的两大介质——译者与社会，尝试细化“二次折射”理论以此重构翻译机制及其动态过程，并将“二次折射”理论与勒菲弗尔翻译观相比较，挖掘统一与差异的思想内涵。

3. 从“一次折射”到“二次折射”

勒菲弗尔在批评埃文—佐哈尔（Itamar Even-Zohar）多元系统论时指出，翻译作为一种折射现象，实际是两种文化系统之间的对话，这是因为“作品总是在一个特定的背景下被人理解的”，而译语文化系统也在经历变化，它所形成的“折射的棱镜在时光流逝的过程中也可能改变”（Lefevere，1982：4）。同时，勒菲弗尔也意识到，翻译的对象并非是翻译语言学派认为的一种静态、不变的文本，它在译语文化中亦受到意识形态、诗学、赞助人等多元因素的规约。

在此意义上，勒菲弗尔的折射理论为翻译学提供了二元文化动态对话机制的新思路，但他的理论构建也存在一定缺陷。首先，以希斯（Hoffman Reynolds Hays）、本特利（Eric Bentley）、曼海姆（Ralph Manheim）与威利特（John Willett）四位译者三个不同时期的译本《大胆妈妈和她的孩子们》（*Mutter Courage und ihre Kinder*）为例，勒菲弗尔在比对不同时期读者接受译本的差异后指出，两个文化系统之间的折射程度“取决于作家在其自身文学系统中的声望”（Lefevere，1982：7）。换言之，勒菲弗尔过分强调了折射中“译语文本读者”和“源语文本作家”之间的心理协商机制，忽略了源语文本最初进入译语文化所需经过的协商机制制定者与创造人的译者存在，尽管勒菲弗尔翻译理论重视改写者的重要性，并将其贯穿于整个理论体系，但他从未对译者拥有过多的强调（耿强，2017：65）。换句话说，他只关注了翻译外部因素，也就是泰纳（Hippolyte Adolphe Taine）提出的文化性“环境”（milieu）因素（Taine，1873）。其次，根据上文折射定义，我们发现，勒菲弗尔翻译思想中的折射过程只发生一次，仅仅注重译语文本与译语读者之间的心理折射，单纯地将折射视为异域文化“接受论”，有意排斥源语文本与译者所处两个文化系统之间的首次折射关联。此外，他虽然强调折射理论中“意识形态、诗学、赞助人”等外部因素，却忽视了译者的内部因素对译本的影响，而这些因素在翻译行为中亦起到极为重要的作用。

正如劳伦斯·韦努蒂（Lawrence Venuti）摘引莫里斯·布朗绍（Maurice Blanchot）的评述指出："翻译是纯粹的差异游戏：翻译总得涉及差异，也掩饰差异，同时又偶尔显露差异，甚至经常突出差异。这样，翻译本身就是差异的活命化身。"（转自冯全功，2019：6）勒菲弗尔之所以认为翻译是折射而非反射，是因为翻译是一种处理差异性文化的复杂行为，而非对源语文本的简单复制，其本身就是一种折射，因其文化的差异性导致了源语文本与译者、译语文本与译语读者无法经常以类似"直射"的方式穿透异域文化介质，无法最快地获取对方真实的思想与内涵。基于此，在源语文本与译者之间，译者需要主动操控源语文本在译语文化之下译者介质中所形成的光路，使其在随后的译语文化社会介质中获得与源语文化类似的心理映射。但是，第一次主动操控光路所形成的"（译者主动操控性）折射"并非随心所欲，它要受到译语文化社会接受程度的考验。这一点正如李力（2019：21）所指出的，"源文本是一个相对固化的客观存在（虽然读者对其意义的理解是动态、主观、多元的）。作者和原作相对而言是一个不变量，像地心引力般对或顺服或逃离的译者随时发挥作用，将译文拉向自己，使整个翻译过程呈现出一种动态的张力"。当译语文本打破这种"张力"的时候，它与源语文本之间也就失去了本该具有的折射关系，甚至造成无法进入译语文化社会的极端状况，造成"完全反射"现象的产生。因为，作为翻译活动的主体——译者兼顾多重身份，他首先是源语文本读者，其次是译语文本的输出者。从更加宏观与多元的视角看，他又是一名"社会人"，从事的翻译活动也是一项社会活动。而社会活动的接受程度又是以源语文本进入译语文化受到"检验"之后的效果为主。在此意义上，作为源语文化的基本组成，社会介质与译者介质之间必然存在联系与区别。如果说，译者介质是在源语文化与译语文化双重影响下，由译者的生活环境、教育背景、职业道德、双语熟练程度、跨文化交际能力等微观因素构成，那么意识形态、经济、宗教、出版社以及读者心理预期等宏观因素则影响译语文本的社会性接受程度。

因此，在"二次折射"理论中，作为"光路"的源语文本通过译者与译语社会这两个介质会造成一定的折射，其二者折射程度（折射角）的大小与假定直射的路径比较，不仅能够清晰、直观地呈现源语文本、译者、译语读者三者之间极为复杂的关系，同时也能廓清、梳理勒菲弗尔曾经模糊的折射概念与理论。据此，“二次折射”理论可简化为图 1 所示的译介过程。

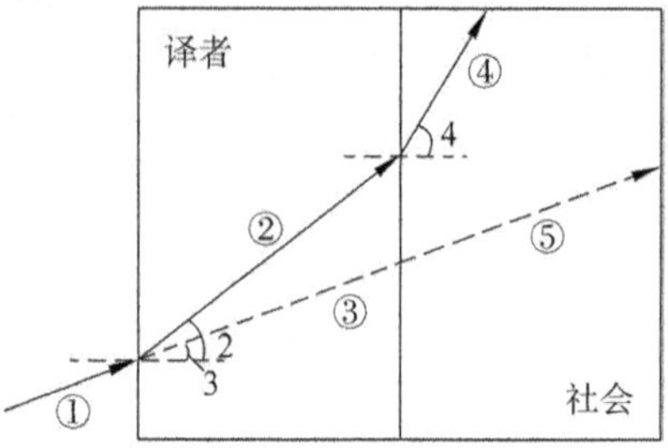

图 1 “二次折射”译介过程

在图 1 中，入射光线①（源语文本）首先进入译者，产生第一次“操控性折射”②（译语文本），它与译者中的假想直射光线③所形成的折射角度（程度）越大，代表译者对源语文本“操控”的力度越大，反之，折射角度越小也就意味着译者对源语文本“操控”力度的减弱。随后，经过译者所形成的第一束折射光线②进入译语社会，再次形成被动“接受性折射”④，它与假想直射光线⑤差异的大小，直观反映译语文本在译语文化中接受程度的高低。

4. 从“操控性折射”到“接受性折射”：“二次折射”理论细化

由于“翻译并非是一套固定意义的文字转换，而是具有动态意义的语言行为”（陈琳、林嘉新，2015：149），翻译理论框架中的二次折射亦是一种动态过程，只有从边界化的特殊状态着手，遵循先特殊、再一般的研究路径，才能覆盖二次折射的所有状态，并且能够准确认识源语文本、译者、译语社会之间的多元关系。

4.1 正操控性折射与正接受性折射的译介模式

在该模式中，译者的翻译行为对源语文本呈正操控状态，即译语文本通过译者造成的折射角大于入射角，形成正操控性折射。随后，作为译语文本的折射进入译语社会中，由于多因素的积极推动，导致该折射得到很好的接收与传播。由此，两次折射共同组成正操控性折射与正接受性折射的译介模式。例如：

例 1：

原文：通形者，先居高阳，利粮道，以战则利。

（孙武，1962：84）

译文：With regard to ground of this nature, be before the enemy in occupying the raised and sunny spots, and carefully guard your line of supplies. Then you will be able to fight with advantage.

(Giles, 1910: 93)

首先，《孙子兵法》中的“居”在汉语中常意为“居住、处于”，而英国汉学家翟林奈（Lionel Giles）却发现该汉字在此处最为精准的含义——“占领”(occupy)。至于“利粮道”中的“利”，他译为 guard（保卫），另一译者塞缪尔·格里菲思（Samuel B. Griffith）则认为是 convenient（便利）(Griffith，1963：124)，二人存在较大分歧。然而，在《孙子兵法》的权威注释本《孙子十家注》中，杜牧对此句的解释是“每于津阨或敌人要冲，则筑垒或作甬道以护之”(孙星衍，1985：169)，杜佑亦认为该策略是“无使敌绝己粮道”(同上)，可见，“利”为“保卫”，更符合孙武兵法思想。译者作为译语社会文化中协商机制的核心制定人与创造者，不仅要在翻译行为中正确把握源语文化概念，还要以强烈的主动操控方式调整源语文本进入译语文化社会介质的折射角，使它在译语社会中得到相应的反馈。翟林奈对折射的正操控行为无疑是成功的。他不仅准确地将“利”译为 guard，而且还附了极为充分、准确的注释。例如：

The general meaning of the last phrase is doubtlessly, as Tu Yu says, “not to allow the enemy to cut your communications.” In view of Napoleon’s dictum, “the secret of war lies in the communications”, we could wish that Sun Tzu had done more than skirt the edge of this important subject here and in I. ss. 10, VII. ss. 11. Col. Henderson says:

> "The line of supply may be said to be as vital to the existence of an army as the heart to the life of a human being. Just as the duelist who finds his adversary's point menacing him with certain death, and his own guard astray, is compelled to conform to his adversary's movements, and to content himself with warding off his thrusts, so the commander whose communications are suddenly threatened finds himself in a false position, and he will be fortunate if he has not to change all his plans, to split up his force into more or less isolated detachments, and to fight with inferior numbers on ground which he has not had time to prepare, and where defeat will not be an ordinary failure, but will entail the ruin or surrender of his whole army."
>
> (Giles，1910：93)

该注释不仅包含杜佑、杜牧、梅尧臣等名人的观点，译者还联系了西方真实的历史事件，以第二次世界大战中洛夫顿·亨德森少校（Col. Henderson）率领"无畏式"俯冲轰炸机参与中途岛海战为佐证，印证《孙子兵法》的合理性与实用性。这种"正操控性折射"的译者行为必然受到推崇，以至于翟译的《孙子兵法》（*Sun Tzu on the Art of War: The Oldest Military Treatise in the World*）自1910年初版伊始便不断再版，虽然在之后百余年间相继涌现多达30余种相关英译本，但只有翟译的《孙子兵法》成为公认的权威译作。

当然，第一次"正操控性折射"和第二次"正接受性折射"必然与译者介质和两种文化的亲密性有关。翟林奈出身汉学世家，并在大英博物馆从事近40年的汉籍管理工作，谙熟中华文化，这为他翻译中国典籍带来了得天独厚的条件。在翻译《孙子兵法》这部军事著作之前，他亦已涉猎多部中外军事名作，对军事颇有了解。与此同时，"20世纪初，英国政府大力推进汉学，促成了汉学的繁荣。1906年，财政大臣组成一个专门委员会，考虑在伦敦设立东方学研究机构。这种对中国文化的热忱实际上起源于大英帝国的商业利益"（转引自罗天，2015：76）。翟译的《孙子兵法》适逢其时，迎合了当时英国国家的政治倾向与经济需求。因此，该种二次折射模式可简化为图2所示的译介模式。

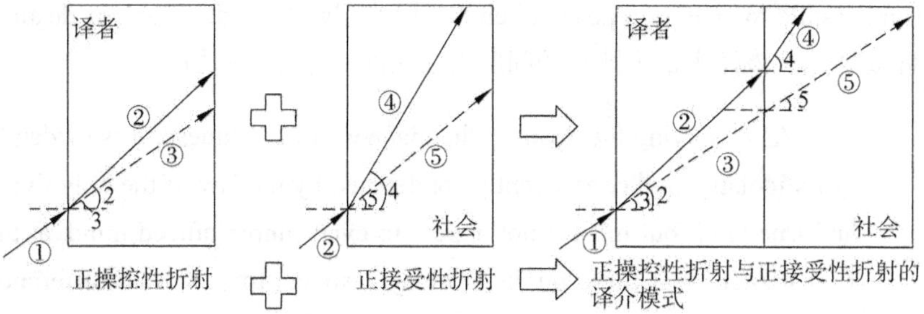

图 2　正操控性折射与正接受性折射的译介模式

4.2　负操控性折射与正接受性折射的译介模式

由于自身能力有限以及其他因素使得译者无法充分驾驭源语文本，导致对源语文本呈负操控状态。之后，作为负操控性折射的译语文本进入译语文化社会中，却能够受到多种外在因素的积极推动，使得该折射得到广泛的接受与认可，由此构成负操控性折射与正接受性折射的译介模式。

例 2：

原文：闵子侍侧，訚訚如也；子路，行行如也；冉有、子贡，侃侃如也。子乐。“若由也，不得其死然。”

（朱熹，1985：155）

译文：Min Tsze stood by with steady mildness in his looks, Tsze Loo appeared firm and bold. Yen Yew and Tsze Kung manifested a soft pliability. Confucius was pleased, but said, Yew will not die a proper death.

（Collie，1828：*HEA LUN*：48）

在汉语中，“侃侃”指说话理直气壮、从容不迫的模样，英华书院（Anglo-Chinese College）第三任校长柯大卫（David Collie）却将其理解为“manifested a soft pliability”（从容不迫），失去了“侃侃”最为基本的“理直气壮”的内涵。另外，源语文本“不得其死然”实指“不得善终”

（impossible to acquire a peaceful end），而非“will not die a proper death”。除误译外，该译本最为严重的问题出现在评注部分。例如：

> As to serving the dead, in the manner of the Chinese, it is evidently gross idolatry, and consequently condemned by the law of the only living and true God: but must it not appear to every unprejudiced mind, at the first glance, that there ought in many respects to be a vast difference between the services which we render to God, and that which we render to our fellow creatures! And is it not a palpable fact, that many are in a great measure acquainted with their duty to man, who are at the same time totally ignorant of the very first principles of their duty to God. Thus confounding things which are so vastly different, is one of the fatal effects of being unacquainted with the revealed will of God.
>
> (Collie, 1828: *HEA LUN*: 48)

柯大卫贬斥儒学，将儒学误认为是一种“盲目崇拜”（gross idolatry），且中国人“不了解上帝的意志”（the will of God），不重视“对上帝负有的责任”（their duty to God），也未对上帝与人类的服务进行区别。可以说，柯大卫并未成功地担当起两个文化之间协商人的角色，而是囿于译语文化的视角，批判源语文化，错误地将东方世界的一切置于西方传统文化视域，其宣扬基督教的“意图”昭然若揭，而这也是勒菲弗尔宣称的“重写者经常带着自己的议程，在同化或经典化过程中发挥最重要的作用”（Lefevere，1998：109）的内因。可见，译者本应实施积极操控的折射行为，被柯大卫有意反向操控，最终导致对源语文本负操控性折射的产生。

尽管西方世界首部“四书”英译本——《四书译注》（*The Chinese Classical Works, Commonly Called the Four Books, Translated and Illustrated with Notes*，1828）未合理弘扬中华文化基质，甚至在诸多方面给予西方读者较为负面的印象，但该译作自出版以来，深受西方世界追捧。美国杂志《日晷》（*The Dial*）在1843年10月发表的文章中指出，该译作是“目前所能见到的中国文献中最有价值的贡献”（Cady，1961：21）。此书也对超验主义代表爱默生（Ralph Waldo Emerson，1803—1882）、梭罗（Henry David Thoreau，1817—1862）的思想产生了重要影响（郭磊，2017：78）。这一现象表明，原本薄弱的第一次主动操控性折射进入译语文化的社会中所形成的第二次被动接受性折射意外获得巨大成功，反映出“正接受”的状态。

这种奇怪的译介现象值得深究。首先，在翻译“四书”之前，柯大卫学习汉语的时间仅有两年，翻译工作从开始到结束也仅历时三年。同时，作为新教（Protestantism）传教士的柯大卫在担任校长期间开展了一系列富有成效的传教工作，翻译“四书”便是他传教的方式之一。粗浅的汉语语言知识、极短的翻译时间、不当的“意图”和错误理解是导致源语文本在翻译行为中造成折射角过小的主要因素。不过，当时西方社会普遍存在的文化偏见为该译本的正接受与广泛传播提供了有利条件，这一点正如学者邓联健（2014：94）认为的：“从基督教视角出发，频频运用语言暴力，对儒家学说和理念横加指责，滥作诋毁，‘传教士帝国主义’在这批传教士儒典翻译的副文本中得到了充分的显示……他们要将自己心目中‘不过尔尔’的儒家典籍‘原样’呈现给西方读者以获取国内对其传教事业的信心与支持。”尽管当时大多数西方读者对柯大卫有意弱化、曲解中国优秀传统文化全然不知，也少有人真正领略《大学》《中庸》《论语》《孟子》等中华典籍中的全貌，但是在他们眼中，柯译的《四书译注》不仅是一部投合西方文化的中国读本，也能够在中西文化的交流当中加深他们对“基督教的认知”，于此产生正接受、广传播的二次折射模式，如图 3 所示。

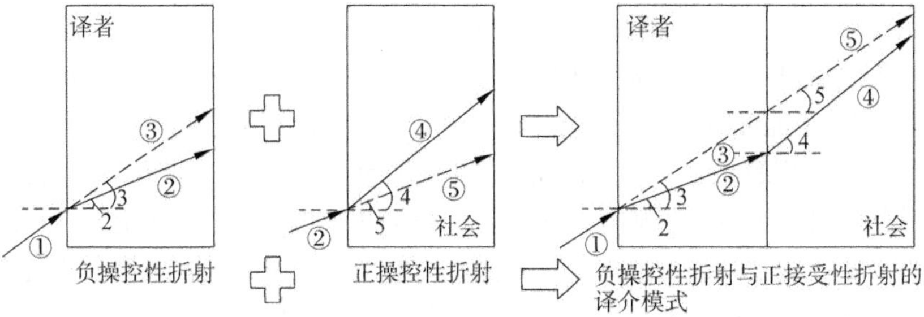

图 3　负操控性折射与正接受性折射的译介模式

4.3 正操控性折射与负接受性折射的译介模式

与上述模式完全相反，正操控性折射与负接受性折射的译介模式即为译者正操控下所形成的译语文本在译语文化社会中遭到冷遇。例如：

例 3：

原文：Oh, won't that be something! Me comin' into the Boston stores with you boys carryin' my bags. What a sensation!

（Miller, 1949/1998：19）

译文：噢，这可好！我走进波士顿的商店，你们哥儿俩提着我的样品箱子。这可不够瞧老大半天的！

（阿瑟·密勒著，姚克译，1970/2004：80）

例 4：

原文：I just can't take hold, Mom. I can't take hold of some kindof a life.

（Miller，1949/1998：39）

译文：我就是扎不下根儿，妈。我不能死钉坑儿地过着一种生活。

（阿瑟·密勒著，姚克译，1970/2004：171）

该译本于 1970 年完成，选自美国剧作家阿瑟·米勒（Arthur Miller）的话剧《推销员之死》（*Death of a Salesman*，1949）。该剧作的社会背景设定为当时最为喧嚣的美国城市纽约，其中充斥着大量口语、俚语。在充分理解源语文本语言特点的基础上，中国翻译家、剧作家姚克大胆启用北京方言，再现原作中生动有趣的语言形式，如将"What a sensation!"译为"这可不够瞧老大半天的！"，"can't take hold"甚至采用"扎不下根儿""不能死钉坑儿"两种译法，这让译本充满了浓厚的中国语言文化色彩。毫无疑问，这一正操控性折射是成功的。姚克自大学起沉迷于戏剧，并创作出名噪一时的剧本《清宫怨》，随后拍成电影《清宫秘史》。而且，自小熟读古文诗词的他不仅具备浓厚的中华文化积淀，亦能熟练使用英语。他曾翻译过鲁迅的《阿 Q 正传》等多部文学作品，鲁迅对他"以西文介绍中国现状"的作用予以很高的评价。这也就不难理解姚克为何能够胜任此项艰难的翻译工作。

遗憾的是，在中国历史性曲折探索时期，姚克因改编电影《清宫秘史》广遭批评，最终被迫漂泊他乡，也正是在这一时期，他完成了《推销员之死》的翻译工作。但是，译者的尴尬身份导致了译本不受当时国内欢迎，最终造成正操控性折射与负接受性折射的译介模式，如图 4 所示。

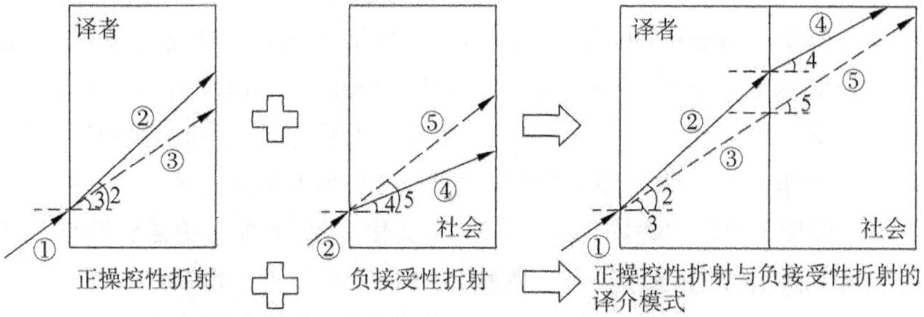

图 4　正操控性折射与负接受性折射的译介模式

4.4　负操控性折射与负接受性折射的译介模式

如果源语文本历经译者与社会所形成的两次折射效果均不令人满意，也就是说，译者并未正确传达源语文本的意义，也未获得译语文化的认可，那么这两次折射共同构成了负操控性折射与负接受性折射的译介模式，比如：

例 5：

原文： Sorrow is hushed into peace in my heart
like the evening among the silent trees.

（Tagore, 1917：10）

译文： 痛在我心里渐渐平和，
夜在树林里一字不说。

（泰戈尔著，冯唐译，2015：10）

例 6：

原文： The world puts off its mask of vastness to its lover.
It becomes small as one song, as one kiss of the eternal.

（Tagore, 1917：3）

译文： 大千世界在情人面前解开裤裆，
绵长如舌吻，
纤细如诗行。

（泰戈尔著，冯唐译，2015：3）

在上述译文中，当代作家冯唐的翻译虽然对仗工整，但存在严重的误译。首先，silent 一词修饰的是 trees 而非 evening。其次，small 的搭配成分是 as one song 与 as one kiss of the eternal，冯唐却将后者遗漏。再者，泰戈尔至纯至真、至善至美的诗句在冯唐笔下成为颇为低俗的性爱诗。该译作一经出版，便引发巨大争议。2015 年 12 月，《人民日报》等主流媒体以《莫借“翻译”行“篡改”（文化世象）》等为题猛烈批驳：“如冯唐者如此随意地翻译经典，既缺乏对经典的尊重，也缺乏对翻译本身的尊重。”（周飞亚，2015）一周后，出版商迫于社会压力主动下架该译著（田超，2015）。

这种“从心所欲”的翻译工作实则是一种似“强”实“弱”的主动操控性折射，即便进入译语社会，甚至受到勒菲弗尔（1982：7）所说的“作家在文学系统中的声望”的影响，最终构成巨大的推力，却依然无法在更加广泛的译语文化中取得寸进，终以虚弱的第二次折射为代价，甚至导致反射的失败终局。因此，这种极为特殊的译介模式可简化图 5 所示的译介模式。

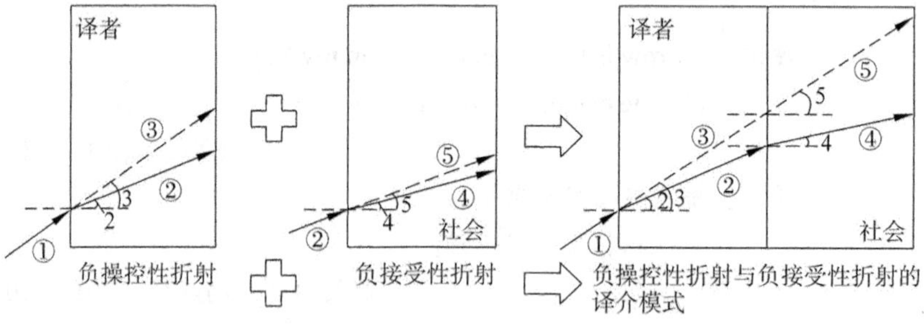

图 5　负操控性折射与负接受性折射的译介模式

5.“二次折射”理论与勒菲弗尔翻译观

吕俊（2000：45）指出：“不论是什么样的艺术形式都是共性中的个性体现，没有共性与规律性艺术本身也会解体，没有个性与差异性、独特性，它又不会成为艺术。”而二次折射理论将翻译视为一种科学与艺术结合的客观实际出发，论证了该观点的正确性。首先，在译介中，译语文化译者介质与社会介质中所形成的折射很少具有一致性，并且随着译者与译语社会共时与历时的变化，其折射角度亦不断变化，这让每一个源语文本在译语文化中都具有了独特的二次折射现象。同时，所有的译介活动都隶属于上述二次折射译介模式中的一种，我们可借助这些特殊模式全面把握整个译介过程。此外，在四种译介模式中，虽然负操控性折射与负接受性折射不甚理想，但最为不佳的译介是负操控性折射与正接受性折射的译介模式，因为由负操控产生的带有诸多讹误的译本在译语文化中被广泛接纳，所造成的不良影响大于其他模式。

其次，正操控性折射和负接受性折射的译介模式，与负操控性折射和正接受性折射的译介模式截然相反，但前者必然优于后者，究其原因，二次折射模式是一个不可逆的译介过程，只有在译者完成主动操控性折射后，方能赋予被动接受性折射发生的可能性，这也就赋予了主动操控性折射的首要地位。同时，“真正的文学经典以其不变的艺术价值面对不断变化粉墨登场的政治意识形态话语。真正的经典经得起政治意识形态的解构”（宋学智，2017：70）。在此，对“意识形态”概念范畴加以扩大，我们就可以得出社会文化的基本属性，即便当前学界发现了姚译《推销员之死》的魅力（李海兰，2013；陈晨，2016），也能意识到柯大卫的《四书译注》对中国传统思想存在严重的偏见（邓联健，2014），但在特定的历史时期，其二次折射在译语文化社会的接受程度必然受到诸多因素（特别是意识形态）的制约。因此，整合上述探讨，按理想的译介程度，二次折射排序应为：负操控性折射与正接受性折射译介模式 < 负操控性折射与负接受性折射译介模式 < 正操控性折射与负接受性折射译介模式 < 正操控性折射与正接受性折射译介模式。

不过，在注重译文读者接受程度的勒菲弗尔看来，合格的翻译只涉及负操控性折射与正接受性折射与正操控性折射与正接受性折射两种译介模式，他一直坚持译语文化“作为对读者、作者和改写者施加的一系列的制约因素发挥着不可替代的作用”（Lefevere，1985：225），从而将其他译介状态置于被忽视的理论角落。这一观点实与其一直秉持的“译语中心”翻译理论观相一致，即对折射理论中的译介根源不以为然，甚至无视翻译学界一直秉持的翻译忠实准则，默许脱离源语文本近似“再创作”的翻译方式。虽然在之后的理论探讨中，勒菲弗尔也曾意识到译者“可以顺从或反对这些制约因素”（Lefevere，1986a：222），“总会有个体的赞助人和专家，作者和改写者并不遵循某个时期系统的意识形态和/或诗学”（Lefevere，1986b：5），却从未展开具体、深入的讨论。基于此，构建二次折射理论的价值就在于弥补勒菲弗尔翻译观的基础——折射理论中被忽略的译者一极，承接英年早逝的勒菲弗尔未竟的理论探索，并在结合实践的基础上，对折射理论乃至勒菲弗尔的翻译观细化、丰富，使其更加完整，更为系统。

6. 结语

借由译介文化接受观，勒菲弗尔构建了极富创新的折射理论，该理论是“对已经完成的翻译的描述，是对‘实然的翻译’或‘翻译事实’的描述”（黄德先、杜小军，2009：78）。它详细探讨了译语文化中影响被动接受性折射的意识形态、诗学、赞助人等多个外部因素，但同时忽略了翻译的内部因素。在此基础上，我们对二次折射理论的丰富与构建，关注译者、社会、读者等多个主体发挥的差异性作用，将操控性折射与接受性折射视为不可分割、必不可少的内在统一体，不仅弥补了折射理论的欠缺，亦从更加科学与客观的视角诠释了翻译机制及动态过程。

参考文献

[1] 阿瑟·密勒. 推销员之死：选评 [M]. 姚克，译，思果，评. 北京：中国对外翻译出版公司，2004.

[2] 陈晨. 译者主体性在戏剧翻译中的体现——以《推销员之死》两个中译本为例 [J]. 周口师范学院学报，2016（1）：55-58.
[3] 陈琳，林嘉新. 跨界的阐释：美国当下比较文学翻译研究的研究范式 [J]. 中国比较文学，2015（3）：139-151.
[4] 邓联健 . 从柯大卫英译《四书》"点评"看新教传教士之"译儒攻儒"[J]. 外语学刊，2014（2）：90-95.
[5] 冯全功. 试论归化和异化的生成动因与三个层面 [J]. 中国翻译，2019（4）：5-13，188.
[6] 耿强. 重返经典：安德烈·勒菲弗尔翻译理论批评 [J]. 中国比较文学，2017（1）：53-69，38.
[7] 郭磊. 首部"四书"英译本——柯大卫《四书译注》初探 [J]. 国际汉学，2017（4）：77-86，203.
[8] 何绍斌. 作为文学"改写"形式的翻译：André Lefevere 翻译思想研究 [J]. 解放军外国语学院学报，2005（5）：66-71，108.
[9] 黄德先，杜小军. 对勒菲弗尔"改写论"的误读 [J]. 广东外语外贸大学学报，2009（6）：77-79.
[10] 李海兰. 舞台表演的剧本需要"度身定译"——从戏剧翻译的特点比较《推销员之死》的两个中文译本 [J]. 现代交际，2013（1）：31-33.
[11] 李力. 译者选择的类坐标系模式 [J]. 中国翻译，2019（5）：17-27，188.
[12] 刘满芸. 共生理念下的翻译学维度考察 [J]. 南京理工大学学报（社会科学版），2014（3）：62-68.
[13] 罗天. 翟林奈译《孙子兵法》与军事典籍翻译中的文化聚合 [J]. 外国语文，2015（4）：72-77.
[14] 吕俊. 关于翻译研究中的两种范式问题——读《翻译学：一个未圆且难圆的梦》[J]. 外语与外语教学，2000（9）：42-45.
[15] 宋学智. 翻译文学经典研究中的问题与思考 [J]. 外语学刊，2017（1）：67-72.
[16] 孙武. 今译新编孙子兵法 [M]. 郭化若，编译. 北京：中华书局，1962.
[17] 孙星衍. 孙子十家注 [M]. 吴人骥，校. 北京：中华书局，1985.

[18] 泰戈尔. 飞鸟集 [M]. 冯唐，译 . 杭州：浙江文艺出版社，2015.
[19] 田超. 出版方下架冯唐译版《飞鸟集》翻译风格引发争议 [EB/OL].（2015-12-29）[2020-10-02]. http://media.people.com.cn/n1/2015/1229/c40606-27987824.html.
[20] 王树槐. 学术定势折射的多棱文化镜像——《阿 Q 正传》三个译本的文化折射率与译者学术定势比较 [J]. 外语研究，2019（5）：70-76.
[21] 邢杰，黎壹平，张其帆. 拉图尔行动者网络理论对翻译研究的效用 [J]. 中国翻译，2019（5）：28-36，188.
[22] 张广奎，黄素因. 反射与折射：在介质中穿梭的文学经典——论经典译介的流变 [J]. 北京工业大学学报（社会科学版），2012（3）：71-74.
[23] 张璐. 从 Python 情感分析看海外读者对中国译介文学的接受和评价：以《三体》英译本为例 [J]. 外语研究，2019（4）：80-86.
[24] 周飞亚 . 莫借"翻译"行"篡改"（文化世象）[EB/OL].（2015-12-24）[2020-10-02]. http://zj.people.com.cn/n/2015/1224/c186960-27388995.html.
[25] 朱熹. 四书集注 [M]. 长沙：岳麓书社，1985.
[26] Bassnett, S. Translation Studies [M]. London: Routledge, 2002.
[27] Cady, L. Thoreau's quotations from the Confucian Books in Walden [J]. American Literature, 1961(1): 20-32.
[28] Collie, D. The Chinese Classical Work Commonly Called *The Four Books* [M]. Malacca: Mission Press, 1828.
[29] Damrosch, D. What Is World Literature? [M]. Princeton: Princeton University Press, 2003.
[30] Giles, L. Sun Tzu on the Art of War: The Oldest Military Treatise in the World [M]. London: Luzac & Co, 1910.
[31] Griffith, S. B. Sun Tzu: The Art of War [M]. Oxford: Oxford University Press, 1963.
[32] Hermans, T. Translation between poetics and ideology [J]. Translation and Literature, 1994(3): 138-145.
[33] Lefevere, A. Translated literature: Towards an Integrated Theory [J]. The Bulletin of the Midwest Modern Language Association, 1981(1): 68-78.

[34] Lefevere, A. Mother Courage's cucumbers: Text, system and refraction in a theory of literature [J]. Modern Language Studies, 1982(4): 3-20.

[35] Lefevere, A. Why waste our time on rewrites? The trouble with interpretation and the role of rewriting in an alternative paradigm [A]. In Hermans, T. (ed.). The Manipulation of Literature: Studies in Literary Translation (pp.215-243) [C]. London: Croom Helm, 1985.

[36] Lefevere, A. On the processing of texts or what is literature? [A]. In D'Haen, T. (ed.). Linguistics and the Study of Literature (pp.218-244) [C]. Amsterdam: Rodopi, 1986a.

[37] Lefevere, A. Power and the canon, or How to rewrite an author into a classic [J]. Journal of Literary Studies, 1986b: 1-14.

[38] Lefevere, A. Acculturating Bertolt Brecht [A]. In Bassnett, S. & Lefevere, A. (eds.). Constructing Cultures: Essays on Literary Translation (pp.109-122) [C]. Clevedon: Multilingual Matters, 1998.

[39] Matthiessen, C.M.I.M. Choice in translation: Metafunctional considerations [A]. In Kunz, K., *et al.* (eds.). Caught in the Middle — Language Use and Translation: A Festschrift for Erich Steiner on the Occasion of His 60th Birthday (pp.271-333) [C]. Saarbrücken: Saarland University Press, 2014.

[40] Miller, A. Death of a Salesman: With an Introduction by Christopher Bigsby [M]. New York: Penguin, 1998.

[41] Muñoz-Martín, R. Cognitive and psycholinguistic approaches [A]. In Millán, C. & Bartrina, F. (eds.). The Routledge Handbook of Translation Studies (pp.241-256) [C]. New York: Routledge, 2015.

[42] O'Brien, S. The borrowers: Researching the cognitive aspects of translation [J]. Target — International Journal of Translation Studies, 2013(1): 5-17.

[43] Tagore, R. Stray Birds [M]. New York: Macmillan, 1917.

[44] Taine, H. A. The Philosophy of Art [M]. New York: Holt & Williams, 1873.

后 记

原本计划在 2023 年 6 月第十届亚太论坛召开一周年之际正式推出这本论文集，以这一更具仪式感的方式赋予论坛和论文集更多的意义。但 2022 年年底的疫情暴发打乱了原有的安排，所有相关工作都被迫延后。所幸在大家的共同努力下，我们得以在第三届国家翻译能力学术研讨会召开之际将论文集出版。

感谢中国翻译协会会长、中国外文出版发行事业局局长杜占元先生，他不仅在第十届亚太翻译论坛开幕式上致辞，还应允我们将他的发言稿整理成文收入论文集。感谢亚太翻译论坛联合委员会主席、中国外文出版发行事业局副局长兼总编辑、中国翻译协会常务副会长高岸明先生将其在论坛上所做的主旨报告赐稿于我们。感谢北京外国语大学校长杨丹教授对论坛的大力支持，以及他在发言中对论坛主题的精彩诠释。三位决策者的发言题目和内容为会议和论文集定下了合作、发展、共赢的主基调。

李宇明教授每次的主旨发言都极具洞见，令我受益匪浅。感谢他容忍我不胜其烦的催促，百忙中拨冗将发言内容整理成稿。感谢另两位学者、国际主旨发言人，加拿大渥太华大学的 Lynne Bowker 教授和瑞士苏黎世应用科学大学的 Gary Massey 教授，他们不仅发言内容精彩，而且慷慨赐稿于我们。

感谢论文集所有其他作者的赐稿，对修改意见和建议的及时回复，以及对论文集延期出版的耐心与宽容。

感谢北京外国语大学高级翻译学院和国家翻译能力研究中心的同事为第十届亚太论坛的顺利举办以及本论文集的出版所做出的重要贡献，他们是（以姓氏拼音为序）：樊晶、方显、葛冬冬、胡晓虹、江璐、姜业宏、李长栓、李雪丽、刘宇波、骆津晶、马仲武、王洪涛、王华树、王苏阳、徐秀玲、姚斌、余丹妮、曾佳宁、张潆洁、赵田园、朱玉犇等。还有数量众多的硕士研究生，因篇幅所限，无法一一具名，一并致谢。

感谢外语教学与研究出版社社长助理李会钦、编辑李海萍的帮助和支持。

本书的出版得到北京外国语大学“双一流”建设重大（点）标志性项目“国家翻译能力理论框架与国家比较”（项目批准号：2022SYLA002）经费以及北京外国语大学国家翻译能力研究中心专项经费的支持，在此表示感谢。

任 文

北京外国语大学西院

2023 年 7 月 26 日